# International Conference on Legal Perspectives on the Internet (COPEJI 6.0)



## The Right to the Confluence of Two Universes: Where to?

Held online

SHS Web of Conferences Volume 177 (2023)

Iasi, Romania
29 - 30 October 2022

**Editors:**

**Carmen Tamara Ungureanu**
**Ioana Maria Costea**

ISBN: 978-1-7138-8350-0

**Printed from e-media with permission by:**

Curran Associates, Inc.
57 Morehouse Lane
Red Hook, NY 12571

**Some format issues inherent in the e-media version may also appear in this print version.**



For additional information, please contact EDP Sciences – Web of Conferences
at the address below.

EDP Sciences – Web of Conferences
17, Avenue du Hoggar
Parc d'Activité de Courtabœuf
BP 112
F-91944 Les Ulis Cedex A
France

Phone: +33 (0) 1 69 18 75 75
Fax: +33 (0) 1 69 28 84 91

contact-edps@webofconferences.org

**Additional copies of this publication are available from:**

Curran Associates, Inc.
57 Morehouse Lane
Red Hook, NY 12571 USA
Phone: 845-758-0400
Fax: 845-758-2633
Email: curran@proceedings.com
Web: www.proceedings.com

# TABLE OF CONTENTS

# Preface

*Carmen Tamara* Ungureanu

The 'Legal Perspectives on the Internet' Conference made its debut in 2017 as a part of the anniversary celebrations the Faculty of Law holds in October to mark the occasion of its founding in 1830. The conference's goal was to create a discussion forum for academics, PhD students, practitioners, and computer scientists concerned with the legal side of their work in order to come up with solutions for the challenging interdisciplinary connections caused by the use of the Internet. The Faculty of Informatics had been an 'ally' of the conference from the beginning.

Starting with the third edition in 2019, the conference's organizers have decided on one subtitle for each of the following editions as a way to both condense the range of topics that can be covered in this vast field and to keep up with technological advancement. As a result, the conference's 2019 theme, 'Evolution of Law through Technology', also signified the conference's expansion to a worldwide audience. In that edition, a novel strategy was introduced: lawyers attempted to trace the evolution of conventional legal institutions by incorporating a variant, the Internet, with the assistance of their computer scientist colleagues.

The sub-theme of the conference in 2020 was 'The Ubiquity of Law in Cyberspace', where it was argued that regardless of how admirable the attempts at self-regulation of cyberspace have been and are, the rules are consistently broken and those whose rights were/are ignored or violated look for solutions. Laws must be followed whether they are wished for or not. Legal experts cannot handle everything on their own when it comes to interpreting the current norms, trying to adapt them to the new circumstances (sometimes like on a Procrustean bed [1]), or developing new norms. This conference's edition placed a strong emphasis on the necessity of a partnership between computer scientists and attorneys in order to address current technological concerns.

At the 2021 edition, 'Cyberspace, The Final Frontier? Concluding and Performing Agreements', the starting point was the premise that cyberspace is becoming more and more like a jungle, with rules imposed by the strongest. Regardless of the risks of 'living' online, it cannot be avoided because it is a space that has become important to all of us, from public state authorities to international organizations and private players, whether professionals or simple users, consumers, or employees. Non-human additional participants, such as algorithms, make the environment more unpredictable and tough, similar to actual hunger games [2].

In 2022, the sixth edition of the conference, with the subtitle 'COPEJI 6.0. The Right to the Confluence of Two Universes: Where to?' had as its core focus new technological advances, with an emphasis on metaverses. We have admitted that the growth of technology leads to pessimistic conceptions of the human being's present and future, whether he or she lives in a physical world or 'enjoys' the promises of the metaverse [3]. The law has the resources to meet the needs of both worlds and to safeguard both the participant in the flesh in social life and his avatar. In this 6th edition of the conference, the aim was to find smart ways to reconcile the two worlds for the benefit of all their inhabitants.

All in all, the conference has evolved into an international conference with great potential, which combines legal issues with tech ones, more from the legal point of view.

The volume of the 6th edition of the *International Conference Legal Perspectives on the Internet. 'COPEJI 6.0. The right to the confluence of two Universes: where to*?', comprises articles written by academics and doctoral students. It covers the subjects from four panels of the conference: *Legal Dimensions of Businesses in the new Digital World*, *Legal Aspects of the Emergence and Use of New Technology*, *Virtual Criminality and Criminal Proceedings in the context of the Digital World*, *The Consumer and the Data Subject in the Digital World.*

We are confident that the volume will contribute to a better understanding of the intricate legal issues triggered by Internet and its new metamorphosis. In the same time, we are expecting the conference to continue to grow and attract more specialists from different fields interested in legal tech.

## References

1. R. Buxton, *The Complete World of Greek Mythology* (Thames & Hudson, 2004)
2. S. Collins, *Hunger Games* (2008)
3. N. Stephenson, *Snow Crash* (1992)

# Statement of Peer review

In submitting conference proceedings to *Web of Conferences*, the editors of the proceedings certify to the Publisher that

1. They adhere to its **Policy on Publishing Integrity** in order to safeguard good scientific practice in publishing.
2. All articles have been subjected to peer review administered by the proceedings editors.
3. Reviews have been conducted by expert referees, who have been requested to provide unbiased and constructive comments aimed, whenever possible, at improving the work.
4. Proceedings editors have taken all reasonable steps to ensure the quality of the materials they publish and their decision to accept or reject a paper for publication has been based only on the merits of the work and the relevance to the journal.

Title, date and place of the conference

Title: **International Conference Legal Perspectives on the Internet. COPEJI 6.0. The right to the confluence of two Universes: where to?**

Date: **October 29-30, 2022**

Place: **Iaşi, Romania**

Proceedings editor(s):

**Carmen Tamara UNGUREANU**

**Ioana Maria COSTEA**

Date and editor's signature

# Workers' non-discrimination in the metaverse

*Felicia* Rosioru[1*]

[1] Faculty of Law, Babes-Bolyai University, Cluj, Romania

**Abstract.** Technology is evolving and the workplace is radically changing; remote work is possible for activities that we never sought that could be done elsewhere than in a workplace organised by the employer. Digitalization enables automated production lines, but also automated decisions related to the employees, replacing human control and making platform work possible. The impact of innovation on labour law was very important during the pandemic, accelerated by the need of the so-called `social distance`. Several platforms, like Google Meet, Microsoft Teams, Zoom, Webex Meet were rapidly adapted to allow live interaction for those who could not meet in-person. Online meetings, online lectures, online administration etc. have become quite rapidly the `normality` of those days. In this context, an old idea has found fertile ground for development: the metaverse. Even if the metaverse doesn't exist yet, work in virtual worlds advertised as metaverses has become a reality, challenging the traditional structures of labour law. One of the concerning issues related to the metaverse is related to workers' discrimination in the virtual world and the possibilities to tackle it.

## 1 From telework to the metaverse. An introduction

When we speak of workers' non-discrimination in the metaverse, several questions come into mind: `what is the metaverse?`; `does it really exist?`; `is it possible to work in the metaverse?` (assuming that the answer to the second question is positive); and, of course, `why would anyone do that?`; or, even more (for those who are rather sceptical) `how did we get here?`. Well, the path was rather long and unpredictable, mixing science-fiction literature with technology and the unexpected pandemic.

The pandemic has generated a 'migration' from the typical workplace to work from home or to a mixture of remote and office work. Telework has developed unprecedently and many workers whose workplace was organised by the employer had to adapt to the new situation and to work remotely. For some workers, remote work has become a way of life, as it has enabled them to travel to different places or it has simply given them the freedom that they needed. Telework has challenged the traditional structures of labour law and raised many issues, among which monitoring and working time aspects, work-life balance issues and health and safety problems. Sometimes teleworkers are intensively monitored: the obligation to turn their camera on during their working programme is very common. Highly intrusive or extensive monitoring techniques were sometimes reported, such as a software that was permanently monitoring the teleworkers' eyes in order to see whether they are focusing on

* Corresponding author email: felicia.rosioru@law.ubbcluj.ro.

their work or they are rather absent, leading to work-induced anxiety. Health and safety issues due to isolation were also commonly reported.

However, it seems that telework is here to stay, as many workers and many employers started to prefer remote work. Workers spare time, often enjoy flexible working arrangements and they can manage their family responsibilities better or travel more easily; employers save money for electricity, heating and rent for the office buildings. Some workers are more efficient when they enjoy some flexibility, other need a more organised environment. But the feeling of isolation remains, at least for workers who choose to work remotely for family responsibility reasons; there are limited opportunities to collaborate with team members and these opportunities are more often organised, nor spontaneous and sometimes less effective; in addition, less experienced workers lack the support and/or guidance of their colleagues [1]. In this context, the „VR (Virtual Reality) work environment" is seen as a palliative for the worker's sense of isolation, representing 'a step change in what is possible when it comes to working at home' [2], to remote work, more generally.

Virtual Reality (VR) spaces for meeting with colleagues were created since 2021, giving them the illusion of being in the same room. As it is commonly said, a person in VR spaces is not using the Internet, she or he is *in* the Internet. *Horizon Workrooms*, created by Meta and *Webex Hologram*, created by Cisco, were launched in 2021; *Mesh* was created by Microsoft for Microsoft Teams in 2022, but there are also many other VR work environments, created by: Pixel Mat, NextMeet, Gather, Connec2, Glue, Immersed, MeetinVR, Meeting Room, Rumii, and vSpatial [2]. Such virtual reality spaces enable meetings with colleagues offering a similar experience to that of a usual office-meeting. Unlike the small windows, that are typical to *Zoom*, *Google Meet*, *Microsoft Teams*, *Webex Meet* etc. and have the merit of enabling 'live' interaction, Virtual Reality spaces combine the flexibility of working from different locations with the feeling of community, of belonging to a team, as the avatars - the person's representation in virtual reality spaces - are in the same room and around the same table. Just imagine that it would be possible to work in an office built on *Minecraft*, but with a *Fortnite* graphics and sound, to move with the help of your avatar, to chat with colleagues and (eventually) have a virtual coffee instead of working in front of a screen, having a bad hair day, in shorts or pyjama combined with a formal shirt, exposing a part of your home and (eventually) of your family members.

But VR work environments are just a part of working in a three-dimensional, virtual world. The next step of remote work is the so-called 'work in the metaverse' - an 'immersive and constant virtual 3D world' [3,4] where people interact through their avatars. Work in the metaverse (the \`meta-universe\`) – or in a world that shows itself as a part of it – is another aspect of humans working remotely in a virtual world. Initially a science-fiction novel topic, the metaverse is seen as the next generation of Internet, a 'fully immersive virtual world' [5], but, at the same time, raising many data protection issues, aspects related to mergers and acquisitions, to competition, cybercrime and workers' protection, ownership of cryptocurrencies and non-fungible tokens. Will there be a place for small and medium enterprises in a virtual world controlled by giant techs, given the practice of \`killer acquisitions\` of nascent competitors in order to halt their innovation? For the moment being, there is a great risk that existing anti-competitive practices, such as companies favouring their own products and influencing users' behaviour and decisions, will be perpetuated in the metaverse. Will there be an opportunity for everyone to live and work in the metaverse, given the high chances for big companies to \`monopolise\` it? Is it a new born democracy, completely self-governed, or the existing rules are also applicable in the metaverse? There is no clear answer, as there is no clear vision of the shape the metaverse will take. The \`community form\`, suggested by the blockchain technology, involves communities that would build and establish the rules of their own worlds. On the other hand, for the moment being, big companies build their virtual worlds and govern them, as an incipient form of `privatised metaverse` [3]. Even if some of these questions may be answered by the Digital Markets Act, other questions remain to be debated. Among them, the issue of workers' non-discrimination in the metaverse.

## 2 Work in the Metaverse

The metaverse raises a lot of legal questions, related to discrimination, hate speech, harassment and protection of human rights more generally. There are issues related to the applicable law and jurisdiction, as persons residing in several countries work in a virtual world that doesn't seem to be governed by the laws that we are used to. There is also the question if there is any law that could be applicable in the virtual worlds based on blockchain technology, characterised by their decentralization and the lack of a central authority that could establish and enforce rules.

### 2.1 What is the Metaverse and why is it so popular?

Metaverse was initially a literature topic, imagined by Neal Stephenson in *Snow Crash*, a fantasy novel in which the old fairy tales are re-invented, humans are replaced by avatars and dragons by software dragons, all living in the cyberspace. Snow Crash is a cyberdrug and a computer virus, but if taken by the avatar, it infects also the person behind it [6]. `The people are pieces of software called avatars. They are the audiovisual bodies that people use to communicate with each other in the metaverse` [3].

For someone who is not committed to hard science fiction, the novel resembles strongly to a nowadays video game: the main character, Hiro Protagonist, delivers pizza, but he is a warrior prince in the Metaverse. The vision seems quite simple, but one should not forget that the novel is more than 30 years old, at a time when less than one million computers were connected to the Internet. Ever since, Internet and video games have developed unprecedently; smartphones are being used widely; three-dimensional (3D) worlds are common in many video games, with multiplayers connected to the same game. A parallel world is created, where people not only play games, but they meet, go to the cinema, to concerts (a livestreamed online concert was held on *Fortnite*), shop or work together. *Second Life* and *Minecraft* are among the first more famous 3D multiplayer video games. Nowadays, Virtual Reality (VR) and Augmented Reality (AR) headsets (such as Google glass and Meta Oculus) and controllers enable computer-mediated interaction in 'virtual-physical blended environments' [7]. Virtual Reality spaces are three-dimensional online environments, but in order to `enter` them, a dedicated headset that is connected to a computer or game console is necessary. Augmented Reality (AR) shows computer-generated items in the virtual world [3].

Actually, nobody knows what the metaverse is, as it doesn't exist (yet). The question still remains if the metaverse is a simple trendy buzzword, amplified by the severe sense of isolation that many people have witnessed during the pandemic, or the future of Internet, transformed form a `task-oriented work and entertainment platform in a place to spend our lives happily' [8]. For the moment being, there is no metaverse as such, as it supposes a single virtual world, immersive and universal; there are rather several 3D virtual worlds, focusing on gaming and leisure, but also on commercial and professional interactions, as well as on financial transaction. After the success of non-fungible tokens, one of the most profitable investments seems to be buying a piece of (virtual) land in the virtual world (a person has bought a virtual plot for €396 000, because he or she wanted to be the virtual neighbour of Snoop Dog [3]) or building offices and opening shops, cinemas and even law offices. There is a whole virtual world based on consumerism, in which one can buy almost everything, from land to eyebrows, make-up, hair-cut or clothes for his/her avatar or from Messi's World Cup T-shirt's representation to a (virtual) Antique Oriental Buddha.

There are (still) some technical problems related to the opened and universal character of the metaverse, as well as to the interoperability of the different virtual `worlds` that exist and are controlled by different entities [7]. Or, the metaverse is conceived as an immersive cyberspace and it should be universal, a single cyberworld and not a network of 3D virtual spaces, as the situation seems to be today. Unlike the Web, which is opened and interoperable, the Metaverse is built on the model of a massive multiplayer online game, such as the French *Deuxième Monde*, the `first European metaverse` [9], enabling interaction in a virtual Paris, or *Second Life*, advertised as `an inclusive haven of self-expression` [10]. The blockchain technology, used by *Decentraland* [11], for example, is seen as a solution for decentralisation and interoperability of the metaverse, the content being stored on distributed servers. In addition, blockchain involves a democratic process, as users have rights, they establish and vote on the rules related to allowed and forbidden behaviours in the virtual world. But even in this democratic world, discrimination could reign when rules are established by the majority, if the world is dominated by certain groups of people.

Furthermore, blockchain technology still depends on a parent company and it has the disadvantage of going against the `right to be forgotten` [7, for arguments against 12], guaranteed in the EU by Article 17 of the GDPR Regulation and Article 8 of the EU Charter of Fundamental Rights. The Court of Justice of the European Union has had the opportunity to protect the right to be forgotten and stated that any information that is considered to be `inaccurate, inadequate, irrelevant, no longer relevant or excessive for the purposes of data processing` should be `erased` by search engine operators by removing links to web pages, in the list of results of a search carried out for a certain name [13]. The respect of the person's private life prevails both over the economic interest of the search engine operator and the general interest of the public to have access to such data, unless the protected person has played an important role in public life [13]. The right to be forgotten applies to search engines with domain names associated with EU Member States [14].

Many companies already use the term `metaverse`, but they only offer virtual 3D worlds that look more like a game and that have the great disadvantage of lacking to be interconnected. They are more like `incompatible closed gardens` [8]; one can visit *Decentraland* metaverse, *Second Life* metaverse, eventually *Meta* metaverse, but not the promised integrated world created for fun and leisure – and also for work. Work in the existing `close gardens`, as well as in the future metaverse, raises a lot of challenges. If the metaverse is the next step of the Internet, work in the metaverse is the next step of digital work and of the labour issues that are related to it.

### 2.2 Labour law in the Metaverse

Due to the fact that the existing 3D virtual worlds look more like a game, some people are not aware that they are actually working. In this situation, it might be difficult to define what work is: where does playing stop and where does work begin? In some other cases, the work performed is obvious: employers organise meetings of their employees in Virtual Reality spaces, apparently moving work from the `zoomiverse` [15] to the `metaverse`; *Decentraland* hires persons to work, through their avatar, in virtual casinos, and they are being paid in the platform's cryptocurrency, which is Mana. Ideally, with the use of Artificial Intelligence (AI), avatars will work independently in the virtual world, performing repetitive or rather boring jobs, so that humans can perform more creative or complex work. For the moment being, avatars represent in the virtual world human beings who perform work.

*Decentraland*'s workers are being paid in Mana, the currency used in this virtual world and they can spend it only in *Decentraland*, to buy land, buildings or items for their avatar, as there is a fashion also in the virtual world, not just on Earth. They are captive in this virtual world, contrary to the International Labour Organisation Convention no 95 on the protection of wages, prohibiting any payment `in the form of promissory notes, vouchers or coupons, or in any other form alleged to represent legal tender` (Article 3 § 1). Or, in this case, Mana is alleged to represent the legal tender in Decentraland, but it enables the worker to buy items only in this virtual world, not in the country where he or she lives. According to the same international instrument, 'the term *wages* means remuneration or earnings, however designated or calculated, capable of being expressed in terms of money and fixed by mutual agreement or by national laws or regulations, which are payable in virtue of a written or unwritten contract of employment by an employer to an employed person for work done or to be done or for services rendered or to be rendered'. Is there a possibility to convert Mana in `real` money – that is, to a currency that can be used in the physical reality? Apparently, yes [16]. Are the common standards also applicable in the virtual world? The question is still debated as to which rules and how many regulations are applicable in these worlds, as their creators often advertise them as democracies where the rules are set and voted by the users, so that the majority decides. Therefore, especially in virtual worlds built on blockchain technology, there is no central authority to establish or to enforce rules.

The situation of employees working in Virtual Reality spaces, in meetings organised by their employer is radically different than work performed for a 'virtual employer', even if, in both cases, the person is represented through his or her avatar. When there is an employment contract signed by the employee and his/her physical employer, the Earthly laws will apply and the parties may regulate some aspects through their contract. Even in these cases, there might be issues related to the applicable minimum wage, jurisdiction, as well as to working time and the worker's possibility to enforce his or her rights.

Work in the virtual space has raised or it might raise multiple issues related to discrimination and the appropriate means to tackle it. Workers are represented in the metaverse (for the moment being, in the virtual world) through an avatar, thus one might claim that the avatar is the victim of discrimination, not the person behind it. A very complex question will arise when (ideally), as a consequence of the use of Artificial Intelligence, only the avatars shall work, without any human being backing them. Until then, the reality is that, behind the avatars that move and work in the virtual world, there are humans. The existing virtual worlds accommodate many discriminatory situations, that may be perpetuated in the future metaverse. Human dignity and equality are fundamental rights that must be protected anywhere, in this universe or beyond it, in the metaverse (as the literal meaning of the metaverse is `beyond universe` [3]).

## 2.3 Workers' non-discrimination in the Metaverse

One of the most important aspects of work (in)equality in the metaverse is related to disability discrimination. In order to participate in the virtual work environment, the person has to wear a headset, placed over the eyes, but also to use stereoscopic lenses, in order to make images appear three dimensional [2]. Their use is not always easy, as VR helmets are bulky and they induce nausea to some users [17], raising additional health and safety issues. Eye, head and neck fatigue may also become rather common. Depending on the type of disability, some workers might be excluded of the labour market, even if they could perform work in a physical environment. In addition, some employers might find too burdensome to make the necessary accommodation in order to enable disabled workers to participate in the virtual work environment. In the field of employment, the existing EU equality rules, set by Directive 2000/78/EC establishing a general framework for equal treatment in employment and occupation, aim to grant equal access, participation in and advancement in employment for disabled persons. Under Article 5 of this directive, employers have to take the appropriate measures for that purpose, unless such measures would impose a disproportionate burden on the employer. Recital 21 of the above-mentioned directive establishes the main criteria for the assessment of the disproportionate burden, by taking into account the financial and other costs entailed by the accommodation measures, the scale and financial resources of the employer, as well as the possibility to obtain public funding or other form of assistance. If the disability policy of the Member State concerned provides for measures to assist employers in adapting the working place or in taking any other necessary measures of reasonable accommodation for persons with disability, including public funding, if necessary, the burden is not considered to be disproportionate. Currently, the financial burden might be real, as adapted VR headsets and gloves are still at early stages and rather experimental and expensive. Motion capture gloves are also necessary, `to accurately capture your expressions, body language, and the quality of (…) voice' [Bill Gates quoted by 17].

On the other hand, one of the initiatives aims to develop technology AI-powered avatars for people with motor disabilities, who would be able to navigate the Virtual Reality world with the use of their eye movements and not through 'the typical motion sensors' [2] (most commonly by the use of VR controllers or, most recently, by VR gloves, that capture the moves of hands and fingers) [19]. For example, after being diagnosed with motor neuron disease, Dr. Peter Scott-Morgan has converted into Peter 2.0, the `first human cyborg in the world` for scientific purposes, in order to adapt technology to the needs of persons with severe disabilities [18]. Peter 2.0 DXC Technology has concluded a partnership with Scott Morgan Foundation to use advanced technologies in order to help people with extreme physical disabilities, as well as 'other life challenging conditions' to overcome them [18]. VR contact lenses were successfully used at the end of 2022, but their cost is very high and they cannot be purchased yet. If there is a hope for persons with motor disabilities, workers with intellectual, sensory or learning disabilities, who should be fully integrated in social life and participate in the life of the community, including through employment, according to Article 15 paragraphs 2 and 3 of the revised European Social Charter, among other international instruments, might simply be excluded from the labour market and replaced by AI powered avatars, 'trained' to perform less complex or rather repetitive work. Or, persons with disabilities have the right to work on an equal basis with others, in a 'labour market and work environment that is open, inclusive and accessible' (Article 27 paragraph 1 of the UN Convention on the Rights of Persons with Disabilities) to them. Genuine social inclusion also means the right to the opportunity to gain a living by means of work that is freely chosen or accepted by the persons with disabilities, reasonable accommodation being also provided by Article 27 paragraph 1 i) of the UN Convention on the Rights of Persons with Disabilities). Given the effects on the health of some persons of VR headsets, work in the virtual world may enhance long term impairments and might lead to a new category of persons with disabilities from a social and work environment perspective. According to the settled case-law of the Court of Justice of the European Union, the concept of disability is not medically defined, by placing the person in a certain degree of disability established according to medical scales. The EU has ratified the United Nations Convention on the Rights of Persons with Disabilities (by Council Decision 2010/48/EC of 26 November 2009). Following this event, the Court of Justice of the European Union has adopted a broad concept of 'disability', understood as a limitation that results from long-term physical, mental or psychological impairments, hindering 'the full and effective participation of the person concerned in professional life on an equal basis with other workers' [20, 21, 22], in interaction with various barriers that exist in the social environment [23]. Constant neck and head pain, due to the use of VR helmets, would significantly reduce the possibility of the person to work in the VR work environment, leading to a disability in the European sense of the concept. It is irrelevant whether the person has contributed or not to the onset of his or her disability, which must be understood as a hindrance to the exercise of a professional activity and not only to the impossibility of exercising it [23].

Disability discrimination is – for the moment being – obvious in the emerging metaverse. Some people who can perform work in the `real` world will simply be excluded of the virtual labour market. But, also, age discrimination should be a hot topic when speaking of the metaverse or of work in the virtual world. Elder workers might face genuine challenges in keeping up with the ever-developing technologies. Age gap, which is already a feature of platform work, will simply be transposed in the virtual world. Children protection would be another problem, as they might perform work under the appearance of an adult avatar, affecting their mental and intellectual development and the completion of compulsory schooling, contrary to the International Labour Organisation's Convention no 1973 on minimum age (1973).

Access to metaverse is based on a technology which, for the moment being, is rather expensive. There are several VR headsets models, with a variety of prices, but the more immersive experience is given by the more expensive headsets (Google Cardboard has the lowest price and HTC Vive Pro has the highest price [2]. There are many VR headsets available, such as: PlayStation's VR helmets, Microsoft's HoloLens, Facebook's Oculus). Even if there is no specific regulation at EU level, many European States prohibit discrimination based on socioeconomic status. Poverty, as well as important family responsibilities may hinder access to work in the metaverse. If the employer is organising meetings in virtual spaces, it is important to provide the same technology to all employees, otherwise they will have different experiences depending on the type of VR headsets and gloves they can afford.

There is, of course, also the issue of gender discrimination, as the tech industry is dominated by male employees. In the US, the proportion of women holding tech-related jobs is of only 26.7% [24]. Besides role models and stereotypes, managers have the tendency to recruit persons who are culturally similar to them [25], or the great majority of managers in tech companies are male. The same concerns raised by algorithmic discrimination in platform work may be perpetuated in the metaverse. An algorithm `used` only to male avatars will automatically declassify women, reflecting societal biases if it was trained only on certain demographic groups [26]. Of course, in this case, discrimination could be avoided by choosing a male avatar, but do we want a metaverse populated only by certain demographic groups?

Workplace biases often lead to workplace harassment. Telework has already raised multiple workplace harassment issues, as it had opened a window on the worker's work environment (often his/her home) and family members, revealing them accidentally, as well as on different personal objects (for example, with religious connotations). Besides of the protected grounds at EU level, digital harassment may be linked to the worker's family responsibilities, socioeconomic status or 'quarantine fashion'. These can be transposed also in the metaverse, even if the worker will not directly expose his or her home anymore. As there is a virtual world fashion, workers with important family responsibilities or those with a low income will not afford to buy a virtual Prada bag for his or her avatar, nor to buy eye-brows or different hair-cuts, being less fashionable and stylish than other avatars. In this context, the in-office unwanted conduct, related to a protected ground and having the purpose or effect of violating personal dignity and of creating an intimidating, hostile, degrading, humiliating or offensive environment may easily be transposed online, where less rules seem to be applicable, as it is often an informal work environment. In addition, the victim might encounter difficulties to report incidents, as a face-to-face conversation is not always possible and the 'digital alternative' is to address e-mails or other messages. Thus, the victim lacks moral support and might fear that his or her complaint is not taken seriously or that it will be made public [27]. Tackling digital workplace harassment might force the employer to increase surveillance and monitoring of workers, leading to a vicious circle, as their personal data and private life would be threatened in this case.

Three-dimensional work environments and work in the metaverse (more generally) bring new challenges, as workers perform work in virtual offices, but without the constraints of a face-to-face interaction. A researcher has raised the issue of sexual harassment, her avatar being the victim during an online meeting in a 3D work environment. A person testing the Meta *Horizon Worlds* has reported that she had been groped by a stranger in the virtual world. Meta has enabled a tool called `Safe Zone`, a protective bubble that users can activate when they feel threatened. The disadvantage of the tool is that, once activated, the avatar cannot interact with others, until they lift the `Safe Zone` (`A woman was sexually harassed on Meta's VR social media platform. She's not the first—and won't be the last` [28]). The debate caused by this fact was quite vivid: can we assimilate the human behaviour in the augmented reality with the one in the physical, 'real' reality? Is it possible to claim that there was a form of harassment if the avatar was actually the victim? In this context, it has to be reminded that sexual harassment is not limited to a physical conduct, but it encompasses any other form of unwanted conduct, verbal or non-verbal, of a sexual nature. The effect or the purpose of such conduct consists in violating the dignity of the victim, in particular by creating an intimidating, hostile, degrading, humiliating or offensive environment [Article 2 paragraph 1 d) of Directive 2006/54/EC on the implementation of the principle of equal opportunities and equal treatment of men and women in matters of employment and occupation (recast)]. Could it be accepted that the degrading, humiliating or hostile environment can also be virtual? If we start from the idea that VR workspaces give you the impression of actually being in that space, then we must admit that there may be harassment also in the virtual world. Furthermore, at least some avatars are to be trained to perform work autonomously. Who can be held reliable for the avatar's unwanted conduct and how can it be stopped? The person for whom the AI powered avatars work will be held reliable, but do we have to search for it on Earth or there will also be virtual courts and authorities? These are just some of the shades of digital workplace harassment, entailing complicated issues related to applicable law and jurisdiction.

## 3 Tackling discrimination in the Metaverse

Tackling discrimination in the Metaverse is strongly related to how the person is represented in the virtual world by his or her avatar. For the moment being, a person participating in virtual world activities can choose an avatar from an existing list and the customizable human depictions are similar to a cartoon character. In this case, the Metaverse should be built as an inclusive heaven, where everyone can find a proper representation for his or her avatar, and not just the most common category of users (in order to allow a proper representation of every persona, Meta has many options of avatar features – more than one quintillion different combinations –, including assistive devices for people with disabilities [29]. The main idea of Meta avatars is that `your avatar is a digital expression of your personality (or personalities)`. Surprisingly, they are called `MetaHuman Avatars` [30]). But, as the virtual worlds are not so popular as advertised and the technological costs are still prohibitive, 3D avatars are now available on *Facebook*, *Instagram* and *Messenger* for users in the United States, Mexico, and Canada. A *Facebook* user may be represented as an avatar in the profile picture, as well as in comments, stickers or stories [29]. It might be a step taken by Meta in order to attract more *Facebook* and *Instagram* users in the virtual world, as, for the moment being, `I don't see someone strapping a frigging screen to their face all day and not wanting to ever leave` [31].

In other cases, the person may create an avatar after 'buying' body shapes, haircut, eyebrows etc. for his or her virtual representation (for example, in *Decentraland*). It means that the avatar doesn't (have to) look like the person behind it and this situation may complicate equality protection. For example, if a white male chooses a female avatar and the avatar is discriminated on grounds of gender, can he argue that he is the victim of discrimination? Furthermore, a person belonging to a discriminated group might choose an avatar having features of the majority; for example, an older worker may choose an avatar representing a young person; a Muslim woman might choose to be represented as a white male, in order to overcome the barriers of the labour market. But forcing people to hide their identity is definitely not a form of protection of human dignity and of non-discrimination.

Non-human avatars are also available for users (although we have to mention that the `Metahuman Avatars` are created starting from the person's profile picture). Non-human avatars might enhance merit-based evaluations in the workplace, putting more weight on the person's work than on his or her appearance. This way, both 'mirrortocracy' (an unconscious favourable evaluation for similar colleagues [2]) and or the so-called grooming gap, where the worker is discriminated based on appearance (disproportionately affecting women in case of telework) would be avoided. Beyond the advantages, the question remains whether we would like a virtual world populated only by animals, such as cats and dogs, performing human work. In case of an affirmative answer, such a `dehumanised` world might lead to the multiplication of discriminatory and harassing behaviours, considering that there is no appearance of violating the dignity of a human being. By definition, harassment is an unwanted behaviour, creating an intimidating, hostile, degrading, humiliating or offensive environment, directed towards a person (Article 2 paragraph 1 c) of Directive 2006/54/EC on the implementation of the principle of equal opportunities and equal treatment of men and women in matters of employment and occupation, recast). On the other hand, using `non-human` avatars would affect one of the main functions of work as a source of social identity [32, 33]. The use of avatars leads to a dilemma, as an avatar that looks similar to the person behind it raises many issues related to personal data protection, but using `non-human` avatars would deprive work of its social and moral value.

There is, of course, the issue of the applicable rules on equality and non-discrimination. Do the EU legal framework and the national legislations apply? We have relied in our analysis on the long-established concepts of discrimination and harassment, but can they be transposed in the metaverse? It would be a mistake to believe that the metaverse can function without or with other rules than the `real` universe. We should distinguish between two situations. The first hypothesis is rather simple: when the employer organises meetings in virtual spaces, it is responsible for tackling non-discrimination. Therefore, precise procedures and rules should be established by the employer's internal regulation and discriminatory acts should be sanctioned. In this case, the Labour Codes and other regulations apply as such, according to the law governing the employment contract. For example, if a Romanian worker has concluded an employment contract with a Romanian employer, there is no reason to disapply the Romanian Labour Code, even if work is performed in virtual spaces. Article 2 of the Romanian Labour Code establishes the applicable legislation and, specifically for the discrimination cases, article 5 of the Labour Code, as well as the Government's Ordinance no 137 of 2000 on preventing and sanctioning all forms of discrimination would apply. The second situation is more complicated, as for workers who are hired online and perform work only in the metaverse there will be a question of establishing the applicable law to the contract, as well as the applicable jurisdiction. The international Conventions and the EU regulation tend to establish the law of the country where the work is performed and, since there is no specific country in the metaverse, it should normally be the country from which the worker performs work (according to Article 8, paragraph 2 of Regulation (EC) No 593/2008 on the law applicable to contractual obligations - Rome I). It should also be noted that, for harassment, hate speech and other forms of discrimination, some virtual world creators undertook the task to develop rules to metaverse content moderation [34]. The EU is also trying to shape the future metaverse and the use of artificial intelligence on ethical principles [3].

## 4 Metaverse and the Future of Labour Law. Some conclusive remarks

In this paper, we have highlighted the risks and weaknesses of the existing virtual worlds, that may be perpetuated in the metaverse. It is not sure that the metaverse will ever be created, the only reality is that there is a great interest of tech companies to invest in what seems to be the future and only the future will tell if the metaverse will ever exist. Until then and if the metaverse is going to be created, one should not forget that people will still actually live on Earth and that we would still need persons to work in hospitals, schools, supermarkets, restaurants, factories etc.

For the moment being, virtual worlds have proven their utility, mainly in training and customer support. In the healthcare sector, the metaverse (actually, virtual working spaces) were used to perform virtual therapy and remote surgeries: for example, *Medivis*, which is a surgical technology company, started using Microsoft's HoloLens technology and has established procedures to train medical students on 3-D anatomy models; other technologies (such as Embodied Labs) have used 360-degree video in order to train medical workers to establish a proper diagnose of Alzheimer's Disease and age-related audio-visual impairments; augmented reality was used for testing learning nursers' skills in specific scenarios. Oculus Quest headsets were used for training technicians on electric vehicle maintenance at *Bosch* and *Ford Motor Company* [35]. The US Army is also taking into consideration to use virtual environments for soldiers' training; consultation and civil service can be provided as avatars by public administration (such as the city of Seoul, planning to open a 'Metaverse 120 Center' in 2023) [3].

Virtual work can also replace the trial period in the employment contract: at MGM Resorts, candidates may try out a specific job in the VR work environment before accepting an offer. This way, the employee doesn't spend time with a job that is not suitable for him or for her; the employer doesn't spend money by training persons who will shortly leave [35]. The metaverse provides real-time feed-back and it encourages conversations and cooperation in a team or even between different teams working on a same project; it can replicate the `in-person brainstorm sessions` [35]. The use of virtual worlds broadens the scope of potential candidates for a certain job, as work in the metaverse it is basically a form of remote work, but it risks to perpetuate the problems and inequities of platform work, occasioning `evermore invasive and relentless forms of algorithmic surveillance` [36].

For the moment being, metaverse seems to be built as the democracy of the majority, but its distributed architecture, which is essential to cyber-democracy, entails security and privacy threats [37]. A huge volume of data is collected and used in the metaverse, raising questions related to user content, but also to cyber security, such as the protection against identify theft of the avatar [3]. One should not imagine, however, that the metaverse is 'the wild west', especially in terms of labour protection [36]. Many issues have to be regulated, but many regulations have already been adopted and many proposals are being debated [3]. In terms of labour protection, in many situations the `Earthly` laws would be applicable. There is, however, the risk of workers misclassification and complicated issues related to the applicable law and jurisdiction may arise, aspects that are also specific to platform work. Shall we be forced to imagine a Labour law of the virtual space? Only the future will tell...

## References


1. K. Kalcheva, *Remote Work Statistics in 2023 and How They Influence the Workplace*, Squaretalk, URL: https://squaretalk.com/remote-work-statistics/, accessed: 01.03.2023 (2023)
2. G. Lordan, P. Will, *8 ways the metaverse can change inclusion at work*, FastCompany, URL: https://www.fastcompany.com/90766687/8-ways-the-metaverse-can-change-inclusion-at—work, accessed: 01.03.2023 (2022)
3. T. Madiega, P. Car, M. Niestadt, L. Van de Pol, *Metaverse. Opportunities, risks and policy implication*, European Parliament Briefing, 24 June 2022, URL: https://www.europarl.europa.eu/thinktank/en/document/EPRS_BRI(2022)733557, accessed: 01.03.2023
4. Council of the European Union, Analysis and Research Team, *Metaverse – Virtual World, Real Challenges*, 9 March 2022
5. K. Laeeq, *Metaverse: Why, How and What*, URL: https://www.researchgate.net/publication/358505001_Metaverse_Why_How_and_What/citations#fullTextFileContent, accessed: 01.03.2023 (2022)
6. N. Stephenson, *Snow Crash*, (Penguin Books Ltd., London, 2011)
7. L.H. Lee, P. Zhou, T. Braud, P. Hui, *What is the Metaverse? An Immersive Cyberspace and Open Challenges*, 7 June 2022, URL: https://doi.org/10.48550/arXiv.2206.03018, accessed: 01.03.2023
8. Kriptomat, Crypto but Simple, *Ce Este Metaversul Și De Ce Ar Tebui Să-i Pese Cuiva?*, URL: https://kriptomat.io/ro/blockchain/ce-este-metaversul/, accessed: 01.03.2023
9. Mémoires du 2eme Monde, URL: https://www.bimondiens.com/, accessed: 01.03.2023
10. Second Life, URL: https://www.secondlife.com, accessed: 01.03.2023
11. Decentraland, URL: https://www.decentraland.org, accessed: 01.03.2023
12. P. Deegan, *The Relational Matrix: The Free and Emergent Organizations of Digital Groups and Identities*, in J.H. Clippinger, D. Bollier (eds.), From Bitcoin to Burning Man and Beyond: The Quest for Identity and Autonomy in a Digital Society, Institute for Institutional Innovation by Data-Driven Design, Amherst, Massachusetts (2014)
13. CJEU (Grand Chamber), 13 May 2014, *Google Spain SL and Google Inc. v Agencia Española de Protección de Datos (AEPD) and Mario Costeja González*, Case C-131/12, ECLI:EU:C:2014:317
14. CJEU (Grand Chamber), 24 September 2019, *Google LLC v Commission nationale de l'informatique et des libertés (CNIL)*, Case C-507/17, ECLI:EU:C:2019:772.
15. L.A. Stutz, *Employment Law in the Metaverse and Zoomiverse: Everything Old Is New Again*, New Jersey Law Journal, 8 November 2022
16. Kraken, *How to Sell Decentraland (MANA)*, URL: https://www.kraken.com/learn/sell-decentraland-mana, accessed: 01.03.2023
17. Adecco Group, *Work in the Metaverse? How the metaverse is shaping the future of work*, 10.02.2022, URL: https://adeccogroup.com/future-of-work/latest-insights/how-the-metaverse-is-shaping-the-future-of-work/?utm_medium=social&utm+source=linkedin&utm_campaign=The+Adecco+Group&utm_keyword=ThoughtLeadership%2CGlobal&utm_content=cf1369a2f75f4f599b677ebe8bb65d79-1929, accessed: 01.03.2023
18. P. Scott-Morgan, S. Gill, *Dr. Peter Scott-Morgan becomes Peter 2.0.*, DXC Technology, URL: https://dxc.com/uk/en/about-us/inclusion-and-diversity/dr--peter-scott-morgan-becomes-peter-2-0, accessed: 01.03.2023
19. Manus, *Virtual Reality Gloves*, URL: https://www.manus-meta.com/vr-gloves, accessed: 01.03.2023

20. CJEU, 11 April 2013, *HK Danmark v Dansk almennyttigt Boligselskab and HK Danmark v Dansk Arbejdsgiverforening*, joined Cases C-335/11 and C-337/11, ECLI:EU:C:2013:222
21. CJEU, 18 March 2014, *Z. v A Government department and The Board of management of a community school*, Case C-363/12, ECLI:EU:C:2014:159
22. CJEU, 22 May 2014, *Wolfgang Glatzel v Freistaat Bayern*, Case C-356/12, ECLI:EU:C:2014:350
23. CJEU, 18 December 2014, *Fag og Arbejde (FOA) v Kommunernes Landsforening (KL)*, Case C-354/13, ECLI:EU:C:2014:2463
24. A. Trachim, P. Chmielewska, *Women in the IT industry,* ItCraft, 29.09.2020, URL: https://itcraftapps.com/blog/women-in-the-it-industry/, accessed: 01.03.2023.
25. Next Generation, *Why Aren't There More Women in Tech?*, URL: https://www.nextgeneration.ie/blog/2018/08/why-arent-there-more-women-in-tech?source=google.com, accessed: 01.03.2023
26. European Union Agency for Fundamental Rights, *Bias in Algorithms – Artificial Intelligence and Discrimination*, Luxembourg: Publications Office of the European Union, (2022)
27. L. Alton, *Identifying and Avoiding Digital Harassment*, 7 June 2022, URL: https://www.adp.com/spark/articles/2022/06/identifying-and-avoiding-digital-harassment.aspx, accessed: 01.03.2023
28. T. Basu, *The Metaverse Has a Groping Problem Already*, Mit Technology Review, 16 December 2021, URL: https://www.technologyreview.com/2021/12/16/1042516/the-metaverse-has-a-groping-problem/, accessed: 01.03.2023
29. A. Shorman, *More Options, More Platforms and Super Bowl LVI Shirts for Avatars,* Meta, 31 January 2022, URL: https://about.fb.com/news/2022/01/updates-to-avatars/, accessed: 01.03.2023
30. Meta, *Introducing the Meta Avatars Store,* 20 June 2022, URL: https://about.fb.com/news/2022/06/introducing-the-meta-avatars-store/, accessed: 01.03.2023
31. B. Marr, *The 10 Best Metaverse Quotes Everyone Should Read*, 15 August 2022, URL: https://www.forbes.com/sites/bernardmarr/2022/08/15/the-10-best-metaverse-quotes-everyone-should-read/?sh=c30ba81225dc, accessed: 01.03.2023
32. M. Doherty, *When the Working Day is Through: the End of Work as Identity?*, in *Work, Employment and Society*, **23**, Issue 1 (2009)
33. A. Supiot, *L'identité professionnelle*, in *Les tendances sociales du droit contemporain*, Études offertes au Professeur Jean Savatier (Presses Universitaires de France, Paris, 1992)
34. A. Bosworth, N. Clegg, *Building the Metaverse Responsibly,* Meta, 27 September 2021, URL: https://about.fb.com/news/2021/09/building-the-metaverse-responsibly/, accessed: 01.03.2023
35. A. Fernandez, *The Metaverse: The Future of Work*, Forbes Business Council, 18 March 2022, URL: at:https://www.forbes.com/sites/forbesbusinesscouncil/2022/03/18/the-metaverse-the-future-of-work/?sh=1cd87d734267, accessed: 01.03.2023
36. A. Aloisi, N. Countouris, V. De Stefano, *The metaverse is a labour issue*, 16 June 2022, URL: https://www.equaltimes.org/the-metaverse-is-a-labour-issue-21651?lang=en#.Y_hp9XZByyI, accessed: 01.03.2023
37. Y. Wang, Z. Su, N. Zhang, R. Xing, D. Liu, T.H. Luan, X. Shen, *A Survey on Metaverse: Fundamentals, Security, And Privacy*, IEEE Communications Surveys & Tutorials, URL: https://doi.org/10.48550/arXiv.2203.02662, accessed: 01.03.2023 (2022)

# The new challenges of hybrid working (part office, part home)

*Raluca* Dimitriu[1*]

[1]Faculty of Law, University of Economic Studies, Bucharest, Romania

**Abstract.** Although not expressly regulated - hybrid work is a reality that cannot be fully encapsulated in the concept of telework. It has several advantages: it allows employees to freely choose where they work, while not losing contact with colleagues. For companies, hybrid working allows a reduction in utility costs and a downsizing of office space, while still being able to benefit from the direct presence of workers. Therefore, hybrid work is the expression of a compromise, which can indeed lead to work-life reconciliation, but it can also have a number of disadvantages. The latter mainly come from the lack of concern of the Romanian legislator for the category of workers who combine remote work with in-office work. The paper describes hybrid work from a legal point of view – at the intersection between willingness and reluctance.

## 1 Context

One of the indicators of today's labour market is, alongside the number of teleworkers, the number of jobs that can be performed remotely (*teleworkable*). Even if the company in question has not actually implemented telework arrangements, this indicator reflects the potential to do so in the future. With regard to teleworkable jobs, some studies show that they account for almost 40% of dependent employment in the European Union [1].

Of course, this does not mean that telework can be equated with teleworkable jobs; for many of the latter, work will continue to be carried out in the traditional system at the employer's premises. Indeed, there are many different aspects (other than the simple nature of the activity) which may be taken into account by the parties when deciding where to carry out the work: the existence of technology and information equipment accessible in the employee's place of work, the distance between the home and the employer's premises, the cost of utilities, the digital skills of the employee concerned, issues relating to the confidentiality of the information processed by the employee, and the degree of security offered by the server used. However, when labour market analysts look to the post-pandemic workplaces of the future, they have in mind this type of work that is susceptible to being carried out remotely, even if this potential cannot always be fully exploited.

During the pandemic, the imposition of social distancing rules has reshaped the role of work in the worker's time economy. Working from home, or from another space organised by herself, the worker:

* Corresponding author email: raluca.dimitriu@drept.ase.ro

-spent more time working for the employer (although often less productive than when working on the company's premises);

-re-internalised a number of activities that he had outsourced (the notorious "pademic-haircut" and other activities that had previously been carried out by third parties in return for remuneration);

-opted for different budget allocations than in the past (fewer purchases of durable goods, lower expenditure on services and goods of the entertainment industry, transport, etc., higher expenditure on training, courier services or dedicated to the purchase of display screen equipment, operating system and software licences). Also, part of the household's current expenditure no longer benefited the family as a whole, but also the employer, through the allocation of space to carry out activities for the employer's benefit, as well as the use of electricity and heat for teleworking purposes;

-in many cases, the worker and her family have left metropolitan areas and large conurbations in favour of less populated rural communities, etc.

But perhaps the most significant change in the realm of labour relations is isolation, which is one expression of the unprecedented expansion of remote work. Any worker doing even partially 'teleworkable' work was sent to work remotely, and this change was sometimes implemented by agreement, but often unilaterally by the employer (the so-called 'forced telework') [2].

The pandemic period was not only a period in which attempts were made to make full use of the potential for remote working, in premises organised by the employees themselves (often their own homes), but also to develop ways of designing jobs [3], defined as the set of objectives, tasks, authority and responsibilities that are assigned to a person in the organisation on a permanent basis, in such a way as to make it possible to separate, in the job description, activities which can be carried out remotely, using information and communication technology, from those for which the physical presence of the employee is indispensable. Firms have thus sought to ensure as much social distance as possible, with as many employees as possible working remotely. According to the legislation applicable in Romania during the state of emergency, they were even obliged to do so, with Government Emergency Ordinance No 192/2020 providing that the employer must order, by unilateral act, the provision of teleworking. Art. 17 of Law no. 55/2020 as amended by Government Emergency Ordinance no. 192/2020 as well as amending letter a) of Art. 7 of Law no. 81/2018 stipulated: 'During the state of alert, employers shall arrange work at home or teleworking, where the specific nature of the activity allows, in compliance with the provisions of Law no. 53/2003 - Labour Code, republished, with subsequent amendments and additions, and Law no. 81/2018 on the regulation of teleworking activity'. By Decision No 50/2022, the Constitutional Court declared unconstitutional Government Emergency Ordinance No 192/2020. It should be noted, however, that the ordinance came out of force anyway, once the state of emergency ended, therefore the effects of the declaration of its unconstitutionality are limited.

However, the effects of this new way of organising activity continued to be felt after the end of the state of alert. The emergence of the new indicator of 'teleworkable' work has highlighted the persistence and even the deepening of the separation between white-collar and blue-collar jobs, between intellectual and physical work and between low-paid and well-paid jobs. **There are basically two distinct classes of employees.** Such differences meant that, during the pandemic, some workers were more protected from the risk of infection than others, because they were able to move less or not at all in the workplace community, due to the very type of work they performed. Workers in areas such as transport, construction, hospitality, restaurants and tourism were not only disadvantaged in terms of health protection measures, but faced technical unemployment (suspension of the employment) and even redundancies. Thus, in a context where social distancing rules were implemented precisely to limit the effects of the Covid 19 pandemic, employees working in companies were more exposed than those who stayed at home. They took on a number of additional risks, which they could not limit by avoiding contact with colleagues and the working environment.

After the end of the pandemic, an 'elite' has emerged among today's workers, who benefit from jobs that are stable but also safe from a health point of view.

Of course, even this 'elite' is not immune from employer abuse and has its own challenges. They face difficulties in quantifying working time and ensuring a fair work-life balance, which has also led to the adoption of new draft directives, such as the one on teleworkers' right to disconnect. But essentially, beyond these concerns, the lives of teleworkers have proven to be more protected than those of employees working in non-teleworkable jobs.

Indeed, elements of working time arrangements statistically impacted the overall level of job satisfaction, revealing a certain pattern. Romanian employees are more satisfied working the same number of hours per day, but more willing to have flexibility in the number of days per week, and this behaviour significantly influences the overall level of their satisfaction. In the last few years, more and more Romanian employers allowed their own employees to either work from home or have a shorter Friday, or a totally free day, and this is also reflected in the level of satisfaction [4]. Ideally, hybrid working would ensure a reconciliation of the two types of jobs and, consequently, of workers. It would enable staff who usually work remotely to overcome the social deficit that telework entails, and those who only work at the company's premises, as a result of the redefinition of jobs, to carry out part of their work remotely.

In reality, however, hybrid working is only an option for workers with teleworkable jobs and who have therefore been able to work remotely, teleworking, also during the state of alert. Because while it is easy to include in the structure of such jobs activities that involve travelling to the company (meetings, direct communications), it is much more difficult to include in the structure of directly productive jobs activities that can be carried out remotely (and related to which the workers also have the necessary equipment and digital knowledge to carry out).

## 2 Hybrid work in Romanian legislation

Hybrid work is work that is performed partly remotely, teleworking, and partly at the employer's premises.

Although there is no express reference in the legislation to hybrid work, the way telework is regulated implicitly recognises the possibility of organising work in this way. Moreover, I would go so far as to say that hybrid work organisation is the rule in this area.

Thus, the Telework Law no. 81/2018 defines telework as a form of work organisation whereby the employee, on a regular and voluntary basis, performs the duties specific to his or her position, occupation or job in a place other than the workplace organised by the employer, using information and communication technology. As a result, employees working in a hybrid system are still considered teleworkers (all the more so as the original text of the law even referred to teleworking as work performed remotely at least one day per month). Indeed, according to Article 5(2)(b) of Law No 81/2018, the teleworking contract must cover the period and/or days during which the teleworker works at a workplace organised by the employer. It is thus accepted that a teleworker may work partly at the workplace organised by the employer and partly at a freely chosen workplace.

In addition, according to Law 296/2020, which amended the Tax Code, the employer is entitled to support, free of tax, the cost of utilities at the place where the teleworker works, up to a ceiling of 400 lei, corresponding to the number of days in the month on which the person works as a teleworker. This legal provision also implicitly recognises hybrid work. It should also be pointed out that the provisions of this legislation did not cease with the end of the state of alert; they continue to have effect.

We would point out that it is not necessary to amend the employment contract for the period during which the work is performed at the employer's premises. The worker remains a teleworker even on these days. Thus, a worker who performs hybrid work is legally a teleworker.

## 3 The place of work

Employees working in hybrid jobs have a dual workplace: for some days, it is the employer-organised space, and for others it is another, non-employer-organised space, for example the teleworker's home.

Government Emergency Ordinance No 36/2021 on the use of electronic signatures in the field of labour relations and amending and supplementing certain regulations has removed the requirement to specify the place of telework, so now the teleworker can choose any place of work and can change it at any time, without notifying the employer. We should mention that, however, in some opinions (sometimes embraced by labour inspectors) since Article 5 (2) of Law No 81/2018 provides that the telework contract should also include the elements provided for in Article 17 (3) of the Labour Code, the place of telework may be even today a mandatory element of the telework.

Anyway, in the case of hybrid work, at least the obligation to establish the place of work on days when the work is carried out in a workplace organised by the employer has to be maintained; even if the hybrid worker is still legally a teleworker, for part of his working time he should have the legal status of a standard employee.

Here we may come up against another rather complex practical problem in the case of teleworkers: how can they be delegated? Delegation is the temporary performance by an employee, on the employer's instructions, of work or tasks corresponding to the duties of his job outside his place of work (Article 43 of the Labour Code). In practical terms, it may be necessary to send the hybrid employee on posting:

- Both on days when the work is carried out in the workplace organised by the employer. This is easier because the place of work is known, therefore the travel order can be issued and travel expenses can be calculated and paid;
- As well as on days when the work is carried out remotely. In this case, the employer may not know where the work is performed, so that posting the employee becomes difficult from a practical and tax point of view.

Article 118 of the Labour Code, as amended by Law no. 283/2022, enshrines the right of employees to request switching to an individualized work schedule, with the employer's obligation to provide a reasoned response to such a request. The matter ends up being of interest to the issue of telework, because in Article 118 (7) the flexible schedule is defined as "the possibility for employees to adapt the work schedule, including through the use of remote work formulas (...)". I think that this definition confuses the temporal plan with the spatial plan: the work schedule has nothing to do with the place of work performance. Although teleworkers and employees performing hybrid work can have (like standard employees) different work schedules, the simple fact that they work remotely does not affect their schedule at all.

Finally, teleworkers have been described as 'digital nomads', in the sense that they are no longer tied to a particular place of work, but could travel anywhere, within the country and beyond, to work. This benefit does not fully apply to hybrid employees, who have to return to the employer's premises a few days in a month or in a week. They would then not be able to travel too far from the company to return on time on the days they are scheduled to do so.

This makes hybrid work more inflexible than pure or full telework, and makes this way of organising work less attractive.

Tangentially, we mention that, according to Law No. 69/2023 amending and supplementing Law No. 227/2015 on the Fiscal Code, foreigners (i.e., non-EU workers) who qualify as digital nomads are not subject to income tax and social contributions for the activity performed in this capacity if they are present in the territory of Romania for a period or multiple periods that do not exceed 183 days during any consecutive 12-month interval ending in the relevant calendar year.

## 4 Activities

The Telework Act applies to areas of activity where teleworking is possible. We note that there is no list of activities in which teleworking is possible, unlike, for example, in the case of day labourers, where Law No 52/2011 provides in Article 13 a list of NACE codes where this type of activity is possible.

So who determines that a particular activity can be performed as teleworking? We also faced this problem during the Covid 19 crisis, when employers had not only the possibility, but even the obligation, to send employees on teleworking, if the specific nature of the activity allowed it. Territorial labour inspectors in some cases, imposed teleworking on employees simply on the basis of a review of the job description, without taking into account other aspects of the work performed (such as restrictions on the confidentiality of information). Nowadays, things are easier, since teleworking, and consequently hybrid work, is only carried out by agreement, an activity is 'teleworkable' to the extent that both parties agree that it can be.

In this respect, some studies [5] differentiate three categories of activities:

a) Activities which in principle are not suitable for being carried out at a distance. These include activities involving dexterity, using and moving objects and equipment, inspecting equipment, structures and materials, operating mechanised vehicles and equipment, activities in agriculture, forestry and fishing, construction, mining, etc.;

b) Social activities, some of which may be performed at a distance. These include sales activities, teaching and training, working with the public, cultural and recreational activities, counselling, care and assistance to others, etc;

c) Information processing activities, which are fully suitable for remote working.

In relation to the job description, hybrid work will reflect how these activities are scaled and can be carried out on-site or remotely with similar results.

However, there can be no spontaneous choice to work at home or at the company; this choice must be anticipated in the employment contract. This contract must specify the periods during which the employee works at the company's premises and at another workplace organised by the employer, thus resulting the days during which the employee works remotely.

The distribution of teleworking days and days worked at the employer's premises is not recorded in ReviSal. But this information must be mentioned in the employment contract with a teleworking clause.

As this is a contractual clause, the employer cannot unilaterally determine or change the days worked at the employer's premises. As we have shown, it was only during the state of emergency that the employer had the possibility and even the obligation to unilaterally order teleworking. In this case, the employer's unilateral act also had to include provisions on working hours, i.e. the number of days on which remote work was to be carried out and the days on which the employee was required to report to the workplace organised by the employer. Thus, during the period of the alert, hybrid work was carried out as a result of the employer's decision, without the employee's consent being required.

However, at present, any determination or change in the distribution of days worked at the employer's premises/remotely will require a renegotiation and an addendum to the individual employment contract – a cumbersome system which can limit the flexibility of the use of hybrid work.

## 5 Content of the hybrid worker's contract

In the case of teleworking, the employment contract shall contain, in addition to the elements referred to in Article 17 (3) of the Labour Code a number of specific items. Since, from a legal point of view, the hybrid worker is also a teleworker, they must also be included in the employment contract:

a) an express statement that the employee works on telework. Failure to comply with the provisions relating to the obligation to expressly stipulate in the employment contract or in the additional act to the contract that the employee is teleworking is punishable by a fine of 10,000 lei per person. The penalty is intended to ensure that the legal provisions on undeclared work are not circumvented by invoking remote working. In other words, if the labour inspector who comes to inspect finds that an employee who is listed as "present" is absent in the records drawn up in accordance with Article 119 of the Labour Code, the employer must prove this by means of the appropriate clause in the employment contract and the work schedule established for the hybrid employee;

b) the period and/or days during which the teleworker works at a job organised by the employer. We would argue that this provision could be replaced by reference to a timetable of activities, which would be updated periodically, by agreement of both parties, so that it would not be necessary to amend the individual employment contract by an additional act whenever the need for the employee's presence in the company arises or, conversely, whenever the employee's presence is no longer necessary. Such an approach would be in line with the Directive (EU) 2019/1158 on work-life balance for parents and carers and repealing Council Directive 2010/18/EU. Indeed, it should be noted that one of the aims of implementing hybrid work is to establish a better balance between work and family life, but the excessive rigidity that accompanies such a clause would in fact lead to a reduction in the hybrid employee's chances of achieving such a balance. Both employer and employee may face unforeseen situations requiring the hybrid employee to be present at one or another of their workplaces without the parties having time to amend the employment contract accordingly;

c) the timetable within which the employer is entitled to check the teleworker's work and the concrete way in which the check is carried out. Similar regulations exist in the Labour Code also with regard to the home-working contract (Article 109 (b)). As have been noted, "for access to the home, the employee's consent must be prior and special. Therefore, in this case, we cannot speak of an unexpected check with the aim of surprising the reality of the employee's compliance with the conditions for carrying out the activity" [6]. Besides, this time we may face a problem: if the teleworker works in the private/public space of a third party (e.g. in a café), the employer's access may be restricted, depending not only on the consent of the teleworker, but also on the consent of the third party – the owner. In addition, the employer may not even know where the hybrid employee carries out the activity, which makes it impossible for him to exercise his right of control;

d) recording the hours worked by the teleworker. The number of hours worked, as well as the start/end time of the activity, under the terms of Article 119 of the Labour Code, can be recorded by monitoring the time of logging in, for the days when the activity is carried out remotely. We have, therefore, a dual system: one monitoring system (such as, for example, the attendance record) which can be used on days when the employee is present in the workplace organised by the employer and another system (such as the presentation of timesheets containing the activity and its hours) on days when the employee works remotely;

e) the responsibilities of the parties agreed according to the location(s) of the teleworking activity, including occupational safety and health responsibilities. The OSH training will need to be conducted twice, depending on the location and the specific risks to which the employee is exposed, in both locations;

f) the employer's obligation to ensure the transport to and from the place of teleworking of the materials that the teleworker uses in his or her work, where applicable;

g) the employer's obligation to inform the teleworker of the provisions of the legal regulations, the applicable collective labour agreement and/or internal rules on the protection of personal data and the obligation of the teleworker to comply with those provisions. Teleworkers can use their own equipment in the course of their work, which sometimes creates issues regarding the confidentiality of the information they work with. That is why the employer can impose specific rules and restrictions regarding the internet networks used. On the contrary, the protection of the teleworker's data does not form the object of an express regulation within the law. Indeed, the law simply states that the employer has the right to check the activity of the teleworker mainly through the use of information and communication technology, under the terms established by the employment contract, the internal regulation and/or the applicable collective labour agreement;

h) the measures the employer takes to ensure that the teleworker is not isolated from other employees and that the teleworker has the opportunity to meet colleagues on a regular basis;

i) the conditions under which the employer bears the costs of teleworking. In particular, the employer may bear the costs of providing the information and communication technology facilities itself or may share these costs with the teleworker. If the use of the teleworker's own means is chosen, this must be expressly stated in the contractual agreement. Moreover, agreement is required in this case, even if teleworking has been unilaterally decided during the period of the state of alert.

## 6 Proportionate granting of rights

In the case of hybrid work, problems may also arise with the granting of allowances for difficult, harmful or dangerous working conditions. For example, by Decision No 1068/2021 of 16 Sept. 2021 – the Timisoara Court of Appeal ruled that "during the period of work at home, the institution's staff do not receive any bonus for difficult, harmful or dangerous working conditions". But what will be the solution if the employee works under such conditions at the workplace organised by the employer, while part of the time is spent on teleworking? The increase should be granted in proportion to the time actually worked in such workplaces.

Travel costs should also be granted proportionally, if the employer has assumed that they will be granted for the employee's travel from home to the company.

The amount of 400 lei is also granted proportionally, under the terms of Law No 296/2020 amending and supplementing Law No 227/2015 on the Tax Code.

## 7 Legal aspects of hybrid work

From a legal perspective, there are certain aspects of hybrid work that need to be considered:

-The place of work depends on the type of work organisation. For example, if the teleworking contract states that the employee is present in the company on Mondays and then from Tuesdays to Fridays works in a freely chosen workplace, it is not necessary to specify in the contract which workplace it is. It could be the employee's home, or any other place. Only for Monday is the place of work known, as it is predetermined in the contract;

-Teleworkers did not receive days off for supervising children learning online, as provided for in all successive legislation regulating this issue, including Government Emergency Ordinance No 110/2021 on the granting of paid days off to parents and other categories of persons in the context of the spread of the SARS-CoV-2 coronavirus, approved by Law No 163/2022. The regulation did not distinguish between days when work was still performed at the employer's premises and days when it was performed at home, so employees who worked in a hybrid regime did not benefit from days off even when they were at the employer's premises;

-Hybrid workers can also be posted. But delegation, which is a unilateral change of workplace, can only be ordered for days when, according to the employment contract, the work is carried out at the employer's workplace. Delegation may not be ordered during the period spent at home or at another freely chosen place, not specified in the contract;

-As employees who work in a hybrid system are also considered teleworkers, it follows that the way in which the working hours are to be recorded will be established by the employment contract (according to Article 5(e) of Law No 81/2018) and not unilaterally by the employer, according to Article 119 (1) of the Labour Code. This record is mandatory for the days when the employee works from home and for the days when he or she works at the company;

-The working hours are determined by mutual agreement in the contract with the teleworking clause (Article 4 (1) of Law no. 81/2018). It may be different on days when the employee works in the company than on days when he or she works at the workplace of his or her choice;

-By establishing hybrid work, the employer implicitly fulfils its obligation to take measures to ensure that the teleworker is not isolated from the rest of the employees and to ensure that the teleworker has the opportunity to meet with colleagues on a regular basis (Article 5 (2) (i) of Law no. 81/2018).

## 8 Challenges

Hybrid working seems to meet the needs of most employees as it allows them to freely choose where they work, while not losing contact with colleagues.

For companies, hybrid working allows a reduction in utility costs and a downsizing of office space. Increased productivity and reduced office fit-out costs are among the most frequently cited benefits for employers. In practice, it is sometimes decided to provide fewer offices than employees. They come to work on a rotational basis, based on appointment. The office is no longer personalised, but on a „first-come, first-served" basis.

The formulas used are various: 1-3 days a week at the employer's place of work and the rest remotely; 2 weeks at the employer's premises, 2 weeks at home; all work carried out remotely, except for 1-2 days a month when certain meetings are held – or any other variant, provided it is specified in the employment contract.

But hybrid working is a compromise, which, like any compromise, sacrifices some interests in favour of others.

-The hybrid worker is, under Romanian law, a teleworker;

-Working hours must be expressly specified in the employment contract, so the employee cannot spontaneously decide where he or she will work this morning;

-Only jobs that are already "teleworkable" are suitable for hybrid work;

-The space occupied by the employee is double (although not always) – he or she will have an office at home and, separately, an office at the employer's premises, which could involve higher expenses;

-If the work is performed using information and communication technology, often some of the equipment will need to be installed both at the employer's premises and at the employee's workplace;

-Hybrid meetings and work sessions may favour some participants over others (the so-called "proximity bias"). Similarly, hybrid work teams can operate in two speeds, between those who are face-to-face and those who are remote. Social bonds between colleagues are different, and asymmetries are created in the team;

-There may be problems related to data protection and leaks of confidential information, caused by the frequent change of workplace;

-Remote working presents its own challenges in terms of collective relations.

Besides, as has been pointed out, "telework must not become a substitute for childcare. The fact that workers are at home is no reason why childcare and public social care services should not continue to be provided or improved where needed. It is vital that teleworking does not become an excuse to push women to stay at home, to do domestic work and to provide for childcare" [7].

## 9 Perspectives

Digitalisation has brought with it a new shift in the way we relate to work. It is no longer necessarily a collective experience, but a solitary one... The boundaries between private and professional life are blurred; the digital worker has already incorporated productive work into family time, and few people are able to draw firm boundaries between these two worlds.

Indeed, today, work done within the family, in one's own household, has begun to take on a relevance that no one suspected it would regain in the context of modern society. The physical separation from colleagues, a pre-existing phenomenon, but no doubt accentuated by the Covid 19 crisis, contemporary management methods geared towards autonomy, and the increasingly direct relationship with the customer, have turned the worker into a lone wolf, who obtains his resources in a universally competitive context and is expected to adopt a more entrepreneurial attitude. Hardly anything that used to define the work carried out in large industrial companies, which gave rise to labour law based on solidarity between workers working shoulder to shoulder, is indispensable today. If we look, for example, at the ILO's 2006 Recommendation No 198 on employment relationships, as well as the indicators considered to be decisive for identifying an employment relationship, we can see how much dependent work has changed in the last 15 years.

Digitalisation has changed not only the way work is actually performed, but also the way we perceive it. Disengaging from a physical workspace can lead to repositioning work throughout our lives. Already the most recent generations to enter the labour market no longer value work as their parents did, but tend to place leisure time and life experiences (not necessarily professional) at the centre of their existence [8].

Governments have reacted differently to the explosion of hybrid employment contracts. Ireland, for example, has passed legislation which allows any employee to request to work, at least in part, remotely [9], and while the employer is of course not obliged to accept such a request, it cannot penalise in any way the employee who submitted this request. Any refusal on the part of the employer must be justified, and the law lists the possible reasons for such a refusal. These include, for example, the speed of the internet in the space proposed by the employee for carrying out the work.

**The right of access to hybrid work is not a universal right.** Once again, it reflects disparities in the labour market, favouring the category of workers – professionals, generally well-paid and digitally literate, at the expense of those who are not digitally literate and are physically active, often poorly paid. Encouraging telework, an object for many European governments during the pandemic and even after its end, should take this into account. Differences also exist between Member States, with some countries, such as the Nordic countries, having a clear advantage before the pandemic, while other Member States have sought to catch up. Differences also exist between companies, with larger companies more likely to successfully implement hybrid working than smaller ones [5].

As far as Romanian law is concerned, I believe that there are still steps to be taken in the direction of making the hybrid employment relationship more flexible, so that it achieves its purpose. Let us not forget that its widespread use has been associated with a very exceptional situation, i.e. the Covid 19 crisis. However, after the end of the pandemic, the percentage of employees working, even partially, remotely, will never return to the low rates seen before the crisis, so it has become a phenomenon that no longer has health causes but is directly linked to the choices of the parties. Some studies [10] reveal that telework – particularly hybrid models – continued after the pandemic, as its large-scale use has raised awareness of its benefits and shown that obstacles can be overcome. Employees who have gone through a work-life integration and learning process push employers to maintain flexible work models. Besides, hybrid work models push companies to rethink the role of the office: the office of the future will be conceived as a place for collaborative and creative work, socialisation, and experiencing company culture.

Finally, the right to disconnect, so frequently discussed at European level in this period, should also be the focus of the Romanian legislator. Teleworking, even partial teleworking, is based on the agreement of the parties, but this does not mean that the employee has also agreed to be permanently available to the employer's requests and messages. His or her rest time should be as well protected as if the employee comes and goes from the company at a certain time. The fact that it is more easily accessible should not presume it to be available without restriction after hours.

## References

1. M. Sostero, S. Milasi, J. Hurley, E. Fernández-Macías, M. Bisello, *Teleworkability and the COVID-19 crisis: a new digital divide?*, A Joint European Commission–Eurofound Report, URL: https://joint-research-centre.ec.europa.eu/system/files/2020-07/jrc121193.pdf, accessed: 01.03.2023 (2020)
2. M. Fana, S. Tolan, S. Torrejon Perez, M.C. Urzi Brancati, E. Fernández-Macias, *The COVID confinement measures and EU labour markets*, Publications Office of the European Union, Luxembourg, URL: https://publications.jrc.ec.europa.eu/repository/handle/JRC120578, accessed: 01.03.2023 (2020). The authors note very different effects from country to country within the European Union: "the fast and largely forced transition to a much more generalised telework regime is likely to have been much more difficult in some countries than others"
3. A. Manolescu, *Managementul resurselor umane* (Ed. Economică, Bucharest, 2003). In human resource management, the job is generally defined as the set of objectives, tasks, authority and responsibilities that are assigned to a person in the organisation on a permanent basis.
4. A.A. Davidescu, S.A. Apostu, A. Paul, I. Căşuneanu, Sustainability, **12**(15), 1-53, 6086, DOI:10.3390/su12156086, accessed: 01.03.2023 (2020)

5. Eurofound, *Teleworkability and the COVID-19 crisis: a new digital divide,* JRC Working Papers Serios on Labour, Education and Technology, URL: https://joint-research-centre.ec.europa.eu/system/files/2020-07/jrc121193.pdf, accessed: 01.03.2023 (2020)
6. S. Panainte, Analele Ştiinţifice UAIC. SSJ, **LXVII**(2), 37-55, URL: http://doi.org/10.47743/jss-2021-67-4-3, accessed: 01.03.2023 (2021)
7. R. Stochiţa, *Costul telemuncii: sarcinile domestice cad pe umerii femeilor*, Cartel Alfa, URL: https://www.cartel-alfa.ro/ro/ultimele-noutati-4/costul-telemuncii-sarcinile-domestice-cad-pe-umerii-femeilor-128/, accessed: 01.03.2023 (2021)
8. R. Dimitriu, Analele Ştiinţifice UAIC. SSJ, **LXVII**(2), 25-36, URL: http://doi.org/10.47743/jss-2021-67-4-2, accessed: 01.03.2023 (2021)
9. D. Mangan, *Responses to Covid-19: Remote Work*, Global Workplace Law & Policy (kluwerlawonline.com), URL: https://global-workplace-law-and-policy.kluwerlawonline.com/2022/05/26/responses-to-covid-19-remote-work/?utm_campaign=10293-B%20-%20PA%20KLO&utm_medium=email&utm_source=Eloqua, accessed: 01.03.2023 (2022)
10. C. Vasilescu, *The impact of teleworking and digital work on workers and society*, Policy Department for Economic, Scientific and Quality of Life Policies Directorate-General for Internal Policies, URL: https://www.europarl.europa.eu/RegData/etudes/STUD/2021/662904/IPOL_STU(2021)662904(ANN05)_EN.pdf, accessed: 01.03.2023 (2021)

# Taxing forms in the digital environment

*Ioana Maria* Costea[1]*

[1] Faculty of Law, Alexandru Ioan Cuza University, Romania

**Abstract.** Taxation is a phenomenon of legal adagio to a preliminary juridical relevant relation generated by legal subjects' interactions in a given environment. The traditional milieu is evolving in newer directions as human activity, including markets, are digitalizing. This new domain of legal interaction is addressed also by tax legislation in both substantial and procedural dimensions. This new map of tax relevancy is read by the present study to catalogue classical and emerging instruments of taxation in the digital environment.

## 1 Introduction

The emerging digital world can be seen both as a set of instruments used by conventional interactions and as a new, *sui generis* collaborative space. The fourth industrial revolution is bringing in the traditional framework of human interaction a set of instruments that are replacing conventional ones or even adding to the classical framework. From robots to bots, from brain drain to tax base erosion, from digital assets to digital contracts, all these forms of expressing business intention and materializing transactions have some standard traits and some new individualities. The aim of the study is to identify the taxation relevancy of these economic dynamics and to verify how legal solutions for classical taxation are applicable in these cases and where there is room for new tax regulation.

In writing this paper, a literature review analysis of the relevant business dimensions sustained or generated by the digital environment has been used. The literature review is accompanied by a historical approach as the study focuses on the clash of classical taxation theory with these emerging business tools.

Our working hypothesis is that the digital market remains a market governed by similar rules to the conventional one and that digital advent is a tool both for businesses and fiscal actors.

The relevancy of the study is deriving from the relevancy of the digital environment based on a constant interrogation: how do we interact in the digital environment? A series of characteristics of this interaction has been identified in the literature; the digital interaction is pseudo-anonymous, as it is mediated through a digital persona (avatar, nickname etc.), de-materialized (interaction is ensured in the on-line environment), de-territorialized (actors are no longer bound to a geographical territory, but to a digital territory) and de-intermediated (actors interact directly, even if a support platform is present).

* Corresponding author: ioana.costea@uaic.ro

## 2 Digital environment – what is it good for?

The digital environment has two dimensions; in a classical legal theory it is the place for personal interactions (including forms of social interactions with no patrimonial direct content, such as a digital agora) and for patrimonial interactions. The latter is the foundation of the digital market. Digital market has its roots in the entrainment of Internet in the market [1] and is also known as electronic market. The digital market includes interactions on the World Wide Web, distributed ledger technology, such as blockchain [2] and digital spaces, known as metaverses [3]. The relation between these digital spaces and digital market is that of intersecting multitudes, as the patrimonial dimension is present only in a portion of the digitalized relationships. We will define the digital market as a market in which the economic actors relate at distance using a form of technology. This emerging market is a place of interaction between businesses, consumers and government regulators that raises economic discussions exceeding this study: contract formation, digital marketing, price regulation, consumer protection etc. These focus points are relevant as they do not represent new dimensions of business *per se*, but new forms of expression of classical trade regulation. This permanency of traditional roles is the foundation of our study as it grounds our statement that emerging markets tend to follow tradition patrimonial patterns (we will use the term patrimonial and not economic since our study is a legal one). A smart contract [4] is a contract nevertheless and the novelty is addressing issues of traditional contracts (enforceability, contractual risks, contractual costs), but is not challenging structural dimensions.

To test our theory, we will first proceed to identifying the utility models of these digital interactions in their patrimonial relevancy with the exclusion of personal, non-economic interactions. We can list at least six domains of the digital space with legal subsequent relevancy. We will use the fiscal relevancy criteria as recognized by classical tax theory: subject and object of taxation, taxable base, collecting method [5] and denounce any subsequent aspects that are ground for other legal fields, such as protection of the parties or enforcement issues. Secondary, we will underline, if the case, the novelty of the relationship as to its content, dividing the matter into two arenas: traditional dimensions altered by digital performance and new spectrums of social relations, digital relations.

Primarily, digital spaces are used as frame for work relationships: digital labour [6] and digitally mediated labour [1]. Although labour relations are not entirely part of the market as they are governed by different rules, their patrimonial dimensions raise the question of taxation. We choose to firstly address this space, as labour relations' volatility increased under the COVID pandemic [7]. Digital labour is a form of cultural labour, that we will treat from a taxation perspective and dissociate it as a form of independent activity. Digitally mediated labour is a form of dependent activity in which the digital connectors mediated the interactions between employer and employee in domains that are prone to such an interaction (controlling services, software development, distribution of products, management functions, gaming services). Some forms of labour are emergent ones, such as 'immaterial labour', part of the digital environment where work has shifted from factory to society [8] in taxation perspective; the materiality of a patrimonial activity is part of the traceability process and proof of the dependency relation. For example, working on a product for an employer from home or using a platform to identify clients to deliver work has a material dimension; creating a digital product for a company loses this dimension and qualifies as immaterial work. The digital context also fashions new spaces for problematic activities, such as '24-7 electronic sweatshops', the emergence of 'net-slaves' [9]. Though the ethical aspect of work is not the object of this study, since our analysis focuses on taxation, the patrimonial relevancy of the activity and the inherent organization of work relationships are significant in determining tax relevancy and tax collection. Digital labour and digitally mediated labour bring through the mediation of the on-line spectrum some particularities to the traditional labour taxation forms

[10] the lack of concomitant physical presence, as a constant of digital environment allows employers and employees to form contractual bounds with an extraterritoriality dimension. Also, the digitally mediated work tends to dilute the traditional dependency between the employer and the employee and transfer some of the risks and obligations to the employee, as a free worker. This autonomy has significant implications in taxation. In all cases, the digital environment is a place that mediates interactions and offers an alternative to on-site work. In the spectrum of labour relations, the fourth industrial revolution introduces a new actor: robots and AI as 'workers'. Even if the issue is relatively new and undergoing, some discussions have risen about the taxation of this work form; from taxation of robots as goods for VAT purposes to taxation of robots or AI as revenue generators, even subject of tax law [11] the implicit replacement of traditional workers by robots or bots generates a shift in the subject of taxation debate. As their autonomy is still at bay, these contributors to the taxable base are not seen as subjects of taxation, but as forms of action of a traditional tax subject natural or legal person.

Secondly, the digital environment is a digital market, as a space that mediates interactions between supply and demand. This market is a market governed by traceability as all information is stored forever [12]. The purposes of this traceability are obvious (product liability, product information etc.); the tax relevancy is implicit as all transactions are collected in a digital registry and are potentially available to the tax authority. The digital market has a prime relevancy as a substitute for conventional market as it brings together the participant to the supply chain, and even generates new supply chains – digital supply chains [13]. Contracts are formed at distance between partners from different jurisdictions, accessibility of products increases as information asymmetries decrease [1]. In this context, contracts are relevant considering a feature for VAT theory as to the object of the contract: supply of goods and supply of services. The VAT theory limits the concept of supply of goods to material, mobile goods and assimilates immaterial goods to services. This construct is useful in taxation as it generates an algorithm for distribution of the power to tax between involved jurisdictions in a digital transaction. A role in the digital market is undertaken by the intermediary platforms both as significant retailers in business to consumer dimension (Shopify, BigCommerce, AdobeCommerce, Amazon, Alibaba) or consumer to consumer contracts (e-Bay, Bonanza, Facebook Market). Other actors are the on-line payment agents that manage payment information: account holders, card activity, digital wallet activity (traditional banks, Chargebee, Paddle, Revolut). The platforms in both cases have a relevant role as they aggregate transactions and information about transactions. This triangulation (supplier-platform-buyer) could be a facilitator for tax collection as the platforms hold all information about the transactions.

The digital market has a second relevancy as a market for 'products' generated and used in the digital environment. This market is bringing together digitally native suppliers [14] with their clients in all forms of transactions b2b; b2c; b2pc. The applications are infinite, from gaming to education, from media to AI services, from crypto assets to data market. The legal relevant dimensions are given by the immateriality of the product, hence our prior statement that digital products are mostly qualifiable as services, by the immediate and digitalized execution of the contract, by data administration and by cyber-security issues. In this context, some taxing directions are to be identified. There is a market for digital products, which raises questions about the place of taxation, such as delivery of digitalized content (regardless of the object: on-line courses, music, media content, gaming etc.). Since the transactions ensuring the transfer of these products are entirely digitalized, the real issue is the place of taxation. We will ensure an analysis on this issue, as we will address the clash between classical permanent establishment theory and the new criteria of digitally relevant presence. The digitalization of the product moves the accent in the jurisdictional matter from the place of supplier's establishment (the common rule derived from VAT theory) to the place of reception of the content. Even more, as content and subsequently the pricing are highly fragmented, a gross manner of determining the volume of transaction is required. In the vast realm of digitalized products, there are some emerging categories. Firstly, the product may present itself as a content usually mediated through a platform (Instagram, Twitter, YouTube, Patreon, Only-fans etc.), with a professional title (that gets further and further from classical professional recognition such as formal occupational classification) or a personal title, known as user generated content, susceptible of instant fame. The vast category of influencers [15] and content creators are a subset of digital labourers as they deliver a generated content which integrates a pricing dynamic (directly or indirectly). Influencers are information or art creators, hence authors in a traditional approach, and their revenues are relevant as intellectual property rights revenues. The integration of these forms of revenues in traditional classification of the taxable base is rather easy due to the similarities in the consumer's approach. Contemporary tax legislations have already undergone this process of integration. In a procedural dimension, the platform ensuring the interactions between creator and consumer plays a patrimonial role and may have a tax collection role. Platforms associate a patrimonial content to the relation between the creator and the follower, directly, through a subscription or indirectly, through deliverance of controlled content, such as advertising. YouTube has a subscription for ad-free content; Patreon allows variable pay-outs to access content; Facebook is free of charge but includes paid services such as promoting your posts. Where content is accessible without fees (Twitter, Instagram, TikTok), social-media-based metrics [15] such as number of followers, frequency of posts, reading of posts, usage of uppercase letters, usage of distinct words, and even hashtags may allow the identification of such influencers and the analysis of their fiscal behaviour. Subsequent contractual dynamics may be revealed with patrimonial relevancy, such as promoting a brand or a product. Secondly, the digital content can be represented by a digital asset or a crypto asset, such as a cryptocurrency (Bitcoin, Ethereum, Dogecoin – on coinmarketcap.com, there are 8864 such instruments listed), stable-coin (USDC, Binance USD), investment token (DAI), game token (GALA) or a non-fungible token (BAYC). Here as the digital market accrued, regulations emerged. The DAC regulation (Directive of Administrative Cooperation) focuses explicitly on the exchange of information between tax administration and the latest proposal reacts to use of crypto assets and e-money. These instruments as they are significantly relevant to patrimony dynamics, highly mobile and imply a certain occult dynamic due to their extremely digitalized algorithm, undergo a process of regulatory approach with the European Union – MiCA regulation. We do not intent to analyse these regulations, but rather point out the jurisprudential approach of the ECJ, confirming our working hypotheses; a cryptocurrency is just a currency [16, 17] and should be treated as such by assimilation to e-money and digitalized payment forms. The secondary patrimonial dynamic as an investing instrument has more fiscal relevancy, but also assimilable to the treatment of revenue in corporate or personal taxation (with no VAT implications) [18]. A relevant emerging market, in a business manner seems to be the data commerce [19]; the concerns for equal access to business opportunity and hence the emerging of data cooperatives is not relevant to our study. We will only state that the commercial relevancy of these new instruments is like any other commerce with immaterial goods.

The digital market users are flirting with the idea of a digital life of humans. The promoted idea of a digital verse, a Meta-verse as an alternative or a complement to our physical existence is conceptualizing a marginal economic ecosystem, as a scalable and networked environment using digital interactions of avatars. The source of such a persona is identifiable in the gaming experience, where interactions with other humans through their digital persona is a constant. Transferring activities from the physical world to the Meta-verse may have a variety of purposes: shopping, gaming, learning, working, meeting others etc. [20, 21]; it is characterized using an avatar, in 'an immersive Internet as a gigantic, unified, persistent, and shared realm' [22]. The experience is an alternative, phenomenological in a philosophical sense, where a real person creates a persona and lives through it. The content is ensured by a platform that allows personas to interact; like any other human interactions the metaverse contact may become legally relevant. It may lead to the need of protection some values, either inherent or metaverse generated; it may generate a patrimonial content such as a transaction of a metaverse 'product' or 'service'; it may gain at certain point a fiscal relevancy. Since the metaverse has a God [23] and that God is omniscient, the platform facilitating the content is also controlling all the information. It may not control all interactions, hence allowing the statement that avatars have free will, as a projection of the person controlling them, but it will codify and archive all interactions. Eating an apple in the garden of the Metaverse will leave a recorded trace in the code and will allow further legal treatment, including a tax response where a taxable base is formed. It is to God to scan all records and identify the primordial sin. Selling 'land', training skilful avatars, performing a cultural act for a price, paying for goods or services are all part of our Universe and transferable to the Metaverse, as encrypted in the code of our human interactions.

The digital life is not reserved only to humans; bots inhabit the Internet and 'live' there too and even AI powered bots. These presences, even if not human in a legal sense, replicate a human presence and engage in social interaction. The quality of this 'replica' [24] is not an issue for our study; its presence is legally relevant as it simulates, replaces, or supplements a human activity [25] and therefore bears similar legal significances. In a legal sense, and especially in the field of tax law, the measure for relevancy is not authenticity, but purpose, refined as patrimonial content [11]. A service provided to a human being by a Bot or an AI application is as relevant for fiscal purposes as a service provided by another human being. The legal analysis may raise inquiries about the subject of taxation or means of taxing but not to the existence of an object of taxation. At this moment in the Internet revolution, as we do not acknowledge to these presences the quality of law subject, legal debates are mere philosophical approaches [26, 27, 28] and despite their newness, we are not in the presence of an alteration of the classical paradigms.

All environments that sustain interactions with legal relevancy contain two types of relations which are qualifiable as licit or illicit [29]; therefore, this rule applies to the internet mediated interactions too. In the context of our study, this rule allows a subsequent qualification of transactions as transparent for tax purposes or means of tax avoidance and tax evasion. The digital interactions due to their aptitudes in relation to traceability may be viewed as opaque in relation to the classical means of identifying transactions, but also more transparent in relation to newer ways of communication with tax authorities. This bipolarity reshapes tax compliance and consequently tax evasion and determines an adaptation of the means of implementing taxation not only for the taxpayer, but also for tax authorities [29]. A possible scenario implies that tax authorities using digital means become invisible, 'this is one possible scenario that could evolve from today's landscape of cashless payments, cash registers and digital-invoicing tools that are connected directly to accounting software, and digital tax registries—that is firmly established and maturing in many countries'.

## 3 What tax challenges are arising?

In this landscape of the digital market, seen both as a subset of the classical markets and a space for new transactions, taxation is under pressure for change both in a material and procedural dimension. The classical theory of taxation organizes around the concept of taxation matter, which is the core of the legal context and a permanency in all markets. Taxation is a secondary legal relation; it derives from a legal interaction with patrimony relevancy, which occurs in each market and has its own existence and purpose. The scope of a patrimonial activity is not taxation; taxation is an external effect, imposed by public force.

The patrimonial activity has an autonomous existence that orientates the behaviour of both participants and tax authority. One can identify subsets of taxation in relation to their subject and their object. A classical dichotomy artificially organises taxation around the type of the subject: personal taxation and company taxation. This artificiality of the dichotomy derives from the fact that the form of organising an activity and does not affect its taxing relevancy as a core, but merely transposes a public policy towards types of business. For example, a lighter tax regime for small farms does not qualify all revenues deriving from farming as non-taxable but transposes a policy of the tax sovereign towards a group of taxpayers: small farmers. Therefore, taxation's main core is not the form of organizing an activity but the content of that activity; one can organize taxation around its content as capital taxation (inert or invested in a business), work taxation (seen as activity delivered in the frame of a labour contract or even independently), consumption taxation (as an effect of consuming products or services) and property taxation.

Taxation is a reflection of the public authority and hence it is strongly related to the space of domination; fiscal authority encompasses the power to decide the object and the level of taxation. Hence, fiscal jurisdictions are heterogeneous; one activity may be taxable in one jurisdiction and exempted from taxation in another. This heterogeneity is a result of fiscal autonomy and part of the state autonomy. Consequently, the place of a transaction is relevant in determining the fiscal effects of the transaction. The classical theory of taxation has produced a set of legal rules to address the potential conflict of jurisdictions synthesized as treaties for avoiding double taxation that rely on a liaison element such as residence or permanent establishment [30]. These two concepts bear a high relevancy of the geographical connection to a certain tax jurisdiction and are under significant pressure as digital market is not mapped [31, 32]. The current tax system is built taking into consideration the actual geographical location of the participants in a legal relation. This location is relevant differently: in capital taxation its ties the business to the geographical source of decision; in work taxation it ties the revenue to the location where work is delivered; in consumption taxation it connects taxation to the location of either the buyer or the seller; in property taxation it gives relevancy to the place where the goods are stored. In this context, digital market brings two new dimensions: one is the shift in the relevance of physical place for a transaction (parts of the transactions have vague connections to a physical, geographical place) and the second is the surplus of mobility that may led to tax erosion. This new reality imposes the rewriting of the classical paradigm for determining the place of taxation; it may be treated as an international taxation matter, but from a certain level on it is a digital taxation matter where territory as seen in the classical theory loses its relevancy. In an analysis of emerging business models [33] regarding Amazon and other digitalized distribution channel is obvious that geography does not serve any role. An alternative solution is required [33, 34] an inventory of relevant factors includes: quantitative facts such as number of active users, number of registered users, amount of costs, etc. and qualitative elements: availability of local domain, local digital platform etc. The emerging taxing models, for implementing a digital permanent establishment (*sic!*) may rely on introducing flat tax for digital market in relation to users located in a certain jurisdiction or taxing the revenues at source under the concept of significant digital presence [35].

A secondary dimension in taxation is the burden of proof; the main characteristic of tax law is the absent creditor. The creditor for tax duties is absent at the tax relevant event; the event in the classical form or digitalized takes unfolds as an act or legal fact between private entities. The public creditor is absent; he does not perceive the event, nor its dimensions. The public creditor is informed through tax formalities about the occurrence of such event by the debtor. This emphasis on transparency from the debtor is a vulnerability of the tax collection system and puts pressure on the proof dynamic in tax law. As to classical business context proof is assured by a concoction of written and material elements, such as invoice, banking turnovers, accounting evidence. In the digital context, as all interactions are mediated by a computational environment, proof and traceability are always obtainable. So, tax audit is evolving in two directions: (1) a synchrony one where digital invoicing is connected to a tax authority server and data processing can signal red flags in taxpayers' behaviour; (2) an a-synchrony one where tax audit investigates digital content in its prior mention omniscient dimension to retrace fiscally relevant transactions.

### 3.1 Substantive dimensions in taxing digital economy

Tax law is facing the digital economy both in a material and procedural dimension. The material elements revolve around the classical or emerging transactions, as tax law is a legal domain after the economic dynamic. Traditional tax theory considers two elements in a rather specific manner: the object of taxation and the subject of taxation. Both components have a classic dimension and newer forms in digital environments.

The most intuitive and direct dimension of digital environment taxation maintains the traditional subject and object and follows its transfer in the digital world. Economic actors, both companies and natural persons will owe tax for the transactions concluded and executed in digital form in identical conditions. A transaction considering its object will be taxed both in case of goods or services material or digitalized, paid in cash, through banking in fiduciary or crypto currency. The relevant tax in this context might be corporate tax or revenue tax, depending on the tax subject. The determination of the tax matter is also ruled by the general provisions of applicable legislation; it might be actual or flat-rate determination; it might be due annually or for smaller fractions of time.

In a more autonomous stage, emerging tax subjects or taxable personas gain fiscal relevancy. This gain is not autonomous completely, it roots also in the transfer of taxable subject or taxable object from physical transactions to digital transaction, with or without a connection to the natural world. It is the case in taxing e-taxpayers, such as the digital workers or the emergent agents such as influencers, facilitators, platforms.

Finally, taxes are due for digital content; such is the case of digital 'goods' or more precise digital services, and of digital personas. In this dimension, as though the digital existence seems entirely autonomous, it is not yet the case. The digital content or the digital persona are projections of a real world will; at this moment in time, even the most autonomous digital existence, such as an avatar in the Metaverse or an AI bot is still related immediately or 'mediately' to the will of a real person, a natural person.

In a very non-sophisticated, direct, and straightforward way, tax law has a unifying duty in addressing economy; it will assure in a normative frame the necessary resources for the budgetary dynamics without significant attention to transactional nuances. 'Render unto Caesar that which is Caesar's' transposes in contemporary dimensions in the flexibility of taxation norms in defining taxable subjects (extended to any legal entity) or taxable matter (especially when it comes to legal entities), but a certain inflexibility in sparing economic dimensions. The normative frame might consider, due to national legislator's preferences, some variables tending to modulate some economic sectors or to favour some vulnerable subjects. For example, promoting digital companies through fiscal incentives upon the salary tax might be a sign of encouraging the economy or adjusting tax evasion in the field.

In the most pragmatic manner, direct taxation is devised between two main sources: taxing businesses and taxing employees. These two main directions target different economic contexts; the first is focusing on professional revenue generated by the difference between a product or a services cost and its selling price regardless of the context, content or market; the second is deriving a tax consequence from delivering labour as an inherent component of any services, including digital ones.

## 3.2 Procedural dimensions in taxing digital economy

The procedural dimensions of taxation include personal obligations under the principle of loyal cooperation. The tax creditor is an absentee landlord; the tax authorities are a shadow presence in all markets, unequipped to supervise all transactions, working on risk evaluation. The debtor and other third parties are traditionally obliged to communicate the existence of the tax debt and to facilitate its audit. This declarative context puts supplementary pressure on the taxpayer and generates consequences as tax avoidance and tax evasion. The procedural dimensions include even preliminary procedures such as corporate authorization and tax purposes registration [5] that are a formal barrier to contractual freedom. In the traditional markets, actors tend to follow through these procedures, as traceability of the activity is easier through physical evidence. In the digital markets, actors are more fluid, so their fiscal dimension is also uncertain. The connection to a fiscal jurisdiction is diluted, so the classical *permanent establishment* needs a new cloth. This concept is related to the traditional way of determining tax jurisdiction as the form of distributing power between states. The new concept of *relevant presence* within a market it seems to answer this difficulty as it shifts accent within taxation from the physical point of connection between business and territory and answers better to the new frame of action. The concept of relevant presence was formulated by European legislation and addresses the market by considering not the source of them economical would but the destination. This new paradigm of taxation allows states to give significance in fiscal matters to the emerging economic dimension and to recognize their power to tax regardless of the source of the good or service and thanking into account only the destination. In this new context even the notion of eroding tax source gains new significance; tax avoidance and tax evasion not only embrace new forms but also demand newer fighting measures.

Identifying the source of the revenue and identifying relevant jurisdiction are more than ever related to the procedural dimensions of taxation. This puts a supplementary pressure on audit capacity of tax administrations. Hence newer forms of audit are required for addressing the transition from the traditional ones to digital ones, as the face-to-face audit is replaced by digital audit. Tax audit inhabits the digital environment and tax authorities are called upon to implement measures of supervising digital transactions. In a recent study, the digital environment [29] was approached as a world, requiring tax authorities to intervene with the same means. These means address several stages of the tax administration activity, such as tax registration, declaring activities and providing information for determining taxes and implementing audit procedures. As information is very fluid in a first-hand approach, digital tax administration should be easier was algorithm would help identifying fraudulent transactions and would allow tax authorities to process faster relevant information. A well-adjusted algorithm would allow tax authorities to extract relevant information about taxable transactions from the very environment that generated them. Secondary, the information once extracted, further processing would reveal the amount of tax due to certain jurisdiction.

The premises of this dynamics is also declarative; someone, either the taxpayer or the platform accommodating transactions, must declare the relevant information in due time and to a certain fiscal jurisdiction. The companies will face a supplementary burden as main collectors of information; the costs of such compliant behaviour might be relevant but it is subsidiary to the access to a certain market. In some cases, the traditional line between companies and physical persons, between professionals and non-professionals will become blurry and will create a generalization of the professional model. One could assert that in the digital environment actors assuming an active role all become professionals. For example, the traditional not so challenging role of an employee, as a protected taxpayer through withholding measures, will diminish in order accommodate the mobility given by the digital context. Processing banking data, VAT information, direct taxation information are part of the business model in the digital environment. It is a 'take it or leave it' moment. Once the information processes to a certain form, accessible to the tax administration, tax effects will occur. Secondary, instruments of tax cooperation would find a suitable environment to exchange automatically or upon request relevant fiscal information about the digital transactions of residents. The administrative cooperation in fiscal matters finds in the digital environment both a challenge and a new form for action.

## Where to?

Taxation is a clash between public and private; forces are confronting each other in a patrimonial dynamic. The traditional way to address this clash is to consider the public realm as stronger; but in fact, the public realm is a projection of the private will in a conglomerated manner. There is no public money, as Margaret Thatcher stated; maybe there is also no direct public will, but a filtered private will through lenses of power [36]. Hence, the stronger part in this dynamic is the private actor, that which mobilizes will and resources. In this spectrum, patrimonial and personal, the private dimension will always be more resourceful. The computational power of the private actors combined is no match for the public sector. Nor should it be. In economic dynamics state intervention is secondary and counter-reactive; it follows private evolutions and adjusts to them. Hence, taxation as a second level, normative influenced intervention will always oppose a reaction to the evolutions in the private sector. This transfer of instruments might be infused with derived normative interventions, but these are a mere reaction, transfer, lend from the private environment.

## References

1. M.D. Smith, J. Bailey, E. Brynjolfsson, Understanding digital markets: Review and assessment, (MIT Press, Massachusetts, USA, 2009)
2. M. Nofer, P. Gomber, O. Hinz, D. Schiereck, Bus Inf Syst Eng, **59.3,** 183-187, DOI: 0.1007/s12599-017-0467-3, (2017)
3. J. Anderson, R. Lee, The metaverse in 2040, URL: https://www.pewresearch.org/internet/wp-content/uploads/sites/9/2022/06/PI_2022.06.30_Metaverse-Predictions_FINAL.pdf, accesed: 1.03.2023, (Pew Research Center, 2022)
4. Z. Zheng, S. Xie, H.N. Dai, W. Chen, X. Chen, J. Weng, M. Imran, Future Generation Computer Systems, **105,** 475-491, DOI: 10.1016/j.future.2019.12.019 (2019)
5. I.M. Costea, Drept financiar. Note de curs, ed. a 8-a, [Financial Law. Course. 8th ed.] (Hamangiu, Bucharest, 2023)
6. C. Fuchs, M. Sandoval, Open Access J. Global Sustainable Information Soc., **12.2**, 486-563, DOI: 10.31269/triplec.v12i2.549, (2014)
7. G.M. Cortes, E. Forsythe, ILR Review, **76.1**, 30-55, 023, pp. 30–55, DOI: 10.1177/00197939221076856, (2023)
8. R. Gill, A. Pratt, Theory, Culture & Soc, **25.7-8**, 1-30, DOI: 10.1177/0263276408097794, (2008)
9. T. Terranova, Social text, **18(2),** 33-58, (2000)
10. I.M. Costea, Perspectives Bus L J, **1,** 320-331, (2012)
11. I.M. Costea, Analele Ştiinţifice UAIC. SSJ, **65.2-bis,** 7-14, (2019)
12. J.M. Song, J. Sung, T. Park, Procedia Comp Sc, **162,** 119-122, DOI: 10.1016/j.procs.2019.11.266, (2019)

13. M.M. Queiroz, S.C. Farias Pereira, R. Telles, M. C. Machado, Benchmarking: an international J, **28(5),** 1761-1787, DOI 10.1108/BIJ-12-2018-0435 (2019)
14. G. Wang, J Product Inn Man, **39(1),** 95-118, DOI: 10.1111/jpim.12605, (2021)
15. P. Harrigan, T.M. Daly, K. Coussement, J.A. Lee, G.N. Soutar, U. Evers, Int J Information Man, **56**, 102-246, DOI: 10.1016/j.ijinfomgt.2020.102246, (2021)
16. D.M. Ilucă, Analele Ştiinţifice UAIC. SSJ, **65(2-bis),** 219-234, (2019)
17. D.M. Ilucă, Analele Ştiinţifice UAIC. SSJ, **63(2),** 311-326, (2017)
18. ECJ, C-264/14, Skatteverket Vs. David Hedqvist, ECLI:EU:C:2015:718, URL: https://curia.europa.eu/juris/liste.jsf?num=C-264/14, accessed: 1.03.2023, (2015)
19. C.T. Ungureanu, Analele Ştiinţifice UAIC. SSJ, **68(3),** 7-23, DOI: 10.47743/jss-2022-68-3-, (2022)
20. M. Sparkes, What is a metaverse, (Elsevier, 2021)
21. B. Kye, N. Han, E. Kim, Y. Park, S. Jo, J Educ Eval Prof, **18,** 18-32, DOI: 10.3352/jeehp.2021.18.32, (2021)
22. L.H. Lee, T. Braud, P. Zhou, L. Wang, D. Xu, Z. Lin, A. Kumar, C. Bermejo, P. Hui, J Latex Class Files, **14(8)**, 1-46, DOI: 10.48550/arXiv.2110.05352, (2021)
23. C. Leaua, C., The Greek Gods and the Metaverse: Legal Order in the Layered Universe, URL: https://irishtechnews.ie/greek-gods-metaverse-crenguta-leaua-efi-pylarinou/, accessed: 1.03.2023 (2020)
24. D.J. Chalmers, *Science fiction and philosophy: From time travel to superintelligence,* in S. Sneider (eds.), The singularity: A philosophical analysis, 171-224, (John Wiley&sons, US, 2016)
25. C. Codrea, Hermeneia, **15**, 145-157, (2015)
26. P. Čerka, G. Jurgita, S. Gintarė, Computer law & security R, **33(5)**, 685-699, (2017)
27. S. Wojtczak, AI & Society, **37(1),** 205-213, (2022)
28. V.A.J. Kurki, T. Pietrzykowski, Legal personhood: Animals, artificial intelligence and the unborn, (Spriger, 2017)
29. B. Bertagnoll, J. Davis, J. Dimson, K. Kamath, J. Rebolledo, Reimagining tax authorities for the future, URL: https://www.mckinsey.com/industries/public-and-social-sector/our-insights/reimagining-tax-authorities-for-the-future, accessed: 1.03.2023 (2023)
30. A.A. Skaar, Permanent establishment: erosion of a tax treaty principle, (Kluwer Law International BV, 2020)
31. J.A.G. Requena, Intertax, **45(11),** 732-741, DOI: 10.54648/taxi2017063, (2017)
32. B. Hoffart, NJ Techn & Intell Prop, **6,** pp.: 106-117, (2007)
33. W. Schön, *Ten questions about why and how to tax the digitalized economy*, Working Paper of the Max Planck Institute for Tax Law and Public Finance, **11,** 1-31, (2017)
34. I.M. Costea, I.M., Analele Ştiinţifice UAIC.SSJ, **64.1-bis,** 211-220, (2018)
35. R.A. Petruzzi, V. Koukoulioti, European taxation, **58.9**, 391-400, (2018)
36. C. Codrea, Logică juridică. Curs universitar [Legal Logics. University course] (Hamangiu, Bucharest, 2023)

# Direct taxation of the digital economy

*Florentin Gabriel* Nanu[1]*

[1] University of Bucharest, Romania

**Abstract.** The objectives of the study are to analyze the future of direct taxation of the digital economy in the field of corporate income tax. Digitalization has grown steadily, spreading to all areas, especially the economic sector, i.e. the economic activity carried out by taxpayers. In this context of development of the digital economy not only at a national level, but also at the European or global level, there is a need to analyze which state is responsible for taxing the profits obtained through the digital economy. The main research tools were the legal provisions on direct taxation, the literature analyzing and interpreting this field, and the identification of conclusions from the specific practice of taxpayers who have encountered problems, have asked the same questions or perhaps have found the answers necessary for this research. The implications of the study are both theoretical and practical. The topic aims to analyze a modern direct taxation mechanism. On the other hand, companies and countries will be able to determine where the tax has to be paid by the taxpayer.

## 1 Introduction

This study requires in advance answers to the following questions – what is 'direct taxation' and what does the 'digital economy' mean?

### 1.1 Direct Taxation

Taxes are classified as direct tax and indirect tax, where the former is levied directly on the profit/income or wealth of the taxpayer, while indirect tax is imposed on the price of goods and services [1].

Direct tax, which is the subject of this paper, therefore refers to the tax levied on the profits of legal persons or on the income of micro-enterprises or on the income of individuals who are both taxpayers in the sense of payers (those who pay the tax) and payers in the sense of payers (those who bear the tax).

* Corresponding author: nanu_florentin@yahoo.com

A brief distinction should be made here between corporation tax, which is a direct tax, the taxpayer being both the person who pays and the person who bears the corporation tax, and VAT, which is an indirect tax paid (effectively to the state budget) by the person collecting the VAT but borne by the final consumer. Indirect tax is levied on the person who consumes the goods and services and is paid indirectly to the budget.

Thus, in what follows we will analyse direct taxation of the digital economy, referring in particular to the subject of corporate income tax, providing the opportunity for the analysis of indirect taxation of the digital economy, namely the application of VAT, to be dealt with on another occasion in a separate research.

### 1.2 Digital Economy

Digital economy, at a first glance, could be equated with e-commerce, but in reality, when we talk about the digital economy, we must bear in mind that economic activity is not just about e-commerce, but is carried out through several channels such as telecommunications, audiovisual, software, computer networks, computer services, online services and content.

The digital economy involves a range of economic processes, transactions, interactions and activities that rely on digital technologies, and this economic activity conducted through various digital channels should be taxed.

This paper aims to establish how to tax the profits made by corporate taxpayers through the digital economy.

## 2 The importance of direct taxation of the digital economy

In recent years, digitalization has grown steadily, spreading to all areas, especially the economic sector, i.e. the economic activity carried out by taxpayers. The existence of travel restrictions during the pandemic period has considerably affected economic activities carried out in physical format and has accelerated this process of digitalizing the economy, with more and more corporate taxpayers carrying out their activity online. Taxpayers, once familiar with the digital economy which offers a whole range of advantages, as they will have access to more information and will reduce costs, they will have to comply from a tax point of view [2].

It should not be forgotten that the EU Economic Recovery Plan requires each Member State to allocate at least 20% of its budget to the digital switchover [3].

In this context of development of the digital economy not only at a national level, but also at the European or global level, there is a need to analyze which state is responsible for taxing the profits obtained through the digital economy.

## 3 Legal framework

According to art. 13 para. (1) of the Romanian Tax Code, the following categories of persons are obliged to pay corporate income tax in Romania:

'a. Romanian legal persons, with the exceptions provided for in art. 13 para. (2) of the Tax Code;

b. foreign legal persons carrying on business through a permanent establishment/several permanent establishments in Romania;

c. foreign legal persons resident in Romania according to the place of effective management;

(...)

e. legal entities with a registered office in Romania, established under European legislation'.

Thus, according to art. 7, item 29 of the Romanian Tax Code, a Romanian legal person is any legal person that has been established and operates in accordance with Romanian law. According to the methodological norms for applying the Romanian Tax Code, this category of legal persons includes national companies, national corporations, autonomous regions, companies - as regulated by Law no. 31/1990 on companies - regardless of the legal form of organisation, including those with foreign capital participation or wholly foreign capital.

## 4 Fixed establishment

A 'fixed establishment' includes a place of management, a branch, an office, a factory, a shop, a workshop, as well as a mine, an oil or gas well, a quarry or other natural resource extraction site.

A fixed establishment involves a construction site, construction project, assembly or erection or related supervisory activities only if the site, project or activities last more than 6 months.

The fixed establishment thus implies a physical presence of the foreign legal entity on the territory of Romania, and the Romanian tax system does not currently consider that the permanent establishment is represented by an online platform, a domain with the '.ro' ending, which represents not a physical presence but a digital (online) presence on the territory of Romania of the foreign legal entity.

Although a location at which automated equipment is operated by a company may constitute a permanent establishment in the country in which it is situated, a distinction must be made between the computer, which may be installed at a location so that it may under certain conditions constitute a permanent establishment, and the data and software used by or stored on that equipment. Thus, an Internet website which is a combination of software and electronic data does not constitute a tangible asset, does not have a location which can constitute a 'place of business' and there is no 'location, such as buildings or, in some cases, equipment or tools' in respect of the software and data which constitute the website. The server on which that website is stored and through which it is accessible is equipment that has a physical location and the physical location may constitute a 'fixed place of business' of the company operating the server.

The distinction between the website and the server on which it is stored and used is important because the company operating the server may be different from the company conducting business through the website. It is common for a website through which a company carries out activities to be hosted on the server of an Internet service provider. Although the fees paid to an internet service provider under this arrangement may be based on the size of the disk space used to store the software and data required for the website, under these contracts the server and its location are not at the company's disposal, even if the company has been able to establish that its website will be hosted on a particular server in a particular location. In this case the company has no physical presence in that location because the website is not tangible. In such cases, the company cannot be considered to have acquired a place of business by arranging the hosting of the website. If the company conducting business through a website has the server at its disposal, owns or leases the server on which the website is stored and used and operates this server, the location of the server constitutes a permanent establishment of the company if the other conditions of art. 8 of the Romanian Tax Code are met.

A computer in a particular location may constitute a permanent establishment only if it meets the condition of having a fixed place of business. A server must be located in a particular place for a particular period of time to be considered a fixed place of business.

In order to determine whether the business of a company is conducted wholly or partly through such equipment, it should be considered on a case-by-case basis whether such equipment provides the company with facilities where the business functions of the company are carried out.

Where a company operates a computer at a particular location, there may be a permanent establishment, even if no employee of the company is required to be present at that location to operate the computer. The presence of staff is not required for a company to be considered to be operating partly or wholly at a location where the presence of staff is not required to operate at that location. This situation applies to e-commerce to the same extent as it applies to other activities where the equipment operates automatically, such as in the case of automatic pumping equipment used in the exploitation of natural resources.

A fixed establishment cannot be deemed to exist where the e-commerce operations carried out by computer at a particular location in a country are limited to preparatory or ancillary activities as described in art. 8 para. (4) of the Romanian Tax Code. For the purposes of determining whether certain activities carried out in such a location are covered by Art. 8 para. (4) of the Romanian Tax Code, they have to be analyzed on a case-by-case basis, taking into account the various functions performed by the company through the respective equipment. Preparatory or ancillary activities include in particular:

a) the provision of a communications link - much like a telephone line - between suppliers and customers;

b) advertising goods or services;

c) transmission of information via a mirror server for security and efficiency purposes;

d) collecting market data for the company;

e) provision of information.

There is a permanent establishment when these functions constitute an essential and significant part of the company's business or when other principal activities of the company are carried out by computer, the equipment constituting a fixed place of business of the company, since these functions go beyond the activities referred to in art. 8 para. (4) of the Romanian Tax Code.

The principal activities of a particular company depend on the nature of the business carried on by that company. Some internet service providers are in the business of operating their servers for the purpose of hosting websites or other applications for other companies. For these ISPs, the operation of servers providing services to customers is a component of the business activity which is not considered to be a preparatory or ancillary activity.

In the case of a company called an 'e-tailer' or 'e-merchant' whose business is the sale of products over the internet and whose business is not the operation of servers, the performance of services at a location is not sufficient to conclude that the activities carried out at that location are more than preparatory and ancillary activities. In such a situation it is necessary to consider the nature of the activities carried out from the perspective of the activity carried out by the company. If those activities are strictly preparatory or ancillary to the activity of selling products over the internet and the location is used to operate a server hosting a website which is used exclusively for promotion, for the presentation of the product catalogue or for providing information to potential customers, it applies. art. 8 para. (4) of the Tax Code and the location shall not constitute a fixed establishment. If the typical sales-related functions are carried out at that location, such as by concluding the contract with the customer, processing payment and delivering the products which are carried out automatically by equipment located at that location, these activities cannot be considered strictly preparatory or auxiliary.

An Internet service provider who provides the service of hosting the websites of other companies on a server shall not be subject to the provisions of article 8 (5) of the Tax Code, because ISPs are not considered agents of the companies to which the websites belong, do not have the authority to enter into contracts on behalf of these companies and do not normally enter into such contracts, they are considered independent agents acting in accordance with their normal business activity, which is also evidenced by the fact that they host websites for different companies. Since the website through which a company carries out its business is not in itself a 'person' as defined in art. 7 of the Romanian Tax Code, art. 8 (5) of the Tax Code cannot apply to deem a fixed establishment to exist by virtue of the website being an agent of the company within the meaning of that paragraph, if no employee of the company is required to be present at the location to operate the computer. The presence of staff is not required for a company to be regarded as carrying on business partly or wholly at a location where the presence of staff is not required to carry on business at that location. This situation applies to e-commerce to the same extent as it applies to other activities where the equipment operates automatically, such as in the case of automatic pumping equipment used in the exploitation of natural resources.

An example would be the company that owns the furniture brand Videnov which had a showroom, a shop in Bucharest, but decided that it preferred to close this shop - permanent headquarters - and to continue to carry out economic activity in Romania through digital channels (having a website for this purpose) as the corporate tax in Bulgaria is 10% as opposed to the corporate tax in Romania which is 16%.

## 5 Place of effective management

Art. 13 para. (1) letter c) of the Romanian Tax Code establishes that foreign legal persons having their place of effective management in Romania shall also pay corporate income tax in Romania. According to art. 7 item 18 of the Romanian Tax Code, the place of effective management is 'the place where, unless proven otherwise, the foreign legal person carries out operations corresponding to real and substantial economic purposes and where at least one of the following conditions is fulfilled:

a) the economic-strategic decisions necessary for the management of the activity of the foreign legal person as a whole are taken in Romania by the executive directors/members of the board of directors; or

b) at least 50% of the executive directors/members of the board of directors of the foreign legal person are residents'.

The place of effective management, according to tax provisions, refers to the place where strategic economic decisions are taken by the directors/members of the Board of Directors, this concept coming from international taxation which qualifies the tax residence of a company according to the place where key decisions are taken (e.g. management, commercial policy).

Thus, the place of effective management is a different concept from the permanent seat.

Foreign legal entities are required to declare by 30 June each year that their place of effective management is in Romania so that the tax authorities can recognise their tax residence on Romanian territory and apply to them the corporate income tax regulated by the Romanian Tax Code.

Basically, in order to apply the corporate income tax, it must be demonstrated that the place where economic-strategic decisions are taken is in Romania. This proof is possible by providing supporting documents such as: corporate documents of the foreign entity, proof of operation of the place of management in Romania and contracts concluded with the executive directors, together with the questionnaire (to be submitted by 30 June).

## 6 Tax residency

Why is it important for companies to establish their tax residency? Firstly, to know exactly what rate of corporation tax is payable. Thus, legal entities with a Romanian tax residence may be subject to 1% turnover tax (if they have at least 1 employee) for micro-companies with an annual turnover of up to €500,000 or 16% profit tax for companies whose turnover exceeds €500,000. Secondly, establishing the tax residency is important in order to avoid possible fines, penalties and interest for late payment if a company with tax residence in Romania does not fulfil its obligations for tax registration, declaration and payment of taxes.

If a foreign legal person is deemed to be resident both in Romania and in a state that is a signatory to a double taxation convention to which Romania is a party, the residence of this person will be established according to the provisions of the double taxation convention.

According to art. 7 of the OECD Model Convention (valid with Spain, Turkey), 'The profits of an enterprise of a Contracting State shall be taxed only in that State unless the enterprise carries on business in the other Contracting State through a permanent establishment situated therein. If the enterprise carries on business in that manner, the profits of the enterprise may be taxed in the other State, but only that part of them which is attributable to that permanent establishment'.

## 7 EU Law on direct taxation on digital economy

The European Commission has issued a proposal for a Directive on a tax on digital services, a proposal for a Directive on the introduction of a digital permanent establishment concept and recommendations to Member States to implement this concept in their double tax treaties.

The new Digital Services Tax (DST) was supposed to apply from 1 January 2020, but its application has been postponed. DST will be levied at a flat rate of 3% of gross revenue.

The digital services tax applies to certain digital services, such as services relating to the provision of virtual spaces for advertising, services relating to the provision of common digital 'marketplaces' facilitating direct transactions between users, services relating to the sale of user data, while services relating to digital content or payment services, as well as trading venues for financial instruments and platforms facilitating investment services, covered by Directive 2014/65/EU, would be excluded from the scope of this tax.

Businesses that would cumulatively meet the following thresholds would be subject to the digital services tax: total annual global revenues of more than €750 million at the level of the multinational group to which the company belongs, and annual revenue from the provision of digital services in the EU of at least €50 million. If the entity is part of a consolidated group, these thresholds will be analyzed at group level.

The digital services tax should be payable in the Member State where the users are located. If users are located in different Member States, the proposal states that the tax base should be distributed in the Member States concerned on the basis of allocation keys.

The notion of 'significant digital presence' is based on the existing concept of a permanent establishment and covers any digital platform such as a website or a mobile application that meets one of the following criteria: the annual revenue from the provision of digital services in a Member State exceeds €7 million, the annual number of users of such services exceeds 100,000, the annual number of online contracts concluded with users in a given Member State exceeds 3,000.

The Directive would apply to EU taxpayers as well as companies established in a non-EU jurisdiction with which there is no double tax treaty with the Member State where the taxpayer is identified as having a significant digital presence. However, this measure does not affect taxpayers established in a non-EU jurisdiction where a double tax treaty exists, unless such treaty includes a similar 'digital permanent establishment' provision.

The aim of taxing digital activity is to structure tax reform on two pillars, in order to allocate basic taxing rights between the countries from which income is extracted.

Pillar I aims to introduce taxing rights for countries where taxpayers have market jurisdictions, even if the company has no physical presence there. For some businesses, such a measure could mean taxing part of their profits in the jurisdictions where the users are located. As regards the conditions and the amount of profits to be allocated to these jurisdictions, a definitive formula has not yet been reached, but in principle at least part of the residual profits earned by the group is taken into account. Another approach proposed by Pillar I is the introduction of a standard level of remuneration for basic marketing and distribution activities carried out for affiliated persons (companies within the same group) and the introduction of mechanisms to ensure efficient resolution of potential disputes on profit allocation between tax authorities in different jurisdictions [3].

Pillar II, for its part, introduces the novelty of imposing a minimum level of taxation on profits at global level. This involves, on one hand, reaching a consensus on the harmonisation of reporting systems and on the other hand, introducing mechanisms to allow the taxation at a minimum level of profits which, in some jurisdictions, are now taxed at very low rates or not at all. It is important to note that the proposals included in Pillar II cover groups in all industries, with certain exceptions - investment funds, pension funds, government bodies and non-profit organisations. In addition, the rules are to apply to groups with annual revenues above €750 million, so that Pillar II is in line with the value threshold described in the country-by-country reporting requirements [4].

## 8 If Taxpayers don't declare tax anywhere?

In 2021, the Council adopted new rules aimed at improving administrative cooperation in the field of taxation and addressing the challenges of the digital platform economy.

An increasing number of individuals and businesses are using digital platforms to sell goods or provide services. However, income from digital platforms often goes unreported and leads to unpaid taxes, especially when digital platforms operate in more than one country. As a result, Member States lose tax revenue and traders using digital platforms have an unfair advantage over traditional businesses.

These new rules regulate the situation of economic activities carried out on digital platforms and will apply from 1 January 2023, when digital platform operators will be obliged to report the revenue made by sellers on their platforms and Member States will be obliged to exchange such information automatically.

## 9 Conclusions

There is a need to obtain a reasonable balance between the reallocation of corporate tax liability between net exporting and net importing countries and between producer and consumer countries, so as not to jeopardise, *inter alia*, the ability of countries to meet their social and environmental objectives.

In addition, the entry into force of the new Digital Services Tax (DST) could solve the problems concerning the competence of Member States' tax bodies to tax the digital economy.

## References

1. D. D. Saguna, D. I. Radu, *Tax Law*, Ed. 3, C.H. Beck Publishing House, Bucharest, 2009, page no. 81.
2. *Economia digitala. Avantaje si dezavantaje de care trebuie sa fim constienti*, URL: https://www.ratb.ro/economia-digitala-avantaje-si-dezavantaje-de-care-trebuie-sa-fim-constienti/, accessed 01.03.2023 (2021)
3. Parlamentul European, *Transformarea digitală: strategia UE explicată*, URL: https://www.europarl.europa.eu/news/ro/headlines/society/20210414STO02010/transformarea-digitala-importanta-avantaje-si-politici-ue, accessed 01.03.2023 (2021)
4. M. Iacob, C. Matei, *Necesitatea taxării echitabile a economiei digitale, urgentată de pandemia de COVID-19*, URL: https://www2.deloitte.com/ro/en/pages/business-continuity/articles/necesitatea-taxarii-echitabile-a-economiei-digitale-urgentata-de-pandemia-de-covid-19.html, accessed 01.03.2023 (2020)

# Collective management of copyright and related rights - fiscal implications

*Andreea Iuliana* Prisacariu[1*]

[1] Faculty of Law, Alexandru Ioan Cuza University, Romania

**Abstract.** Creative activities are a constant in all the periods and changes that humanity has gone through, they enriched life, improved living conditions and contributed to the progress made in different areas of activity. In today's highly digitized context, social networks, YouTube, Spotify and Netflix are representative means by which intellectual creations reach the public. In this equation, it is legally required to answer the question - how do creators, authors and holders of related rights receive appropriate compensation for the use and exploitation of their works? Collective management organizations provide an answer, they provide a way through which copyright and related rights may be exercised. As a consequence of their contribution to the exploitation of copyright and related rights, collective management organizations also play a fiscal role. Some aspects require clarifications, such as identification of taxable persons, direct and indirect tax applied to the achieved income, as well as non-patrimonial tax obligations.

## 1 Introduction

The concept of 'collective management of copyrights and related rights' is relatively recent in the millennial history, as for a long time the works of intellectual creation have not benefited from protection, especially from a patrimonial perspective. The notion of 'copyright' is in place nowadays to safeguard original works of authorship and ensure their protection under the law. This guarantees certain privileges for copyright-holders, which include both non-monetary and monetary aspects that can be exercised either individually or collectively. We aim to shape the general framework of collective management, when it appeared and how it has evolved, what role has the World Intellectual Property Organization (WIPO) played, which are the primary provisions at the European level, as well as the way in which collective management is regulated in Romanian legislation. In the second part of the paper, we will discuss the main fiscal implications of obtaining income through the collective management organization (CMO), aspects related to direct taxation, indirect taxation, taxable persons and non-pecuniary tax obligations.

* Corresponding author: andreea.iuliana.prisacariu@gmail.com

## 2 The collective management - classical input and Internet-mediated forms

The concept of copyright reunites all legal rules related to the creation and use of a literary, artistic, or scientific work [1], assuming both patrimonial and non-patrimonial aspects. From a legal perspective, the concept of 'related rights' is similar to copyright, with the distinction that these are assigned to performing artists, interpreters and show organizers [2]. Both copyright and related rights (CRR) involve a monetary extent that can be (and in some cases must be) individually or collectively exercised. The main patrimonial right implies using the work by authorizing the reproduction, distribution, hire, broadcasting, or public communication. Individual management represents the natural and common way for CRR administration and derives from the personal nature of the copyright [2]. The author or his successors authorize the ways in which the work will be used when the right is individually managed. Individual management is almost impossible and economically inefficient for certain categories of works of art and the corresponding rights, for example, in the case of a musical work, the author must grant licenses for each public communication or broadcasting of his work and his repertory may contain dozens of songs. This conclusion led in time to the appearance of the collective management of CRR.

Collective management is carried out by the CMOs, which are CRR owners' associations and it can be optional or mandatory. The cases and conditions in which collective management is mandatory will be part of every national legislation. The concept of collective management of copyrights and related rights (CRR) appeared in France in the 18th century. Its starting point was marked by the authors' efforts to get their patrimonial and non-patrimonial rights respected. The first CMO appeared in France in 1777 and still carries out its activity today under the name of *The society of dramatic authors and composers* [3], (originally called - *The Office of Dramatic Legislation*). Another CMO was founded by Honoré de Balzac in 1837 (Victor Hugo, who had a significant role in drafting the Berne Convention for the Protection of Literary and Artistic Works in 1886, and Alexandre Dumas also contributed) and it was named *The society of men of letters*. *The civil society of multimedia authors* - SCAM [4] detached itself from *The society of men of letters*. A defining moment for the collective management system was the famous trial between the owner of the restaurant *Les Ambassadors* and 3 authors of intellectual works of creation. In 1847, considering it unfair that they must pay for food and drinks, while the owner had no obligation to pay them for their musical pieces performed by the local orchestra, two composers and one writer refused to pay for food and drinks if they were not being paid for their performances. With the support of their editor, they decided to sue the owner of the restaurant. Unexpected for those times, their action was admitted and the defendant was forced to pay a large sum of money as remuneration for using their songs in the restaurant [5]. For composers and lyricists, this decision opened a new path. They realized that the need to coordinate efforts is imperative and because individual management of copyright was almost impossible in some cases, they founded the *Society of Authors, Composers and Publishers of Music - SACEM*, the most advanced and efficient CMO today in France. In 2004 it collected 725 million Euros from users. In 2008, 128,000 authors were members of SACEM, including 15,500 foreign members and it collected 755.8 million Euros. The society has more than 37 million musical works in the repertory and 1425 employees [6].

The collective management system has been used and improved over time as it is both necessary and useful to ensure complete and efficient protection of CRR. Due to their characteristics, intellectual property rights (IPR), despite all diligence, cannot be protected only through individual management. Authors organized themselves according to categories of works and many CMOs were founded. Subsequently, collective management was extended for related rights [2]. France always had one of the most performing, if not the most performing CRR protection system. Even though the system of collective management was constantly developed, mixed and improved, this was detailed and precisely regulated in 1985 [2].

Nowadays, an additional and important element is represented by the Internet, a system architecture used for communications and commerce 'by allowing various computer networks around the world to interconnect' [7]. By 2020, approximately 4.5 billion people, or more than half of the world's population, were estimated to have access to the Internet [7]. The role played by the Internet is crucial, as it provides a means by which the authors' work reaches the public. In this context, it is almost impossible to exclusively exercise copyright individually, because that would imply each author to track the number of public communications or broadcasting of his works and grant a license for each user. Websites and applications like Youtube, Spotify or Netflix are used as much as classical methods to bring the authors' work to the audience, as 'Publishing rights holders earned $3.5 billion from streaming overall in 2020, a sum that is more than publishing revenue from CDs and downloads any year in the 21st century so far, even during the peak of the CD era' [8]. Spotify paid more than 7 billion dollars in royalties in 2021, according to a transparency report [8], this being the highest amount paid by such a service in 2021 and a record for the highest amount paid annually by a single retailer in history, according to the same report . The conclusions of the report highlight the importance and necessity of the collective management of CRR. According to this, streaming revenue in 2021 alone exceeded total industry revenue from 2009 to 2016, with Spotify payments representing around a third of that streaming total. More than 1000 artists generated 1 million dollars on Spotify alone, 450 artists generated more than 2 million dollars on Spotify, an increase of 110% in five years and 130 artists generated over 5 million dollars, an increase of 160% in the same period. Moreover, Spotify's royalty payments increased by $2 billion in 2021, up from $5 billion in 2020 [9].

The mechanism used by the Spotify platform involves payments to the right-holders, such as the record labels, distributors and CMOs, whom 'artists allow putting their music on the platform and who in turn pay the artists revenue from the earnings on the streaming service' [9]. Artists cannot upload their own music on Spotify, because there are 3 parties involved in this activity, the platform, the intermediary (CMOs, record labels, distributors) and the artist, which makes it important to our study. According to the transparency report published by Spotify, streaming has made it easier for artists to share their music and accelerated the path to finding a global fan base, meaning artists can go from their first single to their first significant paycheck fast. Over 10% of artists (5300) who generated more than 10,000 dollars on Spotify in 2021 released their first song ever in the last two years. In 2021, 350 of them generated 100,000 dollars from Spotify alone. Also, 'streaming revenue is bringing real scale to the music industries of emerging markets, making it increasingly possible to pursue a professional career as an artist in countries around the world. In 2021, Spotify launched in 80+ markets, introducing these artists to new fans in places all over the world. Of the 52,600 artists who generated more than $10,000 on Spotify in 2021, 34% live in countries outside the IFPI's top ten music markets (Australia, Canada, China, Italy, France, Germany, Japan, South Korea, the U.K. and the U.S.)' [8]. Likewise, the mechanism used by YouTube allows artists to get royalties through intermediaries (CMOs, record labels, etc.), but it imposes certain conditions to be able to monetize. Now, in order for a YouTube video to be eligible for monetization, it must have both of these: at least 1,000 subscribers and 4,000 hours of watch-time over the past 12 months [10]. A difference between Youtube and Spotify is given by the fact that 'artists can upload their releases to YouTube as they would to a traditional streaming service, putting it on YouTube Music as well as the main site' [11]. The mechanism is entirely different from the one used by Netflix, the most popular subscription streaming service in the world in 2022, with more than 225 million subscribers worldwide

[12]. Netflix does not accept any materials that they do not specifically request, so if the individuals have 'an idea about a show, film, game, or other projects the only option is to work through a licensed agent (for example, WME - William Morris Endeavor, CAA - Creative Artists Agency, ICM - International Creative Management and UTA - United Talent Agency [13]), producer, attorney manager, or industry executive, as appropriate, who already has a relationship with Netflix, as the platform does not share any references for these resources' [14]. So, if CRRs are collectively managed, this equation involves four parties, the author (or the related rights-holder), the CMO, the middleman and Netflix.

According to its politics, Netflix does not publicly disclose its deals. There are viewpoints that claim Netflix is currently paying between 100 and 250 million dollars for blockbuster movies, while popular TV shows with multiple seasons have budgets that range from 300 to 500 million dollars [15]. None of the agreements signed with filmmakers are made public. In accordance with some opinions and based on some usual ratios, 'filmmakers themselves get around 10 to 20% of direct profit, without the additional fees, but this is really just a rough estimate, as the exact numbers are not subject to public disclosure' [15].

Numbers speak for themselves. The Internet, through platforms such as Netflix, Spotify and YouTube, contributes nowadays decisively to the exploitation of IPR, generating significant incomes, a fact which requires paying particular attention to the fiscal aspects, as well the intellectual property ones.

## 2.1 The role of The World Intellectual Property Organization

Aspects related to the collective management of CRR were addressed at an international level for the first time in 1975, during a meeting that took place in Washington, on the development of techniques for reprographic reproduction of literary works, with the participation of some committees of the Berne Union. It was concluded that it is up to every state to decide how to approach these new challenges, especially the legal framework for non-voluntary licenses and the authors' royalties, suggesting that the foundation of some CMOs for the right of remuneration may be a solution [16]. Over time, the World Intellectual Property Organization (WIPO) and the United Nations Educational, Scientific and Cultural Organization (UNESCO) constantly recommended and suggested collective management for the works that are stored and reproduced with the help of computer systems and for private copying. Simultaneously, they drafted and passed two statute examples and starting in 1985 published studies about CRR collective management.

Nowadays, according to WIPO, 'managing CRR individually may not always be realistic', thus the collective management of CRR is necessary. This is being done through CMOs, which are not-for-profit entities, either private or public [16]. Regarding the attributions, typically a CMO monitors when, where and how works are used; negotiates tariffs and other conditions with users; licenses the use of protected works on behalf of its members and of other rights-holders it represents; and collects the fees from users and distributes these to the rights-holders [16]. WIPO also developed the *WIPO Good Practice Toolkit for Collective Management Organizations (The Toolkit): A Bridge between right holders and Users*, which 'brings together examples of legislation, regulation and codes of conduct in the area of collective management from around the world' [17]. The document is available in 7 languages: English, French, Spanish, Portuguese, Russian, Chinese and Arabic, the last version is from September 2021.

## 2.2 Collective management of copyright and related rights in the European Union

European Union-wide efforts to create a framework of legal protection for holders of CRR materialized in the adoption of 11 directives and 2 regulations, 'harmonizing the essential rights of authors, performers, producers and broadcasters' [18]. Particularly relevant to the collective management of CRR is the adoption of Directive 2014/26/EU of the European Parliament and of the Council on 26 February 2014 on collective management of CRR and multi-territorial licensing of rights in musical works for online use in the internal market. Before the directive was drafted and adopted, a number of documents regarding to the patrimonial rights of the creators and the administration methods of that rights were adopted in European Union. Among these, Council Directive 92/100/EEC of 19 November 1992 on rental right and lending right and on certain rights related to copyright in the field of intellectual property; Directive 2001/84/EC of the European Parliament and of the Council of 27 September 2001 on the resale right for the benefit of the author of an original work of art; Directive 2001/29/EC of the European Parliament and of the Council of 22 May 2001 on the harmonization of certain aspects of CRR in the information society. Among the targets set through the adoption of Directive 2014/26/EU was 'to provide for coordination of national rules concerning access to the activity of managing CRR by CMOs, the modalities for their governance and their supervisory framework' and also 'to lay down requirements applicable to CMOs, in order to ensure a high standard of governance, financial management, transparency and reporting. This should not, however, prevent Member States from maintaining or imposing, in relation to CMOs established in their territories, more stringent standards than those laid down in Title II of this Directive, provided that such more stringent standards are compatible with Union law' according to points 8 and 9 stated in the considerations.

In this regard, a series of rules and principles relating to financial management, transparency, reporting and transparent operation of CMOs are stated in the directive and must be transposed in member states' legislations. According to the text of the directive, CRR can be individually or collectively managed, collective management being possible, optional, or mandatory. Also, the CMOs must collaborate with similar foreign organizations, grant licenses in a non-discriminatory manner and facilitate quick access to works of art. These provisions exist in the Romanian legislation as well.

## 2.3 Collective management of copyright and related rights in the Romanian legal system

Romanian legislation, in line with Directive 2014/26/EU, provides for both individual and collective management of CRR, in accordance with the guidelines drawn by international and European law. According to art. 144 para. (2) of the law on CRR (Law no. 8/1996), collective management can be optional or mandatory and it can only be done for works previously brought to the public's knowledge and the collective management of the related rights can only be done for interpretations or performances previously fixed or broadcast, as well as for phonograms or videograms previously brought to public knowledge.

The provisions of art. 144 para. (4) indicate some of the rights of authors and copyright holders, such as the right to choose for which categories of rights or types of works it authorizes, based on a written warrant, the CMO, the right to grant licenses for non-commercial uses of any types of works or categories of rights, the right to revoke the management warrant, with a reasonable notice that must not exceed 6 months, to collect the remuneration due to them for the acts of exploitation that occurred before the revocation or restriction of the management warrant came into force, the right to be informed annually about how the remuneration collected from users is distributed to members. In the context of the collective management of CRR, the CMO cannot restrict the exercise holders' rights by imposing the condition that the management of the rights or categories of rights that are subject to revocation to be entrusted to another CMO, according to art. 144, para. (5).

Collective management of CRR is mandatory in certain cases: for the right to compensatory remuneration for the private copy, the right to fair remuneration for the public loan, the right to broadcast musical works, the right to unique fair remuneration recognized to performers and producers of phonograms for public communication and radio broadcasting of phonograms published for commercial purposes or their reproductions, cable retransmission right, retransmission right, the right to fair compensation for orphan works, according to art. 145 para. (1) of Law no. 8/1996. Article 145^1 provides the extended collective management for the right to public communication of a musical work; the right to public communication satellite; the right to reproduction, distribution, public communication, or putting on available to the public of protected works outside the commercial track; the right of reproduction and putting on available to the public of works belonging to the publishers of press publications. At the same time, Romanian legislation provides that in situations where collective management is mandatory, right-holders who have not granted a warrant to the CMO will also be represented, according to art. 145 para. (2) of Law no. 8/1996. Statutory provisions also indicate situations in which collective management is optional. These are listed in the contents of art. 146: the right to reproduce musical works on phonograms or videograms; the right to public communication of works, except for musical works (for the right to public communication of musical works an old version of the Law of CRR provided mandatory collective management; nowadays, according to art. 145^1, the right to public communication is subject to extended collective management) and artistic performances in the audiovisual field; the right to borrow (with the exception of the public loan); the right to broadcast works and artistic performances in the audiovisual field; online rights to musical works; the right to fair remuneration resulting from the assignment of the rental right; the resale right.

Currently, in Romania a number of 14 CMOs are registered at the Romanian Office for Copyright: ADPFR - The Association for Phonogram Producers' Rights in Romania; AOTO - The Association on Theological Orthodox Opera; ARAIEX - The Romanian Association for Interpreters or Performing Artists; COPYRO - CMO for Copyright; CREDIDAM - The Romanian Center for Performers' Rights Management Association; DACIN SARA - The Society for Copyright in Cinemas and Broadcasting; OSRO - CMO for Copyright; PERGAM - The Society of Romanian Authors and Editors of Scientific Works; SOPFIA - The Society of Producers of Film and Broadcasting; UCMR - ADA - Romanian Musical Performing and Mechanical Rights Society; UNART - National Union of Artist from Romania; UPFAR-ARGOA - Union of Romanian Producers of Film and Broadcasting; UPFR - Romanian Phonogram Producers Union; VISARTA - CMO for Copyright in the Field of Visual Arts [19]. Romanian CMOs handle copyrights and related rights for Romanian and foreign artists, based on their scope. For instance, UNART has 8458 member rights-holders [20] and 44 members who have acquired rights by inheritance [21].

## 3 Fiscal implications of collective management

Incomes from intellectual property have constantly diversified and experienced a significant increase [22]. For instance, Canadian rapper Drake (Aubrey Drake Graham) has gained 52,5 million dollars from Spotify, generated from 21,5 billion streams, thus being the artist with the higher gain from the platform [23]. As shown above, Spotify, YouTube and Netflix have been paid billions of dollars in royalties. These payments have fiscal relevancy; hence the need to carefully regulate the fiscal issues, methods of taxation, owners of tax obligations (patrimonial and declarative) and methods for avoidance of double taxation, given the nature of the IPR that can effortlessly be exploited abroad. In line with the international and European efforts in this matter, the Romanian legislator has introduced on March 23, 2019 Chapter II^1 in Title IV of the Fiscal Code with regard to taxation on income gained from IPR.

### 3.1 Taxable persons

In this equation, both copyright or related rights holders and the CMOs have tax obligations. The copyright holder is the taxpayer, being the one who owes the tax [24]. According to art. 72 of the Romanian Fiscal Code, the CMO must calculate, withhold the tax and transfer it to the state budget, all the obligations to establish and identify fiscal claims returning to the CMO. Fiscal dispositions do not stipulate direct or indirect taxes applicable for the amounts collected by CMOs, whatever the commission that members pay based on the statute or the amount collected and distributed to the right-holders. This aspect has generated an uneven practice and extensive jurisprudence, as we will analyze further.

### 3.2 Direct Taxation

Incomes obtained by exploiting IPR by natural persons are subject to income tax according to the provisions of Chapter II^1 in Title IV of the Romanian Fiscal Code. According to the definition stipulated in art. 70 of the Fiscal Code, income from the exploitation of IPR in any form comes from copyright and copyright-related rights, including the creation of monumental works of art, patents, designs, trademarks, geographical indications, topographies for semiconductor products and others like it. In Romania, income is only considered as obtained if it is received from a payer within the country or a non-resident payer with a permanent establishment in Romania. The gross income is represented by the total amount collected during the year and the equivalent in RON (currency of Romania) of income in kind. Net income is calculated by deducting from gross income a flat rate of expenses of 40% [24]. The legislator foresaw in the methodological rules for the application of the Fiscal Code what is included in the flat rate, such as commissions and sums due to CMOs, social contributions owed and other income payers as payment for the services provided for the management of rights by the latter to the rights holders. The tax rate is 10% and is calculated after subtracting from the gross income the flat rate of expenses in the amount of 40%.

There are some situations when the net income is determined by subtracting from the gross income the commission owed to the CMO or other payers who have duties to collect and distribute revenues to copyright holders; these situations are represented by income from inherited IPR, income from artist's resale rights, income from private copying compensation (according to art. 72^1 para. (2) of Fiscal Code). The introduction of Chapter II^1 in Title IV of the Fiscal Code outlined plain provisions on direct taxation incomes obtained from valuing intellectual property by individuals.

Another key aspect related to direct taxation is clarifying the legal nature of the commission charged by the CMO, whether or not it is subject to the profit tax, in absence of clear legal provisions. There were several legal cases in Romania regarding the nature of the commission charged and if it represents a commission within the meaning of art. 7 point 9 of the Fiscal Code and also if the provisions of art. 15 para. (3) of the Fiscal Code should be applied or not. According to art. 7 point 9, any payment in money or in kind made to a broker, general commission agent, or to any person deemed a broker or a general commission agent for services mediated in connection with an economic operation is considered commission. Article 15 of the Fiscal Code stipulates that in the case of non-profit organizations, for the calculation of the fiscal result, other earned income is also non-taxable, up to the level of the equivalent in RON of 15,000 Euros, in a fiscal year, but no more than 10% of the total non-taxable income provided for in paragraph 2.

The Romanian High Court of Cassation and Justice (RHCCJ), The Panel for preliminary Ruling on Questions of Law, ruled in Decision 1788 on April 27, 2020, stating that the commission fees outlined in Law no. 8/1996 are the responsibility of members of CMO, as specified by the rules of each individual organization. These fees are meant to cover the operational costs of the organization and are not directly related to CRR. As such, they cannot be considered part of the definition provided by art. 7 point 9 of the Fiscal Code. Also, according to the provisions of Law no. 8/1996, the remuneration collected by the CMO is not and cannot be assimilated into their income. The RHCCJ provided that these income categories are expressly exempted from the profit tax, regardless of whether the provisions of art. 15 of the Fiscal Code refer to the notion of tax, contribution, or financial contribution, while Law no. 8/1996 uses the notion of commission, as long as both apply to the same income categories, only the names used are different. It follows, therefore, 'that the plaintiff's exemption from paying additional profit tax is determined, on the one hand, by the nature of its activity, as a CMO; and, on the other hand, by the nature of the commission collected by the plaintiff in consideration of the operations of collecting the revenues of the holders of CRR'.

The same judgment in Decision 48 of June 19, 2017, related to pronouncing a preliminary ruling on questions of law [25] was used by The RHCCJ (The Panel for preliminary ruling on Questions of Law) to rule that the commission value is established by law without being related to the other party's services, in any way. According to art. 134 para. 1 (i) of Law no. 8/1996, the commission held by the CMO cannot be higher than 15% of the sums distributed to everyone.

### 3.3 Indirect Taxation

Incomes obtained from the CRR also require the clarification of aspects related to value-added tax, this being the only indirect tax related to which, at a practice and doctrine level, questions have been raised as to whether or not it is applied to the income collected by the CMOs [24]. The main clarification required, in absence of express legal provisions, is the determination of the legal nature of the operation by which CMOs gather sums of money that afterward distribute to CRR holders if that is framed as supplying of services, according to art. 271 para. 3 (c) of the Fiscal Code, having correspondent in art. 2 (c) of the VAT Directive. The practice has provided different answers, thus generating extensive jurisprudence.

The RHCCJ by Decision 1788 pronounced on April 27, 2020 ruled that amounts collected as commission cannot be subject to value-added tax, because in this way 'the value-added tax corresponding to the rendered service by a middleman would have to be applied to value distinct service which was attended and not at the value of own supplied service' [26]. There is a similar reasoning in Decision 48 of June 19, 2017, pronounced by the RHCCJ [25]. Through it, the RHCCJ has ruled that the 'collection of CMO remunerations due to performing artists for the broadcasting or public communication of records containing fixation artistic performances of them does not represent a taxable operation in terms of the value-added tax' (paragraph 124 of the decision). The main arguments the RHCCJ relied on refer to the fact that a direct rapport between the services performed by each party does not exist, CMOs collect amounts due by users under the law or based on an agreement with the owners and not as counter-service for their services.

Regarding this aspect, the decision of the Court of Justice of the European Union (CJEU); pronounced on January 18, 2017, in case C-37/16, following the request for a preliminary decision according to art. 267 of the Treaty on the Functioning of the European Union is relevant. The request was made in a dispute between the Ministry Finansów (Ministry of Finance, Poland), on one hand and Stowarzyszenie Artystów Wykonawców Utworów Muzycznych I Słowno-Muzycznych SAWP (the Society of Performers of Musical Works with or without Words (SAWP), based in Warsaw, Poland), on the other hand, related to the application of value-added tax in the situation of compensatory remuneration for the sale of devices for recording and reproducing works protected by copyright or objects protected by related rights and for the sale of supports used to fix such works or such objects [27].

The relevant EU legal context was represented by art. 2 para. (1) letter (c) of the VAT Directive: 'The following operations are subject to VAT: [...] (c) the supply of services for consideration within the territory of a Member State by a taxable person acting as such'; art. 24 para. 1 of the VAT Directive 'supply of services shall mean any transaction which does not constitute a supply of goods'; art. 25 letter (a) 'A supply of services may consist, inter alia, in one of the following transactions: (a) the assignment of intangible property, whether or not the subject of a document establishing title (...)'; art. 2 of the Directive 2001/29/CE on the harmonisation of certain aspects of CRR in the information society 'Member States shall provide for the exclusive right to authorize or prohibit direct or indirect, temporary or permanent reproduction by any means and in any form, in whole or in part: (a) for authors, of their works; (b) for performers, of fixations of their performances; (c) for phonogram producers, of their phonograms; (d) for the producers of the first fixations of films, in respect of the original and copies of their films; (e) for broadcasting organizations, of fixations of their broadcasts, whether those broadcasts are transmitted by wire or over the air, including by cable or satellite'; and art. 5 para. (2) letter (b) of Directive 2001/29 'Member States may provide for exceptions or limitations to the reproduction right provided for in Article 2 in the following cases (...) (b) in respect of reproductions on any medium made by a natural person for private use and for ends that are neither directly nor indirectly commercial, on condition that the rights-holders receive fair compensation which takes account of the application or non-application of technological measures referred to in Article 6 to the work or subject matter concerned'.

The relevant Polish legal context was represented by the provisions relating to the VAT and the one relating to CRR. Regarding VAT provisions 'The following shall be subject to the tax on goods and services: (1) the supply of goods or services for consideration within national territory'. According to the same law (art. 8), 'The supply of services (...) shall mean any supply to a natural person, legal person or organizational unit without legal personality which does not constitute a supply of goods (...), including the assignment of intangible and legal assets, regardless of the form in which the legal transaction is effected' and 'Where a taxable person acting in his own name but on behalf of another person takes part in a supply of services, he shall be deemed to have received and supplied those services himself'. Regarding CRR provisions, art. 20 of Law on CRR 'Producers and importers of: (1) audio recorders, video recorders and other similar devices, (2) photocopiers, scanners and other similar reprographic devices enabling a published work to be copied in full or in part, (3) blank media for recording or reproducing, for personal use, works or the subject matter of related rights, using devices referred to in subparagraphs 1 and 2, shall be required to pay to CMOs determined pursuant to paragraph 5 and acting on behalf of authors, performers, phonogram producers, videogram producers and publishers, fees in an amount not exceeding 3% of the amount due by virtue of the sale of those devices and media' and art. 20^1 para. (1) 'Possessors of reprographic devices who carry on an economic activity relating to the reproduction of works for the personal use of third parties shall be required to pay, through an organization collectively managing copyright or related rights, fees amounting to 3% of the revenue in that respect to authors and publishers, save where the reproduction is made pursuant to a contract with the right holders. Those fees shall accrue to the authors and publishers in equal parts'.

The main dispute is based on a request made by SWAP to Poland's Ministry of Finance about stating its position on whether or not to apply the value-added tax for the amounts representing compensatory remuneration for unregistered media and recording and reproduction devices, paid by the producers and importers of such devices and supports pursuant to art. 20 of the Law on CRR. In response, on August 20, 2012, the Ministry of Finance issued an individual opinion in which he indicated that the sums paid to the SWAP company by the producers and importers of supports constitute a payment for the use of CRR related to the sale of equipment that serve to copy and fix the works and that, therefore, VAT must be applied.

SWAP requested the cancellation of the opinion in court (Administrative Court of Warsaw Voivodeship) and the request was accepted. The Ministry of Finance filed an appeal and the court of appeal noted that in Poland there is a contradictory jurisprudence on this matter and decided to address the CJEU using the preliminary procedures provided for by art. 267 of the TFEU.

The questions addressed to the CJEU concerned the nature of the provision of the authors to the manufacturers and importers of media, respectively whether this is a supply of services in the sense provided by the VAT Directive and, if the answer is affirmative, must the CMOs issue invoices to the producers, respectively the importers of supports, in which they include the value added tax when they charge compensatory remunerations? According to the VAT Directive, a series of 3 transactions can be classified as supplies of services, including the assignment of intangible property, the referring court requesting to clarify whether the operation in question in the main litigation represents the transfer of an intangible asset within the meaning of the VAT Directive. However, before answering this question 'it should be determined whether such a transaction is carried out for consideration. Under Article 2(1)(c) of the VAT Directive, in order for such a supply of services to be covered by the directive it must, in any event, be made for consideration' (paragraph 24). The Court ruled that it is not a matter of a service provided for consideration in the case. Based on consistent jurisprudence, the court ruled that in the sense of the VAT Directive, a provision of services is performed for consideration only when a relationship between the provider and the beneficiary exists and between them, there are mutual services. However, fair compensation does not constitute the direct consideration for any supply of services, because it is linked to the harm resulting for those rights-holders from the reproduction of their protected works without their authorization (see, to that effect, the judgment of 21 October 2010, *Padawan*, C-467/08, EU: C:2010:620, paragraph 40). 'In the present instance, first, it does not appear that there is a legal relationship pursuant to which there is a reciprocal performance by, on the one hand, holders of reproduction rights or the organization collectively managing such rights and, on the other, producers and importers of blank media and of recording and reproduction devices. Indeed, the obligation to pay fees, such as those at issue in the main proceedings, is owed by those producers and importers by virtue of the national legislation which also determines their amount' (paragraphs 27 and 28). Thereby the CJEU (Eighth Chamber) ruled that the VAT Directive 'must be interpreted in the sense that holders of reproduction rights do not make a supply of services, within the meaning of that directive, to producers and importers of blank media and of recording and reproduction devices on whom organizations collectively managing CRR levy on behalf of those rights holders, but in their own name, fees in respect of the sale of those devices and media'.

A different reasoning has been applied by the Court in case C-501/19, a request for a preliminary ruling under art. 267 TFEU [28] in the proceeding between UCMR – ADA Association for the copyright of composers (UCMR-ADA) and Cultural Association 'Romanian Soul' (the Association). The request concerns the interpretation of art. 24 para. (1), art. 25 (a) and art. 28 of the VAT Directive, regarding the taxation for value-added tax. The EU legal context was represented by the VAT Directive: art. 2 para (1) - 'The following transactions shall be subject to VAT: (…) (c) the supply of services for consideration within the territory of a Member State by a taxable person acting as such;', art. 24 para (1) - 'Supply of services shall mean any transaction which does not constitute a supply of goods', art. 25 - 'A supply of services may consist, inter alia, in one of the following transactions: (a) the assignment of intangible property, whether or not the subject of a document establishing title;' and art. 28 - 'Where a taxable person acting in his own name but on behalf of another person takes part in a supply of services, he shall be deemed to have received and supplied those services himself'.

The Romanian legal context was represented by the provisions of the then Fiscal Code (in the main proceedings, the applicable law was represented by Law no. 571/2003; in 2015, the Romanian legislator has adopted Law no. 227/2015 which replaced Law no. 571/2003): art. 126 - Taxable transactions - 'Transactions that fulfil the following cumulative conditions shall be taxable in Romania for VAT purposes: (a) transactions which, within the meaning of Articles 128 to 130, constitute or are treated as a supply of goods or services, which is subject to VAT, for consideration', art. 129 - '(1) A supply of services shall mean any transaction which does not constitute a supply of goods as defined in Article 128. (2) Where a taxable person acting in his own name but on behalf of another person takes part in a supply of services, he shall be deemed to have received and supplied those services himself. (3) Supplies of services include transactions such as: (…) (b) the assignment of intangible property, whether or not the subject of a document establishing a title, inter alia: the transfer and/or assignment of copyright, patents, licenses, trademarks and other similar rights; (…) (e) services performed by intermediaries acting in the name and on behalf of other persons, where they take part in a supply of goods or services (…)' and the Copyright Law: art. 134 para (3) - 'Royalties paid to CMOs is not revenue of those organizations, nor can it be treated as such'.

The Association had obtained a non-exclusive license from UCMR-ADA to perform some musical works for a public audience during a show it organized and had to pay remuneration for the public performance of those works. For the right of public communication, the national legislation established mandatory collective management. At the point where the facts happened, the Law on CRR provided that the right of public communication is subject to mandatory collective management. In 2019, Law no. 15/2019 modified the Law on CRR and now the right of public communication is no longer subject to mandatory collective management, being subjected to extended collective management, according to art. 145^1. The Association paid only a part of the remuneration claimed and UCMR-ADA brought the matter to court. The court of appeal considered that the transaction involving the collection of remuneration by UCMR-ADA was not subject to VAT and reduced the sum charged to the association by the amount of that tax (according to points 20, 21 and 22 of the Decision). UCMR-ADA claimed that the decision has the effect of making it bear the VAT burden, even though UCMR-ADA is not the end user of the works at issue. The RHCCJ asked, in the first place, whether a transaction by which holders of copyright in musical works authorize performance organizers to use such works could be classified as a supply of services for consideration within the meaning of the VAT Directive. In case of an affirmative answer, the CMO acts like a taxable person within the meaning of art. 28 from the VAT Directive when they receive remuneration from performance organizers for the right to perform musical works for a public audience? With regard to a supply of services made for consideration, in accordance with consistent jurisprudence, including the Decision pronounced in case C-37/16 [27], it is mandatory that a legal contract exists between 'the provider of the service and the recipient pursuant to which there is reciprocal performance, the remuneration received by the provider of the service constituting the value actually given in return for the service supplied to the recipient' (paragraph 31).

The CJEU ruled that the express request of the user, who, in turn, pays the fee due, indicates not only that there is a legal contract pursuant to which there is a reciprocal performance between the service provider and the user, but at the same time it allows a direct link to be established between the service supplied and the actual consideration received (paragraph 35). Thereby, in this situation, the remuneration paid by the user constitutes the actual consideration for the service supplied in the context of that relationship contract. Regarding the first question, due to the fact that the CJEU established that it is indeed a matter about supply of services made for consideration, it must also answer the second question as well: does the CMO act as a taxable person within the meaning of art. 28 of the VAT Directive?

Relating to the second question, the CJEU ruled that when a taxable person acting in their own name but on behalf of another person takes part in a supply of services, that person shall be deemed, under Article 28 of the VAT Directive, to have received and supplied those services itself. Accordingly, that provision creates the legal fiction of two identical supplies of services provided consecutively.

The Court ruled that the CMO must be considered to have acted as a commission agent within the meaning of art. 28 of the VAT Directive, it must be regarded to have, firstly, received the services in question from the holder before providing, secondly, those services to the end users itself. The Court relied on the following arguments: collective management is mandatory for the right to perform musical works for a public audience; an appointed CMO also represents right holders who have not granted it a warrant and who are therefore not members of that organization; it is obliged to grant non-exclusive licenses to users who apply for such licenses; and the remuneration is collected in the name of CMO but on behalf of the copyright holders.

Thereby, the Court decided 'that Article 28 from the VAT Directive must be interpreted in the sense that a CMO which collects, in its own name but on behalf of holders of copyright in musical works, royalties due to them in consideration for the authorization for the public performance of their protected works, acts as a 'taxable person' within the meaning of that provision and is therefore deemed to have received the services in question from those rights holders before providing them to the end user itself. In such a case, that organization is required to issue invoices in its own name to the end user containing the royalties collected from the latter, including VAT. The copyright holders are, in turn, required to issue to the CMO invoices including VAT for the services supplied in respect of the royalties received' (paragraph 52).

We can notice that in interpreting the VAT Directive by relating to the modalities for the exercise of copyrights, the Court established that there is no supply of services in the case of compensatory remuneration for the sale of devices for recording and reproducing works, leading to the conclusion that the sums representing compensatory remuneration are not subject to the value-added tax. On the other hand, there is a supply of services made for consideration in the case of collecting the remuneration for public performance by the CMOs, after they have given in advance a non-exclusive license.

The different treatments of the two rights, both objects of mandatory collective management according to Romanian legislation at that moment, can be explained by the fact that it is easier to track the number of public communications of a work, the user needs a license beforehand, but it is impossible to track the number of private copies that can be made after a written work. For each public communication, we can identify the performance and the payment that has been made, therefore the CJEU considered it a supply of services made for consideration. The number of copies made of a written work cannot be counted; the remuneration for private copies has the function of compensating the author (or the copyright holder) and it does not represent a payment for each copy.

With reference to the application of the value-added tax for other rights, which according to the Law of CRR are subject to mandatory collective management, we consider that the solution pronounced by the Court in case C-37/16 [27] may also be applicable to the right to remuneration for the public loan, being almost impossible to track each loan and working as a remedy and the fair compensation for orphan works. In this situation, we consider that it is not a supply service made for consideration and on those sums of money the value-added tax should not be applied.

Regarding the other rights for which the Law of CRR provides collective management (the right of broadcasting, the right to public communication and broadcasting of phonograms for commercial purposes, the right of cable retransmission), we believe that the same judgment can be applied as in the case C-501/19 [28]. Considering that each use of a work can be identified, payments made can be attributed to performance, like a supply of services made for consideration, so they can be subject to value-added tax.

### 3.4 Double Taxation of Copyright and Related Rights

Nowadays, the Internet creates a facile communication of works of intellectual creation over a country's borders and this leads to the possibility of obtaining a foreign income. One of the most important points discussed regarding the foreign income is the avoidance of double taxation, both in the state where the income was achieved and in the state where the author (or the right-holder) has the domicile. States have taken action to prevent cases of double taxation and the efforts have taken the form of double taxation agreements, which are treaties between two (or more) countries to avoid this on CRR income [29].

Romania has signed many double tax treaties with other countries 'with the main purpose of avoiding double taxation on income both in Romania and in each country that has signed a bilateral agreement with Romania' [30]. A list of all double taxation agreements signed by Romania is published on the tax authority website [31].

International organizations have also created legal instruments to avoid double taxation of income obtained from the CRR [32]. To this effect, the convention signed within the UNESCO, in Madrid, Spain, on 13 December 1979 - the *Multilateral Convention for the Avoidance of Double Taxation of Copyright Royalties, with model bilateral agreement and additional Protocol* [33].

Another international legal instrument was adopted within The Organization for Economic Co-operation and Development (OECD) - *Recommendations of the Council OECD Legal Instruments concerning the Avoidance of Double Taxation with respect to Taxes on Income and on Capital* [34]. This recommends the governments of member states 'to pursue efforts in concluding bilateral conventions for the avoidance of double taxation with respect to taxes on income and on capital with those Member countries with which they have not yet entered such conventions and to revise those of the existing conventions between them which may no longer be keeping up with present-day needs'. The annex to this document included the *Model Convention for the Avoidance of Double Taxation with Respect to Taxes on Income and Capital.*

At the European Union level, Member States have concluded double tax agreements that aim to shape a legal framework to avoid double taxation [35]. Under many bilateral tax agreements, the amount paid in the country where the person works will be offset against the tax owed in the country of residence [36]. In other cases, the income earned in the country where the person works might be taxable only in that country and exempt from tax in the country of residence [36]. These rules also applied to the income obtained through the CMOs, CRR royalties. There are two methods that can be applied: the exemption method and the credit method. If the exemption method is used, the state of residence of the recipient of income does not tax the income derived by and taxed in the other State [29]. On the other hand, the credit method implies that the state of residence calculates the tax on the basis of all taxable income earned, internal and foreign income, deducting afterwards the tax paid abroad [29].

In the circumstance of collective management of CRR, the income is achieved through the CMO, so according to the features of the convention signed between the two countries, one of these two methods will be applied, the credit method or the exemption method. If the exemption method will be applied, the income obtained through the CMO would not be taxed in the state of residence, but it will be taxed according to the tax law of the state where the income was obtained. If the credit method will be used, the income obtained through the CMO will be taxed in the state where the income was obtained, that amount being later decreased from the tax due in the other state [32]. For example, according to Article 12 (paragraph 1) of the *Convention between Canada and Romania - For the Avoidance of Double Taxation and the Prevention of Fiscal Evasion with Respect to Taxes on Income and on Capital* [37], 'royalties arising in a Contracting State and paid to a resident of the other Contracting State may be taxed in that other State', thereby the exemption method is applied. The second paragraph provides the situation of taxing the royalties in the state in which they arise and according to the law of that state, but without exceeding '5 percent of the gross amount of the royalties if they are: (i) copyright royalties and other like payments in respect of the production or reproduction of any literary, dramatic, musical, or other artistic work (but not including royalties in respect of motion picture films nor royalties in respect of works on film or videotape or other means of reproduction for use in connection with television broadcasting); or (ii) royalties for the use of, or the right to use, computer software or any patent or for information concerning industrial, commercial, or scientific experience (but not including any such royalty provided in connection with a rental or franchise agreement); 10 percent of the gross amount of the royalties in all other cases'; in this scenario the credit method is applied for 5 or 10 percent of royalties and the exemption method for the remaining.

## 4 Conclusions

The development of the Internet enables submitting works of intellectual creation to the public, requesting an efficient method through which the right-holders to be remunerated and collective management appears to be the answer. Being a means by which income can be obtained, it is of great importance to clarify the financial aspects related to that. We consider the current legal framework to be favorable, on both the national and the European levels. The distinct regulation in the Fiscal code of incomes obtained from intellectual property was welcomed and we believe that the Romanian legislator must clarify the situation of indirect taxation, especially the value-added tax, given the uneven practice of the courts.

Considering the statements found in the jurisprudence of The CJEU, the Romanian legislator needs to specifically regulate the situation of value-added tax for incomes obtained by and through CMOs, for each type of right that can be collectively managed, whether it is about mandatory or optional collective management.

The role of CMOs will reveal more prominent with the development of the Internet, this leading to the possibility of becoming the principal means for works of intellectual creation to get to the public. This being the case, clarifying and regulating the aspects related to the Internet and the ways in which the authors can use it for bringing the works to the public is crucial. This is also equally for ensuring the right remuneration for the right-holders. Thereby, CMOs ensure the link between authors (or the right-holders) and platforms on the Internet, which in many situations is the only space where they promote and exploit their works.

## References

1. N.R. Dominte, Dreptul proprietății intelectuale. Protecție juridică (Solomon, Bucureşti, 2021)
2. V. Roş, Dreptul proprietății intelectuale, Vol.1. Dreptul de autor, drepturile conexe şi drepturile sui generis (C.H. Beck, Bucureşti, 2016)
3. Société des Auteurs et Compositeurs Dramatiques, *SACD, the Society of dramatic authors and composers,* URL: https://www.sacd.be/en/, accessed 01.03.2023
4. SCAM, *The civil society of multimedia authors,* URL: https://www.scam.be/en/, accessed 01.03.2023.
5. CISAC, *The History of Collective Management,* URL: https://www.cisac.org/sites/main/files/files/2020-11/CISACUniversity_The_History_of_Collective_Management_FINAL.pdf, accessed 01.03.2023.
6. SACEM, *Repertoire of works,* URL: https://repertoire.sacem.fr/en, accessed 01.03.2023.
7. Encyclopedia Britannica, *Internet,* URL: https://www.britannica.com/technology/Internet, accessed 01.03.2023.
8. Loud & Clear, *Spotify and the Streaming Economy*, URL: https://loudandclear.byspotify.com/, accessed 01.03.2023.
9. M. Dellatto, *Spotify Says It Paid $7 Billion In Royalties In 2021 Amid Claims Of Low Pay From Artists*, URL: https://www.forbes.com/sites/marisadellatto/2022/03/24/spotify-says-it-paid-7-billion-in-royalties-in-2021amid-claims-of-low-pay-from-artists/?sh=21d08c46a0db, accessed 01.03.2023.
10. R. Zimmerman, *5 Things You Should Know About YouTube Royalties*, URL: https://blog.symphonic.com/2022/07/15/things-you-should-know-about-youtube-royalties/, accessed 01.03.2023 (2022)
11. RouteNote Blog, *How do YouTube music royalties work,* URL: https://routenote.com/blog/how-do-youtube-music-royalties-work/, accessed 01.03.2023 (2021)
12. All Top Everything, Top 10 Most Popular Subscription Streaming Services, URL: https://alltopeverything.com/most-popular-streaming-services/, accessed 01.03.2023
13. Desktop Documentaries, *How does an independent filmmaker get their movie on Netflix?*, URL: https://www.desktop-documentaries.com/howdoes-an-independent-filmmaker-get-their-movie-on-netflix.html, accessed 01.03.2023
14. Netflix, *How ideas are pitched to Netflix*, URL: https://help.netflix.com/en/node/100386, accessed 01.03.2023
15. A.S. Poe, *How Much Does Netflix Pay for Movies, TV Shows, and Filmmakers?*, URL: https://fictionhorizon.com/how-much-does-netflix-pay-for-movies-tv-shows-and-filmmakers/, accessed 01.03.2023 (2021)
16. World Intellectual Property Organization, *Collective Management of Copyright and Related Rights*, URL: https://www.wipo.int/copyright/en/management/, accessed 01.03.2023
17. World Intellectual Property Organization, *WIPO Good Practice Toolkit for Collective Management Organizations (The Toolkit): A Bridge between Rightholders and Users*, URL: https://tind.wipo.int/record/44374, accessed 01.03.2023

18. European Commission, *The EU copyright legislation*, URL: https://digital-strategy.ec.europa.eu/en/policies/copyright-legislation, accessed 01.03.2023
19. Oficiul Român pentru Drepturile de Autor, *Organisme de gestiune colectivă,* URL: https://orda.ro/organisme-de-gestiune-colectiva/, accessed 01.03.2023
20. Uniunea Naţională a Artiştilor din România, *Lista titular de drepturi UNART,* URL: https://www.unart.ro/wp-content/uploads/2022/11/LISTA-TITULARI-DE-DREPTURI-UNART.pdf, accessed 01.03.2023
21. Uniunea Naţională a Artiştilor din România, *Membri UNART - titulari de drepturi dobândite prin moștenire (moștenitori ai artiștilor decedați)*, URL: https://www.unart.ro/wp-content/uploads/2022/11/MEMBRI-UNART-DECEDATI.pdf, accessed 01.03.2023
22. I.M. Costea, D.M. Ilucă, *Artiștii, aurul și...Codul Fiscal* (TaxMagazine nr. 6, 2021, pp. 413-426)
23. URL: https://lwvworc.org/ro/who-does-spotify-pay-royalties-to, accessed 01.03.2023
24. I.M. Costea, Drept financiar. Note de curs, Ediția a 8-a (Hamangiu, București, 2023)
25. High Court of Cassation and Justice of Romania, Decision no. 48 of June 19, 2017, URL: https://www.iccj.ro/2017/06/19/decizia-nr-48-din-19-iunie-2017/, accessed 01.03.2023 (2017)
26. High Court of Cassation and Justice of Romania, Decision no. 1788 of April 27, 2020, URL: https://www.scj.ro/1093/Detalii-jurisprudenta?customQuery%5B0%5D.Key=id&customQuery%5B0%5D.Value=178982#highlight=##, accessed 01.03.2023 (2020)
27. Court of Justice of the European Union (Eighth Chamber), C-37/16, *Minister Finansów v Stowarzyszenie Artystów Wykonawców Utworów Muzycznych i Słowno-Muzycznych SAWP* (2017)
28. Court of Justice of the European Union (Third Chamber), C-501/19, *UCMR – ADA Asociația pentru Drepturi de Autor a Compozitorilor v Asociatia culturala „Suflet de Român"* (2021)
29. I.M. Costea, Fiscalitate europeană. Note de curs (Hamangiu, Bucureşti, 2016)
30. URL: https://www.romanian-accountants.com/double-taxation-avoidance-treaties-signed-with-romania, accessed 01.03.2023
31. National Agency for Fiscal Administration, *Convențiile pentru evitarea dublei impuneri și protocoalele de modificare a acestora încheiate de România cu alte state,* URL: https://static.anaf.ro/static/10/Anaf/AsistentaContribuabili_r/Conventii/Conventii.htm, accessed 01.03.2023
32. P. Malherbe, Elemente de drept fiscal internaţional (Hamangiu, Bucureşti, 2017)
33. UNESCO, *Multilateral Convention for the Avoidance of Double Taxation of Copyright Royalties, with model bilateral agreement and additional Protocol*, URL: https://en.unesco.org/about-us/legal-affairs/multilateral-convention-avoidance-double-taxation-copyright-royalties-model, accessed 01.03.2023 (1979)
34. OECD, *Recommendations of the Council concerning the Avoidance of Double Taxation with respect to Taxes on Income and on Capital*, OECD/LEGAL/0151, URL: https://legalinstruments.oecd.org/public/doc/471/471.en.pdf, accessed 01.03.2023
35. C.F. Costaş, Drept fiscal. Ediția a II-a (Universul Juridic, București, 2019)

36. Your Europe, *Double Taxation,* URL: https://europa.eu/youreurope/citizens/work/taxes/double-taxation/index_en.htm, accessed 01.03.2023
37. Government of Canada, *Convention between Canada and Romania for the Avoidance of Double Taxation and the Prevention of Fiscal Evasion with Respect to Taxes on Income and on Capital,* URL: https://www.canada.ca/en/department-finance/programs/tax-policy/tax-treaties/country/romania-convention-2004.html, accessed 01.03.2023

# The legality of reverse engineering or how to legally decipher trade secrets

*Carmen Tamara* Ungureanu[1*], *Ştefan Răzvan* Tataru[1**]

[1] Faculty of Law, Alexandru Ioan Cuza University of Iasi, Romania

**Abstract**. Reverse engineering is the process of extracting secret information (trade secrets) by analysing an existing product. To determine whether reverse engineering falls within the limits of legality, the paper explores first the trade secrets (their meaning and forms, their regulation and legal protection). Then, the reverse engineering is brought under scrutiny, pointing out its main issues that of what reverse engineering consists of, what are the conditions that should be met in order to be considered legal, where it could be applied. The paper highlights the usefulness of reverse engineering in the traditional industry, software industry and as well as in the digital twins technology. In this endeavour, beyond the consulted legal literature, European and American caselaw is examined. Finally, the means of protection that trade secrets right holders have at their disposal against reverse engineering are revealed.

## 1 Introduction

Innovation and technological progress are subject to unrestricted access to the latest discoveries, scientific studies and processes or products. The absence of such information would make the work of a researcher difficult and lengthy. Gaining access to the latest technologies, so called 'state of the art' (meaning the level of development a particular field has reached at a particular point in time) [1], allows those who develop products or processes to innovate on an up-to-date scientific basis and save time and resources allocated to experiments or prototypes already tested and whose results have been made public and applied [2]. The same idea was expressed by the English scientist Isaac Newton who said 'If I have seen further, it is by standing on the shoulders of giants', confirming that the work and the scientific results obtained would not have been possible without the previous contribution made by the enlightened minds of the scientific community.

Those who fund the research and development of new products and technologies, do so with the purpose of recovering the investment and maximising the profit. The success of this objective lies in obtaining a monopoly on the market and protecting the innovation

[*] Corresponding author: carmen.ungureanu@uaic.ro
[**] Corresponding author: razvantataru@gmail.com

through the means considered appropriate to the given scientific field. Protection can be secured either by registering intellectual property rights (patent, brand, design or model) or by keeping confidential the information regarding the product's manufacture or the development of the technological process (trade secrets/know-how) [3]. Confidentiality is a safety precaution that blocks the access of unauthorized users to certain information, being at the same time a prohibition and an exception to the normal use of information. Protecting the interests of the parties implies the defence of commercial secrecy and implicitly the acceptance of confidentiality. According to the provisions of the International Standard on Information Security - ISO/IEC 27000:2018, confidentiality is 'the property according to which information is not made available or disclosed to unauthorized persons, entities or processes'.

The business environment at the national and international level has evolved into an extremely competitive one, and the development of products and technologies has become a continuous concern for all enterprises. Thus, as a Business Week headline from 1992 stated, '*Competitive advantage no longer belongs to the biggest or those blessed with abundant natural resources or the most capital. In the global economy, knowledge is king'*. Acquiring 'knowledge' is not easy for everyone, as it involves resources of all kinds (human, financial, and so on) [4]. The concept of Knowledge includes three elements: know-how, know-why and know-what. Knowledge represents an understanding of phenomena. In the context of technological systems, knowledge is an understanding of the principles that underlie their operation, the processes used to create them, and the uses that these technological systems serve. Once achieved, the information holders seek to protect it by preventing any interested party from obtaining it through illegal, non-competitive, or unethical means. In this context, we endeavour to shed light on what trade secrets are and how they can be legally acquired through reverse engineering activities.

# 2 Trade secrets

Reverse engineering is necessary and justified only in the situation where the information and technical principles incorporated in a product are not generally known or easily accessible, being kept secret by their holder and protected against disclosure. Hence, the concept of trade secrets and their legal protection are to be explored hereinafter.

## 2.1 Trade Secrets: Concept and Regulation

The term 'trade secret' [5] originates from the Agreement on Trade-Related Aspects of Intellectual Property Rights (TRIPS). According to art. 39 of TRIPS, member states have the obligation to protect 'undisclosed information', in accordance with art. 10 bis of the 1883 Paris Convention for the Protection of Industrial Property. The TRIPS provisions do not use the notion of know-how or trade secrets, but of undisclosed information which are related to unfair competition.

The Romanian legislator takes over the provisions established in the TRIPS Agreement [art. 39 para. (2)] and defines the term of trade secret within the framework of art. 11 lit. d) from Law no. 11/1991 as 'the information that cumulatively meets the following requirements: 1. are secret in the sense that they are not, as a whole or as presented or articulated their elements, generally known or easily accessible to people in those circles that are usually dealing with the type of information in question; 2. have commercial value given by their secret nature; 3. have been the subject of reasonable measures, under the given circumstances, taken by the person who legally has control over the respective information, in order to keep it secret'.

More recently, the concept of commercial secrecy has been taken up within the provisions of Government Emergency Ordinance no. 25/2019 (hereinafter, G.E.O. 25/2019), which transposes into national legislation the Directive (EU) 2016/943 on the protection of know-how and undisclosed business information (trade secrets) against illegal acquisition, use and disclosure (hereinafter, Directive 2016/943). Although the directive defines the concept of trade secret in art. 2 point 1, these provisions are not taken over in G.E.O. 25/2019, which references to the definition included in Law no. 11/1991.

In the United States of America (USA), The Uniform Trade Secrets Act (UTSA) was adopted in 1979, with amendments from 1985, which is applied in almost all-American states [6]. The provisions of the UTSA are supplemented by guidance from the Unfair Competition Restatement of 1995, which defines a trade secret as 'any information that can be used in the operation of a business or other enterprise and that is sufficiently valuable and secret to afford an actual or potential economic advantage over others' [7].

## 2.2 Protection of trade secrets

The legal literature emphasises that protection of trade secrets means, in certain circumstances, protection against such conduct that is contrary to honest commercial practice [8]. Article 39 para. (2) of TRIPS, without defining the notion of undisclosed information, specifies the conditions that such information should satisfy as to be considered undisclosed and therefore protected. Thus, the natural and legal persons have the possibility of preventing information lawfully under their control from being disclosed to third parties, or acquired or used by others without their consent and in a manner contrary to honest commercial practices, under certain conditions that must be met cumulatively, so long as such information: '(a) is secret in the sense that it is not, as a body or in the precise configuration and assembly of its components, generally known among or readily accessible to persons within the circles that normally deal with the kind of information in question; (b) has commercial value because it is secret; and (c) has been subject to reasonable steps under the circumstances, by the person lawfully in control of the information, to keep it secret.' [9, 10]. Moreover, art. 39 para. (2) of TRIPS emphasizes that there is no absolute property right over undisclosed information. Unauthorized disclosure or use of information must be prevented only if such acts are contrary to honest commercial practices [11]. TRIPS defines "conduct contrary to honest commercial practices", stating that this includes at least practices such as breach of contract, breach of trust, and causing others to violate contractual provisions to which they are bound.

The Directive 2016/943 envisaged the adoption of uniform rules in the member states of the European Union (EU) to ensure the protection of know-how and undisclosed business information, as trade secrets, by establishing appropriate mechanisms of access to justice for the purpose of applying sanctions in the event of the illegal acquisition, use or disclosure of information constituting trade secrets. The Directive 2016/943 provides for a minimum harmonization, which results from art. 1 paragraph (1): 'Member States may, in compliance with the provisions of the TFEU, provide for more far-reaching protection against the unlawful acquisition, use or disclosure of trade secrets than that required by this Directive [...]'.

The Directive 2016/943 was a necessary piece of legislation in the context of a vast diversity of regulations on an EU member states level, since trade secrets did not benefit from protection in all states and where this protection existed, the norms were included in civil law, criminal law, labour law or in unfair competition legislation and intellectual property law [6].

According to the first point in the recitals of the Directive 2016/943, '[...] valuable know-how and business information, that is undisclosed and intended to remain confidential, is referred to as a trade secret'. Next, point (2) of the recitals emphasizes that 'Businesses, irrespective of their size, value trade secrets as much as patents and other forms of intellectual property right. They use confidentiality as a business competitiveness and research innovation management tool, and in relation to a diverse range of information that extends beyond technological knowledge to commercial data such as information on customers and suppliers, business plans, and market research and strategies. [...] By protecting such a wide range of know-how and business information, whether as a complement or as an alternative to intellectual property rights, trade secrets allow creators and innovators to derive profit from their creation or innovation and, therefore, are particularly important for business competitiveness as well as for research and development, and innovation-related performance'.

The concept of trade secrets is also analysed at the point (14) of the recitals of the Directive 2016/943, where it is mentioned that: 'It is important to establish a homogenous definition of a trade secret without restricting the subject matter to be protected against misappropriation. Such definition should therefore be constructed so as to cover know-how, business information and technological information where there is both a legitimate interest in keeping them confidential and a legitimate expectation that such confidentiality will be preserved. Furthermore, such know-how or information should have a commercial value, whether actual or potential. Such know-how or information should be considered to have a commercial value, for example, where its unlawful acquisition, use or disclosure is likely to harm the interests of the person lawfully controlling it, in that it undermines that person's scientific and technical potential, business or financial interests, strategic positions or ability to compete. The definition of trade secret excludes trivial information and the experience and skills gained by employees in the normal course of their employment, and also excludes information, which is generally known among, or is readily accessible to, persons within the circles that normally deal with the kind of information in question'.

From the recitals of the Directive, we come to the point that a secret includes both the know-how and the undisclosed business information.

To be protected as trade secrets, according to art. 2 point 1 of the Directive, the information must cumulatively meet the following requirements:

a. 'To be secret in the sense that it is not, as a body or in the precise configuration and assembly of its components, generally known among or readily accessible to persons within the circles that normally deal with the kind of information in question'. There are no international standards to clarify the meaning of being *generally known* or *readily accessible* to people within the normal business circles [6]. Some authors [12] have proposed that the moment when the last competitor finds out the secret, should be considered the point the secret information is generally known. Nevertheless, in this approach, knowing the secret does not seem advantageous to the information holder, who is almost everyone. Therefore, another method should be used namely that of the case-by-case analysis, bearing in mind that confidentiality agreements are concluded to maintain secrecy [6]. What it is meant by „readily accessible" is also not clear or explained. The term 'readily ascertainable', used in UTSA, similar to 'readily accessible', designates the situation in which 'information is readily ascertainable if it is available in trade journals, reference books, or published materials. Often, the nature of a product lends itself to being readily copied as soon as it is available on the market'. A more controversial hypothesis considers that the disclosure of the secret occurs by simply placing the product on the market [13, 6] – 'if the public is able to discover through reverse engineering the secret information embedded in a product once it is introduced on the market, the secret information embedded in it is no longer a secret and can no longer be protected'[14].

b. To have commercial value by being kept secret. The trade secrets have a commercial value arising from the confidential character of the information embedded within a product or service, which represents a competitive advantage and has the ability to generate an economic benefit to the holder.

c. To have been the subject of reasonable measures, under the given circumstances, taken by the person lawfully in control of that information, to keep it secret. The holder of the trade secret should act in the way of protecting its own patrimony by implementing appropriate technical and organizational measures to preserve the confidential/secret character of the information.

## 2.3 A classification of trade secrets

If it is to be considered the types of information included in the broad concept of trade secrets, they could be divided into know-how and undisclosed business information (confidential information).

### *2.3.1 Know-how*

The know-how is a form of intellectual property and represents a set of unpatented (patentable or non-patentable) and transferable technical knowledge that is used to manufacture a product or develop a process [15] [16] [17].

An essential characteristic of know-how is that its protection is achieved privately, i.e., through contracts concluded between business partners, unlike other forms of intellectual property such as patents, copyrights or trademarks, which are protected by rules developed in national and international legislation [18].

Another essential characteristic of know-how is that it does not have limited validity in time. It exists legally as long as the secrecy is kept. This is one of the reasons why companies prefer the use of know-how to the detriment of patents, which have time expiration. One of the best-kept commercial secrets (know-how) is the chemical formula of Coca-Cola, which has remained undisclosed for over 100 years. The Coca-Cola company preferred trade secrets over the patent, thus avoiding the entry of the formula into the public domain, which would have happened after the patent expired [18].

According to art. 1 lit. (if) of the Commission Regulation (EU) No 316/2014 of 21 March 2014 on the application of Article 101(3) of the Treaty on the Functioning of the European Union to categories of technology transfer agreements, the know-how is: 'a package of practical information, resulting from experience and testing, which is: (i) secret, that is to say, not generally known or easily accessible; (ii) substantial, that is to say, significant and useful for the production of the contract products, and (iii) identified, that is to say, described in a sufficiently comprehensive manner so as to make it possible to verify that it fulfils the criteria of secrecy and substantiality;".

### *2.3.2 Undisclosed business information*

Undisclosed business information or confidential information represents one of the most used and most valuable forms of intellectual property given the absence of any registration procedures or costs and the possibility to benefit from the protection and to 'exploit' the information indefinitely, under the condition of keeping the secret [3]. According to the doctrine, trade secrets are considered a category of goods which benefit from property protection rules, in accordance with art. 1 protocol 1 of the European Convention on Human Rights. [28] [66]

In the absence of a legal definition in the national legislation, we consider that 'confidential information' designates the non-public information, regarding an organization/an enterprise/a company, its activities or the operations in which it is involved, and which have commercial value and are subject to protection measures against unauthorized access or public disclosure.

A definition of the concept of confidential information can be found in the content of the Confidentiality Contract Model developed by the International Chamber of Commerce in Paris, which represents 'any information [...] communicated by or on behalf of the Disclosing Party to the Receiving Party, including, but not limited to, any kind of business, commercial or technical information [...], except for information that is demonstrably non-confidential in nature' [19].

The scope of undisclosed business information is determined by each individual organization/enterprise/company, which establishes the precise categories of information considered confidential and the appropriate protection measures to keep them secret. Companies may consider confidential a wide range of information, including manufacturing technology processes, early-stage inventions, marketing or sales plans and strategies, market prospecting methods, distribution methods, supplier and/or customers databases, investment plans, research and development projects [3] [20].

Due to the similarities of the two concepts, know-how and undisclosed business information, their delimitation by the holder becomes, in practice, unfeasible. For this reason, it appears appropriate to use the notion of trade secrets, delimiting in this way the information used in business activities from other categories of information that must be kept confidential, such as classified or personal information.

The ways of legally acquiring a trade secret are provided in the art. 3 of the G.E.O. 25/2019. While in the art. 3 para. (1) a) the usual ways of creating trade secrets are laid down, more precisely through independent discovery / research-development, under para. (1) b) the methods of acquiring the secrets already incorporated within an existing product or object are presented. In this last scenario, the problem of so-called reverse-engineering arises.

## 3 Reverse engineering and trade secrets

In order to analyse the concept of reverse engineering, a few clarifications are necessary. First, the meaning of the engineering activity should be outlined, as to then could define the reverse engineering and show the conditions of keeping reverse engineering within the limits of legality. Afterwards, the application of reverse engineering in various industries are to be pointed out and, finally, the ways of protection against reverse engineering are to be revealed.

### 3.1 Reverse engineering: concept and regulation

To analyse the concept of reverse engineering, we should first define what the engineering activity is. Engineering means 'the creative application of scientific principles to design or develop structures, machines, devices or manufacturing processes or works' [21]. Thus, engineering involves a process that starts from the principles and ends with the final product. Reverse engineering goes in the opposite direction, being a process that starts with the known product and works backwards to find out the technical principle behind its construction. By reference to traditional manufacturing products and processes, this analysis can be performed by taking apart a machine and analysing its components. Modern methods include chemical analysis of components or electronic scanning of the shape of the product or its parts. Since the advent of computer technology, decompiling or disassembling software programs have become the most widely used methods of reverse engineering [10] [22].

In the specialized literature, there are also opinions that support the existence of an additional concept that of 'forward engineering' or 'advanced engineering', as a conventional process of moving from advanced ideas to their material implementation. This usually includes the preparation of engineering drawings from which models and then moulds are formed for the final stage of mass production [22]. In software development, forward engineering involves the development of a new product based on precisely established requirements that call for the use of advanced knowledge [23].

If initially reverse engineering processes demanded considerable effort on the part of a reverse engineer, nowadays they are facilitated by computer-aided design (CAD) to create three-dimensional virtual models of existing parts and subassemblies. A 3D scanner can create, as well, a CAD design by scanning an existing object [24]. Subsequently, 3D models can be processed with the help of computer-aided engineering (CAE) software programs and manufactured with the assistance of computer-aided manufacturing (CAM) software programs and 3D printers [25].

What does reverse engineering mean? Reverse engineering is the process the secret information is extracted by examining and analysing an existing product. In other words, the reverse engineer studies a product to discover and learn its design, construction, and mode of operation, which are not accessible to the public [8].

As to the regulation of reverse engineering, art. 39 of TRIPS regarding trade secrets, does not clarify the legal situation of reverse engineering. The TRIPS provision does not even explicitly refer to reverse engineering activities. However, it does not make the protection of undisclosed information subject to the impossibility of discovering it by following a reverse analysis, nor does it determine whether reverse engineering is always or only in some situations 'contrary to honest commercial practices' [10].

EU member state legislations take a different approach; for example, in German law reverse engineering is considered an unfair commercial practice [8] [6].

In the EU, it is not clear from the wording of the Directive 2016/943 whether reverse engineering is allowed or not, in what way and within what limits.

According to recital (16) of the Directive, 'in the interest of innovation and to foster competition, the provisions of this Directive should not create any exclusive right to know-how or information protected as trade secrets. Thus, the independent discovery of the same know-how or information should remain possible. Reverse engineering of a lawfully acquired product should be considered as a lawful means of acquiring information, except when otherwise contractually agreed. The freedom to enter into such contractual arrangements can, however, be limited by law'. It could be inferred that reverse engineering is legal under certain conditions. Considering the provisions of art. 4 para. (2) of the Directive, it seems that a case-by-case analysis should be applied as to assess whether the reverse engineering activity represents an anti-competitive behaviour and whether the trade secret was obtained unlawfully.

In the recital (17) of the Directive it is mentioned, as well, that 'In some industry sectors, where creators and innovators cannot benefit from exclusive rights and where innovation has traditionally relied upon trade secrets, products can nowadays be easily reverse-engineered once in the market. In such cases, those creators and innovators can be victims of practices such as parasitic copying or slavish imitations that free-ride on their reputation and innovation efforts'.

As a matter of fact, a reverse engineer could act as an *innovative analyst* or as *an imitative* one. In the first scenario, the reverse engineer tries to expand his own technological knowledge aiming at creating new, innovative products or at improving the existing ones. As *imitative analyst,* on the contrary, the engineer uses the reverse process to *copy* a product. In order to distinguish innovative reverse engineering activities based on legitimate acquisition of trade secrets and creation of a similar competing product from imitative reverse engineering built on non-competitive practices such as servile copying and the creation of a low-cost identical product, a case-by-case method should be used. In USA, for instance, in *Bonito Boats v. Thunder Craft Boats*, the American Supreme Court held that '[I]mitation and refinement through imitation are both necessary to invention itself, and the very lifeblood of a competitive economy' [10].

According to art. 4 para. (3) of the European Directive, 'The use or disclosure of a trade secret shall be considered unlawful whenever carried out, without the consent of the trade secret holder, by a person who is found to meet any of the following conditions: (a) having acquired the trade secret unlawfully; (b) being in breach of a confidentiality agreement or any other duty not to disclose the trade secret; (c) being in breach of a contractual or any other duty to limit the use of the trade secret.'. The next paragraph specifies that 'The acquisition, use or disclosure of a trade secret shall also be considered unlawful whenever a person, at the time of the acquisition, use or disclosure, knew or ought, under the circumstances, to have known that the trade secret had been obtained directly or indirectly from another person who was using or disclosing the trade secret unlawfully within the meaning of paragraph 3.'.

In USA, the notion of reverse engineering was defined by the US Supreme Court in *Kewanee Oil v. Bicron Corporation* [26] as a form of information discovery, starting with a known product and analysing/working backwards to its origins to reveal the process that helped create, develop and manufacture it. If we are to admit the legality of reverse engineering, setting limits to trade secret protection, this is an essential step towards innovation [6].

Reverse engineering mainly concerns trade secrets, but it can also affect other intellectual property rights, such as those protected by patents or copyrights. Patents give inventors protection for twenty years and exclusive rights to make, use, and market the patented product, but only in exchange for public disclosure of significant technical details about their inventions. It seems that as long as the inventor is asked to disclose sufficient information about the invention and about how it is made, reverse engineering is not necessary and does not affect patent law. However, an infringement becomes possible when a 3D scanner is used for scanning an object, which is then printed with a 3D printer. The result is a copy of the original product protected by a patent [24].

In terms of copyright, which protects the expressed ideas but not the ideas themselves, reverse engineering is possible in the case of computer programs, as it was made clear in a case decided by the Court of Justice of the European Union (CJEU) [27]. In *SAS Institute v. World Programming Ltd* (C-406/10) on an infringement of copyright on computer programs and manuals relating to IT database system brought by SAS Institute the court stated that: '[...] neither the functionality of a computer program nor the programming language and the format of data files used in a computer program in order to exploit certain of its functions constitute a form of expression of that program [...]. To accept that a functionality of a computer program can be protected as such (copyright) would amount to making it possible to monopolise ideas, to the detriment of technological progress and industrial development'.

In order to avoid reverse engineering, parties may enter agreements or include clauses that prohibit reverse engineering into computer programs [6].

Reverse engineering is not expressly mentioned in art. 10 TRIPS either relating to computer programs. In the USA reverse engineering is legal, both according to the caselaw of the Supreme Court of Justice [6] and to the Uniform Trade Secrets Act (UTSA). The US Supreme Court stated in Kewanee Oil v. Bicron Corp. that 'a trade secret law, however, does not offer protection against discovery by fair and honest means, such as by independent invention, accidental disclosure, or by so-called reverse engineering'.

At the international level, the World Intellectual Property Organization WIPO clarifies the controversy surrounding the activity of reverse engineering, considering it as a legal activity, in accordance with honest practices; information protected as trade secrets can be obtained lawfully by reverse engineering [27, 28] [30] [31].

## 3.2 Reverse engineering legality conditions. Applicability of reverse engineering in industry

In the common law, the first condition that should be fulfilled for the reverse engineering to be legal is the *ownership* of the product that is "disassembled". Ownership must have been lawfully acquired. In the case of *Mars UK Ltd v. Teknowledge Ltd*, a British court stated in 2000 that "what the owner has is the full right of ownership. With that goes an entitlement 'to dismantle the machine to find out how it works and tell anyone he pleases" [6].

In the EU the condition demanded is not the ownership, but the legal *possession* of the product. Alternatively, the object/product, subject to a reverse engineering, should have been made available to the public. The Directive 2016/943 establishes in art. 3 paragraph (1) (b) these conditions stating that the observation, study, disassembly or testing should be carried out on a product or an object that has been made available to the public or on a product/ object that is lawfully in the possession of the person who acquired the information and to whom no legally valid contractual obligation to limit the acquisition of the trade secret applies. This leads to the idea of licensing agreements, such as software licenses.

As we mentioned previously, the reverse engineering process can be applied to any product or process, presenting different particularities depending on the field of activity / industrial sector to which the object subject to reverse engineering belongs. In the specialized literature, reference is often made to three main areas: the manufacturing industry (traditional), the semiconductor industry (production of microchips) and the software industry. From our point of view, the manufacturing industry includes the semiconductor one, the technical peculiarities that the latter encompasses not justifying the creation of a distinct category. However, a new field is gaining momentum, which includes elements from the traditional industry, the data economy and the software industry: the use of reverse engineering for the creation of digital twins (which will be shortly analysed). Another particular domain is evolving, as well: 3D bioprinting technology, nanotechnology and tissue engineering technology. It combines cutting-edge machinery, electronic circuitry, software, materials, and processes (which will not be addressed in this paper) [32].

### *3.2.1 Reverse engineering in manufacturing industry*

Traditional products and manufacturing processes can be reverse engineered starting from simple, common products such as boats or children's toys to complex military, pharmaceutical or automotive products.

The motivation of reverse engineering processes can vary. James Pooley, university professor and international expert in the field of trade secrets, identifies six reasons behind reverse engineering: acquiring new information for a better understanding and use of a product; modification or reparation of a product; provision of an associated service; development of a compatible product; clone creation; improvement of the product [2]. In the industrial production sector, the economic goal of reverse engineering is the development of a similar competitive product or an improved object. Reverse engineering undertaken for the purpose of repairing a purchased product may well affect the manufacturer's aftermarket (eg. for parts or service), but this will generally have less economic effect on the manufacturer than it would have a new reverse engineered competing product [2]. However, the process of developing similar competing products is time-consuming, difficult and expensive, so that an innovator should not fear the reverse engineering; he/she has actually a significant period of time to enjoy market exclusivity, sufficient for the recovery of product research and development expenses [2].

If reverse engineering is carried out for the purpose of developing a new, improved product, banning it would hinder innovation. The economic effects can be at least partially positive, including the situations when reverse engineering serves only to providing information for servile copying, because such copying tends to break up monopolies and reduce market prices.

### *3.2.2 Reverse engineering in the software industry*

In the software industry, reverse engineering is a common practice used to understand how each module of the software program works and how it interacts with other systems [33]. Unlike industrial manufacturing products and processes, software programs are information-rich and incorporate a lot of know-how, which explains the efforts to restrict reverse engineering in this area.

The most common tools for reverse engineering computer programs are disassemblers, debuggers, and decompilers [34]. Decompilation is a form of reverse engineering that involves translating object code into a human-readable form, largely through trial and error. Part of the decompilation process can be computer assisted; there are, for example, disassemblers that will translate object code into an intermediate form of assembly language that is more decipherable for skilled readers, namely source code [35] [36].

Some authors consider that a 'software engineer that has to reverse engineer a computer program for education and interoperability purposes, will always be protected by the ECJ and has not to worry any legal action by the software owner', even if the software engineer does not have any permission from the owner. Moreover, a reverse engineer will not infringe any rights if he/she wishes to re-engineer the software, taking into account only the 'principles' or 'ideas' of the original [33].

In a different opinion [37, 2] decompilation and disassembly should be illegal from the point of view of copyright and trade secret law. A reverse engineering cannot be completed without unauthorized copies of the program, and this violation makes decompilation and disassembly to be an improper means of obtaining trade secrets. In the US, courts have allowed software to be copied during decompilation or disassembly if necessary to achieve fair purposes, such as interoperability between software programs or between a program and a hardware platform.

The European rule is similar in that it is purpose-based, with decompilation permitted when and if it is done to achieve interoperability [10]. In the software industry, the provisions of Directive no. 2009/24/CE on the legal protection of computer programs apply. According to art. 1 paragraph (2) and (3) the protection is provided to any form of expression of a computer program. The ideas and principles underlying an element of any computer program, including those underlying its interfaces, are not protected by copyright. A computer program is protected if it is original, in the sense that it is an intellectual creation of the author.

As art. 6 of Directive no. 2009/24/CE reads reverse engineering in the form of decompilation is allowed for the reproduction of the object code, if the aim is to ensure interoperability. Thus, the reproduction of the object code and its decompilation is permitted without the authorization of the holder when it is indispensable for obtaining the information necessary to achieve the interoperability of a software program created independently of other programs [36] and subject to the following conditions: '(a) those acts are performed by the licensee or by another person having a right to use a copy of a program, or on their behalf by a person authorised to do so; (b) the information necessary to achieve interoperability has not previously been readily available to the persons referred to in point (a); and (c) those acts are confined to the parts of the original program which are necessary in order to achieve interoperability'. According to art. 6 para. 2 lit. c), the information thus obtained cannot be used for 'development, production or marketing of a computer program substantially similar in its expression, or for any other act which infringes copyright'.

Art. 5 para. (3) provides for another form of allowed reverse engineering: '(3) The person having a right to use a copy of a computer program shall be entitled, without the authorisation of the rightsholder, to observe, study or test the functioning of the program in order to determine the ideas and principles which underlie any element of the program if he does so while performing any of the acts of loading, displaying, running, transmitting or storing the program which he is entitled to do'.

Decompiling, making a copy and analysing, studying or testing the operation of the program in order to identify ideas and principles cannot be restricted by contractual clauses. Such agreements would be null and void (art. 8, para. 2) [36]. Recently, the CJEU ruled in the case *Top System SA v. Belgian State* (C-13/20) that a 'lawful purchaser of a computer program who wishes to decompile that program in order to correct errors affecting the operation thereof is not required to satisfy the requirements laid down in art. 6 of Directive 2009/24/EC. However, that purchaser is entitled to carry out such a decompilation only to the extent necessary to affect that correction and in compliance, where appropriate, with the conditions laid down in the contract with the holder of the copyright in that program' [38].

The reverse engineering is legal according to the Directive 2016/943, unless the one who acquired the information is subject to any legally valid contractual obligation that prohibits reverse engineering. Recital 16 of the directive stated that 'Reverse engineering of a lawfully acquired product should be considered as a lawful means of acquiring information, except when otherwise contractually agreed. The freedom to enter into such contractual arrangements can, however, be limited by law', leaving it to the discretion of the EU member states to limit the party autonomy. The Romanian legislator did not deal with this issue in G.E.O. 25/2019 transposing the directive.

In the US, restricting the right to reverse engineering by contract is controversial. In the 1988 case of *Vault Corporation v. Quaid Software Limited*, prohibition of reverse engineering was declared unenforceable [6]. In 2005, in another case, it was considered valid and effective (the case of Davidson & Associates v. Jung [39]) - where the court considered that: 'In Vault, plaintiffs challenged the Louisiana Software License Enforcement Act, which permitted a software producer to impose contractual terms upon software purchasers provided that the terms were set forth in a license agreement comporting with the statute. [...] Unlike in Vault, the state law at issue here neither conflicts with the interoperability exception under 17 U.S.C. § 1201(f) nor restricts rights given under federal law. Appellants contractually accepted restrictions on their ability to reverse engineer by their agreement to the terms of the TOU and EULA. [...] By signing the TOUs and EULAs, Appellants expressly relinquished their rights to reverse engineer [6]'. Subsequently, the case law of the American courts' records equally different and controversial rulings.

Restricting the right to conclude contracts, which imposes an obligation not to reverse engineer, would aim to promote innovation and ensure progress with effects also on a healthy commercial competition. Allowing contractual 'not to do' obligations can lead to unfair competition, giving the trade secret holder the possibility to impose market conditions, including price-related criteria (which would affect consumers, as well), ensuring its dominant position on the market, and the impossibility of innovation.

An example could be the case *Microsoft v. European Commission* (T-201/04) [40], decided in 2007, whereby Microsoft was required to provide access to the information, documents and 'source code' of relevant Microsoft products under violation of art. 102 TFEU for dominant market position (as it refused to provide the interoperability information and authorize its use).

The most relevant US software reverse engineering case is *Sega Enterprises Ltd. v. Accolade Inc.* [41]. In this case, Accolade, an American computer game company, disassembled Sega's software programs in order to obtain the information necessary to make its games compatible with the Sega Genesis platform. Accolade was subsequently able to market independently developed games in direct competition with those produced by Sega and by licensed third-party developers. Sega sued Accolade claiming copyright infringement by copying and disassembling the object code. The Ninth Circuit court did not consider the commercial purpose of Accolade's copying, as it was done 'solely to discover the functional requirements for compatibility with the Genesis platform — aspects of Sega's programs that are not protected by copyright'. Reverse engineering was, in fact, the only way Accolade was able to gain access to this information. Even if Accolade had copied the object code of the software programs developed by Sega in the process of reverse engineering, the court did not consider this aspect relevant, as it constituted an intermediate stage in the development of Accolade's software. Although the court found that the Accolade games adversely affected the Sega game market, it found that the copyright on the Genesis console was not affected. The court did not legitimize all reverse engineering activities on the object code of the software developed by Sega, but only those that have been undertaken for the purpose of ensuring interoperability and only if they 'provide the only means of access to those elements of the code that are not are protected by copyright' [2] [42].

The US Court of Appeals for the Ninth Circuit reaffirmed this reasoning in *Sony Computer Entertainment Inc. v. Connectix Corp.* [43], in which Connectix disassembled Sony's object code in order to ensure the interoperability of other hardware devices with games developed exclusively for the Sony Playstation platform. In this case, Connectix developed emulation software (Virtual Game Station) that allowed games developed exclusively for the Sony Playstation platform to run on other devices. The Court of Appeal ruled in favour of Connectix, holding that there is no relevant difference between decompiling for interoperability purposes for the development of competing platforms and developing a virtual platform for game interoperability.

The analysis of the reverse engineering purpose in the *Sega v. Accolade* and *Sony v. Connectix* cases demonstrates that reverse engineering in the software industry has other motivations than those in the manufacturing industry, namely, ensuring the interoperability of one software program with another or with a hardware system. Reverse engineering for software programs is far too difficult and resource consuming to be cost-effective and to be used for the purpose of developing a similar competing product [2].

### *3.2.3 Reverse engineering, digital twins and Metaverse*

Technology has opened up immeasurable possibilities for reverse engineering. By using real-world models, with the contribution of the data industry, the AI (Artificial Intelligence) and the software industry, digital twins can be created.

What is a digital twin? Although it would seem that the digital "twin" is the virtual replica of a physical object, in fact, digital twin means more than that. While the digital replica, which a reverse engineer could make with a 3D scanner, does not receive data from the original [44], the digital twin or the virtual 'twin' of an object, process or even a service, allows data analysis and its monitoring through simulation in virtual space [45]. In other words, the digital twin is the mirror image of its real-world counterpart [46], which it is interdependent with; the real-world object/process/service can be adapted, improved according to the feedback generated by its digital twin, which is 'fed' real-time 'sensory data' from the real world, recreating the environment and conditions of the actual object/process/service [46].

Digital Twin Technology is often confused with CAD (Computer-Aided Design). What distinguishes it from this is that CAD technology only provides the digital image/representation of the real-world object, while digital twin technology aims to create an interdependence between the virtual and the real representation [47].

What a digital twin could be used for? There are various domains where digital twins would be useful: in ensuring the good functioning of a driverless vehicle (autonomous car) [47], in the agri-food sector (in the food processing industry) [44], in medicine, in the manufacturing industry, in the distribution chain, etc. [48]. Finally, digital twins are present in the Metaverse[3].

Digital replicas have already been run, for instance in the virtual reality Second Life (a platform that has been offering Metaverse-specific experiences since its inception in 2003 until now), where General Motors, Nissan and other vehicle manufacturers have opened dealerships since 2005 [49]. Ferrari is present in the game Fortnite since 2021 [50]. Car manufacturers create digital twins for models to be launched in the real-world market, and afterwards, the 'twins' 'learn' from each other, contributing to the improvement of their performances, as is done for example by the Renault group [51], Hyundai [52] and others, and not least Tesla Motors [53]. However, these professionals do not need reverse engineering to create digital twins, as they have at their disposal all the data/information that is the basis of their products, from the real world or the virtual world, protected by intellectual property mechanisms.

Could a digital twin be created by reverse engineering? Advances in technology make the answer affirmative. Reverse engineering is a booming activity supported and powered by technology. Trade secrets, whatever form they take, can be deciphered.

There are platforms that offer reverse engineering services, one example being CadCrowd [54], registered in Canada, which offers freelance services provided by licensed and qualified engineers. On the opening page of the platform, the legality of the services offered is mentioned: 'Items, products, or programs that are purchased by an entity from a competitor can be reverse engineered legally as long as any patented or protected material is not used in a new product. This is often done to figure out just how a new product or program operates so that the information discovered can be used as the basis for improvement' [54]. In the adhesion contract imposed by the platform (Terms of Service) [55] at point 4(a) it is stipulated that 'Any Designs submitted, input, or uploaded by a Service Buyer will be owned by the Service Buyer or its licensors. Cad Crowd claims no rights in such Designs;'. Therefore, the condition of ownership of the object to be 'disassembled', or the condition of possession of the object under a license agreement is necessary to be fulfilled for the legality of the reverse engineering services. In addition, the new reverse-engineered "product" must not contain patented or otherwise protected information.

The possibility of obtaining a digital twin through reverse engineering emerges equally from the tools available on the market. For example, the Artec 3D platform (Artec Europe

[3] The notion of Metaverse was first used by the American writer Neal Stephenson in his book *Snow Crash*, published in 1992, where the Metaverse is a 3D virtual reality. Currently, Metaverse illustrates the same concept, of a virtual reality, built on the infrastructure of the Internet, in which blockchain technologies, virtual currencies and NFTs (non-fungible tokens) are used. In this regard, see [66].

SRL) [56], specialized in the sale of 3D technology (scanners and scanning software), offers the necessary equipment for this. Andrei Vakulenko (Chief Business Development Officer at Artec 3D), said that '[…] 3D scanning lets you conduct precise inspections of the real-world versions of these digital twins in mere minutes, thus ensuring intelligent analyses of manufacturing variances and product performance' [57].

Digital twins of collectable cars or of unique models are created. For example, The Bridgade [58], a design studio based in New York, creates digital twins of rare cars (using reverse engineering equipment), which can be accessed using tokens on platforms such as Opensea [59]. A Mercedes model is to be offered for sale on the Opensea platform, with a link to a 3D configurator [60].

As virtual realities develop, to offer users experiences comparable to those in the real world or even more spectacular, digital twins will occupy an important place. Reverse engineering will provide the 'supply' of 'twins' where real-world model owners are unwilling or unable to participate in the Metaverse marketplace.

### 3.3 Protection against reverse engineering

To reduce the risk of losing trade secrets, their holders could employ different methods of protection against reverse engineering activities, among which: licensing agreements; confidentiality agreements; increasing brand awareness (of the innovative product) and implementing other measures to attract and keep customers; using trade secret protection systems that make reverse engineering difficult.

Licensing agreements are an easy way to reduce the threat of reverse engineering. The holder of the trade secrets can grant licenses, thereby controlling the entry of new competitors into the market. By granting a license, the licensor is able to recover its research and development expenses through licensing revenues and prevent the licensee from selling the product at prices that would have a destructive effect on the market [61]. Licensing agreements create the premise of obtaining the same secret information and economic advantages as in the case of reverse engineering, but without the allocation of financial, human and time resources to carry out the entire reverse engineering process [2]. Also, as long as reverse engineering is permitted by law, trade secret holders will be willing to offer licenses on favourable terms to drive the opportunity cost against reverse engineering. In economics, *opportunity cost* means „the cost of a benefit that must be forgone to pursue an alternative" or, in other words, potential gains missed by choosing one option over another [62].

Confidentiality agreements could be chosen, as well, as means of protecting trade secrets, in every stage of the business relations. Even reverse engineers may be required to enter into confidentiality agreements with the enterprise/natural or legal person to whom they provide reverse engineering services. For example, the freelancing platform CadCrowd imposes confidentiality rules on engineers through the adhesion contract available on the platform (Terms of Service). In Appendix 1 to the Terms of Service it is stated that: 'Restrictions. The Service Provider understands that the Information is owned by the Service Buyer or its licensors, and is confidential to the Service Buyer or its licensors, and shall not be used or disclosed, except in accordance with the terms of this Appendix. To ensure protection of the Information, Service Provider will: 1. maintain the Information in strict confidence; 2. not copy or use the Information or any part thereof in any way, except as required for the purposes set out in Section 4; 3. not disclose the Information or any part thereof directly or indirectly to any other party without in each instance having first obtained the prior express written consent of the Service Buyer; 4. not alter, modify, disassemble, reverse engineer, or decompile the Information or any part thereof in any way except as required for the purposes set out in Section 4; 5. protect the Information against unauthorized disclosure' [55].

An indirect path to contrabalance reverse engineering could be the increasing of brand awareness by carrying out marketing campaigns. In this way, the innovative product would keep its market share and would be easily distinguishable from any other similar product introduced later on the market. For instance, the promotion of the Coca-Cola brand, a product that also incorporates trade secrets (the manufacturing recipe), determined notoriety at the international level, even if several competing similar products entered the market.

Last but not least, the trade secret holder can implement protection measures against reverse engineering starting from the design and manufacturing stage of the product. Thus, the trade secret holder may use sealing systems or construction materials that break down in the disassembly process and make reverse engineering difficult, if not impossible. The manufacturer or developer can use different techniques in this context, such as: encapsulation of hardware components to make non-destructive disassembly almost impossible; mislabelling or marking components to mislead a potential reverse engineer; adding some 'locks' on the product components or within the software program [2].

In addition to the measures taken by the manufacturers themselves a few state legislators have enacted regulations that punish the illegal use of trade secrets and the anti-competitive practices of using information obtained through reverse engineering to make slavish imitations. In the US, since the 1970s, several states have adopted regulations prohibiting the creation of moulds as a way of reverse engineering some products already on the market [63]. Through these rules, US states forbade the use of a mould to manufacture identical products in direct competition with the moulded product [2].

In Romania, in the same vein, the Law no. 344/2005 regarding some measures to ensure compliance with intellectual property rights in customs clearance operations states in art. 3 paragraph (2) the fact that moulds are assimilated to goods that infringe an intellectual property right, provided that their use infringes the right holder. According to art. 4 para. (5) from Directive 2016/943, 'the production, offering or placing on the market of infringing goods, or the importation, export or storage of infringing goods for those purposes, shall also be considered an unlawful use of a trade secret where the person carrying out such activities knew, or ought, under the circumstances, to have known that the trade secret was used unlawfully within the meaning of paragraph 3'. By 'infringing goods' should be understood, according to art. 2 point 4 of Directive 2016/943, goods, the design, characteristics, functioning, production process or marketing of which significantly benefits from trade secrets unlawfully acquired, used or disclosed.

At EU level, trade secret holders are entitled to apply to the competent court for the enforcement of measures, procedures and remedies provided by law to prevent, restrain, or obtain redress for, the unlawful acquisition, use or disclosure of their trade secrets.

Unlike patents, where the information becomes part of the prior *state of the art*, trade secrets are not made public and therefore do not provide 'defensive' protection to the holder. In the absence of this type of protection, for example, if a manufacturing process of a product has been protected as a trade secret, any person can obtain a patent for the same technological process as long as he independently developed / discovered the information [29].

The World Intellectual Property Organization (WIPO) states that 'a trade secret owner, however, cannot stop others from using the same technical or commercial information, if they acquired or developed such information independently by themselves through their own R&D, reverse engineering or marketing analysis, etc' [29].

Recently, norms belonging to an international organization have been adopted with reference to reverse engineering. Thus, the FIA (Fédération Internationale de l'Automobile), revised the technical regulations for Formula 1 from 2021, prohibiting the use of reverse engineering regarding the design of rival competitors [64]. In the new regulation, reverse engineering is not permitted: 'No competitor may design its Listed Team Components (LTC) based on reverse engineering of another competitor's LTC. For the purpose of this Article, 'reverse engineering' shall mean: 1. The use of photographs or images, combined with software that converts them to point clouds, curves, surfaces, or allows CAD geometry to be overlaid onto or extracted from the photograph or image. 2. The use of stereophotogrammetry, 3D cameras or any 3D stereoscopic techniques. 3. Any form of contact or non-contact surface scanning. 4. Any technique that projects points or curves on a surface so as to facilitate the reverse-engineering process. Listed Team Components are defined by the regulations as components whose design, manufacture and intellectual property is owned and/or controlled by a single Competitor or its agents on an exclusive basis. On occasions where there is deemed to be significant similarities between listed components on different team cars, the FIA has the right to investigate the matter asking a team to prove that their design was independently created' [65].

However, the FIA does not completely prohibit reverse engineering, but only that which looks at the design of rival competitors. Creating digital replicas of rival cars with improved performance, even digital twins, does not seem to be off limits.

According to the opinion of some authors [31], 'Information and knowledge diffusion (and free competition) are the rule and intellectual property protection is the exception'. Because of this rule, all intellectual property protection regulations are limited in various ways. Trade secret regulation is no exception. In fact, since the protection is not conditional on a disclosure or *quid pro quo*, the holder's rights are more limited.

## 4 Conclusions

Protecting the valuable information to a business by designating it as a trade secret is a necessity on the today's ultra-competitive global market. Businesses need a protected, confidential environment with a view to developing new products and generating business strategies. By means of trade secrets, the developer of a product has the ability to insulate all information from disclosure, irrespective of the product stage (from the research and development phases until the application for a patent protection, if wanted so); or the developer could keep protecting the information as trade secrets, if the threat of reverse engineering is mild.

An effective protection of an innovative product can only be achieved in a strategic way, by combining available and complementary intellectual property protection methods, through technical and organizational data security measures within and out of the organization. According with this line of reasoning the product and its manufacturing process could be protected both by an invention patent and by means of trade secrets, the latter as to the information that is not required to be disclosed in the patent application, but which is relevant to the success of the product and the effectiveness of the manufacturing process. These protection methods can be supplemented, where possible and appropriate, by registering other intellectual protection rights (trademark, design and utility model).

Given the particularities of trade secrets and their value within businesses/companies/organizations, it seems that they can be viewed as genuine intellectual property rights. However, the activity of reverse engineering as a means of legally acquiring trade secrets should be included in the field of competition law, its main impact being felt in the competition on the market, whether the market is traditional or virtual (located in Metaverse).

To sum up the reverse engineering represents an easy, adaptable and indispensable tool for 'deciphering' trade secrets and at the same time an incentive for innovation, generating competition on the market and indirectly, competitive prices and the desire to improve the existing products.

## References


1. D. Barford, *Intellectual Property and Patent Information*, World Intellectual Property Organization, URL: https://www.wipo.int/export/sites/www/tisc/en/ppt/Philippines/state_of_the_art_search.pdf, accessed 12.10.2022 (2011)
2. P. Samuelson, S. Scotchmer, The Yale Law Journal, **111(7)**, 1662 (2002)
3. Ş.R. Tataru, Analele Ştiinţifice UAIC, SSJ, **Tomul I(LXVI)**, 261-277 (2020)
4. R. Garud, Advances in Strategic Management, **14**, 83-85 (1997)
5. R. Dincă, Protecţia secretului comercial în dreptul privat (Universul Juridic, Bucureşti, 2009)
6. G. Surblyte, Enhancing TRIPS: Trade Secrets and Reverse Engineering, 731 in H. Ullrich, R. M. Hilty, M. Lamping, TRIPS plus 20 From Trade Rules to Market Principles (Springer, 2016)
7. American Law Institute, *Restatement of the Law 3rd, Unfair Competition*, URL: https://wipolex-res.wipo.int/edocs/lexdocs/laws/en/us/us216en.pdf, accessed 12.10.2022 (1995)
8. D. Arcidiacono, European Papers, **1(3)**, 1076, DOI:10.15166/2499-8249/83 (2016)
9. C.T. Ungureanu, Dreptul comerţului internaţional. Contracte de comerţ international (Hamangiu, Bucureşti, 2014).
10. Ohly, Reverse Engineering: Unfair Competition or Catalyst for Innovation? in W. A. Pyrmont, Patents and Technological Progress in a Globalized World, MPI Studies on Intellectual Property, Competition and Tax Law Vol. 6, DOI:10.1007/978-3-540-88743-0_37 (Heidelberg: Springer, Berlin, 2009)
11. O.-M. Florescu, Economie teoretică şi aplicată, **6(501)**, 67 (2006)
12. N. P. de Carvalho, The TRIPS Regime of Antitrust and Undisclosed Information (Kluwer Law International, Haga, 2008)
13. S. H. Leong, *World Intellectual Property Organization*. URL: https://www.wipo.int/edocs/mdocs/sme/en/wipo_smes_uln_13/wipo_smes_uln_13_o_leong.pdf, accessed 12.10.2022 (2013)
14. S.H.S. Leong, presentation titled 'In Confidence' - Putting in Place a Trade Secret Protection Program from the Training of the Trainers Program on Effective Intellectual Property Asset Management by Small and Medium Sized Enterprises (SMEs), organized by the World Intellectual Property Organization (WIPO), Mongolia, Ulaanbaatar, October 8-10, 2013
15. I. Macovei, Tratat de drept al comerţului internaţional (Hamangiu, Bucureşti, 2014)
16. C.T. Ungureanu, Dreptul comerţului internaţional (Hamangiu, Bucureşti, 2018)
17. J. Reichman, Vanderbilt Law Review, **42(3)**, 656 (1989)
18. W. F. Fox, International Commercial Agreements and Electronic Commerce (5th ed.) (Kluwer Law International 2013)
19. International Chamber of Commerce, ICC Model Confidentiality Agreement, ICC Services Publications Department, Paris, URL: https://epdf.pub/icc-model-confidentiality-agreement.html, accessed 12.10.2022 (2006)

20. Kumar, P. Mohanty, R. Nandakumar, Journal of Intellectual Property Rights (JIPR), **11(6)**, 397-408, DOI: 0971-7544 (2006)
21. United States Engineers Council for Professional Development, Britannica.com, URL: https://www.britannica.com/technology/engineering, accessed 12.10.2022 (2022)
22. S. Guernsey, *Competition, Non-Patented Innovation, and Firm Value*, DOI: 10.2139/ssrn.3074622 (2019)
23. *Difference between Forward Engineering and Reverse Engineering*, URL: https://www.geeksforgeeks.org/difference-between-forward-engineering-and-reverse-engineering/, accessed 12.10.2022
24. M. Weinberg, *When 3D Printing and the Law Get Together, Will Crazy Things Happen?* 15 in Van den Berg, B, Van der Hof, S., Kosta, E. (Editors), 3D Printing Legal, Philosophical and Economic Dimensions, DOI: 10.1007/978-94-6265-096-1 (Springer, ebook, 2016)
25. Michigan State University, *What is the Difference between CAD, CAE and CAM?*, Michigan State University, URL: https://online.egr.msu.edu/articles/cad-vs-cae-vs-cam-what-is-the-difference/, accessed 12.10.2022 (2021)
26. USA Supreme Court, 416 U.S. 470, *Kewanee Oil Company v. Bicron Corporation et al.* (1974)
27. Court of Justice of the European Union, C-406/10, *SAS Institute v. World Programming Ltd*
28. G. Faludi, *Balancing The Relevant Legitimate Interests In The Legal Protection Of Trade Secrets In Hungarian Law*, WIPO Symposium on Trade Secrets and Innovation, Geneva, Switzerland, URL: https://www.wipo.int/edocs/mdocs/mdocs/en/wipo_ip_inn_ge_22/wipo_ip_inn_ge_22_p4.pdf, accessed 12.10.2022 (2022)
29. World Intellectual Property Organization - Trade Secrets section, World Intellectual Property Organization, URL: https://www.wipo.int/tradesecrets/en/tradesecrets_faqs.html, accessed 12.10.2022
30. J. Watal, *Balancing Legitimate Interest in the Trade Secret System under the WTO TRIPS Agreement*, WIPO Symposium on Trade Secrets and Innovation, Geneva, Switzerland, URL: https://www.wipo.int/edocs/mdocs/mdocs/en/wipo_ip_inn_ge_22/wipo_ip_inn_ge_22_p3.pdf, accessed 12.10.2022 (2022)
31. K.S. Sandeen, *Balancing Legitimate Interests in the Trade Secret System*. WIPO Symposium on Trade Secrets and Innovation, Geneva, Switzerland, URL: https://www.wipo.int/edocs/mdocs/mdocs/en/wipo_ip_inn_ge_22/wipo_ip_inn_ge_22_p5.pdf, accessed 12.10.2022 (2022)
32. E.D. Ferrill, K. Rajan, *3D Bioprinting, Nanotechnology, and Intellectual Property*, 505-523 in L.G. Zhang, J.P. Fisher, K.W. Leong, (Editors), 3D Bioprinting and Nanotechnology in Tissue Engineering and Regenerative Medicine, Second edition (Elsevier, 2022)
33. P. Ciancarini, D. Russo, A. Sillitti, G. Succi, *Reverse Engineering: a European IPR perspective*, SAC'16: Proceedings of the 31st Annual ACM Symposium on Applied Computing. DOI: 10.1145/2851613.2851790 (2016)
34. URL:https://hack.technoherder.com/reverse-engineering/, accessed 12.10.2022
35. D. Varadarajan, Iowa Law Review, **103**, 1596 (2018)
36. U.-M. Mylly, ICC, **52**, 1323, DOI: 10.1007/s40319-021-01120-3 (2021)

37. R. Grogan, *Decompilation and Disassembly: Undoing Software Protection*, Computer Law (1984)
38. Court of Justice of the European Union, C-13/20, *Top System SA v. Belgian State* (2021)
39. Davidson & Associates, doing business as Blizzard Entertainment Inc; [...] v. Tim Jung, URL: https://h2o.law.harvard.edu/collages/45578, accessed 12.10.2022
40. Court of First Instance (Grand Chamber), T-201/04, *Microsoft Corp. v. Commission of the European Communities* (2007)
41. United States Court of Appeals, *Sega Enterprises Ltd. v. Accolade Inc.* (Ninth Circuit 1992, URL: https://h2o.law.harvard.edu/cases/4486, accessed 12.10.2022
42. K. Love, Technology & Intellectual Property Law, **4(1)** (1993)
43. U.S. Ninth Circuit Court of Appeals, Sony *Computer Entertainment Inc. v. Connectix Corporation*, 203 F.3d 596 (2000)
44. Koulourisa, N. Misailidis, D. Petrides, Food and Bioproducts Processing, **(126)**, 317-333 (2021)
45. M. Alba, *Finally Digital Twins get their own consortium*, URL: https://www.gafcon.com/engineering-com-digital-twins-get-their-own-consortium/, accessed 12.10.2022 (2020)
46. G. Bhatti, H. Mohan, R.R. Singh, Renewable and Sustainable Energy Reviews, **141** (2021)
47. F. Tao, F. Sui, A. Liu, Q. Qi, M. Zhang, *Digital twin-driven product design framework*, International Journal of Production Research, DOI: 10.1080/00207543.2018.1443229 (2018)
48. P. Augustine, Advances in Computers, **117(1)**, DOI: 10.1016/bs.adcom.2019.10.008 (2020)
49. *Bridging the real and the virtual for the automotive aftermarket*, URL: https://peel-3d.com/blogs/news/bridging-the-real-and-the-virtual, accessed 12.10.2022
50. *Test Drive The Ferrari 296 Gtb In Fortnite*, URL: https://www.epicgames.com/fortnite/en-US/news/test-drive-the-ferrari-296-gtb-in-fortnite, accessed 12.10.2022 (2021)
51. *Vehicle Digital Twin: when physical and digital models unite*, URL: https://www.renaultgroup.com/en/news-on-air/news/vehicle-digital-twin-when-physical-and-digital-models-unite/, accessed 12.10.2022 (2022)
52. *Hyundai Motor to adopt digital twin in latest move of virtual technology use Digital twin technology set to be introduced at HMGICS, allowing the automaker to create a digital replica of a real car for simulation not only in virtual space but also in the physical world*, URL: https://www.kedglobal.com/tech/newsView/ked202107050009, accessed 12.10.2022 (2021)
53. D. Piromalis, A. Kantaros, *Digital Twins in the Automotive Industry: The Road toward Physical-Digital Convergence,* Applied System Innovation, URL: https://www.mdpi.com/2571-5577/5/4/65(2022), accessed 27.08.2022
54. URL: https://www.cadcrowd.com/hire/reverse-engineering, accessed 12.10.2022
55. URL: https://www.cadcrowd.com/page/termsofservice, accessed 12.10.2022
56. Terms of Use, URL: https://www.artec3d.com/terms-use, accessed 12.10.2022

57. T. Kevan, *Introducing the New Reverse Engineering*, URL: https://www.digitalengineering247.com/article/introducing-the-new-reverse-engineering/design, accessed 12.10.2022
58. URL: https://brigade.tv/about/, accessed 12.10.2022
59. URL: https://opensea.io/, accessed 12.10.2022
60. *Bridging the real and the virtual for the automotive aftermarket*, URL: https://peel-3d.com/blogs/news/bridging-the-real-and-the-virtual, accessed 12.10.2022 (2022)
61. J.H. Reichman, *Legal Hybrids Between the Patent and Copyright Paradigms*, Columbia Law Review, 2441, URL: https://scholarship.law.duke.edu/cgi/viewcontent.cgi?article=1075&context=faculty_scholarship, accessed 12.10.2022 (1994)
62. B. Haghpour, E. Sahabeh, H. Halvari, International Journal of Consumer Studies, **46**, 1942–1959 (2022)
63. D.W. Carstens, Harvard Journal of Law & Technology, **3(Spring)**, 174-175 (1990)
64. *Reverse engineering clampdown and super licence revisions approved by FIA*, URL:https://www.formula1.com/en/latest/article.reverse-engineering-clampdown-and-super-licence-revisions-approved-by-fia.4S2ZYwi3X37jsnkJNlOxxW.html, accessed 12.10.2022
65. *Formula 1 Bans 3D Scanning and Reverse Engineering*, URL: https://metrology.news/formulae-1-bans-3d-scanning-and-reverse-engineering/, accessed 12.10.2022 (2020)
66. T.F. Aplin, *Right to Property and Trade Secrets* in C. Geiger, Research Handbook on Human Rights and Intellectual Property, 421-422, Edward Elgar
67. M.D. Murray, *Trademarks, NFTs, and the Law of the Metaverse*, DOI: http://dx.doi.org/10.2139/ssrn.4160233 (2022)

# On the normative equivalence paradigm in cyberspace

*Carmen* Moldovan[1*]

[1]Faculty of Law, Alexandru Ioan Cuza University of Iaşi, Romania

**Abstract.** Constant evolution of communication technology and expansion of Cyberspace has had a pervasive effect on all areas of human life, activities and interactions, that law unsuccessfully tried to regulate. Cyberspace was for a long period of time considered uncharted territory, an unlimited and open space outside the control of States and the limits on the admissible or accepted conduct of states and other stakeholders were blurred. In this context, the most important challenge and pressing need is to identify normative guidelines applicable in this environment considering its specific features (being unlimited, world-wide availability, anonymity). The aim of the paper is to challenge the elements of the so-called normative equivalence that was developed by several international bodies first in relation with human rights safeguards and extended as generally applicable with some special approaches at the level of the European Union (protection of personal data, strategy on cybersecurity) which will not be addressed.

## 1 Special architecture of Cyberspace

There is no terminological consistency to designate Cyberspace and terms like *cyberspace, digital space, cyber space* or even *digital ecosystem* [1], are used as interchangeable. Cyberspace is not defined by International Law or used as such, instead the terms "Information and Communication Technology" (ICT) are used and favoured by the United Nations in different reports and documents. The term Cyberspace in the sense used now has its origins in the 1984 book *Neuromancer* by William Gibson, who described it as follows:

'*Cyberspace. A consensual hallucination experienced daily by billions of legitimate operators, in every nation, by children being taught mathematical concepts... A graphic representation of data abstracted from the banks of every computer in the human system. Unthinkable complexity. Lines of light ranged in the nonspace of the mind, clusters and constellations of data. Like city lights, receding*' [2].

Previously, it was used by the Danish artist Susanne Using in the late 1960s when she and the architect Carsten Hoff constituted *Atelier Cyberspace*, which had nothing to do with the current sense given to this term (it represented a series of installations and images entitled "sensory spaces" that were based on the principle of open systems adaptable to various influences, such as human movement and the behaviour of new materials) [3].

* Corresponding author: carmen.moldovan@uaic.ro

Unlike the state territory which has a material and physical dimension, Cyberspace is entirely human made [4] and constitutes a complex global network, a logical space, unlimited, imperceptible, non-materialized, time-dependent [5] and constantly changing, who cannot exist without the physical support of infrastructure [6], an interconnected information system created by non-state actors, with no borders [7], parallel to the physical territory.

All these features make it a *sui generis* phenomenon [8], that it is probably one of the greatest creations of humanity. At the same time, we should highlight that Cyberspace is not only civil and commercial space, it is also a military space being used for military purposes and activities.

In order to justify regulation of Cyberspace, it was characterised as chaotic, anarchic [9] and asymmetric in relation to resources and capabilities in cyberspace [6] that protect the interests of States in relation to other States, affirming this principle does not resolve all the subsequent issues: state responsibility, consequences on the interests and rights of private persons and non-state actors. The complexity of the environment itself, the diversity of its users (States, non-state actors, private companies, private persons) actually determined multiple layers and different types of relationships between its users, depending on their quality and of the nature of the acts. Hence, the environment can be divided technically and legally in several parts: public networks accessible to everyone and not restricted by internal borders, with free access; territorial networks such as military intranets or government networks with limited access; exclusive networks - for e-government services, business, finance - the access is limited to authorised persons [10].

Due to the lack of a standard or objective definition of Cyberspace, it is generally used regarding any aspects of using computer and internet networks [5] and the term "cyber" has been used to describe almost anything that has to do with networks and computers, especially in the security field. Etymological, the term Cyberspace comes from 'cybernetics', which in turn is derived from the Ancient Greek 'kybernētēs', which means 'steersman, governor, pilot, or rudder'. Norbert Wiener defined the term 'cybernetics 'in the title of his book as "Cybernetics: Or, the Control and Communication in the animal and the machine". The idea that humans can interfere with machines and that the resulting system can provide an alternative environment for interaction provides a foundation for the concept of Cyberspace [5].

Legally defining Cyberspace may be impossible due to its dynamic nature and the unpredictability of its future evolution. However, the environment cannot be considered as unregulated or uncharted, rather a regulated as a multistakeholders model [11].

## 2 Attempts to define and regulate Cyberspace

States did not succeed in the task of completely regulate Cyberspace and to clarify the norms and obligations incumbent to them and to other stakeholders in this environment. There are very few treaties or regional legally binding instruments governing issues of Cyberspace: Convention on Cybercrime [12], its Additional Protocol [13], Shanghai Cooperation Organisation's International Information Security Agreement [14], the International Telecommunication Union Constitution and Convention [15] and International Telecommunication Regulations [16].

All these instruments are limited in scope and terms and do not contain a definition of Cyberspace or of the meaning of state responsible behaviour in this environment. Budapest Convention on Cybercrime has a limited scope to criminal behaviour of persons through informatic systems and does not clarify the jurisdiction issues. The Shanghai Organization (led by Russia and China) [17] defines cyberwarfare but does not tackle other elements of state behaviour or applicable rules of International Law [18].

It also proposed, in 2015, the International Code for Information [19] with very little effect and reaction from other States. From the perspective of the terms used, the International Code for Information security is interesting, yet it has only a declarative purpose. At least partially and formally, the purpose of this code of conduct is similar to the recommendations established within UN, as it *"is to identify the rights and responsibilities of States in the information space, promote constructive and responsible behaviour on their part and enhance their cooperation in addressing common threats and challenges in the information space, in order to establish an information environment that is peaceful, secure, open and founded on cooperation, and to ensure that the use of information and communications technologies and information and communications networks facilitates the comprehensive economic and social development and well-being of peoples, and does not run counter to the objective of ensuring international peace and security.*" [20]

It refers to the Charter of the United Nations and especially to the principles of sovereignty, territorial integrity and political independence [21]. Overall, it refers to all the rules of International Law that may be related to the cyber activity of States. As opposed to other instruments, this Code uses and focuses on information society, not on cybersecurity [22].

A relevant example of a regional effort in identifying rules applicable to cyber operations is the *Tallinn Manual 2.0 on the International Law Applicable to Cyber Operations* (The Tallinn Manual 2.0) [23] considered to be the most comprehensive academic publication on the subject of cyber activities [24]. It contains useful findings concerning the principles of sovereignty and non-intervention in Cyberspace yet, it does not provide an answer to all questions and focuses on issues related to use of force in peacetime, preventive self-defence, cyber-attacks and evaluating imminence of cyber-attacks. As estimated, the Tallinn Manual proved highly influential in matters concerning the activity of States in Cyberspace [25].

There are also several private initiatives on rules applicable in Cyberspace. The *Paris Call for Trust and Security in Cyberspace* [26] was launched in 2018 as a multistakeholder initiative and formulated nine principles - principle number 9 refers to International norms - promotes the widespread acceptance and implementation of international norms of responsible behaviour as well as confidence-building measures in Cyberspace. A *Digital Geneva Convention* proposed by Microsoft in 2017 underlines the importance of international humanitarian law in cyberspace, without giving details on how this is applicable and to what extent and it is at the same time appreciated [27] and criticised [28].

## 3 Consensus that International Law applies in Cyberspace

As a result of the works of different bodies within the United Nations on norms applicable in Cyberspace, it is generally accepted that International Law is applicable to cyber operations [29, 30] and this consensus puts an end to the controversy in this regard, and to the idea that States should not be involved in regulating this environment and affect the free internet. One legal consequence of this finding is that States should comply with the correlative rights and obligations in their activities therein [31].

The conclusions found in recent *soft law* acts by the United Nations through different working groups [32] refer to voluntarily non-binding norms, rules and principles of responsible state behaviour in cyberspace, that International Law rules apply in cyberspace, the need to implement confidence-building measures to build trust between States, and to increase global capacity when it comes to ensuring cyber security [29]. These reports are considered to be one of the first United Nations initiatives in this regard [33].

The common feature of all legal instruments related to state activity in Cyberspace is that they all recognize that the existing International Law actually provides the framework for regulating the conduct of States in cyberspace [34]. However, neither of them provides any indication on exactly how this conclusion may be transferred into practice and it cannot be considered as elements of international custom. State practice continues to be ambiguous or silent, although States enjoy the prerogative of engaging themselves in formally adopting rules of conduct applicable in Cyberspace [24].

## 4 Overview of the relevant conclusions of the UN GGE

Within the United Nations, the Group of Government Experts on Developments in the Field of Information and Telecommunications in the Context of International Security (hereinafter UN GGE) was created in 2004 [35] as an exclusive body [24] having at the beginning 15 member States: Belarus, Brazil, China, France, Germany, India, Jordan, Malaysia, Mali, Mexico, Russia, South Africa, South Korea, United Kingdom, United States of America [36]. Further, a number of 25 States were members of the UN GGE [37]. The GGE reports to the General Assembly of the United Nations. Several sessions were held and the most important ones are those from 2013 [38] and 2015 when it was stated that the principles of the United Nations Charter apply to States' conduct and operations in Cyberspace [41]. Although a small group, its work is generally considered as the first step in identifying cyber norms and addressing the question of responsible behaviour of States in Cyberspace [39].

One of the most relevant conclusions of the 2013 Report of the UNGGE [40] is

*"that State sovereignty and the international norms and principles that flow from it apply to States' conduct of ICT-related activities and to their jurisdiction over ICT infrastructure with their territory".*

All in all, the report contains recommendations and uses as interchangeable the notions of principle, norms and rules [39]. Despite and beyond this vagueness, the report directly and repeatedly associates state sovereignty and international norms to ICT related activities and jurisdiction of States over ICT infrastructure within their territory. It mentions that it

*''offers the following non-exhaustive views on how International Law applies to the use of ICTs by States: (b) In their use of ICTs, States must observe, among other principles of international law,* State *sovereignty, sovereign equality (....)"*and comply with their international obligations, which corresponds to general rules of international law. [41]

The 2015 UN GGE Report confirms the rules and principles of International Law found applicable by the previous report in similar terms. Moreover, it asserts that it considered how International Law applies to the use of ICTs by States [42] but a thorough lecture and analysis does not reveal clearer issues than the previous ones. The 2015 Report also contains a series of recommendations [43], as voluntary norms, rules and principles for the States' behaviour in Cyberspace. That was the maximum result of the UN GGE because in 2017 it ended in a deadlock as it was not able to adopt a consensus report [44]. The points of divergent views for States were particularly on the right to self-defence and the applicability of international humanitarian law to cyber conflicts. [45]

## 5 The deadlock of the UN GGE and the creation of the OEWG

From a critical point of view, the findings of these reports are actually limited as they hold the application of International Law rules and enunciate fundamental principles and the need for cooperation between States and other stakeholders in Cyberspace but they emphasize the lack of consensus on how they apply [46], which is the most important issue to be addressed. Moreover, the findings of the UN GGE have at most the meaning of recommendations or *soft law* as a legal nature and the fact that the Group is currently experiencing deadlock cannot lead to the conclusion that there is *opinio juris* among States. As a consequence, the UN created in 2018 an *Open-ended Working Group* (OEWG) [47] with similar prerogatives. In 2018 also, the UN General Assembly established a new GGE to work on these issues starting from 2019. [48]. In contrast with the UN GGE, the OEWG is inclusive [29], as it is open to all interested United Nations member States, thus creating the possibility for a larger number of States to participate in and express their opinion. Hence it is a more open and accessible framework for discussion.

The objective expressed in resolution A/RES/73/266 *"was to provide all Member States the opportunity to engage in interactive discussions and share their views on issues under the GEE's mandate."* [48].

The first Substantive meeting took place in December 2019 and it found „*broad agreement ... that the cumulative outcomes of the previous GGE reports should serve as a basis for discussions in both the GGE and the OEWG*" and established that „*the new GGE should focus on moving beyond what was already agreed in 2015*" and that the 2015 recommendations should be respected [49].

The fact that the UN GGE failed to give clear guidance on how the principles of International Law apply in Cyberspace was considered whether a "blessing in disguise or a major setback" [45]. Yet, this situation does not automatically determine the unregulated character of Cyberspace. All these actions reflect a genuine concern and interest from States and United Nations, yet it is rather unlikely that the future work of international bodies within the United Nations or other international organizations will be clearer on issues connected to cyber sovereignty.

The existence of two working groups having similar mandates may prove inefficient and highly politically influenced. Instead of obtaining transparency and predictability, the position of States could continue to remain ambiguous. The failure in reaching consensus on how International Law applies is determined by the political nature [44] of these special working groups. However, it must be stressed that the role of the reports of the GGE and OEWG is not a normative one because they may not adopt cyber norms [44], a term subject to criticism and considered inappropriate [50].

## 6 Legal uncertainty on the extent to which rules of International Law is applicable in Cyberspace

The norms regarding State responsible behaviour in Cyberspace, identified by the works of the two working groups are generally considered norms voluntarily accepted by States [42]. This assertion is partially inadequate and presents the great disadvantage of their non-binding force; therefore, they are not part of the *hard law* and no international obligations may derive from them. Such an assertion is highly relevant as an example, from the perspective of applying the sovereignty principle in Cyberspace, for establishing jurisdiction and other legal consequences. Therefore, these conclusions lead to legal uncertainty.

However, works of the OEWG highlight the essential role of the 2015 Report of the UN GGE, the need for the implementation of the voluntary norms identified in order to ensure the public core of the internet, all through a human rights approach [51]. Furthermore, on 30th October 2020, the document *The future of discussions on ICTs and Cyberspace at the UN* [52] of the OEWG proposes the establishment of a *Programme of Action for advancing responsible State behaviour in Cyberspace* with a view to ending the dual track discussions (GGE/OEWG) and establishing a permanent United Nations forum to consider the use of ICTs by States in the context of international security, taking into account the *acquis* of the previous GGEs and OEWG`s work in order to ensure a secure, stable, accessible and peaceful Cyberspace.

The positions expressed within OEWG are in perfect congruence with the concept of *global digital cooperation* proposed by the United Nations Secretary General in its 2019

*Report The Age of Digital Interdependence* [53] as referring to "ways of working together to address the societal, ethical, legal and economic impacts of digital technologies in order to maximise benefits to society and minimise harms" and as a means of exchanging knowledge and ideas. The approach of the UN in this regard is in accordance with the idea of an open Cyberspace and access to every person to this environment intended to be an inclusive digital economy and society [53].

All forms of rules proposed on cyber activities of States and international organizations-reports, statements or guides of best practices, codes of conduct, scholarly works are not binding and in a generic manner, all could be included in the category of *soft law* [54] or *quasi-norms* [55].

The main legal consequence of this situation is the fact that their violation does not determine the international responsibility of States (in the sense of the *Draft Articles on State Responsibility*) [56] and does not involve the same legal remedies [57]. For example, as a general rule, a breach of an international obligation gives rise to reparations [58]. Applying this principle to cyberoperations, if a State`s cyber activity violates another`s State sovereignty, the State victim has the right to reparations [57], and this particular issue is still unclear.

Regulating Cyberspace appears to be in its beginning phase. In the future process of clarifying the content of rules applicable to States in Cyberspace the evolutive interpretation of existing norms and framework in this environment may prove useful. In this regard, it may be relevant the opinion of the International Court of Justice expressed in the *Advisory Opinion on Namibia*, which held that an

*"international instrument has to be interpreted and applied within the framework of the entire legal system prevailing at the time of interpretation"* [59].

and thus, taking into consideration the development of the legal system.

## 7 What is the meaning of normative equivalence?

Affirming the idea that the same rules and principles are applicable in the offline and online environment and to the same extent is a solution to solve the dilemma of an uncharted Cyberspace. However, it is not the complete solution and raises many questions and uncertainties as well, given the special features of this environment. As previously mentioned, the equivalence was promoted in the human rights field, as well, by several international bodies, jurisdictional and non-jurisdictional. Moreover, it was anticipated by international legal instruments providing that human rights and fundamental freedoms must be respected regardless of frontiers. This is the case of freedom of expression, enshrined in several universal and regional instruments that are legally binding or part of *soft law*. For example, Article 19 of the Universal Declaration of Human Rights provides that

"Everyone has the right to freedom of opinion and expression; this right includes freedom to hold opinions without interference and to seek, receive and impart information and ideas through any media *and regardless of frontiers."*

The same terms – *regardless of frontiers* - are used by the International Covenant on Civil and Political Rights in its Article 19, the European Convention on Human Rights and Fundamental Freedoms in its Article 10, American Convention on Human Rights in its Article 13. Therefore, States have the obligation to respect freedom of expression in any environment, having a negative and a positive obligation at the same time [60].

Since 2012, the Human Rights Council stressed

*"that the same rights that people have offline must also be protected online, in particular freedom of expression, which is applicable regardless of frontiers and through any media of one's choice, in accordance with articles 19 of the Universal Declaration of Human Rights and the International Covenant on Civil and Political Rights;"* [61]

and at the same time

*"2. Recognizes the global and open nature of the Internet as a driving force in accelerating progress towards development in its various forms;*

*3.Calls upon all States to promote and facilitate access to the Internet and international cooperation aimed at the development of media and information and communications facilities in all countries;"*

The UN Human Rights Council reiterated these conclusions in 2014 [62].

Previously, the Report of the Special Rapporteur on the promotion and protection of the right to freedom of opinion and expression, Frank La Rue underlined the implications of the internet for the freedom of expression and access to information [63].

Also, at the universal level, UNESCO had an assiduous activity usually by cooperation with other entities in supporting Internet freedom and access to information and published a dedicated series on Internet Freedom, in connection with media freedom and pluralism [64]. These works are particularly relevant taking into consideration the moment they were adopted and divergent to the idea of applying cyber sovereignty as a form of control over the national territory. For example, *Declaration of Principles Building the Information Society: a global challenge in the new Millennium* [65], drafted in collaboration with the International Telecommunication Union highlights the importance of access to information for the information society and for the development of persons and society in its entirety.

Restrictions on the exercise of freedom of expression and access to information are admissible if they are in accordance with the requirements of the limitation clause provided by paragraph 3 of Article 19. The 2011 *General Comment no. 34* on freedom of expression of the Human Rights Committee [66] also underlines this conclusion in the following wording:

*"Any restrictions on the operation of websites, blogs or any other internet-based, electronic or other such information dissemination system, including systems to support such communication, such as internet service providers or search engines, are only permissible to the extent that they are compatible with paragraph 3. Permissible restrictions generally should be content-specific; generic bans on the operation of certain sites and systems are not compatible with paragraph 3. It is also inconsistent with paragraph 3 to prohibit a site or an information dissemination system from publishing material solely on the basis that it may be critical of the government or the political social system espoused by the government."*

Free access to Internet and digital networks without any barriers, technical, structural or educational is also supported by the OSCE [67]. The Council of Europe had the same approach of application of the same standards recognized for the offline environment to the online [68].

Not least, even the 2015 UNGGE Reports also expressly mention the respect of fundamental rights including the right to freedom of expression and the resolution and report adopted by the Human Rights Council and General Assembly [42]. As a consequence, there must be a balance between the admissible actions of States that constitutes interferences with the normal exercise of this right and its content. Establishing full state control over the infrastructure, flux of data and information as an effect of state cyber sovereignty would impact the right to access to information in a disproportionate and illegitimate way.

The general opinion on this issue determined the idea of fundamental digital rights [69] that actually show that the equivalence paradigm does not completely solve the problem on the framework applicable to human rights in Cyberspace. It is the same situation in respect of the rules and principles of International Law applicable in Cyberspace.

Scholars and works of different international bodies have revealed that the existing framework may not be completely adequate to address the complications determined by the special features of Cyberspace, especially in regard of human rights.

Exploring the efforts and works of different bodies within the United Nations clearly show that the challenges still exist and in time the topics to be addressed became more complex, which shows that a specialized approach is needed. At the moment, at the United Nations level, following the unsuccess of previous working groups, that are still active and they continue their mandate (in 2020, OEWG was renewed for the period 2021-2025 [70]) and, at the initiative of over 40 States, Programme of action on cybersecurity (PoA) was established; it will become a permanent mechanism after the 2021-2025 OEWG, more inclusive and will address comprehensively the issue of international norms in Cyberspace [71].

## 8 Conclusions

Applying the same normative framework to the online environment is clearly the best solution against considering the Cyberspace unregulated. However, the challenges posed by this environment that is continuously developing at a very rapid pace must be addressed and at the moment this is one of most sensitive topics of International Law. The normative equivalence must be also analysed through a critical lens which emphasizes the need for new human rights norms and implementation strategies specifically designed for application in cyberspace.

Further work from States and international bodies is needed to define the content, scope and limits of International Law principles and rules, by reference to those already established. The fact that different bodies within United Nations were not able to successfully develop International Law rules through diplomatic means and channels suggests this need and the inadequacy of the equivalence paradigm for this environment. Although its work and findings were incomplete and sometimes criticized, the United Nations continues to be the most appropriate and legitimate forum open to all States for discussing all types of issues related to cyberspace. Nevertheless, reaching a common view is more difficult but discussions and debates in the General Assembly would offer the premises of *opinio juris* on State behaviour and a global governance of Cyberspace.

All interests of multi stakeholders are interrelated and interconnected in Cyberspace. As an example, connected to International Law issues, the concept of cyber sovereignty, founded on the principle of sovereignty, is opposed to the idea of global governance of Cyberspace and does not take into account the interests of other stakeholders such as private companies and private persons, to whom Cyberspace is opened to. There is no obstacle in International Law in regulating Cyberspace and conduct of States and other stakeholders by reference to principles and rules already established that may be adapted to the special features of this environment. As it appears, state sovereignty in Cyberspace is limited and it does not have the same scope as the physical territory between its borders. The best approach in this regard would be taking into account that state sovereignty in Cyberspace relates to elements of physical infrastructure on which the existence of Cyberspace depends, yet the issues related to state jurisdiction and extra-territorial effects and what constitutes a breach of sovereignty in Cyberspace should be clarified.

Most States are silent and do not publicly express their position on how International Law applies. A possible interpretation is that they are reluctant to bind themselves to new rules until they are sure of how those rules will apply and how the technology and cyber environment will develop in the foreseeable future. Another possible interpretation is that silence provides the framework for any type of activity. This makes finding common ground on how International Law applies more difficult, but not an impossible task.

## References

1. E. Donahoe, *The Need for a Paradigm Shift on Digital Security* in eds. F. O.Hampson, M. Sulmeyer, *Getting beyond Norms New Approaches to International Cyber Security Challenges Special Report*, Centre for International Governance Innovation, 31 (2017)
2. W. Gibson, Neuromancer (Ace Books, first published 1984)
3. J. Lillemose, M. Kryger, *Commentary Artikel på dansk, The (Re)invention of Cyberspace, Who invented cyberspace?,* URL: https://kunstkritikk.com/the-reinvention-of-cyberspace/, accessed 16.02.2023 (2015)
4. M. Baezner, P. Robin, *Trend Analysis: Cyber Sovereignty,* Risk and Resilience Team Center for Security Studies (CSS), ETH Zürich, 8 (2018)
5. R. Ottis, P. Lorents,. *Cyberspace: Definition and Implications. In Proceedings of the 5th International Conference on Information Warfare and Security*, Dayton, OH, US, 8-9 April, Reading: Academic Publishing Limited, 267-270, URL: https://ccdcoe.org/library/publications/cyberspace-definition-and-implications/, accessed 16.02.2023 (2010)
6. Y. Shen, Chinese Political Science Review, **1:81**. 93, 82 (2016)
7. K. Nyman Metcalf, Tallinn Paper, **10**, 2 (2018)
8. D. Broeders, L. Adamson, R. Creemers, *Coalition of the unwilling? Chinese and Russian perspectives on cyberspace,* in The Hague Program For Cyber Norms Policy Brief, 2, URL: https://www.thehaguecybernorms.nl/research-and-publication-posts/a-coalition-of-the-unwilling-chinese-and-russian-perspectives-on-cyberspace, accessed 10.02.2023 (2019)
9. S. Arsène, *Global Internet Governance in Chinese Academic Literature. Rebalancing a Hegemonic World Order?,* China Perspectives 2016/2 What Kind of International Order Does China Want, 28 (2016)
10. J. Zeng, T.Stevens, Y. Chen, Discourse of 'Internet Sovereignty', Politics & Policy, **45 (3)**, 432-464, 451 (2017)
11. M. Mueller, *Sovereignty and Cyberspace: Institutions and Internet governance,* Essay presented at the 5th Annual Vincent and Elinor Ostrom Memorial Lecture, given at the University of Indiana October 3rd 2018, URL: http://dlc.dlib.indiana.edu/dlc/bitstream/handle/10535/10410/5th-Ostrom-lecture-DLC.pdf?sequence=1&isAllowed=y, accessed 12.02.2023 (2018)
12. *Convention on Cybercrime*, 23.XI.2001, ETS No.185.
13. Additional Protocol to the Convention on Cybercrime, concerning the criminalisation of acts of a racist and xenophobic nature committed through computer systems, Jan. 28, ETS No. 189 (2003)
14. Agreement between the Governments of the Member States of the Shanghai Cooperation Organisation on Cooperation in the Field of International Information Security, 61st Plenary Meeting, Dec. 2 (2008)
15. Constitution and Convention of the International Telecommunication Union, Dec. 22, 1825 UNTS 330 (1992)
16. *The International Telecommunication Regulations* and their Appendices, adopted by the World Conference on International Telecommunications, Dubai, 2012/ International Telecommunication Union, Final Acts, of the World Conference on International Telecommunications (Dubai, 2012) (2013)

17. N. Pijović,. *The Cyberspace 'Great Game'. The Five Eyes, the Sino-Russian Bloc and the Growing Competition to Shape Global Cyberspace Norms*, 13th International Conference on Cyber Conflict Going Viral, T. Jančárková, L. Lindström, G. Visky, P. Zotz (Eds.) 2021NATO CCDCOE Publications, Tallinn, 215-231 (2021)
18. Annex to the letter dated 9 January 2015 from the Permanent Representatives of China, Kazakhstan, Kyrgyzstan, the Russian Federation, Tajikistan and Uzbekistan to the United Nations addressed to the Secretary-General, UN Doc A/69/723, URL: https://digitallibrary.un.org/record/786846?ln=en, accessed 12.02.2023
19. Annex to the letter dated 9 January 2015 from the Permanent Representatives of China, Kazakhstan, Kyrgyzstan, the Russian Federation, Tajikistan and Uzbekistan to the United Nations addressed to the Secretary-General, Sixty-ninth session Agenda item 91 Developments in the field of information and telecommunications in the context of international security, A/69/723, URL: https://digitallibrary.un.org/record/786846?ln=en, accessed 12.02.2023
20. International Code of Conduct, para 1.
21. International Code of Conduct, para 2 (1).
22. D. Broeders, L.Adamson and R.Creemers (n 15) 2
23. M.N. Schmitt (ed.), Tallinn Manual 2.0 on the International Law Applicable to Cyber Operations (Cambridge University Press, Cambridge, 2017)
24. F. Delerue, François, ESIL Reflections, **7:4**, 2 (2018)
25. E. Talbot Jensen, Georgetown Journal of International Law, **48**, 735-778 (2017)
26. *The Paris Call for Trust and Security in Cyberspace.* 2018, URL: https://pariscall.international/en/, accessed 12.02.2023
27. J. Guay, L. Rudnick, *What the Digital Geneva Convention means for the future of humanitarian action,* The Policy Lab June 25, URL: https://www.unhcr.org/innovation/digital-geneva-convention-mean-future-humanitarian-action/, , accessed 12.02.2023 (2017)
28. V. Jeutner, Journal of International Humanitarian Legal Studies, **10 (1)**, 158–170 (2019)
29. M. Tolppa, *Overview of the UN OEWG developments: continuation of discussions on how International Law applies in cyberspace,* URL: https://ccdcoe.org/library/publications/overview-of-un-oewg-developments-continuation-of-discussions-on-how-international-law-applies-in-cyberspace/, accessed 10.02.2023 (2020)
30. CCDCOE. *Trends in International Law for cyberspace*, URL: https://ccdcoe.org/uploads/2019/05/Trends-Intlaw_a4_final.pdf, accessed 12.02.2023 (2019)
31. S. Kanuck, Texas Law Review, **88**, 1575 (2010)
32. UNODA, *Fact Sheet - Developments in the field of information and telecommunications in the context of International Security*, URL: https://unoda-web.s3.amazonaws.com/wp-content/uploads/2019/07/Information-Security-Fact-Sheet-July-2019.pdf, accessed 12.02.2023 (2019)
33. I. J. van Os, *The United Nations, Global Cyberspace, and the Route to Hegemony,* Leiden University, URL: https://openaccess.leidenuniv.nl/bitstream/handle/1887/75333/Final%20Master%20Thesis%20GPE%202%20%281%29.pdf?sequence=1, accesssed 10.02.2023 (2019)

34. H. Moynihan, *Power Politics Could Impede Progress on Responsible Regulation of Cyberspace,* URL: https://www.chathamhouse.org/expert/comment/power-politics-could-impede-progress-responsible-regulation-cyberspace, accessed 10.02.2023 (2019)
35. UNODA, *Developments in the Field of Information and Telecommunications in the Context of International Security,* Fact Sheet, URL: https://unoda-web.s3.amazonaws.com/wp-content/uploads/2019/07/Information-Security-Fact-Sheet-July-2019.pdf, accessed 10.02.2023
36. M. Kaljurand, *United Nations Group of Governmental Experts: The Estonian Perspective*, in A.-M. Osula, H. Rõigas (eds.), *International Cyber Norms, Legal, Policy & Industry Perspectives*, NATO CCD COE Publications, Tallinn, 114, URL: https://dig.watch/processes/un-gge, accessed 10.02.2023 (2016)
37. UNGGE members in 2019-2021: Australia, Brazil, China, Estonia, France, Germany, India, Indonesia, Japan, Jordan, Kazakhstan, Kenya, Mauritius, Mexico, Morocco, Netherlands, Norway, Romania, Russian Federation, Singapore, South Africa, Switzerland, United Kingdom, United States, and Uruguay, URL: https://www.un.org/disarmament/group-of-governmental-experts/
38. United Nations General Assembly, Group of Governmental Experts on Developments in the Field of Information and Telecommunications in the Context of International Security, para. 19, U.N. Doc. A/68/98, June 24, para 19, URL: http://undocs.org/A/68/98, accessed 10.02.2023 (2013)
39. A.-M. Osula, H. Rõigas, *Introduction*, in Anna-Maria Osula and Henry Rõigas (eds.), A.-M. Osula, H. Rõigas (eds.), *International Cyber Norms, Legal, Policy & Industry Perspectives*, NATO CCD COE Publications, Tallinn, 17, URL: https://dig.watch/processes/un-gge, accessed 10.02.2023 (2016)
40. United Nations, General Assembly, *Report of the Group of Governmental Experts on Developments in the Field of Information and Telecommunications in the Context of International Security*, A/68/98, 24 June (2013)
41. United Nations, *General Assembly, Report of the Group of Governmental Experts on Developments in the Field of Information and Telecommunications in the Context of International Security*, A/68/98, 24 June, paras 20, 27, 28 (2013)
42. United Nations General Assembly, *Report of the Group of Governmental Experts on Developments in the Field of Information and Telecommunications in the Context of International Security*, A/70/174 (2015)
43. P. Meyer, *Norms of Responsible State Behaviour in Cyberspace*, in M.Christen, B. Gordijn, M. Loi (eds.), *The Ethics of Cybersecurity,* The International Library of Ethics, Law and Technology, **21**, 353 (2020)
44. E. Tikk, M. Kerttunen, Mika, *The Alleged Demise of the UN GGE: An Autopsy and Eulogy*, in Cyber Policy Institute, 14 (2017)
45. S. Soesanto, F. D'Incau,, *The UN GGE is dead: Time to fall forward. Commentary,* URL: https://www.ecfr.eu/article/commentary_time_to_fall_forward_on_cyber_governance accessed 10.02.2023 (2017)
46. B. Lété, Bruno, P. Chase, Peter, *Shaping Responsible State Behavior in Cyberspace*, in The German Marshall Fund of the United States Workshop Briefing Paper, 6 (2018)
47. UN General Assembly, General Assembly, *Developments in the field of information and telecommunications in the context of international security*, UN Doc A/RES/73/27, URL: https://undocs.org/A/RES/73/27, accesed 10.02.2023 (2018)

48. UN General Assembly General Assembly, *Resolution adopted by by the General Assembly on 22 December 2018 on Advancing responsible State behaviour in Cyberspacein the context of international security*, UN Doc A/RES/73/266, URL: https://undocs.org/en/A/RES/73/266, accessed 10.02.2023 (2018)
49. UN GGE Chair`s Summary, URL: https://www.un.org/disarmament/wp-content/uploads/2019/12/gge-chair-summary-informal-consultative-meeting-5-6-dec-20191.pdf. accessed 10.02.2023 (2019)
50. T. Maurer, Hague Journal on the Rule of Law,**12**, 283–305 (2020)
51. Statements by the Republic of Finland Open-Ended Working Group on Developments in the Field of Information and Telecommunications in the Context of International Security Virtual Informal Consultations 19 June and 2 July 2020, Statement 2 delivered 2 July 2020, URL: https://front.un-arm.org/wp-content/uploads/2020/09/oewg-informal-virtual-meetings-statement-by-finland-19-june-and-2-july-2020.pdf, accessed 10.02.2023
52. *The future of discussions on ICTs and Cyberspace at the UN,* URL: https://front.un-arm.org/wp-content/uploads/2020/10/joint-contribution-poa-the-future-of-cyber-discussions-at-the-un-10302020.pdf, accessed 10.02.2023 (2020)
53. United Nations High-Level Panel on Digital Cooperation, *The Age of Digital Interdependence, Report of the UN Secretary-General's High-level Panel on Digital Cooperation*, URL: https://www.un.org/en/pdfs/DigitalCooperation-report-for%20web.pdf, accessed 09.02.2023 (2019)
54. D. Shekton, *International Law and 'Relative Normativity*', in ed. M. D. Evans, International Law, Fourth Edition. 159 (Oxford Universrity Press, Oxford, 2014)
55. T. Erskine, M. Carr, *Beyond 'Quasi-Norms: The Challenges and Potential of Engaging with Norms in Cyberspace*', in A.-M. Osula, H. Rõigas (eds.), *International Cyber Norms: Legal, Policy & Industry Perspectives*, 100 (NATO CCDCOE Publications, 2016)
56. International Law Commission. 2001, *Draft Articles on Responsibility of States for Internationally Wrongful Acts*, by the Commission at its fifty-third session, in 2001, and submitted to the General Assembly as a part of the Commission's report covering the work of that session, annex to General Assembly resolution 56/83 of 12 December 2001, https://legal.un.org/ilc/texts/instruments/english/commentaries/9_6_2001.pdf, accessed 09.02.2023
57. M. N. Schmitt, L. Vihul, *The Nature of International Law Cyber Norms*, Tallinn Paper No. 5 Special Expanded Issue, 31, URL:https://ccdcoe.org/uploads/2018/10/Tallinn-Paper-No-5-Schmitt-and-Vihul.pdf. accessed 10.02.2023 (2014)
58. Cour permanente de Justice internationale, *Chorzow Factory Case*, 1928 PCIJ., (ser. A) No. 13, at 28.
59. International Court of Justice, Legal Consequences for States of the Continued Presence of South Africa in Namibia (South West Africa) notwithstanding Security Council Resolution 276,Advisory Opinion, I.C.J. Reports 1971, 16. para 53 (1970)
60. G. Rona, Gabor, L. Aarons, Journal of National Security Law & Policy, **8:503**, 505-506 (2016)
61. Human Rights Council, *The promotion, protection and enjoyment of human rights on the Internet*, United Nations A/HRC/20/L.13, 29 June (2012)
62. United Nations General Assembly, *The promotion, protection and enjoyment of human rights on the Internet*, A/HRC/RES/26/13 26/13, URL: https://documents-dds-

ny.un.org/doc/UNDOC/GEN/G14/082/83/PDF/G1408283.pdf?OpenElement, accessed 10.02.2023 (2013)

63. Human Rights Council, *Report of the Special Rapporteur on the promotion and protection of the right to freedom of opinion and expression*, Frank La Rue, A/HRC/17/27, URL: https://www2.ohchr.org/english/bodies/hrcouncil/docs/17session/A.HRC.17.27_en.pdf, accessed 10.02.2023 (2011)
64. UNESCO, URL: https://www.unesco.org/en/freedom-expression-online, accessed 10.02.2023 (2022)
65. World Summit on the Information Society Geneva 2003-Tunis 2005,WSIS-03/GENEVA/DOC/4-E, 12 December, URL: https://www.itu.int/net/wsis/docs/geneva/official/dop.html, accessed 20.02.2023 (2005)
66. Human Rights Committee, *General comment No. 34, Article 19: Freedoms of opinion and expression*, CCPR/C/GC/34 July 2011, para 43 (2011)
67. Organization for Security and Co-operation in Europe, *The Representative on Freedom of the Media Amsterdam Recommendations, Freedom of the Media and the Internet,* URL: https://www.osce.org/files/f/documents/4/a/41903.pdf, accessed 12.02.2023 (2003)
68. Council of Europe, Recommendation CM/Rec(2014)6 of the Committee of Ministers to member States on a Guide to human rights for Internet users (Adopted by the Committee of Ministers on 16 April 2014 at the 1197th meeting of the Ministers' Deputies), URL: https://rm.coe.int/CoERMPublicCommonSearchServices/DisplayDCTMContent?documentId=0900001680645b44, accessed 10.02.2023 (2016)
69. D. Dror-Shpoliansky, Y. Shany, EJIL, **32(4)**, 1249–1282, DOI: 10.1093/ejil/chab087 (2021)
70. United Nations General Assembly, *Developments in the field of information and telecommunications in the context of international security*, Resolution adopted by the General Assembly on 31 December 2020, A/RES/75/240, URL: https://documents-dds-ny.un.org/doc/UNDOC/GEN/N21/000/25/PDF/N2100025.pdf?OpenElement, accessed 12.02.2023 (2021)
71. United Nations General Assembly, *Developments in the field of information and telecommunications in the context of international security*, Resolution adopted by the General Assembly on 7 December 2022, A/RES/77/37, URL: https://digitallibrary.un.org/record/3991743?ln=en, accessed 10.02.2023 (2022)

# Advertising in the metaverse. A quasi-legal overview

*Aura-Elena* Amironesei[1*]

[1]Faculty of Law, Alexandru Ioan Cuza University of Iaşi, Romania

**Abstract.** Maybe it started as traditionally and old-fashion as possible, just with billboards and postcards. Then radio. Television. Digital billboards on the streets. Telephones. Internet. And from the internet.. things just exploded – an unprecedented explosion. The internet was maybe the Big Bang of the advertising. The moment advertising have started expanding everywhere and in any possible shape: videos, photos, articles, bots, GIFs, voices, online advertising, personalised advertising, targeted advertising, display advertising, search advertising, programmatic advertising, advertising by use of the internet-of-things (IoT). When one could say that the state of arts in advertising was reached and that expanding advertising universe started to cool down, technology went further again. A virtual and limitless world has been created and with it, the potential of advertising has been once again unveiled. Advertising was re-born in a new universe, the metaverse, claimed to be lawless. This paper will focus on how 'lawless' is the advertising in the metaverse and what possible legal issues might be encountered by publishers, advertisers, influencers and consumers.

## 1 Introduction. The metaverse and the advertising industry: coming together

There is no consensus on the definition of the metaverse [1], but it is generally agreed that it can be described as a virtual [2] alternative parallel [3] world. Starting with Neal Stephenson, who imagined in 1992 a virtual world filled with advertisements, and coming to these days, when building that world for subsidiary declared marketing purposes has become the goal of one of the largest tech companies in the world, one can notice that the metaverse is an environment more than suitable for advertising. Lately, there has been a worldwide focus on the potential of advertising in the metaverse, also reflected by one of the largest tech companies changing its name from 'Facebook' to Meta. The change comes as a metaphor for the transition from online personalised advertising on the social media to online personalised advertising in the metaverse. The high compatibility between metaverse and advertising has been also acknowledged by the European Parliament [4], which recognizes that the advertising strategies already started to include the concept of metaverse.

* Corresponding author: elena.amironesei@uaic.ro

So, the metaverse inspired the name of one of the tech giants, more than 30 years after being introduced to the world for the first time. Now, the idea of building a metaverse is more alive than ever, even if during these 30 years many other dreams and attempts have been born and died one after the other. As the metaverse is a copy of the real life, and real life includes advertisements almost everywhere, then the metaverse will also include them, being a new environment for advertising.

The scope of this paper is to identify the general and particular rules that are applicable to the metaverse advertising, also focusing on distinct features of the metaverse and their legal implications, such as the avatars. Legal fields such as data protection and intellectual property will be further discussed in the context of the advertising in the metaverse. The directions that will be followed throughout the paper start with describing the immersion of advertising in the metaverse, continues with the relevant marketing features of the virtual world, the contractual architecture and in particular the six most frequent objects of the contract for advertising services in the metaverse. Finally, for a better understanding of the metaverse and the contractual clauses agreed upon by consumers (and not only) for entering the virtual world, a study-case of a metaverse for marketing purposes will be presented in details.

## 2 Advertising in the metaverse

Each metaverse aims at being populated, highly populated, which means being accessed by large numbers of users. The reason behind this ambitious goal is elementary – it cannot exist an alternative digital world if it is not populated; it simply won't be a world anymore. One could argue that bypassing this requirement is easy by using bots and simulate virtual human interactions. Nothing could be truer, but when considering the advertising purposes of a metaverse, the requirement of numerous human users is not desirable to be sidestepped.

A metaverse has to attract people, real ones, and convince them to become users. The importance of this is revealed by quite a famous example of an unsuccessful event in the metaverse: the European Commission organised a rave party in the digital world [5], but only 6 participants showed up, while the costs of the event amounted to EUR 387 000. European Commission's action was highly disputed afterwards, as the costs have been unjustified, and the event was labelled as a major failure. This particular example shows the importance of having a populated metaverse, also in light of the costs for supporting such technology. A high revenue should be generated in order to cover the costs for creating and maintaining the virtual world and its entire digital infrastructure. Having this in mind, when a brand decides to make use of a metaverse, the costs incurred should be at least covered by the revenue generated, meaning that the return on investment (ROI) should be mandatory positive. If the ROI is negative, it means a loss on investment, so the project of the metaverse has caused nothing but a loss of money for the brand who invested in the marketing idea.

We came to the conclusion that a metaverse needs users. As most of them are consumers in real-life, the metaverses are the new 'places' where consumers can be found, especially in the post-pandemic times, after experiencing a mass movement towards online shopping, virtual social interactions and digital leisure activities. Metaverse technology represents a new channel for the brands to reach their consumers [2]. It is deemed to intensify the brand experience [6] and to also allow brands to create new experiences [7] for their customers, otherwise impossible in the physical world. Increasing brand awareness means not only more sales, but also a highest valuation of the brand as when it is known, it is considered 'to represent a significant component of the overall value of a company' [8].

At the same time, as it simulates close to real-life experiences, consumers are allowed and provided with the tools to have a behaviour as normal and natural as possible. When the metaverse gives out of ordinary experiences, consumers are given the opportunity to explore new actions and behaviours, inaccessible in the physical world. So the consumers are able to replicate their daily behaviour in the metaverse, while also going beyond the laws of physics and experiencing new actions and reactions – everything in a digital and brand-controlled metaverse. As consumers' activity is already tracked in the online world, the metaverse represents a new source for data about consumers, their decision mechanism and behaviours.

In the light of the above, the metaverse has a double usefulness from a marketing [9] point of view: a new channel for advertising and a new environment for data on consumers to be collected. It represents the scene of experiential marketing [10] which focuses on consumer experiences and their overall greater satisfaction. The ultimate goal when used for advertising purposes remains influencing their commercial decision and establishing or enhancing the relationship with the brands and the products and/or services they have to offer.

But as we already had videogames, also qualified as virtual worlds, what does the metaverse bring new? As explained, the metaverse revolves around the idea of a new, alternative world, where the impossible is possible and even more. The videogames promise only playing (in the end, it is just a game), the metaverse promises much more – traveling, working, social experiences, events studying, malls, restaurants. Universities as Stanford already created their metaverses for online studies. Marketplaces exists, events exists (*e.g.* Decentraland Metaverse Fashion Week 2023 [11]). However, even with these new activities available, the core idea remains the same – we do play in the metaverse: we play our avatar, we play by attending events, but we also go beyond simply playing.

Notwithstanding, there might be a significant difference between a metaverse and a videogame, important also from a legal perspective. As any brand has to adapt to the local market, this is also applicable for the metaverse. This would be one of the major differences between videogames and metaverses: while videogames are indeed global and the same game and rules are applicable and available for any player, the metaverse, globally available, should be adapted to the local culture, especially the ones built exclusively for advertising purposes. This strategy is best reflected by Circle Square's motto 'Work global, think local' [12].

Meta's objective is closely following the general goal of a metaverse: to shift the real world's social and economic interactions in their own virtual world. This would also lead to transferring the electronic commerce [13] in the metaverse, a fact already proven by the creation of marketplaces (*e.g.* the marketplace available on Xclusiverse [14]) and the arrival of phigital products (also available on Xclusiverse [15]). Phigital products are merging the offline world products with the digital ones, being mostly used in offline to online (O2O) marketing strategies [16].

The electronic commerce is based on advertising – the products or the services should be first advertised, made known to the customers, meaning that advertising should actually precede any other commercial activity. After the name change, Meta company is expected to also transfer the personalised advertising into the metaverse, as this economic activity is acknowledged to be immensely 'profitable' [17], in particular for it. The advertising purpose is also acknowledged by other metaverses providers, such as Roblox [18], which states in the terms and conditions of the platform that the use of their metaverses is permitted for advertising purposes [19] among others.

## 2.1 Advertising-relevant features of the metaverse

The metaverse makes way for a new type of advertising to take off – the immersive advertising, which is now deemed to be the most engaging type [20]. This is the form of advertising that consumers can interact with, in contrast to the more traditional advertising which they could only observe [21]. The consumers, as users of the metaverse, are practically immersed into the advertising, which is no longer only a bidimensional visual representation. Consumers are immersed in the advertising itself, especially when the metaverse is entered via virtual reality (VR) technology [22]. In this way, the metaverse provides tools for the marketers to enrich the consumer experience and to enhance their sensorial perception.

There are also metaverses that do not imply using VR technology for accessing them. These might be accessed upon creating an avatar, which can be metaphorically described as the key to the door of the metaverse.

### *2.1.1 Avatars: metaverse-owned and user-generated content*

Consumers could enter the metaverse after creating an avatar, which is afterwards used for participating in the digital life. Consequently, creating and controlling an avatar might be one of the most important steps and features of the metaverse. An avatar is the visual digital appearance taken by the users and which helps any other participants to the metaverse to identify them in the virtual interactions. It has a visual appearance, decided by the users, and a name (the latest might not be necessary in all the metaverses). The appearance is decided by the users, but it is limited to the options provided by the developer of the metaverse (for example, the user can choose the style and colour of the hair of the avatar, as well as the clothes to be worn by the avatar, based on the available options. At the same time, there might be metaverses that allow users to create new items for their avatars, also providing them with the tools to do so. However, even this freedom to create is limited to the tools available, meaning that new clothes could be created only by using the features developed by the provider of the metaverse.

As users have a significant input in the process of creating their avatars, either by unique combinations of the already existing items or creating completely new items for their avatars, an avatar is a mixture of user-generated content and the content created by the developer of the metaverse. Due to the potential of being qualified as user-generated content, metaverses include in their terms and conditions certain related rights. Such an example would be Roblox [19]; however, under the same terms and conditions, the users agree to grant Roblox a license for using the avatar they created, the license being *perpetual, worldwide, non-exclusive, royalty-free* [19], with the subsequent right to sublicense. This is why it would be advisable for brands which include in their designs real-world protected IP work (including logos [8], trademarks, designs) to pay attention to such clauses and eventually to conclude a separate agreement when they enter the metaverse through avatars as means of marketing. As an example of good practices in this respect, Roblox specifies expressly in terms and conditions that the license and right to use cover *any trademarks owned or controlled* by the creator of the avatar, uploaded in Roblox for the purpose of creating it. Nevertheless, this is not applicable when the user creates virtual items (not the avatar itself). In this last case, the user still keeps the intellectual property rights in full over '*the copyrighted material owned or controlled (...) that has been published off of the Platform prior to the time that it was uploaded by Creator onto the Platform*'. For example, if the marketing team from Dior brand would reproduce in the metaverse a Dior suit or gown, the right to use the virtual items will not be licensed to Roblox.

### *2.1.2 Virtual items*

The metaverse is filled with virtual items, inspired (or not) from the real world. For reflecting everything around us in the daily life, real-products might have their virtual replica in the metaverse. However, this raises the question of the intellectual property rights over these real-life products, brought in the digital worlds for making it more 'real', more convincing.

This issue has been raised in the past in relation to filmmaking, which sometimes has the same core guideline: reflect the reality as much as possible. For example, in many movies one might see on the streets the same cars usually encountered in real life. The same is applicable for clothes and many other products – filmmakers do not design and create everything from scratch just for the movie (imagine the costs). This does not imply directly asking for the permission of all the brands for the use of all the products that appear in the movie. A similar conclusion has been reached to in 2017 in the context of videogames, when the developer of a game named The Call of Duty, copied the model of a real-world vehicle produced by AM General [23]. AM General sued the producer of the game, but the court decided that as the video game was intended to reproduce the reality, it is allowed to copy elements from the actual world [24]. Consequently, the ruling was in favour of the video game. There is a hypothesis that the same reasoning might apply to the metaverse [25]. However, there have also been cases when the courts decided that the brand creators might have gone too far with copying products, as in the case of the recent Metabirkins lawsuit [26], which has been won by the brand (Hermes [27]). Anyway, the particular details of the lawsuits should also be considered, as Metabirkins lawsuit did not focused specifically on the metaverse, but on NFTs traded individually.

## 2.2 Contractual aspects of advertising in the metaverse

Entrance in the metaverse is preceded by concluding a contract with the metaverse provider or owner, which takes the shape of 'terms and conditions' when it comes to normal users. However, the same is not applicable when brands enter the metaverse for advertising purposes. The contract agreed upon by the owner of the metaverse and the user has is one of adhesion and is in general 'for free'. As metaverses intend to make profit out of advertising in the new world, they will conclude advertising contracts with the brands that wish to benefit of the new digital raising worlds. This is how the metaverses bring money to their developers or owners, when are offered for free to the public.

### *2.2.1 Contractual parties*

The parties to the contract for advertising services in the metaverse are not different from the traditional ones. The basic structure of an advertising contract involves the publisher and the advertiser. In the case of metaverse, the publisher would be its owner, who is not necessarily the creator or the developer. The advertiser is the brand who wishes for its products and/or services to be promoted in the metaverse. Sometimes, this structure might be tripartite and additionally involve a marketing agency. These agencies are constantly adapting themselves to the new types and means of marketing, meaning that agencies that help brands with choosing the suitable metaverse and intermediating the contractual relationship already exist [28]. Just as how in the past they adapted to influencer marketing and ended up with an impressive portfolio of influencers ready to collaborate, now they have the tools for metaverse advertising.

### *2.2.2 Influencers as a party to the metaverse advertising contract*

When it comes to influencer marketing in the new digital world, one could argue that the two types of advertising are mutually exclusive. The reality is just the opposite, influencers are not excluded from the metaverse, but are rather more present than ever as they go hand in hand for the digital marketing campaigns. What is different is that now there are two categories of influencers used - real life and metaverse influencers, the last category being further divided into two types: human influencers and virtual influencers. Metaverse influencers that also exist in real life might appear just as a replica of the real person – the so-called 'digital twins' [29], a concept also applicable to celebrities that have an identical digital representation/appearance. The virtual influencers might be creations of the developer of the metaverse or other users', even AI-generated [29], with their existence limited to the digital world.

The metaverses need, as previously explained, to be populated. If they do not have a high human traffic, then there would be almost no ROI because there won't be generated any commercial decision or brand awareness. Currently, there are many metaverses for consumers and some people might not even be tempted to join one, so they must somehow be attracted to these new digital worlds. This is the moment when the influencers step in: they no longer advertise only the brand, but also its metaverse, hence inviting their audience to join the digital world of the brand they're promoting. Of course, they have to lead by the power of example, so often they create their own avatars in the metaverse, for encouraging their community of followers to do the same. A concrete example would be the metaverse created by Circle Square for Lacoste, which resembles more to a game and it involves influencers who are supposed to play and share their score on social media in order to raise awareness among customers [30]. Shiseido is also among the brands that use influencers for promoting their metaverses.

A different perspective is that the metaverses might actually be the new social media platform for the new influencers to grow or for the old ones to migrate to. Consequently, the same social media influencers would now be available for interactions with the users in the metaverse and for the same advertising activities. As a result, influencers could also be hired for continuing their activity further in the metaverse, notwithstanding they keep the status of influencer. At the same time, new influencers might appear solely in the metaverse, without existing on any other platform. Someone might create an avatar, have a lot of interactions and outstanding activity, gain popularity and 'followers', hence becoming an influencer in the metaverse. These users could also conclude advertising contracts for products and/or services advertising to the users in the metaverse.

Finally, within the metaverse the avatars could not even be human-created and controlled, but computer-generated, even by use of artificial intelligence. These avatars could adopt a human-like behaviour, gain popularity and become virtual influencers. There are already plenty of them with no real existence. Amazon, Puma, Lexus, Samsung, Dior, Toyota, Dr. Pepper, Porsche, Calvin Klein and KFC are brands that have already used bots for their marketing campaigns. Air Asia has the virtual influencer Miss Ava. The fully digitally-generated influencers are also known as computer-generated imagery influencers [31] or computer-generated fictional characters [32]. The difference between this type of influencers and real human beings will raise more issues and worries in relation to the effect of the influencer marketing on the consumers. These digital influencers are flexible, with no control, and might actually be created to be perfect from all points of view: the perfect party to the contract that performs the contract precisely, and a flawless appearance, voice and behaviour, desirable by any user of social media. Brands might want to 'contract' with these influencers so they have their products and/or services promoted in the metaverse. In this situation, the digital influencer will not be party to the contract, but the person (moral or physical), that owns and controls it.

Advertising in the metaverse and specific marketing campaigns do not impact only the advertising contract, but also any other international trade law contracts that imply clauses related to advertising, such as distributorship, dealership and franchise. The contractual clauses providing rights and/or obligations for advertising the products that are distributed and the services that are franchised might be shaped up but the characteristics of the advertising in the metaverse.

### *2.2.3 The right to advertise in the metaverse: distributorship and franchise contracts*

In a franchise or distributorship contract, the franchisor and the distributor are the parties in charge of marketing the products and/or the services on the local market in which they are doing business and performing the contracts. Sometimes, the marketing campaigns are not coordinated in a centralised manner, but rather the local teams take care of it, meaning that the franchisor or the distributor handles entirely the local marketing. In general, these parties are allowed to advertise the products and/or services only locally, without being allowed to interfere with the consumers from areas in which another franchisor or distributor has exclusivity. Consequently, the license granted for the use of intellectual property rights and even the right to advertise are narrowed to a precise territory [33].

Online advertising in a designated area is possible thanks to geo-localisation services together with the possibility to select the customers from a certain area to be targeted. Nevertheless, it is still debatable whether the metaverses will provide the same tools for being able to choose the location of the customers who see the advertisement. Of course, a few metaverses will likely have this option, but as some metaverses are built to be global and accessible from everywhere, advertising in the context of franchise and distributorship contracts might need to be reconsidered.

Finally, as the metaverse is not linked directly to a territory, there might be issues concerning the choice of advertising the products and/or services in the metaverse that replicates the real world – will the same real territory limitations apply in the metaverse? Meaning that if the distributors have exclusivity only for Europe and the metaverse reproduces the entire globe, will they be allowed to advertise the products in the digital United States of America? These are questions still to be provided with an answer.

### *2.2.4 Object of the metaverse advertising contract*

In the context of advertising in the metaverse, the object of the advertising contract differs depending on the type of the metaverse, marketing campaign and the advertising methods and tools chosen by the brand. The limitless virtual worlds inevitable lead to, well, not limitless objects of the contract, but at least quite a large variety. We will further discuss six of these which we deem to be the most common.

Even if they are different, all of the contractual objects might imply the same performance – paying for the computer code, which would be available in the code/software of the metaverse for the agreed contractual period. Subsequent services such as IT maintenance/service might also be included.

### 2.2.4.1 Product placement

The object of the contract for metaverse advertising could be product placement, which is the root of embedded advertising [29] and takes a really different shape in the virtual world. If in the real-world placing a product is generally used in audio-visual advertising such as television, online videos, and it implies placing a well-known or at least recognizable product of the brand in the landscape/scenario, in the metaverse, a virtual world, the real product is of course no longer used. What is used instead is a digital replica of a real product. The product is nothing but lines of computer code, read by a specific computer programme that can then display the visual representation of the code. It could be branded clothes for dressing up the avatar or simply branded products available to be bought by avatars. A new and specific type of product placement is making phigital products available in the metaverse – physical products that can be visualised and even controlled from the digital environment.

Product placement is more likely to be experienced in metaverses with a worldwide dimension and availability, built by companies who aim to develop a 'major virtual world' and to 'attract massive amounts of users' [34].

In general, one would experience this type of advertising while watching television or any other audio-visual content on a digital device (laptop, telephone, tablet etc). In that content, at some point, either someone consumes a branded product intentionally, either it is placed around the characters/people or in the surrounding with the aim of being noticed by the viewers. Nevertheless, that content and the product that is placed is the same for all the viewers, meaning that everyone who watches for example a TV show will see the exact product being placed.

The metaverse changes the game in what concerns product placements. It allows for this advertising method to be personalised [35], just as ordinary display online advertising does. This means that while someone is in a metaverse, if he/she goes in a bar, then that person might see on the tables only coke (if he/she does not drink alcohol), and another avatar might see only beer (if they usually drink it and in particular if it is their favourite alcohol beverage). The products will be placed around the users depending on their preferences. Everyone's ads and placed products will be possibly tailored, meaning that the metaverse has the potential to be different depending on the user, thus personalised.

Nonetheless, the personalisation of advertising in the metaverse might increase the level of polarization in societies. As in general the personalised advertising is based on algorithms that recommend the users certain products/services, it will further appear as a filter that will lead to creating virtual existential bubbles in which each avatar (real-life consumer) will digitally live and see only what they are interested in, while shut off from alternative products and services [34]. The metaverse will definitely influence the products and services consumers are exposed to [17].

### 2.2.4.2 'Buying' land

The second object of the contract would be buying virtual 'land' in the metaverse and 'building' a virtual presence. For example, McDonald's might decide to be permanently present in the metaverse. Let's assume they would re-enter the metaverse by placing there a long-lasting McDonald's restaurant. Of course, the real aim is advertising, as they will not be actually selling food and making profit – avatars, obviously, do not need food as humans. Similarly, a law firm in the United States of America bought digital land for building up their digital presence through an office in the metaverse [36].

An example of a metaverse oriented towards selling digital land is Decentraland [37]. The terms and conditions of Decentraland acknowledge the possibility of doing advertising by using their site and the tools provided, as these also provide the liability for advertising [38] and unauthorized advertising [39], which implies the opposite, *i.e.* the existence of *authorized* advertising. Making land available to be bought is a win-win situation, because populating a metaverse with familiar places might attract users and increase traffic in the metaverse. It would also maybe make it easier for the developer, as it does not have to imagine places, but rather use the architecture of the existing ones.

From a legal point of view, selling land in the metaverse equals to granting a right to use and to modify and/or have modified the computer code lines that turn into the visual representation of the 'land' that is bought. If the metaverse is providing tools for building on that land, the actual activity of building will reflect in the computer code lines that will be modified. If agreed, the buyer might even ask the developer to build the construction it wishes, which means that the developer will modify the computer code for having the precise design of the building ordered by the buyer to appear on his digital land.

### *2.2.4.3 Hosting an event*

Advertising can also be done by hosting events. Now, these events can take place virtually, in the metaverse. We deem that sometimes, behind these events there might be a co-branding contract [40]. This is applicable especially when in the out-of-the metaverse advertisements for promoting the event, there is a noticeably focus also on the brand that owns the metaverse. Popular examples are related to the Super Bowl: a commercial of the Super Bowl made available only in the metaverse [41] - so for seeing it, people were 'forced' to join the metaverse; and a future concert also in relation to the Super Bowl [42], available only in the metaverse – once again, for attending the concert, people have to only enter the metaverse. Another example is the Fashion Week organised by Decentraland in 2022, to which brands have been invited to attend. Estee Lauder [33], Philipp Plein and Forever 21 have been among the attendees. The metaverse also hosted digital parties, art expositions and even panels on fashion [43], such as Gucci Garden Experience [44] [45], held in Roblox [46] metaverse.

When hosting an event in the metaverse, one that is popular and highly looked after in the physical world, basically, both parties of the contract win – the fans of the advertiser enter the metaverse for their brand (especially when a unique event is organised, available only in the metaverse, as it has already happened), hence increasing the 'population' of the metaverse, while the advertiser benefits from the already existing users on the metaverse. These types of events also lead to highly increasing brand awareness both in the metaverse and outside (as the events are also promoted in the real world, being generally announced as partnerships).

### *2.2.4.4 The metaverse itself as an advertisement*

Brands might contract developers of metaverses for having created their own branded-metaverse. Examples of such a developers are Keiichi, which listed among its client Nike, Bulgari, Sony, Nokia [47], and Circle Square [48], who worked for brands like Lacoste, Toblerone, NARS, Kiehl's, Nestle and Godiva. NARS [49] brand came up with a beauty-verse, defined as a 'brand world' [50] and named 'NONSTOP NARS universe'. Dior [51] also contracted for a metaverse that combines retail with tester experience; the result has been a 'timeless' and 'location-free' [52] virtual shop. This is also applicable to the beauty-verses, digital worlds built just for advertising beauty products of a particular beauty brand. Shiseido [53] is another example of beauty brand that choose to have a beauty-verse for marketing purposes.

Similarly, there are metaverse providers that already allow brands to use their tools and to create their own small virtual world on their platform with multiple metaverses. For instance, Roblox allows brands to design branded metaverses on the platform; Nike is one of the brands who already benefitted of these services and created 'Nikeland' [54].

In all of the above specific cases, there is no actual advertising contract concluded with the developer of the metaverse, even if the final goal of the brand is to use it in the context of a marketing campaign, for advertising purposes. The brand orders the developer to create a metaverse, based on the instructions it provides. After completion, the brand will own and control the metaverse. However, due to the complexity of such computer programming work, the metaverse might be hosted on the platform of the developer, so it will continue to provide maintenance and eventually software services to the brand, during the entire availability of the metaverse for the user to join it.

What is more interesting is that co-branding contracts might as well result in new metaverses. More specifically, the brands, parties to the co-branding contracts, might agree to create a metaverse dedicated to their contract, with both brands being digitally displayed within the virtual world. Such an example is Mistaverse [55], created by Axe [56] and Fortnite [57], which is basically a virtual reality for playing, based on the Fortnite game and including Axe products. The metaverse itself is the advertisement, not only the products that are digitally placed. Thus, as users enter their website, they will find the disclosure of the advertising: "*The greatest advertisement you will ever play. Our legal team told us to write this.*" This also confirms that the metaverse is the advertisement itself. Fortnite had also collaborations with Balenciaga [58], which led to Balenciaga branded clothes being available in Fortnite's game.

Beauty-verses are going further and offer the opportunity to virtually try the products and check how they would look like on users' avatar or even on the persons themselves, when the avatar is created by using their real physical characteristics. There are also metaverses designed to combine both the typical online shops with the experience of a real shop [51], meaning that users can not only try the products, but also buy them immediately if they wish to – for instance, Dior's beauty-verse 'Atelier of dreams' [59], launched in 2021.

#### *2.2.4.5 Metaverse version of out-of-home and digital-out-of-home advertising*

The object of a metaverse advertising contract might also concern the typical out-of-home (OOH) and digital out-of-home (DOOH) advertising migrated into the metaverse. More specifically, it would imply the OOH and DOOH advertising, transposed in the virtual world, just as it would be displayed on the real streets, buildings and billboards. We deem that the distinction between OOH and DOOH will not be faded by the digital nature of the metaverse, as conceptually they will be perceived in the same way as in real life. Walking down the streets of the metaverse and seeing advertisement on static or digital billboards will only make it resemble better the real world.

The two types of traditional advertising would still be different in the metaverse, even if they are both digital. Conceptually, the OOH is static, simply displaying a content, while the digital OOH implies using digital billboards, with elements in motion, that might be as well recreated/simulated in the metaverse.

In the light of the above, in the context of a contract for OOH and DOOH advertising in the metaverse, the advertiser would pay for its advertisements to be displayed in the virtual world, similar to the physical world. He might opt for the same advertisements already existing or might create new ones adapted to the metaverse world. In contrast to a traditional contract for this type of advertising, contractually establishing the location of the advertisements might not be that relevant. However, clauses related to the period of time for displaying the advertisements are still applicable.

#### *2.2.4.6 Avatars: owning a branded-avatar or 'hiring' a computer-generated one*

The advertising contract can also be based solely on creating an avatar that is emblematic enough in order to advertise the brand through its own appearance. For example, McDonalds has the possibility to enter the metaverse through their mascot, Ronald McDonald, as a brand-controlled avatar. In this case, every user in the metaverse would immediately recognize the brand and it might be even more interactive and thus effective than just displaying the McDonald's logo on a billboard or building. There are also many other relevant mascots and brands that could use the same strategy: Milka's cow, Walt Disney Company's Mickey Mouse, Cheetos' cheetah, Michelin's Michelin Man, and so on. Instead of static logos and advertisements, these would be 'living' avatars, wondering the metaverse and interacting with the consumers.

Not only mascots could be transformed into avatars, but also iconic figures related to brands. Seeing Karl Lagerfeld with his cat in the metaverse, Steve Jobs or Donatella Versace would definitely increase brand awareness among the users, as all of them are representative for their brands.

At first glance, one could say that these avatars do not imply a contract between the metaverse and the brand, as all the users are free to create their own avatars however they want . However, for making an avatar identical to a mascot, celebrity or public figure iconic for the brand, using merely the tools provided by the metaverse platform are not enough. This is more indisputable when it comes to re-creating mascots that do not have an anthropic form, while the metaverse provides tools only for creating human-shaped avatars. Such an avatar should be specially created upon the request of the brand. Having a contract in place also ensures the protection of any intellectual property right implied by the creation and digital display of the avatar.

Avatars used for advertising might not always be created by the brand or imitating a notorious person or logo associated with it. Nowadays brands can also opt for computer-generated avatars, that do not embed any sign linked to the brand, but they are means for a new form or targeted advertising [60] in the metaverse. This type of advertising can be done now through simulated digital people, products and activities [35]. An ordinary avatar from the metaverse could come to an user with a Coke in its hands and say how good it tastes, while another might come dressed in a Dior T-shirt, hug the user and ask him whether he/she have seen the latest and incredibly amazing SS collection from Dior. These could be bots or computer-generated avatars, created and used for advertising purposes. At the same time, real sales-men [35] could create avatars and join this new world full of potential buyers.

In case of computer-generated avatars, it is considered that even the avatar might be special generated just for a certain users [35] so it resembles a person that the user would have trust in, with physical details that are enjoyable to the user. Finally, these avatars could be the means for personalised advertising, especially if they are AI-generated [29], as their discussion and gestures with the user might be tailored based on the profile of the user as a consumer. They might use the exact triggering words and gestures in order to manipulate the user for making commercial decisions.

## 3 Legal framework applicable to metaverse advertising

When the idea of the metaverse was brought again in the spotlight, multiple questions about the applicable regulatory framework have arisen. The metaverse is not new [61], but it has been recently re-invented and even promoted as a new lawless world, where everything is possible. A world without rules, where one can express himself/herself however he/she wants, doing whatever he/she wants. No sanctions, no consequences, just a limitless getaway from the reality. But.. is this true? Is this new metaverse a lawless world?

The freedom specific to the metaverse has been mostly promoted in relation to the 'avatars', for the users that enter the metaverse and materialise their presence through a digital visual representation. For them, the idea of a ruleless world, where they can escape the real world's boundaries, is a great promise for marketing purposes, which indeed attracts them to join the digital environment. In a world where people use all kind of methods for running away from reality, being their true self is a nowadays a trend, discovering and expressing themselves beyond their family, job and materialistic aspects of life is the new goal of the modern world. The metaverse is promising all of these – everything people can't do in their daily life, they can do it there, in their own (virtual) terms (.. which should be compliant to the terms and conditions of the platform that owns the metaverse).

We deem that the metaverse is not so different from a regular video game. Users are provided with a virtual world (less or more similar to real life) and the possibility to create an avatar however they want it to be - they are not limited to their physical appearance, not even their genre, but they can use only the tools already existing on the platform for creating such an avatar. Then there are a (minimum) number of rules to abide. Now let's compare this with a videogame – users (players) can do in a videogame things they are not allowed in real life – murder, steal; even things not physically possible in real life, such as flying or fighting as a superhero – exactly what the metaverse promises. They can choose the 'avatar' to play with or even use VR technology to play a game. Why would the metaverse be so substantially different from the videogames?

If it is not real-life, then it is kind of a playing, and this is what human users generally do in a metaverse. They choose a role and they play it – they play with their avatar, with others' avatars and with the virtual world itself and everything it has to offer. Some metaverses are indeed meant to offer the possibility to explore real life places – a cheaper alternative to travelling, yet exploring the world (another goal of the modern society). Of course, there are also the metaverses that provide the possibility to learn and work. However, one can clearly notice how much the metaverse resembles a videogame. It is argued that the videogames are the precursors of the metaverse, laying its grounds [62]. It is also claimed that games like Second Life and Fortnite are actually early versions of the metaverses [63]. The metaverse is even described as being close to a multiplayer online game [64], and videogames are not outside of law. On the contrary, they are quite thorough regulated in all the world's jurisdictions.

As to the parties involved in the development of the metaverse, they are bind by at least all the rules applicable to videogames. These rules come also with significant differences depending on the users that are targeted to be attracted in the metaverse (special regulation apply for metaverses for children), data processing activities (which further implies data security and privacy [1]), type of intellectual property rights, activities to be conducted or available in the metaverse etc. We might not have already specific laws in place for regulating the metaverse, but the metaverse is not new and does not fully require a specific and particular legal framework.

The legal framework is nevertheless blurred when it comes to metaverses controlled by the users themselves in form of decentralised autonomous organisations [4], also known as open metaverses, as it is almost impossible to identify the holders of the obligations and ultimately the responsible for any breach of law. From a data protection perspective the legal issues involved by metaverses are almost completely reduced in an open type because users are in control of their own data. However, when it comes IP rights, and in particular related infringements, it might be difficult to determine who precisely has the obligation to take down the illicit content [4].

As the existent legal provisions do apply to the metaverse, our research questions are: what are the legal obligations in terms of advertising in the metaverse? What are the legal implications for choosing to advertise in the metaverse and are there any features of the metaverse that might make it harder to comply with the legal framework? Are there any particularities of the metaverse that might trigger legal liability of not paying attention to make sure that the existing rules are being complied with?

### 3.1 General advertising rules

Advertising in the metaverse should comply with the general rules. It should always be legal, truthful [65] and it should exclude the use of subliminal techniques. When the avatar created and/or used for advertising purposes is AI-generated, European Union's proposed AI Regulation prohibits AI practices '*that have a significant potential to manipulate persons through subliminal techniques beyond their consciousness or exploit vulnerabilities of specific vulnerable groups*' [66]. Also, misleading and deceptive advertising is illicit in the European Union (EU), as well as in the United States of America. In the EU, it should comply with the Unfair commercial practices directive (Directive 2005/29/EC) and Directive on misleading and comparative advertising (Directive 2006/114/EC).

Since having multiple new technology booms, initially unregulated, it has become quite a standard practice to draft and implement code of conducts. In respect of self-regulations of the advertising industries, additional requirements are added. Advertising should be '*decent, honest and truthful and by doing so helps create consumer trust in advertising and in brands*' [67]. No distinction is made between advertising depending on the means for doing it, thus the same general soft rules should be also applied in the metaverse.

As advertising is meant to reach the consumers, the legal framework for consumer protection is also relevant to the metaverse advertising. At the same time, an important requirement generally applicable to advertisements is the disclosure of their commercial nature, in particular when it is not obvious or easy to be recognised, for instance in case of endorsements. We will further detail on the disclosure requirement separately in the subsection below.

Finally, the social and ethical norms applicable to online advertising are also fully compatible with the metaverse advertising. For advertising to succeed in the virtual world, the basic social and ethic norms must not only be taken into consideration, but thoroughly implemented. In order to have success with the brand awareness metaverse strategy, advertisers should respect the reason for which the consumers enter the metaverse. Whether it is learning, socializing, playing or traveling, the advertising content should not overcome the content that firstly attracted the consumer in the virtual world. In addition, the advertisers and the publishers should not only make sure that they keep a small percentage of advertising for not overriding the interests of the users, but they should also ensure that the way the advertising is used and interacted with does not affect users' reaching their objectives in the metaverse. What is more, the advertisers might even thing about enhancing, through their advertising content, the experience, activities or interactions the consumers are seeking in the metaverse.

### *3.1.1 Disclosure of the commercial nature – a legal requirement*

Both the publisher (owner of the metaverse) and the advertiser must comply with the disclosure requirements that are mandatory under the law, especially in the European Union and in the United States of America [68]. More specifically, '*clear and prominent disclosure is necessary to ensure that the average consumer is properly informed and not misled as to the commercial nature of a native or content ad*' [69]. If in general the advertiser should ensure that the ad is marked as an ad, disclosing thus the commercial nature, this legal obligation should also be considered by the marketer when developing the metaverse or by the developer, when the marketer is only ordering its creation. The marketer or the developer are supposed to provide the adequate tools [32] for the advertiser to be able to comply with the disclosure requirements. At the same time, provided that the advertiser might use endorsers (such as metaverse influencers or computer-generated avatars), the publisher should ensure appropriate tools for disclosing their commercial purpose [32].

Even if in the online advertising industry complying with the disclosure requirements seems to be easy, as it only takes to mark the advertising content as an ad, in the metaverse this might raise some significant issues, depending on the features of the metaverse. This is why we are deeply in favour of a metaverse compliant both by design and by default with the legal framework applicable to advertising. The metaverse is a more interactive space and the built-in world might be extremely different from the one already existing. Items might be rotated 360 degrees, including logos, placed products and even avatars impersonating notorious brands' mascots. Consequently, the developers of the metaverse must ensure that the disclosure is clearly seen, regardless the angle of perspective and/or the type of interactions with the ad. In a limitless space, if users are allowed to do anything (as some metaverses promise), then they might also be able to avoid the disclosure of an advertising content. Moreover, in the USA, the Federal Trade Commission proposes now that the disclosure must also be *clear and conspicuous* [70], which would imply a 360 degrees readable disclosure in the metaverse. The USA's Federal Trade Commission has already made important steps for regulating the advertising in the metaverse, in a document named *Works on Guidelines for games and virtual reality*. Even the name of the document proves the great similarity between videogames and metaverses, both being ultimately nothing but virtual reality.

Native advertising is very much likely to exist in the metaverse, as it would be hard to distinguish between commercial content and non-commercial. This type of advertising is perfectly incorporated in the context or content where it is placed, making its commercial nature almost unnoticeable (*e.g.* a paid newspaper article for a beauty product, which does not disclose the commercial relation between the newspaper and the beauty brand). Native advertising could take the shape of display advertising [60] or even endorsements from the avatars. What is special about this type of advertising is that it blends perfectly in the surroundings so one could not identify as what it is – an advertisement. Native advertising is against the law, violating the rule of disclosing the commercial nature of an ad. Consequently, such advertising should not be permitted in the metaverse, but even prevented. A solution advanced in the past by International Advertising Bureau (IAB) Europe, suitable nowadays for the metaverse advertising, is putting in place visual demarcations, '*such as the use of different design by the publisher like shading, different fonts, outlines or borders*' which '*should be used to help mark the content out as being different to other (...) content*' [69].

### *3.1.2 Influencer marketing*

As already discussed, influencer marketing is fully compatible with the metaverse and brands might combine influencer marketing with metaverse advertising in their future campaigns. At the moment, one could even assert that influencers are essential for convincing consumers to join the metaverse, where they can be 'fed' new types and forms of ads. As it will continue to be influencer marketing at root, the already existing legal frameworks remain applicable, together with the general advertising rules, regardless of being qualified as 'virtual influencer marketing'. This conclusion is also supported by the opinion released online by the Federal Trade Commission (FTC), in which it established that its guidelines on influencer marketing, performed until now outside the metaverse, are also applicable to virtual influencers [32].

However, it is also claimed that the current provisions are not enough, as influencer marketing might disclose an unforeseen potential in the metaverse, in the light of the newly AI-influencers. Consequently, there are academics and professionals in favour of enacting a new legal framework, applicable only to virtual influencers [71]. In this respect, our opinion is that such a legal framework would not be applicable to virtual influencers per se, as they cannot even be held liable for violations, but rather to the developers of such digital influencers of the advertisers who control/own them afterwards. Even if the avatars might be artificially intelligent, the computer code that stands behind them should comply with the legal framework, both by default (the computer code) and by design. Notwithstanding, there are also advantages in having a virtual influencer, as it can be programmed to perfectly perform the advertising contract, without any deviation/breaches.

## 3.2 Particular advertising rules

Besides the general advertising rules that are applicable to advertising in the metaverse, depending on the type of advertising, there are also special legal provisions that should be considered. For instance, when it comes to sponsorship with a marketing purpose, special legal frameworks are applicable - in the metaverse might be sponsored concerts, events, restaurants or even charity events, as these allow brands to consolidate their digital presence. In addition, depending on the type of advertised products and/or services, the related legal framework for their advertisement will still be mandatory to be complied with in the metaverse. This assertation is more evident when it comes to advertising alcohol, medicines, cigars, medical interventions, vaccines, diet supplements etc.

## 3.3 Non-applicable particular advertising rules: real-world advertising provisions

Not every legal provision generally regulating advertising is applicable in the metaverse. For example, Romanian Government Ordinance no. 43/1997 prohibits placing advertising billboards near street intersections, but this restriction is no longer justified in a metaverse, where there is no danger of causing real car accidents because of lack of visibility; the concept of lack of visibility can be definitely challenged in a virtual world. Another example of advertising regulation unjustified in the digital environment would be the ones prescribed in Romanian Law no. 51/1995 which establish strict rules for lawyers' advertising. For instance, if they choose to display the name of their law firm, the physical displaying support is mandatory to have a predetermined size, measured in centimetres. It is hard to imagine and also pointless to keep such restrictions in a virtual world, that might actually be completely different from the real world. Nevertheless, it is debatable whether lawyers are allowed to advertise themselves in these new digital words, as theoretically, Romanian Law no. 51/1995, as amended, also imposes harsh restrictions on advertising methods and channels for lawyers. This is a situation about which one could argue that there is a legal vacuum in Romania's national law and a legislative future input is welcomed.

Another example of regulation applicable only to real-word and physical advertising would also be the local tax on advertising, payable to local authorities, and regulated by the Romanian Tax Code (Law no. 227/2015, as amended). This tax is due when there is DOOH or OOH advertising, located in public spaces or oriented towards them, so people standing in such places are able to see it, even if it is actually attached to a private building or any other private support.

Similarly, the enforcing regulations that apply to public institutions and/or authorities will also be unjustified in the metaverses, even if some of them might be built as real towns with city halls, police posts, universities, and so on. If in real life one will not see public authorities' inside and outside walls filled with ads, in the metaverse, the virtual representation of such institutions might be a suitable place for advertising – nothing precludes the publisher to design the metaverse as he/she wishes. This type of advertising rules related to the places available for advertising purposes are actually agreed contractually and dependent only on the parties' will and metaverses' technical configuration.

The conclusion is that we could actually narrow the regulations applicable to the metaverse advertising. As it is quite evident that the regulations strictly and directly related to the characteristics of traditional (physical/real word) advertising are unjustified in the metaverse, we could conclude that it can be applicable only the framework in place for online/digital advertising or compatible with this type of advertising.

### 3.4 Data processing in the metaverse

The metaverse represents either a replica of the real word or it goes beyond it, enhancing the real life possibilities. Users could just reproduce the common real activities (going to a concert, studying, shopping etc) or do even more in a world where the laws of physics do not apply. Maybe the concept of the metaverse is not new, but the high number of its users is. More users equal to more online activities digitally tracked, which means more data in the online metaverses [7]. This will also allow marketers to gather more data on the consumers, by analysing their behaviour in the metaverse [7]. It has been predicted that by 2026, a quarter of the world's population will spend minimum one hour per day in the metaverse [35] for activities like shopping, education, entertainment etc. If the 'usual' online tracking consisted of what people click on, how much time they spend on visualising a certain content, what they search online, and their commercial decision, in the metaverse many other activities can be tracked and recorded, such as what and how the work, how they interact with their friends, where they go, what they study etc. It is considered that even the emotional state of a person will be analysed, by processing the voice of the person and even the facial expressions [35], which subsequently implies processing biometric data [72]. Privacy is even more important in the metaverse as sometimes people behave there as they cannot in the real word, revealing maybe some of their deepest wishes, thoughts or intentions. The metaverse also represent the perfect environment for collecting data for neuromarketing purposes [73], especially when VR technology is used for entering it.

Metaverses and related technologies also contribute to datafication [74], by turning the users into numbers and values. The issue is that users are less aware of the amount of data collected and the entities rendering and harvesting data or inferences about them [74]. Data collection will focus on behavioural and biological aspects of the consumers' activity [75]. It is also claimed that in this new digital world, the companies '*will have the unprecedented ability to exploit the full potential of the data they collect*' [24].

The metaverse platforms opted for the same economic strategy as social media – generate revenues out of advertising. While they made the metaverses free for the users, so no fee has to be paid by individuals, they charge brands for advertising their products and services to the users. Consequently, the consumers and their attention become the product that is sold to the brands.

Advertising in the metaverse is closely linked to '*The Three M's of the Metaverse: monitor, manipulate and monetize*' [35]. The metaverse, when used for advertising purposes, might offer advanced-personalised advertising services for the advertisers, which entails different forms of advertising customised in accordance with users' needs and commercial wishes. Considering the volume of data processed in the metaverse, the tailoring process is likely to become one of the most advanced ever. As previously explained, it might be a computer-generated avatar which chats with users and it adapts the speech to the profile of each consumer or simply arranging the OOH and DOOH advertising just for a particular user. When two different users would walk down the same street, they might see completely different advertisements, designed and displayed in accordance with their preferences. Also, it is already foreseen that users will be '*offered product selection based on their behaviours and reactions*' [4], which is possible only after tracking and processing users' activities for then delivering the promised results. The metaverse will imply data processing for it to be able to analyse and then highly personalise the virtual content [6]. Just as currently the online activity of consumers is being tracked, the digital fingerprints left behind in the metaverse will be as well processed for the purpose of targeted advertising [35]. Moreover, the experience of the metaverse itself is wished to be customized in the future for each user, and this is possible only by processing their data [76] and getting to know what each user wants. Worries are frequently expressed in relation to targeted ads in the metaverse, as it is deemed that they will skyrocket and can become very intrusive.

In the light of the above, both metaverse owners (publishers) and advertisers will have to comply with the data privacy regulations. In the European Union, they will have to abide by the provisions of the General Data Protection Regulation (Regulation EU 2016/279 - GDPR) when it comes to any personal data processing.

### 3.5 Intellectual Property Rights

The metaverse implies visual representation (models and designs) of products, trademarks and intellectual creative work, in particular original works of authorship. Consequently, the metaverse is filled with copyrighted works so it is also subject to intellectual property law, which protects the rights over *corpus mysticum* [24] that are to be found in the metaverse. The creators or owners of the metaverse must respect the intellectual property rights (IP rights) of the brands over their distinctive signs [24], which are popular and recognizable by the users, in particular trademarks, designs and models.

In general when it comes to advertising, IP rights are also involved and specific clauses are included in the advertising contracts for ensuring that these rights are accordingly protected. In addition, when ordering the creation of an avatar or a branded-metaverse, the right to use brand's trademark should be granted to the creator. However, before entering the metaverse a brand should ensure that the protection of its IP rights [64] is also extended in the metaverse [33]. Nevertheless, even without joining a metaverse, it would be advisable for the global brands (and not only) to already take the steps to ensure the protection of their IP rights in the new virtual world. Brands that have already proceeded to secure their IP rights are Prada [77] and Gucci [78], who filed applications for protecting their trademarks in the metaverse [33].

From an IP rights perspective, counterfeit still represents a challenge as it will be difficult to assess whether a product is counterfeit or not in the metaverse. This would also mean that brands will have difficulties with tackling counterfeiting in the metaverse, in particular when it comes to phigital products. Such products can be qualified as branded goods for the purpose of enforcing the IP law [1] and preventing counterfeiting. However, it is also questionable who will be held liable for counterfeiting products. There is a notably difference between creating a counterfeit product in real life and creating it in the virtual world. The latest basically entails lines of computer code that can must read by a special programme for displaying the visual representation of the code. Such an example is the case of Hermes who sued an NFT creator for copying the model of their iconic Birkin bags and displaying them in the metaverse as 'Metabirkins'.

Going beyond the already existing IP rights, activity in the metaverse might generate new ones as creating avatars, buildings and products also imply a creative and intellectual input from users or brands. In what concerns the content created by the users, the property over the generated IP rights is settled by the terms and conditions for joining the metaverse.

### 3.6 Video-games legal framework

In a previous section of this paper we came to the conclusion that a metaverse resembles videogames a lot. Consequently, the law applicable to videogames could also apply to the metaverse, depending of course on its type, services and features [4] - for example, a workspace cannot be considered [79] a videogame, but metaverses such as Horizon Worlds [80], Somnium Space [81] and Decentraland might fall under video games' legal framework.

### 3.7 Legal provisions applicable to online and platform activities

In the European Union, the metaverse can be qualified as an information society service, that provides digital content and services, triggering thus the applicability of EU's *Directive on electronic commerce* (Directive 2000/31/EC) and *Directive on certain aspects concerning contracts for the supply of digital content and digital services* (Directive EU 2019/770). Furthermore, also in the EU, metaverses fall under the provisions of the *Digital Services Act* (DSA), which amended the *Directive on electronic commerce*, and *Digital Markets Act* [82] (DMA), even if neither of them addresses directly the topic of virtual reality [4]. Finally, as it might act as a marketplace or intermediate in any other way the provision of services and products of the brands to the consumers, it might also be subject to the provisions of EU's *Regulation on promoting fairness and transparency for business users of online intermediation services* (Regulation EU 2019/1150).

*Directive on electronic commerce,* amended by DSA, compels the metaverse providers to inform users about their identity, address (physical and electronic mail address) and whether they are registered in a trade or any similar register. This Directive also imposes the obligation of disclosure (already discussed in a previous section), as metaverse providers should ensure that the commercial communications which are part of or constitutes their service are clearly identifiable as such and also point to the person on whose behalf the communication is made.

*Directive on certain aspects concerning contracts for the supply of digital content and digital services* will only be applicable for the metaverses for which the consumers will pay for joining. Such an example is at the moment World Horizons, as it is predicted to charge users in the future. Under this Directive, the provider of the metaverse has the obligation to deliver digital services and content that: (i) are fit to the purposes to which they would be normally used; and (ii) possess the qualities and performance features, including in relation to functionality compatibility, accessibility, continuity and security, normal for digital content or digital services of the same type and which the consumer may reasonably expect, given the nature of the digital content or digital service.

The DSA obliges metaverse providers to have in place procedures for taking down the illicit content and acting accordingly if the case. The providers are also compelled to collaborate with national authorities when required, as well as to transmit them the requested information when certain conditions are met. DSA also tangentially handles the subject of terms and conditions and their content, providers of metaverses being obliged to include in the contractual clauses '*information on any restrictions that they impose in relation to the use of their service in respect of information provided by the recipients of the service*'. They are also supposed to inform the users about their internal system for receiving and solving complaints, as well as about the rules of procedure to be followed in case of breaching the restrictions or decisions made by platforms that are considered to be abusive.

The DMA regulates in particular gatekeepers, defined as those platforms that provide a 'core service' and have (i) a size that impacts the internal market; (ii) the control of an important gateway for business users towards final consumers; and (iii) an entrenched and durable position [82]. The applicability of the DMA in the industry of metaverses is a certainty as even the European Parliament acknowledged the possibility of having the metaverse landscape 'dominated by a few big companies' [4]. Meta with its Horizons World is expected to become soon a gatekeeper in the industry.

The metaverses business will provide some companies with the opportunity 'to monopolise digital markets' [4]. When a metaverse will start to do so (which implies attracting more than a significant percentage of users), the owner/vendor of the metaverse will control every business having access to the metaverse - one of the largest virtual environments with one of the highest numbers of consumers. This will once again lead to challenges in terms of competition between the businesses that want to enter the metaverse and depend on the decision of the gatekeeper. In case of not accessing the metaverse, they will have a disadvantage on the market from the start, compared to the brands that entered the virtual world. In the DMA there are also obligations imposed on gatekeepers related to data processing, which might be extremely relevant in the context of the metaverse and related advertising activity. One of them, enshrined in Article 5, is to not mix the personal data collected from core platform services with data from other gatekeepers or third-party services, as well as to not sign up the users to any other service without their consent. Now that metaverses might not be exclusively developed by a single entity and as they started to integrate third party solutions [34], these require more actions and precautions from the metaverse owners. A relevant example is the situation when there is a different provider for the avatars: the metaverse developers create only the metaverse, while the tools for creating the avatars and storing them are offered by a third party; in this case, an avatar can be used in multiple metaverses, all owned by different entities which have the same provider of avatars. Also, creating a metaverse for online shopping (like an online mall), might imply integrating third-party services.

Finally, under the *Regulation on promoting fairness and transparency for business users of online intermediation services*, if the users of the metaverse will be able to search for products and/or services, even virtual influencers or mascots, then the platform should provide an explanatory note on the criteria used by the algorithm behind the search results, in particular for the hierarchy that was displayed to the user.

### 3.8 Avatars: legal issues

The avatars in the metaverse give space for the right of publicity to be infringed. The right of publicity is an intellectual property right [83], which provides celebrities protection against unauthorised commercial use of any references to them [84], such as name, photos, voice, pseudonym, and likeness [84]. The right of publicity comes from the American Law where it is considered an '*appropriation of the commercial value of a person's identity*', in accordance with the *Restatement (Third) of Unfair Competition* [85]. The idea behind granting and protecting this right is to not let people who have not contributed to the success and work of the celebrity to benefit from it [86]. In some jurisdictions, it is not necessary for the celebrities to have previously commercialised their identity in order to enforce the right of publicity (in Japan for example [87]). In others, this right might also be protected after one's death, meaning that brands cannot use familiar figures that passed away for attracting the consumers, without having contractual permission to do so (*e.g.* a brand could not create an Elvis Presley avatar in the metaverse without being allowed to). In the USA, it is recognised '*a related statutory right to protection against false endorsement, association, or affiliation*' [84].

If such a right has been assigned to artist managers (like actors and singers do), then they might exercise the rights and also ask for compensation in case of violations. The right to publicity is for protection purposes too, as it shields consumers from 'deceptive trade practices' [86].

As avatars could impersonate celebrities, and their name and appearance have a financial value/pecuniary worth [85], the controllers and/or creators of such avatars would benefit from the publicly value of celebrities, which is mainly based on their fame [5]. This might happen by simply creating an avatar which resembles to the celebrity, without asking for any permission. In the metaverse, infringing the right to publicity could also imply merely the use of voice or even significant physical similarity [25] (it is not required for the avatar to be a perfect replica).

However, the right of publicity is not absolute and does not outweigh freedom of expression. Consequently, even in the metaverse, the name and/or image of a celebrity could be used if for example the metaverse simulates the availability of news channels on TVs or simply transmits audio-video news from the real world. In this context, displaying celebrities on the TV without a prior consent is licit as long as it is not used for endorsement and advertising purposes [88]. In this situation, it can be argued that as the metaverse aims to simulate as accurate as possible the real-life, and daily life implies such news on the TV, then the news that show celebrities can also be displayed in the metaverse without infringing the right of publicity. This example falls under the doctrine of fair use [89], which allows for references to a celebrity to be used in particular cases [90] in order to balance the right of publicity with other competitive interests [90].

When an avatar of the celebrity already exists lawfully in the metaverse, creating a second similar one without permission implies the act of duplicating the avatar [4]. As the duplicate infringes the right of publicity and it could be proven that such an avatar has already existed, it is questionable whether the duplicated avatar can be qualified as illicit content and thus took down by the metaverse according to their internal procedure, without addressing the issue in the court. We consider that such regulations applicable in case of duplicating avatars or infringing rights might also be included in the terms and conditions of the metaverse, so duplicating an avatar would result in a serious breach of contract, sanctioned accordingly by the metaverse. Metaverse providers should take into account that whenever it comes to illicit content, if they fall under the provisions of the DSA, then they are supposed to have in place a procedure for taking it down and also for filing related complaints.

Duplicating an avatar or infringing the right of publicity might also result in a virtual theft of identity [4], which could further negatively impact the advertising in the metaverse. If an avatar resembles a celebrity or a mascot of a brand and behaves in an inappropriate manner, this would further affect brands' image and make it less desirable in the metaverse. Of course, further questions arise in case the avatar is infringing rules of the digital community or even breaking the real-world laws which continue to apply in the metaverse [91].

## 4 Contractual clauses for services in the metaverse. Case study: Shiseido's beauty-verse and its avatars

Shiseido is one of the latest beauty brands who took advantage of the concept of metaverse and integrated it in its marketing campaign. The result of combining Shiseido with the metaverse is the beauty-verse [92] - the metaverse used by a beauty brand.

Shiseido's metaverse implies a co-branding contract with the brand Douglas, the collaboration between these two brands being also publicly announced by Douglas on social media [93] and also by the CEO of Douglas Romania: '*Tokyo #Beauty-verse is a virtual world where you can create your own avatar and start exploring the city, find Shiseido building and discover many surprises.*' [94]

**Fig. 1.** Screenshot from the Shiseido beauty-verse (10.01.2023).

Their metaverse is different depending on the region of the world where it is used or entered into. In the Asian region, the main characteristic of the metaverse is the resemblance of a part of the beauty-verse to a videogame, in which customers might play games with Shiseido products. It is needless to say that brand identity can be recognized in the entire virtual environment, not only on the products. If in the real world one could see the name of the brand only on its products (and on physical or online advertising), in the beauty-verse Shiseido's name and trademark can be spotted everywhere 'around'. Its advertising metaverse is, as expected, filled with advertising – from billboards to 3D products, stores and the brand being shown almost everywhere possible [95].

For the European region, customers can find virtual beauty-advisors, which will help them to choose the products that suit best their skin, and will even provide the opportunity to virtually try them. The possibility to test the products is one of the first ideas that Shiseido came with in the metaverse world when they started their new metaverse-based marketing journey. In general, the beauty-verse aims to provide as many real-life experiences in the metaverse as possible, including beauty seminars and advice [6].

The Shiseido beauty-verse experience starts as any other typical metaverse journey – concluding a contract that takes the form of 'terms and conditions' and creating the avatar for navigating the virtual world. For using the metaverse, there is granted a license (non-exclusive, free, non-transferable and non-sublicensable).

The metaverse's terms and conditions have at least the typical contractual clauses for the use of an online platform, as follows: the 'as is' clause, (un)availability of the site, acceptable use policy, limitation of liability for accuracy/omission of information, exclusion of obligation to update the information, the right to unilaterally modify the content of the site without any prior notice, and many waivers of liability related to the access to the platform and its use (*e.g.* no liability for not being able to access the website).

By entering into this contract, the consumers become users within the beauty-verse, meaning that any content they generate in this virtual world, would be classified as 'user-generated content'. Over the avatar users created for Shiseido's beauty-verse, they retain no IP rights, as there are set forth clauses for assignment of the IP rights over the avatar. These clauses are included in the context of the acknowledgement that users' creation might be qualified as intellectual/creative work, protected by the applicable legal framework. The users assign the right of use without any limitation and they also agree with waiving any right to remuneration and/or compensation.

Not always creating an account and entering the digital beauty-world is based on free will. As discussed in a previous section, influencer marketing might go hand in hand with the metaverse. Even Shiseido opted for this combination, especially for advertising the existence of their beauty-verse and convincing the consumers to try it. Consequently, for some persons, concluding the contract for entering the beauty-verse might come up as a contractual obligation, included in the advertising contract. Almost all the influencers used by Shiseido have been provided with gifts (the so-called 'freebies'), made of Shiseido products, and required to create an avatar. The entire process of joining the beauty-verse was supposed to be posted for their followers, so they will be attracted by the idea and follow their example. Basically, traditional influencers have now the job to influence consumers to enter the beauty-verse.

When it comes to entering the metaverse following a contractual obligation, we deem that there might be a conflict between the terms that are put forward based on the free will of the user and the advertising contract between Shiseido and the influencer, given that the influencer might have not been priorly provided with the terms and conditions of the beauty-verse.

What is even more specific about Shiseido's beauty-verse, is that a third's party services are used for creating the avatar. Shiseido avoids costs for developing another part of the software in charge with creation of the avatars. This outsourcing also contribute to the interoperability of the metaverses (someone who already has an avatar created on the platform of the same service provider, could instantly export it in the beauty-verse and use it, without creating a new one). As the beauty-verse could be entered only through an avatar, users are literally 'obliged' to also agree with the terms and conditions of the third-party services provider. These terms and conditions involve clauses on data privacy, IP rights, legal treatment of user-generated content, waiver of rights, and limitation of liabilities. The avatar created by the users is qualified as intellectual work, protected by intellectual property laws. It might be also created based on a selfie of the person (Art. 1.1 of End-user Terms of Use for Ready Player Me [96]) and the service provider has the right to keep the avatar in its database [96] (regardless of how it was created). This provision, together with waiver of asserting any right related to the impossibility of licensing a right under the applicable law (Art. 13.4 of End-user Terms of Use for Ready Player Me [96]), is questionable from a data protection law perspective. It entails that an avatar based on the biometric data of the real-person can be commercially stored, exploited and processed anytime in the future, without the data subject being able to exercise the data protection rights.

The third-party service is described as an 'online tool' that has the scope to allow the customer to create the avatar with or without a selfie. The users are granted a right to use the avatar in Article 3.3 [96] of the terms and conditions. Given that third party's services are provided to multiple metaverses, its terms conditions, it reserves the right to retain the avatar in its servers (Art. 5.6 of End-user Terms of Use for Ready Player Me [96]), without differentiating when the avatar is made based on the selfie of the customer or not. This is also one of the clauses that survive termination of the contract (Art. 17.3 of End-user Terms of Use for Ready Player Me [96]). Other specific clauses that are encountered in terms and conditions are the ones related to the acceptable use policy (the avatar cannot be immoral, illegal, abusive or harmful purpose (Art. 7.1 a) of End-user Terms of Use for Ready Player Me [96]) or for damaging reputation of any party). Of course, as entering the metaverses is free, creating an avatar is completely free (Art. 9.1 of End-user Terms of Use for Ready Player Me [96]) for the user. The onerous contractual relationship is established between the owner/developer of the brand and the third-party service provider. If entering the metaverse is free, then what Shiseido gains? As already discussed, the metaverse is part of their marketing strategy. Consequently, in the end will improve their brand awareness and even generate revenues following the immersive advertising.

Nevertheless, brands do not always follow Shiseido's pattern, meaning that they do not create/order an individual and dedicated metaverse each time they go with a marketing strategy that integrates the metaverse. Furthermore, generally, they do not do it internally – it would mean creating a new structure within the company dedicated for this specific and timely work. Instead, they would contract the services of an already specialised company and which would 'build' the metaverse as requested, following the instructions of the client (that are aligned with the marketing strategy in place).

The specialisation goes even further today, as there are companies creating the metaverse's digital environment and companies creating only the tools for the avatars [97] or any other services required that can be separated and then re-integrated. In addition, companies might completely separate the metaverse from the avatar, as in the case of Shiseido's beauty-verse, in which the developer is still the owner of the rights over the avatars and later it might introduce features for the avatars that they might have to pay for (Art. 9.5 of End-user Terms of Use for Ready Player Me [96]) or for damaging reputation of any party). In addition, they also offer the 'portability' of the avatar, meaning that if they created an avatar for another company, then the customer might choose to use, to transfer/migrate/copy the same avatar in the newly created metaverse (Art. 5.5 of End-user Terms of Use for Ready Player Me [96]) or for damaging reputation of any party).

## 5 Conclusion

This paper represents only the tip of the iceberg in what concerns legal perspectives and issues on the advertising in the metaverse, as it was intended to capture a legal overview, without going into specific details. New legal challenges are already emerging in what concerns consumer protection, children advertising and competition (for example, in case a metaverse that is also a potential gatekeeper decides to prohibit the avatars to wear anything but Nike shoes [76], provided that it is not a Nike-owned or controlled metaverse). Personal data protection is a fragile legal land over which the developers and owners of the metaverse seem to walk without caring. As always, legislators do not keep pace with technological advances in the field, but it cannot be claimed that there is an absolute legislative vacuum. As we have shown in the paper, the existing legal framework is applicable to the metaverse.

The world of the metaverse is, at the moment, a never-ending developing one, as new technologies are incorporated and users' experience keeps on being improved. AI is also already predicted to be integrated and used even for advertising purposes, in particular for targeted advertising. Whether there will be an AI-generated avatar [98] who will have tailored conversations with the consumers or simply any other type of advertising content AI-generated, this new technology will change entirely the online advertising, especially in the metaverse. AI could definitely assist with personalised recommendations and improve the immersion of the consumer [99], consequently enhancing the potential of immersive advertising.

## References

1. Clifford Chance, *The Metaverse: What Are the Legal Implications? – Thought Leadership*, 2, 4, URL: https://www.cliffordchance.com/content/dam/cliffordchance/briefings/2022/02/the-metaverse-what-are-the-legal-implications.pdf, accessed: 08.02.2023 (February 2022)
2. M. Ciotola, D. Kincaid, *Enforcement in the Metaverse, NFTs, Crypto and the Metaverse*, CTC Legal Media, 7, URL: https://www.cantorcolburn.com/assets/htmldocuments/Enforcement%20in%20the%20Metaverse%20by%20Michelle%20Ciotola%20and%20David%20Kincaid%20in%20The%20Trademark%20Lawyer%20Magazine.pdf (2022)
3. R. Pateh, Business Law Review, **43(5)**, 188-193, URL: https://kluwerlawonline.com/journalarticle/Business+Law+Review/43.5/BULA2022028, accessed: 08.02.2023 (2022)
4. T. Madiega, P. Car, M. Niestadt, L. Van de Pol, *Metaverse. Opportunities, risks and policy implications*, European Parliament, PE 733.557, 6, 7, 5, 4, 9, URL: https://www.europarl.europa.eu/RegData/etudes/BRIE/2022/733557/EPRS_BRI(2022)733557_EN.pdf, accessed: 08.02.2023 (2002)
5. Question for written answer E-004045/2022 to the Commission. Rule 138. Filip De Man (ID). Metaverse 'rave' party, submitted: 12.12.2022, URL: https://www.europarl.europa.eu/doceo/document/E-9-2022-004045_EN.html, accessed: 10.03.2023
6. Accenture, *Call for change. Finding beauty in every beholder*, URL: https://www.accenture.com/us-en/case-studies/consumer-goods-services/accelerate-personal-beauty-experiences, accessed: 08.02.2023
7. K. Bavanaa, Jus Corpus Law Journal, **2 (3)**, 2, 3, URL: https://www.juscorpus.com/wp-content/uploads/2022/03/2.-K.-Bavana.pdf, accessed: 03.03.2023 (2022)
8. R. Moro-Visconti, The Valuation of Digital Intangibles. Technology, Marketing, and the Metaverse, 2nd edition, 302, 309 (Palgrave Macmillan, 2022)

9. NYU, *Web3's Impact on the Practice of Law: Changes Are Already Underway with Wide-ranging Implications*. October 26, URL: https://www.sps.nyu.edu/homepage/metaverse/metaverse-blog/web3s-impact-on-the-practice-of-law-changes-are-already-underway-with-wide-ranging-implications.html, accessed 12.03.2023 (2022)
10. S. Smilansky, *Experiential marketing. A practical guide to interactive brand experiences*, Kogan Page London and Philadelphia., 6, URL: https://www.iibms.org/pdf/e-library/Experiential-Marketing.pdf., accessed: 12.03.2023 (2009)
11. Metaverse Fashion Weekd by Decentraland, URL: https://mvfw.org/, accessed 15.03.2023
12. Circle Square, URL: https://www.circle-square.com/en/, accessed 15.03.2023.
13. V. Otter, T. Tsukuda, B. Vivenot, *The metaverse. Challenges and regulatory issues*, SciencesPo. 1, URL: https://www.sciencespo.fr/public/sites/sciencespo.fr.public/files/Metaverse-Group-report-final-draft-June-12-1.pdf, accessed: 02.02.2023 (2022)
14. Xclusiverse Marketplace, URL: https://marketplace.xclusiverse.com/, accessed: 02.02.2023
15. Xclusiverse Marketplace's phigital products, URL: https://marketplace.xclusiverse.com/index.php/products/phigital-products.html, accessed: 02.02.2023
16. MJV Team, *Phygital: What It Is and Why It Is Evolving the Customer Experience*, URL: https://www.mjvinnovation.com/blog/what-is-phygital/, accessed: 03.03.2023 (2023)
17. R. Deleveaux, *Regulating the metaverse: issues and regulatory strategies*, 7, URL: https://www.iicom.org/wp-content/uploads/Rodman-Deleveaux.pdf, accessed: 03.03.2023 (2022)
18. Metamandrill, *Roblox Metaverse; One of the Biggest Players in the Metaverse Worlds*, URL: https://metamandrill.com/roblox-metaverse/, accessed: 03.03.2023 (2023)
19. Roblox Terms of Use, URL: https://en.help.roblox.com/hc/en-us/articles/115004647846-Roblox-Terms-of-Use, accessed: 08.03.2023
20. M. Boland, *Can adevrtising scale in VR?*, TechCrunch, URL: https://techcrunch.com/2021/07/08/can-advertising-scale-in-vr/, accessed: 08.03.2023 (2021)
21. Infosys, *The emergence of immersive adveriting*, URL: https://www.infosysbpm.com/offerings/functions/bpm-analytics/insights/documents/the-emergence-of-immersive-advertising.pdf, accessed: 08.03.2023 (2021)
22. According to Wikipedia, 'Virtual reality (VR) is a simulated experience that employs pose tracking and 3D near-eye displays to give the user an immersive feel of a virtual world', URL: https://en.wikipedia.org/wiki/Virtual_reality, accessed: 10.03.2023
23. AM General, URL: https://www.amgeneral.com/, accessed: 10.03.2023
24. A. Ramos, *The metaverse, NFTs and IP rights: to regulate or not to regulate?*, WIPO Magazine, URL: https://www.wipo.int/wipo_magazine/en/2022/02/article_0002.html, accessed: 10.03.2023
25. Priyal Chandrakar, Indian Journal of Integrated Research in Law, **II (I)**, 6 (2022)

26. M. Dellatto, *Hermès Wins Trademark Lawsuit Against Furry 'MetaBirkins' NFTs In First-Of-Its Kind Trial*. Forbes. URL: https://www.forbes.com/sites/marisadellatto/2023/02/08/herms-wins-trademark-lawsuit-against-furry-metabirkins-nfts-in-first-of-its-kind-trial/?sh=385411505acf, accessed: 10.03.2023 (2023)
27. Hermes' official website, URL: https://www.hermes.com/us/en/, accessed: 10.03.2023
28. G. Mileva, *Top 10 Metaverse Marketing Agencies to Help Build Your Brand in the Metaverse*, Influencer Marketing Hub, URL: https://influencermarketinghub.com/metaverse-marketing-companies/, accessed: 08.10.2023 (2022)
29. B. Heller, A. Bar-Zeev, *The Problems with Immersive Advertising: In AR/VR, Nobody Knows You Are an Ad*, Journal of Online Trust and Safety, 3, 7. doi:10.54501/jots.v1i1.21 (2021)
30. Circle Square, *Lacoste. Creativity, collaborationand crocodiles*, URL: https://www.circle-square.com/en/work/lacoste-creative, accessed: 10.03.2023
31. Truth in advertising, *Reality Check: TINA.org Calls on FTC to Address Virtual Influencers. Why the FTC should consider virtual influencers as it reviews its Endorsement Guides*, URL: https://truthinadvertising.org/articles/reality-check-tina-callson-ftcto-address-virtual-influencers/, accessed 10.03.2023 (2020)
32. Federal Trade Commission, *FTC Proposes to Strengthen Advertising Guidelines Against Fake and Manipulated Reviews. Agency Warns Marketers on Child-Directed Stealth Advertising*, URL: https://www.ftc.gov/news-events/news/press-releases/2022/05/ftc-proposes-strengthen-advertising-guidelines-against-fake-manipulated-reviews, accessed: 15.03.2023 (2022)
33. Webber Wentzel in alliance with Linklaters, *Legal Issues in the Metaverse. Part 2: Commercial Opportunities*. 2, 3, URL: https://www.webberwentzel.com/News/Documents/2022/webber-wentzel-metaverse-part-2.pdf, accessed: 08.03.2023 (2022)
34. R. Benjamins, Y. Rubio, C. Alonso, *Social and ethical challenges of the metaverse. Opening the debate*, Telefonica. 7, 11, URL: https://www.telefonica.com/en/wp-content/uploads/sites/5/2022/05/Social-and-ethical-challenges-metaverse-EN.pdf, accessed: 08.03.2023 (2022)
35. L. Rosenberg, ICVARS '22: Proceedings of the 6th International Conference on Virtual and Augmented Reality Simulations, 21, 24, 25, DOI: 10.1145/3546607.3546611, accessed: 01.03.2023 (2022)
36. D. Bindman, *What the metaverse means for lawyers*, Legal Futures, URL: https://www.legalfutures.co.uk/blog/what-the-metaverse-means-for-lawyers, accessed: 10.02.2023 (2022)
37. Decentraland website, URL: https://decentraland.org/, accessed: 28.12.2022
38. Clause 14 of Decentraland's Terms of Use, URL: https://decentraland.org/terms/, accessed: 02.02.2023
39. Clause 12.3 of Decentraland's Terms of Use, URL: https://decentraland.org/terms/, accessed: 02.02.2023
40. A. E. Amironesei, *Legal Silhouettes in Influencer Marketing*, Analele Ştiinţifice UAIC.SSJ, **LXVIII/2**, 143, 144, DOI: 10.47743/jss-2022-68-3-8, accessed: 10.12.2022 (2022)

41. A.-C. Diaz, E.J. Schultz, *See the miller lite super bowl commercial running only in the metaverse*, Ad Age, URL: https://adage.com/article/special-report-super-bowl/see-miller-lites-super-bowl-commercial-metaverse/2400371, accessed: 10.02.2023 (2022)
42. S. Lutz, *NFL Reveals First Super Bowl 'Metaverse' Concert in Roblox*, Decrypt URL: https://decrypt.co/120404/nfl-roblox-saweety-super-bowl-concert, accessed: 08.02.2023 (2023)
43. Decentraland, *Metaverse Fashion Week is here! Dive into four days of runway shows, after parties, shopping, panel talks, and more*, URL: https://decentraland.org/blog/announcements/metaverse-fashion-week-is-here/, accessed: 10.03.2023 (2022)
44. Roblox, *The Gucci Garden Experience Lands on Roblox*, URL: https://blog.roblox.com/2021/05/gucci-garden-experience/, accessed: 10.03.2023 (2021);
45. Gucci Garden, URL: https://guccigarden.gucci.com/#/en/, accessed: 10.03.2023
46. Roblox's website, URL: https://www.roblox.com/, accessed: 10.03.2023
47. Keiichi Matsuda, URL: http://km.cx/about, accessed: 05.03.2023
48. Circle Square, *Work. The power of ideas our selected works*, URL: https://www.circle-square.com/en/work, accessed: 10.02.2023
49. NARS, URL: https://www.narscosmetics.com/, accessed: 10.02.2023
50. Circle Square, *NARS. Step into the beauty-verse*, URL: https://www.circle-square.com/en/work/nars-shiseido, accessed: 10.02.2023
51. EMPERIA, *How beauty brand are entering the metaverse. The making of the beauty-verse*, URL: https://emperiavr.com/2022/05/19/how-beauty-brands-are-entering-the-metaverse-the-making-of-the-beauty-verse/, accessed: 10.02.2023
52. EMPERIA, *Dior Beauty. Atelier of Dreams*, URL: https://emperiavr.com/project/dior-beauty/, accessed: 10.02.2023
53. Shiseido's website, URL: https://www.shiseido.com/us/en/, accessed: 10.02.2023
54. Roblox, *Nikeland by Nike*, URL: https://www.roblox.com/games/7462526249/NIKELAND, accessed: 10.02.2023
55. W. Wright, *Axe and Fortnite to launch the 'Mistaverse'*, The Drum, URL: https://www.thedrum.com/news/2022/06/14/axe-and-fortnite-launch-the-mistaverse, accessed: 10.02.2023 (2022)
56. Axe's website, URL: https://www.axe.com/us/en/home.html , accessed: 10.02.2023
57. Fortnite's website, URL: https://www.fortnite.com/, accessed: 10.02.2023
58. Fortnite, *High digital fashion drops into Fortnite with Balenciaga*, URL: https://www.fortnite.com/news/high-digital-fashion-drops-into-fortnite-with-balenciaga, accessed: 10.02.2023 (2021)
59. EMPERIA, *Dior Beauty. Atelier of Dreams*, URL: https://emperiavr.com/project/dior-beauty/, accessed: 10.02.2023
60. C.T. Ungureanu, *Drept internațional privat european în raporturi de comerț internațional* [*European private international law in international trade relations*] (Hamangiu, București, 2021)
61. EUIPO, *IP and the metaverse*, URL: https://euipo.europa.eu/ohimportal/ro/web/guest/-/news/ip-and-the-metaverse-new-problems-new-rules-1, accessed 10.12.2022 (2022)

62. N. Rosa, *Understanding the Metaverse: A Business and Ethical Guide*, Wiley, 65 – 68 (2023)
63. J. Stiehl, J. Canter, P. Chakrabarti, *Cases Show Real-World Laws Likely Apply In Metaverse*, Law360, 2, URL: https://www.crowell.com/files/20221101-Cases-Show-Real-World-Laws-Likely-Apply-In-Metaverse.pdf, accessed: 10.12.2022 (2022)
64. D. Gilbert, E*merging Issue. Welcome to the Metaverse: Legal Issues Marketers need to Consider*, 2, 5, URL: ttps://www.dglaw.com/wp-content/uploads/2022/06/Welcome-to-the-Metaverse.pdf, accessed 05.02.2023 (2022)
65. Federal Trade Commission, *Truth in Advertising*, URL: https://www.ftc.gov/news-events/topics/truth-advertising, accessed 05.02.2023
66. Proposal for a regulation of the European Parliament and of the Council laying down harmonised rules on artificial intelligence (Artificial Intelligence Act) and amending certain union legislative acts, COM/2021/206 final, URL: https://eur-lex.europa.eu/legal-content/EN/TXT/?uri=celex%3A52021PC0206, accessed: 10.03.2023
67. European Advertising Standards Alliance, URL: https://www.easa-alliance.org/, accessed 02.02.2023
68. Federal Trade Commission, *Native Advertising: A Guide for Businesses*, URL: https://www.ftc.gov/business-guidance/resources/native-advertising-guide-businesses, accessed: 10.12.2022 (2015)
69. International Advertising Bureau Europe, *IAB Europe Guidance. How to comply with the EU Rules Applicable to Online Native Advertising*, URL: https://iabeurope.eu/wp-content/uploads/2020/06/20161207_IAB-Europe-Online-Native-Advertising-Guidance.pdf, accessed: 10.03.2023 (2016)
70. Federal Register, *Guides Concerning the Use of Endorsements and Testimonials in Advertising . A Proposed Rule by the Federal Trade Commission on 07/26/2022*, URL: https://www.federalregister.gov/documents/2022/07/26/2022-12327/guides-concerning-the-use-of-endorsements-and-testimonials-in-advertising, accessed: 28.02.2023
71. Truth in Advertising, *Reality Check: TINA.org Calls on FTC to Address Virtual Influencers. Why the FTC should consider virtual influencers as it reviews its Endorsement Guides*, URL: https://truthinadvertising.org/articles/reality-check-tina-callson-ftcto-address-virtual-influencers/, accessed: 28.02.2023 (2020)
72. Thales, *Biometric data and privacy laws (GDPR, CCPA/CPRA)*, URL: https://www.thalesgroup.com/en/markets/digital-identity-and-security/government/biometrics/biometric-data, accessed: 20.10.2022 (2021)
73. C.T. Ungureanu, A.-E. Amironesei, Challenges of the Knowledge Society. International Conference volume 2021, 317 – 331, URL: http://cks.univnt.ro/articles/15.html, accessed: 10.10.2022 (2021)
74. E. M. Renieris, Beyond Data. Reclaiming human Rights at the Dawn of the Metaverse, 119, 127, 128 (The MIT Press, 2023)
75. A. Sethi, Cyber Security Insights Magazine, **2**, 2 (2022)
76. Kudun & Partners, *The rise of the metaverse: Challenges ahead for the legal industry*, 2, 3, URL: https://www.kap.co.th/wp-content/uploads/2022/01/Thought-Leadership-The-rise-of-the-metaverse-Challenges-ahead-for-the-legal-industry.pdf, accessed: 10.10.2022 (2022)

77. Prada's website, URL: https://www.prada.com/ww/en.html, accessed: 01.03.2023
78. Gucci's website, URL: https://www.gucci.com/ro/en_gb/, accessed: 01.03.2023
79. Accenture's Nth Floor Metaverse. *Going beyond with extended reality*, URL: https://www.accenture.com/us-en/about/going-beyond-extended-reality, accessed: 01.03.2023
80. Meta, *Horizon Worlds*, URL: https://www.meta.com/horizon-worlds/, accessed: 04.01.2023
81. Somnium Space's website, URL: https://somniumspace.com/, accessed: 04.11.2022
82. European Commission. *Digital Markets Act: rules for digital gatekeepers to ensure open markets enter into force*, Press release, IP/22/6423, URL: https://ec.europa.eu/commission/presscorner/detail/en/ip_22_6423, accessed: 12.10.2022 (2022)
83. International Trademark Association, *Right of Publicity*, URL: https://www.inta.org/topics/right-of-publicity/, accessed: 15.03.2023
84. D. Gervais, M. Holmes, Fame, Intell. Prop. Media & Ent. L.J., **25 (1)**, 181, 185 (2014)
85. Right of Publicity, *Restatement (Third) of Unfair Competition, S. 46-49*, URL: https://rightofpublicity.com/statutes/restatement-third-of-unfair-competition-s46-49, accessed: 12.03.2023
86. J. Waller, UCLA Entertainment Law Review, **9 (1)**, 62, DOI: 10.5070/LR891027023 (2001)
87. Getting the deal through, *Right of Publicity*, Law Business Research Ltd, ISSN 2045-4325, 54, URL: https://www.aplawjapan.com/archives/pdf/file/Getting_the_Deal_Through_Right_of_Publicity2012.pdf, accessed: 14.03.2023 (2012)
88. J. M. Garon, Marq. L. Rev, **106(1)**, 230 (2022)
89. Copyright.gov, *U.S. Copyright Office Fair Use Index*, URL: https://www.copyright.gov/fair-use/, accessed: 10.03.2023
90. K.R. Raygor, V.E. Alter, MLR Bulleting **(4)**, 112-114 (2008)
91. B. C. Cheong, International Cybersecurity Law Review **3(2)**, 470, DOI: 10.1365/s43439-022-00056-9 (2022)
92. 101. Shiseido's beauty-verse: Tokyo Beauty-Verse, URL: https://www.tokyo-beauty-verse.com/, accessed: 28.12.2022
93. Douglas Romania's Instagram post with the Tokyo beuatyverse, URL: https://www.instagram.com/p/CnoZiFihJyv/, accessed: 28.02.2023
94. LinkedIn post: '*Tokyo #Beauty-verse is a virtual world where you can create your own avatar and start exploring the city, find Shiseido building and discover many surprises. We are happy to offer this playfull #customerexperience in Romania. Great job everyone!*', URL: https://lv.linkedin.com/posts/laviniadragomirescuivas_exploreaza-shiseido-ginza-tokyo-beautyverse-activity-7021887995209232384-2qKL, accessed: 16.03.2023
95. YouTube, Example of short video for exploring the metaverse https://www.youtube.com/watch?v=CyowQEdpxXc, accessed: 08.03.2022
96. *End-user Terms of Use for Ready Player Me*, URL: https://drive.google.com/file/d/1ER3gBvx1UwXMDiOaZk8akzPmO6LAFfTp/view, accessed: 05.03.2023

97. An example would be WOLF3D. URL: https://wolf3d.io/, accessed: 05.03.2023
98. CMS, *Part 4 - Expected impact of the EU Artificial Intelligence Regulation, the metaverse as a workplace*, URL: https://cms.law/en/int/publication/legal-issues-in-the-metaverse/part-4-expected-impact-of-the-eu-artificial-intelligence-regulation-the-metaverse-as-a-workplace, accessed: 05.03.2023
99. N. Desai, *Metaverse: A New Universe. Legal, Regulatory and Tax Issues,* 9, URL: https://www.nishithdesai.com/fileadmin/user_upload/pdfs/Research_Papers/Metaverse_A_New_Universe.pdf, accessed: 05.03.2023 (2022)

# Using blockchain technology to combat counterfeiting

*Alexandru* Chistruga[1*]

[1]Faculty of Law, Alexandru Ioan Cuza University of Iași, Romania

**Abstract.** Although the globalization of trade entails multiple benefits for both traders and consumers, such as the expansion of markets and the possibility of accessing a wide range of products, it also entails the risk of the spread of counterfeit goods. One of the tools that could be used to combat this trend is blockchain technology. The aforementioned technology presupposes the existence of a single ledger that is shared and synchronized across many sites, organizations, or computers, with participants having the ability to register any type of information. Thus, in the near future, a single ledger could be created in which relevant information about the specific traded good, such as its origin or sanitary certificate, would be recorded. By doing so, the quantity of counterfeit goods on the market will decrease, while consumer confidence will increase. The World Intellectual Property Organization is currently analyzing the possibility of incorporating blockchain technology into several areas specific to intellectual property law, with one of the goals being to combat counterfeiting. Therefore, through this article, we propose to conduct an analysis of the legal provisions of the European Union that aim at fighting against counterfeit goods. Simultaneously, we will investigate the methods used by the private sector in this field, particularly blockchain technology. In this regard, some practical examples that have been used for several years by large retailers such as Walmart and Carrefour will be presented.

## 1. Introduction

One of the most important successes of the European Union is the creation of a single market where products can enter without being hindered by additional barriers. Despite the fact that this phenomenon has many advantages, the prevalence of counterfeit goods coming from both Member States and third countries presents a significant threat.

At the level of the European Union, efforts are being made to put an end to this phenomenon by developing a series of restrictive norms that place additional requirements on companies. However, the desired result seems unlikely to be achieved in the near future. Especially since, as electronic commerce develops, more and more goods from third countries enter the single market, which is beneficial but also risky, because some of these goods violate companies' intellectual property rights.

* Corresponding author email: alexandruchistruga@gmail.com

Therefore, through this article, we propose to conduct an analysis of the legal provisions of the European Union that aim at fighting against counterfeit goods. Simultaneously, we will investigate the methods used by the private sector in this field, particularly blockchain technology. In this regard, some practical examples that have been used for several years by large retailers such as Walmart and Carrefour will be presented.

## 2. An analysis of current EU regulations from a theoretical and practical perspective

To begin with, according to Organization for Economic Co-operation and Development (OECD) data on counterfeiting and international trade, *'the total value of counterfeit and pirated goods was about $1 trillion in 2013 and is expected to grow to close to $3 trillion in 2022'* [1]. In this regard, according to the latest figures published by the OECD, *'footwear accounted for 22 percent of the total value of counterfeit goods seized by customs in 2016, making it the most pirated product category, ahead of clothing, leather goods, and electrical equipment'* [2]. Aside from these, pharmaceuticals, toys, perfumes, and watches are among the most counterfeited products, according to the same statistics [2]. As a result, the likelihood of purchasing a counterfeit product at least once in a lifetime is quite high.

According to specialized literature, *'counterfeit goods are those that illegally imitate, copy, or duplicate a good or use a registered trademark without authorization and, therefore, infringe upon the legal right to copy of the right's owner'* [3]. The interpretation of this definition leads to the conclusion that there are two methods of goods counterfeiting.

The first category includes items that only look like the originals. In their case, the manufacturer takes advantage of the buyers' lack of attention, who may believe they are purchasing an original good. However, most buyers are aware that they are purchasing a counterfeit item due to its lower price.

The second category includes goods that claim to be original and use registered trademarks or other types of intellectual property rights without authorization for this purpose. In their case, an ordinary buyer will not be able to recognize that the item he is purchasing is counterfeit because there is an almost perfect visual similarity. However, the buyers will recognize that something is wrong after a short period of time, usually due to the breakdown of the good. Most likely, they will seek compensation from the manufacturer whose brand was used, but their attempt will be unsuccessful because the goods were never made by that manufacturer. As a result, buyers will most likely no longer purchase any products from that particular brand, and the manufacturer will suffer a loss of profit and reputation.

Even if purchasing a counterfeit good usually results in a monetary loss, there are some cases where the outcome can be fatal. For example, *'recent investigation found formaldehyde in woolen and cotton clothes which was 500 times higher than safe levels should be'* [4]. According to World Health Organization *'the formaldehyde is used to give a permanent-press effect to clothes but high levels (20 parts per million) can cause eye, skin and nasal irritation, respiratory problems, asthma and skin cancer'* [4]. More dramatic examples can be found in the case of counterfeit alcohol products. For example, 34 people recently died in Russia after *'consuming counterfeit vodka'* [5].

To combat the spread of counterfeit goods, the European Union has developed several normative acts. Thus, the current legal provisions impose obligations not only on manufacturers but also on other trade participants, such as importers, in relation to the goods they prepare for sale. For example, according to the Proposal for a Regulation of the European Parliament and of the Council on general product safety amending Regulation (EU) No 1025/2012 of the European Parliament and of the Council, and repealing Council Directive 87/357/EEC and Directive 2001/95/EC of the European Parliament and of the Council (hereinafter, Proposal for a Regulation on general product safety), it is necessary that the goods entering the single market meet the conditions outlined in Article 3, Point 2, which defines the concept of a 'safe product'. According to this legal provision, 'safe product' means *'any product that, under normal or reasonably foreseeable conditions of use or misuse, including the actual duration of use, does not present any risk or only the minimum risks compatible with the product's use, is considered acceptable and consistent with a high level of protection of the health and safety of consumers*'. Relating this legal provision to the previously mentioned example, counterfeit clothes cannot be considered 'safe', as they are dangerous for the health of consumers.

However, these goods could easily fall under the category of 'product presenting a risk' as defined by the provisions of the Regulation (EU) 2019/1020 *on market surveillance and compliance of products* (hereinafter, Regulation 2019/1020). Thus, according to Article 3, point 19, 'the product presenting a risk' *means a product having the potential to affect adversely health and safety of persons in general, health and safety in the workplace, protection of consumers, the environment, public security and other public interests, protected by the applicable Union harmonization legislation, to a degree which goes beyond that considered reasonable and acceptable in relation to its intended purpose or under the normal or reasonably foreseeable conditions of use of the product concerned, including the duration of use and, where applicable, its putting into service, installation and maintenance requirements*. As a result, it is unclear why the European legislator regulated a new concept that brings nothing new to the fight against counterfeiting or other fields. It seems to be a legislative technique to avoid making additional references to previously adopted normative acts.

In addition to these pieces of legislation, the European Union elaborated the Regulation (EU) No. 608/2013, which was created to provide additional protection for both producers and consumers by enforcing intellectual property rights. According to the legal provisions of this regulation if customs officials identify counterfeited goods, they have the option of suspending the release or detaining the goods. In other words, the suspicious goods will be stored in a warehouse while their provenance is investigated. If it is determined that these goods violate another person's intellectual property rights, customs authorities have the authority to destroy them.

For example, the three parallel stripes *'that appear across all Adidas product lines'* are a registered trademark [6]. We could say that the said trademark is one of the most valuable assets owned by the German company. Thus, because Adidas is one of the largest manufacturers of sporting goods, its products are frequently counterfeited. In this regard, according to the data provided by Adidas, *'10% of its current market products may be counterfeit'* [7]. A significant part of this volume is also found on the European Union territory. Considering the enormous volume of production that enters the market under the Adidas brand, it is nearly impossible for supervisory authorities to identify all cases of counterfeiting. However, if some of these goods can be identified, the customs officials can proceed in accordance with the Regulation (EU) No. 608/2013.

According to these legal provisions, one of the primary goals of European Union bodies is to ensure the security of the single market. To put it differently, substantial efforts are being made to reduce the amount of non-compliant goods by implementing preventive mechanisms such as customs control and regulation of new market challenges.

One of these challenges is the expansion of electronic commerce, which has reduced the effectiveness of the Directive 2001/95/EC, which goal is the general safety of products. In this regard, according to the reasons for and objectives of the Proposal for a Regulation on general product safety the application of the directive to all consumer products, *'whether sold in brick-and-mortar stores or online*' jeopardizes *'the safety of EU consumers and the level playing field for compliant EU businesses*'. As a result, there is a risk that products that fall into the category of risk products, as defined by Regulation (EU) 2019/1020, will be introduced on the single market.

To address these concerns, the Regulation proposal on general product safety was drafted which, if all legal requirements are met, will replace the Directive 2001/95/EC. This proposal establishes a set of safety requirements for economic operators and the goods they put into the market. For example, according to Article 8, point 4 from Regulation proposal on general product safety, manufacturers *must include technical documentation on their products, which must include a general description of the product and its essential properties relevant for assessing the product's safety, as well as an analysis of the possible risks associated with the product and the solutions adopted to eliminate or mitigate such risks, including the results of any tests conducted by the manufacturer or another party*. Furthermore, one of the most important obligations that manufacturers must fulfill is the requirement *to indicate on goods their name, registered trade name, or registered trade mark, as well as the postal and electronic addresses at which they can be contacted, on the product or, if that is not possible, on its packaging or in a document accompanying the product (*Article 8, point 7).

Based on the interpretation of these legal provisions, it follows that this Regulation proposal tends to provide additional protection to consumers who use electronic commerce to obtain a specific good. At the same time, the legal texts' obligations and safety measures apply to goods that are introduced to the market in the traditional manner. However, for a variety of reasons, those provisions will have a limited impact on the fight against counterfeit goods.

First, the documents accompanying the goods may be falsified, which may go undetected due to free trade. As a result, such a safeguard would be effective only for products originating in third countries, and only if the supervisory authorities conducted a thorough examination, which would incur additional costs as well as the involvement of a greater number of human resources.

For example, operation OPSON XI targeting food fraud, was coordinated by Europol for EU-wide actions. It took place between December 2021 and May 2022. According to reports, national authorities conducted *'checks in customs areas, physical and online marketplaces, and throughout the food supply chain to detect criminal activity*' [8]. Despite more than 70,000 checks, only 26,800 tons of counterfeit production were discovered. Therefore, in comparison to the time required to discover these quantities of goods and the number of counterfeit goods that enter the single market on a daily basis, the competent authorities appear to have been outpaced.

Second, the obligation to indicate the trademark or any other intellectual property right on product packaging could only be effective if all trade participants acted in good faith. Because counterfeiting involves illegal actions and, as a result, bad faith on the part of the producers, this protective measure will only be effective in a few cases. For example, *'the simplest, and arguably crudest, way to counterfeit wine is to slap the label of a fine wine on to another, similar-looking bottle*' [9]. From a legal standpoint, there is a trademark on the wine bottle, in most cases an original one, but what matters is that the wine is counterfeit. Therefore, the relevant legal provision may only be effective in rare cases where the intellectual property right itself is falsified. However, the possibilities provided by new technologies may be able to counteract this last point.

In addition to the previously mentioned normative acts, the European Union is attempting to increase consumer trust in the authenticity of the displayed products by making several verification tools available to those who are interested.

Consumers, for example, could use the eSearch plus to access the database of the European Union Intellectual Property Office (EUIPO). They can use this platform to compare the authenticity of a trademark or geographical indication on a product to those listed in public registers platform [10]. However, it would be more of a hypothetical situation because it would require knowledge that a buyer might not have, as well as access to the platform and the completion of several formalities. As a result, it is unlikely that a consumer would use this tool solely to verify the authenticity of a product. To limit or even eliminate these inconveniences, *'new technologies such as non-fungible tokens (NFT) and blockchain'* could be used [11].

## 3. The opportunities that blockchain technology provides

The goods are counterfeited for commercial purposes rather than personal use. As a result, the manufacturer or another person who knows that the goods are counterfeit is forced to act like a legitimate trader. This behavior entails locating a market and transporting goods to it. In other words, there are no significant differences in comparison to other legitimate trade participants. Consequently, it is not necessary to draft new normative acts with the sole purpose of establishing new rules to combat counterfeit products. It is critical to capitalize on the new opportunities provided by technology.

For example, one method for combating their activity would be to monitor the entire supply chain, beginning with the manufacturing stage and ending with the sale of the goods. Thus, in order to determine whether a good is authentic, any interested person should be able to identify the date on which it was manufactured, the date on which it was delivered, the date on which it passed customs control, in the case of goods intended for trade in another state, and the date on which it was placed for sale. Even if one could argue that this information is usually displayed on the packaging of the goods, there is no guarantee that it is correct. After all, it is just a piece of paper that anyone with a printer can reproduce.

One of the solutions could be the digitization of the entire supply chain, at least for the most counterfeited items. The digitalization would involve the creation of a web page containing the goods' essential information, such as the date and place of production. However, it is important to note that counterfeit goods producers are evolving, so simple digitization is no longer sufficient. In this regard, it is now common practice to create duplicates of major corporations' websites. The operation entails duplicating a website and selling counterfeit goods on it. Thus, simple digitization of the supply chain could not have a significant impact because it could be easily defrauded by creating a fake site with no exaggerated costs. To minimize these risks, blockchain technology can be implemented.

To better understand what blockchain technology entails, a definition is required. The European Economic and Social Committee defines blockchain technology *'as both a code, i.e., a communication protocol, and a public register, in which all transactions between network participants are recorded one after the other, with a high degree of transparency and in an irreversible manner'* [12]. In doctrine, blockchain technology is defined *'as a distributed, append-only database that enables transactions between human or software agents without the use of a central trusted intermediary'* [13]. The most important thing to remember from these definitions is that *'blockchain is a method of storing data'* [14].

As an illustration, if a product is delivered from the warehouse on November 30, 2022, this information will be recorded in a block and will never be able to be changed. Once the item has arrived at its destination, an additional registration will be made to allow tracking of the duration of the transportation process. What matters is that, compared to classical digitalization, blockchain technology offers a high level of security because the records created through it cannot be changed. This *immutability* is due to a *'combination of factors including the cryptography used in a Blockchain, its consensus/validation mechanism and its distributed nature'* [15].

In addition to immutability, we identify *'interoperability, transparency, traceability, and security as key features of blockchain technology'* relevant to the current work [16].

The IEEE Computer Society defines interoperability as '*the ability of two or more blockchain systems or applications to exchange information and to mutually use the information that has been exchanged*' [17]. In other words, interoperability can be defined as a blockchain's ability to interact with other blockchains or even with technology that is not part of the distributed ledger network. This feature is critical because the respective technology is constantly evolving and must be able to adapt to market demands. For example, while blockchain technology was initially used only for cryptocurrency trading, '*it is now used in a variety of applications such as digital marketing, entertainment, and finance*' [18]. In terms of the supply chain, the United Nations Economic Commission for Europe believes that interoperability '*should also be understood as a concept that supports the implementation of the principle of free movement of goods and services in the digital world*' [15].

The First Decentralized Finance Encyclopedia defines blockchain transparency as '*a characteristic feature of the blockchain that ensures all the transactions and data on the network are available to everyone with access to the system*' [19]. According to this definition, anyone with access to blockchain technology will be able to consult the information that interests him without incurring any costs in terms of money or time. Thus, if we return to the theme of this article, i.e., fight against counterfeit products, transparency will enable any interested party to obtain key information about the product they intend to purchase. For all that, it is necessary to develop a method of interaction with buyers or other people who do not have a contractual relationship with the manufacturer in order to facilitate access to this information for them. The least complex option is to assign each selected product a special barcode or QR code that can be scanned by a smartphone.

For example, by scanning a unique QR Code, any consumer will be able to access vital '*information (data on the producer, location, and manufacturing date of the good, as well as information on health certificates) about the product they intend to purchase without having to navigate through multiple platforms*' [20]. This possibility is offered by traceability, which could be defined as the ability to identify and track a good throughout all stages (production, processing, and distribution).

Aside from monitoring the supply chain, blockchain technology can be used to identify cases where manufacturers use slave labor. In this regard, manufacturers can be '*required to prove that they are not using child labor and/or are paying their workers a living wage*' [15]. The relevant evidence should be pre-registered in the blockchain ledger so that it can be verified. Due to a lack of supporting documentation and an inability to quickly falsify it, some of them won't be able to prove this. As a consequence, the demand for their products may decrease.

Coca-Cola Co., for example, imports sugarcane primarily from the Asia-Pacific region. As a result, the business has received a lot of criticism, including claims that it works with suppliers who use slave labor. In this regard, a recent report '*shows that the company is still using suppliers that use slave labor in China's Xinjiang province*' [21]. To respond to these critiques, '*a private-public partnership spearheaded by the Coca-Cola Company (KO) and the United States Department of State will use blockchain technology to combat forced labor in their supply chains*' [22]. Despite the fact that it seems to be a publicity stunt (meaning *something done just to get the attention of the public* [23]), it still has the effect of expanding the use of blockchain technology in supply chain monitoring.

Last but not least, using blockchain technology in addition to what has already been discussed could aid in the realization of the EU's Green Deal [24]. The strategy perspective calls for a number of actions, such as combating global deforestation and forest degradation caused by EU production and consumption. In this regard, the European Commission elaborated the Proposal for a regulation on deforestation-free products. This normative act requires companies '*to prove that the products are both deforestation-free (produced on land that was not subject to deforestation after 31 December 2020) and legal (compliant with all relevant applicable laws in force in the country of production)*' [25]. Furthermore, '*companies will also be required to collect precise geographical information on the farmland where the commodities that they source have been grown, so that these commodities can be checked for compliance*' [25]. By interpreting this legal provision, it follows that the monitoring process will be carried out by fusing geolocation with remote monitoring via satellite images.

Although it is stated that '*geolocation coordinates are the simplest and most cost-effective way to obtain the necessary geographic information for authorities to be in a position to check whether products and commodities are deforestation-free*' this statement is not entirely accurate [26]. It is unclear how it will be possible to precisely verify the provided data given the enormous amount of wood that is exported. The satellite images can only show that the portion of the forest mentioned in the supporting documents was actually deforested. Therefore, it's possible that some of the trees were cut down in uncontrolled areas.

For example, according to data provided by the European Parliament, 158 million hectares of forest, or 5% of all forest in the world, are found within the EU [27]. A database of the distribution of forests across the European Union's states and regions is also available [28]. However, because the hectares of forests have not been digitized, this information is only statistical data. Consequently, it is essential to build a new database using blockchain technology. Thus, '*through the use of blockchain, this data would be time-stamped and tamper-proof, ensuring EU privacy, data protection and competition rules are fully respected*' [29]. Therefore '*with its enhanced data security and traceability, blockchain can help tackle trust in wood and other natural-resource supply chains to guarantee specific attributes and other relevant identity information*' [29].

## 4. Blockchain technology implementation at the European Union level. Practical examples

Distributed ledger technology, specifically blockchain technology, has advanced in recent years to the point where it can no longer be ignored by European Union bodies. According to information on the European Commission's official website, the EU aims to '*be a leader in blockchain technology*', attempting to lay the groundwork for a '*gold standard*' that includes European values and ideals [30]. The European Union's strategy for achieving this goal includes '*building a pan-European public services blockchain, the foundations of which have already been laid by the creation of the European Blockchain Services Infrastructure*' [31]. This assumes the existence of a peer-to-peer network of interconnected nodes running a blockchain-based service infrastructure, with at least 30 nodes currently operational in each of the 27 EU member states, as well as Norway and Liechtenstein.

Document traceability is one of the key areas where this network is to be implemented. As a result, several pilot projects have been launched to investigate how blockchain technology could be used to create one or more public ledgers where digital documents are registered, with one of the goals being to eliminate paper documents.

One of the most successful projects in this field was carried out by the European Court of Auditors in collaboration with Compellio [32], a Luxembourg start-up. It entails the creation of a single traceability ledger where European Court of Auditors documents are registered, any interested party being able to verify their authenticity by accessing the corresponding network. Because of the blockchain's immutability, '*there is certainty that the documents registered on the platform have not been altered over time*' [33] and present current information without the need for further investigation.

Following the completion of the pilot project, the Court identified three cases in which the aforementioned technology could be used in the near future. The most promising project entails the '*ability to legalize documents registered with blockchain technology without the involvement of a notary*' [34].

The previous example is only one of many possible applications of blockchain traceability by European Union bodies. In this regard, document traceability will be integrated in a number of cases, including '*cross-border recognition of certified digital copies of documents (for example, diplomas, transcripts, etc.); traceability of food or other components; and modernization of document legalization processes, such as apostille*' [34].

In relation to the subject of this article, the European Union Intellectual Property Office (EUIPO) is making significant progress in the battle against counterfeit goods [18]. In this regard, since 2018, EUIPO has been attempting to identify '*methods for incorporating blockchain technology into the field of intellectual property rights protection*' [35].

To begin, EUIPO is not aiming at creating a new platform to compete with the existing solutions, such as '*non-fungible-tokens (NFT) platforms*' but rather is trying to develop EUIPO tools that are already involved in the supply chain, in particular, the TMview and DesignView platforms [36].

These platforms were created to help interested parties to gain access to intellectual property rights registered at both the national and European Union levels. As a result of the fact that the registration of a trademark or design can differ depending on the state in which the right of protection is sought, as well as the language barriers that may arise in some cases, the EUIPO, in collaboration with the national offices, established these two supranational platforms to mitigate the existing disadvantages. Both platforms are digital tools that '*allow any user, free of charge, to search the registered trademarks or designs of all participating national offices*' [37]. For example, through DesignView, users can consult the registers of participating offices or organizations and obtain a variety of information '*regarding industrial designs, such as legal status, representations of industrial designs, owner, representative, and so on*' [38].

The next step was to hold a conference to identify potential applications for the implementation of blockchain technology. In this regard, the EU Blockcathon conference was held with the goal of identifying ways in which blockchain technology could be used to combat counterfeit goods. As a result, the creation of a special digital duplicate of a tangible good—also known as the tokenization of goods—was recognized as one of the potential solutions. For example, if a manufacturer intends to introduce a certain number of goods into the single market, he/she must create a digital copy—in other words, a digital token—for each good, allowing customs authorities or anyone else interested in verifying its authenticity.

However, to make the simple tokenization of goods much more efficient, a register containing the intellectual property rights corresponding to the respective tokenized goods must be created. Of course, finding a way to connect the currently existing registers with the blockchain technology used by EUIPO is an option, but we appreciate that creating a new register would be better and easier.

Finally, all of the previously mentioned registers must be linked to the networks managed by the supervisory authorities. As a result, the time required for customs authorities to carry out the control will be reduced because there will be no need to check documents. In Egypt, for example, following a change in customs law, importers of goods were required to register the documents accompanying the goods '*on the CargoX platform prior to shipment*' [39]. This blockchain-based platform allows Egyptian customs authorities to verify the authenticity of documents before goods arrive at Egyptian ports, allowing them to conduct timely investigations. As a result of this legislative change, '*the time for goods release has been reduced from 29 days to 9 days*' [40].

To make it easier to understand how blockchain technology could be used to prevent counterfeit products from entering the single market, the following practical examples are useful.

Everledger is a blockchain-based platform that provides those interested with a variety of tools for tracking the path of a specific type of good from the time it is manufactured to the time it is purchased by the consumer. Currently, Everledger provides *'tracking services for luxury goods, diamonds, and wine or other spirits'* [41].

In 2019, Everledger developed an *'end-to-end traceability and provenance solution for the wine industry'* [42]. The technology entails the use of plugs with Near Field Communication (NFC) tags that can be read by anyone with a smartphone. These NFC tags are linked to Everledger's blockchain network, which records the majority of the details about each *'individual bottle of wine, including origin, wine characteristics, certifications, varietal name, and carbon footprint'* [43].

In addition to the ability to track the entire journey of a wine bottle from bottling to purchase, Everledger allows users to check whether transport and storage conditions, as well as the temperature recommended by the manufacturer, have been met. This avoids situations in which a genuine good has some flaws that necessitate its withdrawal from the market. Furthermore, the risk of obtaining a counterfeit product is almost entirely eliminated, because the moment the wine bottle is opened, *'a record is made in the blockchain register ensuring that the same bottle cannot be reused for the purpose of counterfeiting'* [44].

Another case in point is Walmart's use of blockchain technology in supply chains for some of their products. In this regard, Walmart, in collaboration with IBM [45], has developed two pilot projects *'aimed at tracking the origin of pork in Chinese stores'* [46], as well as mangoes sold in American stores. Consumers, like in the previous example, can use a smartphone to scan a QR code, which provides *'information on the food's source, geographic location, logistics data, and inspection reports'* [47]. As a result of the implementation of blockchain technology, the food safety of pork and mangoes has increased exponentially, *'while the time required to identify the origin of the goods has been reduced from 7 days to just 2.2 seconds'* [47]. In this manner, contaminated products *'can be removed from the shelves of Walmart stores in a timely manner'* [48], and if these goods have already been sold, *'consumers can check if the purchased good is part of the recalled lot from the market by simply scanning a QR code'* [49].

Following the completion of the above-mentioned pilot projects, IBM created a new network to provide *'the food supply chain with unprecedented visibility and accountability'* [50]. This network, according to IBM, *'links producers, processors, distributors, and retailers via a shared, permanent, permissioned record of food system data'* [50]. Also, through this network, anyone who is interested can find out *'the origin, current location, and condition of any food item'* [51]. Last but not least, organizations can identify *'which foods have been grown or produced in a certified manner, reducing contamination risks and potentially harmful food fraud along the supply chain'* [51].

BrightFarms is an illustration of a business utilizing the technology supplied by IBM. BrightFarms, acording to IBM, *'was founded to simplify and decentralize the supply chain for greens, and to provide consumers with a more sustainable choice'* [52]. Thus, *'the company uses IBM Blockchain on IBM Cloud® to keep data safely encrypted and uploads data to the IBM Food Trust platform through each stage of the process, from the moment seeds are planted until packaged greens arrive at the retailer'* [52]. Furthemore, *'once the greens are on the shelves, the retailer can continue to add data to the platform as well, including how long the greens have been in the store and at what temperature they are being stored'* [52]. From the examples given, it is clear that the uses of blockchain technology that we had initially suggested are already prevalent in the United States, even though in this particular example the supply chain from farm to store is relatively short.

As to the European Union single market, a good example is Carrefour. Carrefour is a *'European leader in food traceability through the gradual application of blockchain technology to its Carrefour Quality Line products'* [53]. For instance, one of the products displayed in Carrefour is the *Purée Mousline*, which has recently been added to this network due to its popularity among French consumers. A barcode is used on the packaging of the respective product that can be scanned by a smartphone to provide consumers with valuable information about the mix they're about to prepare, such as the region where the potatoes were grown and the varieties used, quality control in the Nestlé factory where the product was made, and the places and dates of storage before it arrived at the grocer [54].

## 5. Conclusion

To conclude the blockchain technology can be applied in a variety of contexts and is flexible enough to be adjusted for each circumstance. In other words, even though the article's main goal was to show how effective the blockchain technology can be in the fight against counterfeit goods, we have also shown how it can be applied to other situations. In light of this, we began by simply highlighting the steps that a good takes to get to the shelves of retailers. Then, by requiring the registration of labor contracts, we showed how the aforementioned technology can be used to combat the slave labor. Finally, we demonstrated that by integrating blockchain technology with the registers already in place at the level of the European Union, it is possible to track the origin of deforested trees, removing from the market trees originating from illegal logging.

So, based on the examples given, it is clear that incorporating blockchain technology to facilitate the tracking of goods entering the single market could be beneficial and, more importantly, feasible. Among the main benefits identified in this paper, we highlight traceability, which allows both producers and consumers to trace the origin and authenticity of goods, thereby preventing counterfeit goods from entering the supply chain. Furthermore, transparency is a critical factor in increasing consumer confidence in the goods they purchase, which increases the profit of producers who have integrated blockchain technology. Finally, by utilizing blockchain technology, supply chain members *'can record transactions in real time, reducing current time lags'* [55].

In conclusion, blockchain technology has the potential to positively impact the development of the European Union's single market. Currently, European Union bodies must thoroughly investigate what type of blockchain could be more efficient and easily integrated into the existing production chain. Simultaneously, it must be compatible with other existing distributed ledger networks in the private sector, as well as networks managed by other Union bodies such as customs or supervisory authorities. Product counterfeiting may become obsolete in the near future if blockchain technology is extended to the majority of goods entering the market.

## References

1. R. Handfield, *Counterfeiting is on the rise, and projected to exceed $3 trillion in 2022,* North Carolina State University, URL: https://scm.ncsu.edu/scm-articles/article/counterfeiting-is-on-the-rise-projected-to-exceed-3-trillion-in-2022, accessed: 15.12.2022 (2021)
2. F. Richter, *The Industries Most Affected by Counterfeit Products,* Statista, URL: https://www.statista.com/chart/17410/counterfeit-and-pirated-products-by-category/, accessed: 15.12.2022 (2019)
3. J. Rutter, J. Bryce, Sociology, **42**, 6, DOI: DOI: 10.1177/0038038508096938, accessed: 4.12.2022 (2008)
4. Europol, *Counterfeit products: Why buying fakes can be bad for your health (and more),* Europol's Publications, URL: https://www.europol.europa.eu/publications-

events/publications/counterfeit-products-why-buying-fakes-can-be-bad-for-your-health-and-more#downloads, accessed: 12.12.2022 (2021)

5. O. Whitehead, *Counterfeit alcohol in Russia claims 34 lives,* The Brussels Times. URL: https://www.brusselstimes.com/188971/counterfeit-alcohol-in-russia-claims-34-lives, accessed: 12.12.2022 (2021)
6. Team ZenBusiness, *History and Meaning Behind Adidas Logo*. ZenBusiness INC, URL: https://www.zenbusiness.com/blog/adidas-logo/, accessed: 18.12.2022 (2012).
7. S. Amaro, *10% of Adidas products in Asia are fakes, CEO says*, CNBC, URL: https://www.cnbc.com/2018/05/03/10-percent-of-adidas-products-in-asia-are-fakes-ceo-says.html, accessed: 17.12.2022 (2018)
8. Europol, *Food fraud: about 27 000 tonnes off the shelves, European Union Agency for Law Enforcement Cooperation, URL:* https://www.europol.europa.eu/media-press/newsroom/news/food-fraud-about-27-000-tonnes-shelves, accessed: 25.11.2022 (2022)
9. A. Mukherji, *Counterfeit Wine: 5 Signs You're Sipping on Fraud, FindLaw, URL:* https://www.findlaw.com/legalblogs/small-business/counterfeit-wine-5-signs-youre-sipping-on-fraud/, accessed: 10.12.2022 (2019)
10. European Union Intellectual Property Office, *eSearch plus platform*, URL: EUIPO - eSearch (www.europa.eu), accessed: 26.12.2022 (2022)
11. H. Pun, J.M. Swaminathan, P. Hou, *Blockchain Adoption for Combating Deceptive Counterfeits*, Kenan Institute of Private Enterprise Research Paper No. 18-18, URL: https://ssrn.com/abstract=3223656, accessed: 4.10.2022 (2018)
12. Opinion of the European Economic and Social Committee on *Blockchain and distributed ledger technology as an ideal infrastructure for the social economy*, Official Journal of the European Union C 353/1, 18.10.2019
13. J. Bacon, J.D. Michels, C. Millard, J. Singh, *Blockchain demystified*, Queen Mary School of Law Legal Studies Research Paper Series. No 268/2017, (2017) *apud,* European Commission, Directorate-General for Communications Networks, Content and Technology. *Study on copyright and new technologies: copyright data management and artificial intelligence*, Publications Office of the European Union (2022)
14. A. Haris, *Blockchain—A Short and Simple Explanation with Pictures*, Hackernoon, URL: https://hackernoon.com/blockchain-a-short-and-simple-explanation-with-pictures d60d652f207f, accessed: 27.11.2022 (2019)
15. United Nations Economic Commission for Europe, *White Paper on Blockchain in Trade Facilitation,* United Nation, URL: https://unece.org/fileadmin/DAM/trade/Publications/ECE-TRADE-457E_WPBlockchainTF.pdf, accessed: 14.11.2022 (2020)
16. B. Carson, G. Romanelli, P. Walsh, A. Zhumaev, *Blockchain beyond the hype: What is the strategic business value?*, McKinsey & Company, URL: https://www.mckinsey.com/capabilities/mckinsey-digital/our-insights/blockchain-beyond-the-hype-what-is-the-strategic-business-value, accessed: 29.11.2022 (2018)
17. IEEE Computer Society, *IEEE Draft Standard for Blockchain Interoperability – Data Authentication and Communication Protocol*, IEEE Standards Association, URL: https://standards.ieee.org/ieee/3205/10237/#:~:text=Blockchain%20interoperability%20is%20the%20ability%20of%20two%20or,play%20a%20very%20important%20role%20in%20realizing%20interoperability, accessed: 14.11.2022 (2020)

18. E. Ganne, *Can Blockchain revolutionize international trade?,* World Trade Organization, URL: https://www.wto.org/english/res_e/booksp_e/blockchainrev18_e.pdf#page=137, accessed: 16.11.2022 (2018)
19. DeFipedia, *What Is Blockchain Immutability?,* The First Decentralized Finance Encyclopedia, URL: https://defipedia.com/topic/blockchain-immutability, accessed: 14.12.2022 (2022)
20. M. Higginson, J.T. Lorenz, P.B. Olesen, *The promise of blockchain*, McKinsey & Company, URL: https://www.mckinsey.com/industries/financial-services/our-insights/the-promise-of-blockchain, accessed: 29.11.2022 (2017)
21. F. Walker, *Coca-Cola still using slave labor despite efforts to appear "woke" – report,* Natural News, URL: https://www.naturalnews.com/2021-08-02-woke-coca-cola-still-using-slave-labor.html, accessed: 17.12.2022 (2021)
22. J. Liebkind, *Coca-Cola and US State Dept Use Blockchain to Combat Forced Labor*, Investopedia, URL: https://www.investopedia.com/news/cocacola-and-us-state-dept-fight-forced-labor/, accessed: 18.12.2022 (2019)
23. Merriam-Webster Dictionary, URL: https://www.merriam-webster.com/dictionary/publicity%20stunt, accessed: 08.01.2023.
24. European Council, *European Green Deal*, URL: https://www.consilium.europa.eu/en/policies/greendeal/#:~:text=What%20is%20the%20European%20Green%20Deal%3F%20The%20European,prosperous%20society%20with%20a%20modern%20and%20competitive%20economy, accessed: 14.12.2022 (2022)
25. European Comission, *Green Deal: EU agrees law to fight global deforestation and forest degradation driven by EU production and consumption,* URL: https://ec.europa.eu/commission/presscorner/detail/en/ip_22_7444, accessed: 14.12.2022 (2022)
26. European Commission, *Questions and Answers on new rules for deforestation-free products*, URL: https://ec.europa.eu/commission/presscorner/detail/en/qanda_21_5919, accessed: 12.12.2022 (2021)
27. European Parliament, *The European Union and forests,* Fact Sheets on the European Union, URL: https://www.europarl.europa.eu/factsheets/en/sheet/105/the-european-union-and-forests, accessed: 4.12.2022 (2022)
28. Eurostat, *Forestry data*, URL: https://ec.europa.eu/eurostat/web/forestry/data/database, accessed: 4.12.2022 (2022).
29. Fourth Industrial Revolution, *Blockchain can protect our trees. Here's how,* World Economic Forum, URL: https://www.weforum.org/agenda/2021/03/blockchain-can-protect-our-trees-here-s-how/, accessed: 5.12.2022 (2021)
30. European Commission, *Shaping Europe's digital future, Blockchain Strategy*, URL: https://digital-strategy.ec.europa.eu/en/policies/blockchain-strategy, accessed: 26.09.2022 (2022)
31. European Commission, *Shaping Europe's digital future, European Blockchain Services Infrastructure*, URL: https://digital-strategy.ec.europa.eu/en/policies/european-blockchain-services-infrastructure, accessed: 14.11.2022 (2022)
32. M. Iaconisi, *The European Blockchain Services Infrastructure is coming, and the ECA has a role to play*, European Court of Auditors, URL:

https://medium.com/ecajournal/the-european-blockchain-services-infrastructure-is-coming-and-the-eca-has-a-role-to-play-68b53395c788, accessed: 29.09.2022 (2020).

33. A. Shireesh, N. Petrovsky, JEFC, **7**, 3 (2016)
34. European Blockchain Services Infrastructure, *The purpose of the Document Traceability*, European Commission, URL: https://ec.europa.eu/digitalbuildingblocks/wikis/pages/viewpage.action?pageId=555222715#Highlevelscope(documenttraceability)-High%20levelscope(documenttraceability), accessed: 17.11.2022 (2022)
35. European Union Intellectual Property Office, *IP register on blockchain. Strategic plan 2025,* URL: https://euipo.europa.eu/tunnelweb/secure/webdav/guest/document_library/contentPdfs/Strategic_Plan_2025/project_cards/SD3_IP_Register_on_Blockchain_PC_en.pdf, accessed: 20.10.2022 (2020)
36. European Union Intellectual Property Office, *The Anti-counterfeiting Blockathon Infrastructure*, URL: https://euipo.europa.eu/ohimportal/en/web/observatory/blockathon/acbi, accessed: 20.12.2022 (2022)
37. European Union Intellectual Property Office, *The Tmview platform*, European Union Intellectual Property Network, URL: https://www.tmdn.org/tmview/#/tmview/about, accessed: 29.12.2022 (2022)
38. European Union Intellectual Property Office, *The DesignView platform*, European Union Intellectual Property Network, URL: https://www.tmdn.org/tmdsview-web/welcome#/dsview/about, accessed: 29.12.2022 (2022)
39. S. Lama, *CargoX Becomes Official Blockchain Partner of Egyptian Customs Authorities*, BeInCrypto Team, URL: https://beincrypto.com/cargox-becomes-official-blockchain-partner-of-egyptian-customs-authorities/, accessed: 15.12.2022 (2021)
40. CargoX, *Blockchain document workflows for governments*, CargoXplatform, URL: https://cargox.io/solutions/for-governments/#use-case-egypt, accessed: 14.12.2022 (2019)
41. N. Hackius, M. Petersen, HICL, **23**, Epubli GmbH, Berlin, DOI:10.15480/882.1444, accessed: 14.12.2022 (2017)
42. Everledger, *Everledger and Gübelin*. Everledger, URL: https://everledger.io/everledger-with-avery-dennison-and-wine-trade-network/, accessed: 14.12.2022 (2019)
43. Ledger Insights, *Tencent, Fidelity backed Everledger launches blockchain bottle closures for wine industry*, LedgerInsights Blockchain For Business, URL: https://www.ledgerinsights.com/everledger-blockchain-bottle-closures-wine-anti-counterfeit/, accessed: 29.11.2022 (2020)
44. N. Alzahrani, N. Bulusu, CCPE, **32**, 12, DOI:10.1002/cpe.5232, accessed: 4.11.2022 (2019)
45. R. Hackett, *Walmart and 9 Food Giants Team Up on IBM Blockchain Plans*, Fortune Magazine, URL: http://fortune.com/2017/08/22/walmart-blockchain-ibm-food-nestle-unilever-tyson-dole, accessed: 18.12.2022 (2017)
46. R. Hackett, *Walmart and IBM Are Partnering to Put Chinese Pork on a Blockchain,* Fortune Magazine, URL: https://fortune.com/2016/10/19/walmart-ibm-blockchain-china-pork/, accessed: 18.12.2022 (2016)

47. Pixelplex, *How Walmart Strives for Food Quality And Safety Using Blockchain Technology Solutions*, Pixelplex Blog, URL: https://pixelplex.io/blog/walmart-strives-for-food-safety-using-blockchain/, accessed: 18.12.2022 (2020)
48. S. Higgins, *Walmart: Blockchain Food Tracking Test Results Are 'Very Encouraging*, Coindesk, URL: https://www.coindesk.com/walmart-blockchain-food-tracking-test-results-encouraging, accessed: 19.12.2022 (2017)
49. F. Giles, *Is Blockchain the Future of Food Safety*?, Growing Produce, URL: https://www.growingproduce.com/fruits/blockchain-future-food-safety/, accessed: 19.12.2022 (2018)
50. FoodSafety, *IBM Launches Blockchain Food Traceability Platform*, FoodSafety Magazine, URL: https://www.food-safety.com/articles/5970-ibm-launches-blockchain-food-traceability-platform, accessed: 19.12.2022 (2018)
51. IBM Food Trust, *Focus on food safety,* IBM Corporation, URL: https://www.ibm.com/downloads/cas/KWNWD3ZM, accessed: 20.12.2022 (2020)
52. C. Palmer, *Indoor produce grower BrightFarms uses IBM Food Trust*, IBM Corporation, URL: https://www.ibm.com/case-studies/brightfarms/, accessed: 20.12.2022 (2019)
53. Carrefour, *Food Traceability: Carrefour, A Blockchain Pioneer In Europe, Has Joined The IBM Food Trust Platform To Take Action On A Global Scale*, URL: https://www.carrefour.com/en/news/food-traceability-carrefour-blockchain-pioneer-europe-has-joined-ibm-food-trust-platform-take, accessed: 20.12.2022 (2018)
54. IBM THINK Blog, *Carrefour and Nestlé Partner with IBM to Extend Use of Blockchain to New Food Categories*, URL: https://www.ibm.com/blogs/think/2019/04/tracing-your-mashed-potatoes-on-ibmblockchain/, accessed: 20.12.2022 (2019)
55. M.J. Casey, P. Wong, *Global Supply Chains Are About to Get Better, Thanks to Blockchain,* Harvard Business Review, URL: https://hbr.org/2017/03/global-supply-chains-are-about-to-get-better-thanks-to-blockchain, accessed: 20.12.2022 (2017)

# On the curiosities of the future: meta criminal law

*Laura Maria* Stănilă[1*]

[1] Faculty of Law, West University of Timişoara, Centre for Research in Criminal Sciences, Romania

**Abstract:** The new virtual realm – *Metaverse* – despite its entertaining potential and features, comes with a lot of threats and perils, and tends to seriously challenge the legal system. The lack of regulation, the increasing number of users and the occurrence of new acts that can be committed solely in Metaverse are just a few topics this article aims to address. The author proposes the creation of a new branch of law – Meta - Criminal Law and asks for immediate intervention of the national and international legislators to create a frame system to protect the users of virtual platforms and ensure their safety.

## 1 Metaverse as an Alternate Reality

Criticized by the scholars due to the inequalities risen based on economic limitations, Metaverse keeps being a hot topic in scholarly and Media discussions. „Unlike the previous disruptive iterations of internet-age projects, Metaverse has been proactively grappled with by various types of scholars and writers. The cautionary tales set by *The Matrix, Ready Player One,* and *Snow Crash* already paint a dystopian picture in the popular imagination. The equity markets are also punishing Facebook (meta) for several reasons including the overinvestment and poor reception of the meta project (in addition to declining user base)" [1].

As shown by the foreign literature, the physical world is no longer the necessary arena of human activity. Cyberspace gives us a new, non-spatial arena in which we can conduct many, if not all, of the activities we carry out in the physical world. The availability of this new, conceptual vector for human activity has various consequences for criminal law [2]. And, if that wasn't enough Metaverse as a newly created virtual world comes and further challenges the Law in general and Criminal law.

The term Metaverse is a combination of the prefix *meta* (Greek term for *transcendence*) and the suffix *verse* (short for *Universe*) and is used to denote "a computer-generated world with a consistent value system and an independent economic system connected to the world physics" [3]. *Metaverse* is a term applying to a wide range of technologies that aim to merge the social connections of the real world with the innovations of the digital age. The term *Metaverse* was first used in a 1992 dystopian sci-fi novel by writer Neal Stephenson, *Snow Crash*. The book describes a world where governments have been replaced by corporations, the global economy has collapsed, while citizens escape this bleak reality by accessing a virtual world through headsets. There, their avatars can roam the digital realm, own virtual

* Corresponding author: laura.stanila@e-uvt.ro

property, and socialize with other avatars. This dystopian future imagined by the author does not correspond to the foundation of the emergence and development of the Metaverse in our world. Instead, it has evolved through increased digitization and the emergence of new technologies and multiple innovations such as crypto-assets and blockchain, these configuring the so-called web *3.0 Metaverse* [4].

Metaverse is considered an extended reality platform (*extended reality* - XR), which however, faces multiple problems such as viruses, the current impossibility of imposing age limits on users because many virtual games are Metaverse worlds. This allows adults to interact with minors very easily and engage them in dangerous behaviours. In addition, the exponential growth of users, individuals, or companies, has made this virtual realm extremely crowded and therefore, a regulation and a planning of the situation in the future being as difficult as it is necessary. There are nearly 200 companies operating in the Metaverse. New technologies such as 5G or 6G and Web 3.0 will further accelerate social relations in the Metaverse by connecting the 7.9 billion users in the real world [5].

Because the lack of technical knowledge of non-IT public, it is necessary to define some specific terms used in reference to Metaverse analysis. Virtual reality (VR) and augmented reality (AR) are the main terms in the media, both being used for about 30 years, with VR emerging in the late 1980s and AR in the early 1990s. The key difference between them consists in the perception of the user. In VR, the user feels present within a simulated environment, while in AR the user feels present in a combined world of real and virtual content [6]. *Virtual reality (VR)* is an immersive and interactive simulated environment that is experienced in the first person and provides a strong sense of presence to the user. *Augmented reality (AR)* is an immersive and interactive environment in which virtual content is spatially registered to the real world and experienced in the first person, providing a strong sense of presence in a combined real/virtual space. *Extended reality (XR)* emerged to describe the full spectrum of VR and AR capabilities.

The connection between these terms is explained in the Fig. 1 [6]:

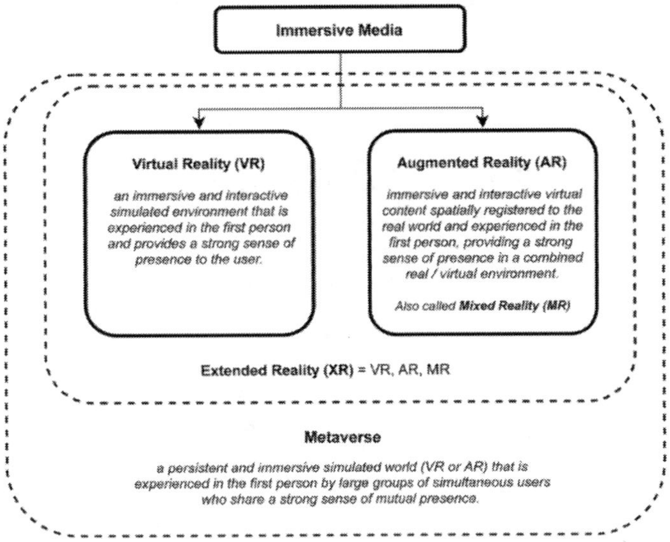


**Fig. 1.** Explanation of VR, AR and XR and the connection between them.

In general, the development of the Metaverse is expected to go through three successive phases (now in progress) as follows: (a) the digital twin, (b) the digital native, and finally (c) the sur-reality [3]. The first phase involves the creation of a mirror world, a digital copy of the real world in which we find the digital twins of people and things in physical reality; In this first phase the Metaverse is a digital representation of physical reality. In this phase, the user's behaviour and emotions are imitations from the physical world, the virtual space being parallel to the physical world. The second phase focuses mainly on native content creation, where digital natives represented by avatars can produce innovations and insights within digital worlds, and these digital creations can only exist in virtual spaces. In this phase, the contents created massively in the digital world become equal to those created in the physical world, and the digital world can transform and innovate the production process of the physical world, thus creating more intersections between these two worlds. Finally, in the last phase, the Metaverse grows to maturity and transforms into a persistent and self-sustaining hyperreality that assimilates reality into itself. The perfect integration and mutual symbiosis of the physical and virtual worlds will be achieved in this phase, where the scope of the virtual world will be greater than that of the real world.

Finally, we must point out that there are several visions as regards Metaverse: for some Metaverse is the evolution of internet, or an embodied internet, for others, Metaverse includes immersive offline experiences that enable users to experience a different reality, or a combination of the physical and virtual world in a type of mixed reality [7]. For sure, Metaverse is one of the core topics of concern for several international bodies, including Europol.

## 2 Should we regulate Metaverse?

In our opinion, the need to regulate metaverse is imperative. It is obvious that Metaverse will bring together a range of digital activities [8] as shown in the Fig. 2 bellow:

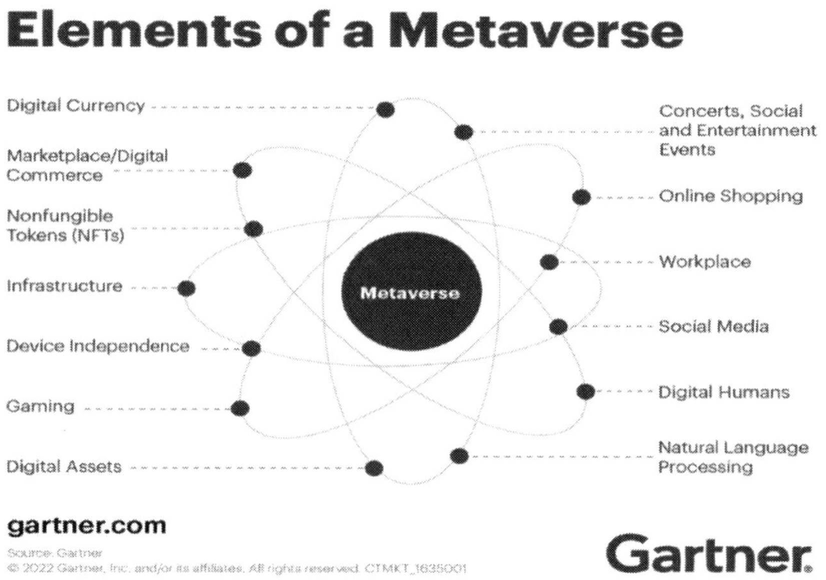


**Fig. 2.** Elements of a Metaverse.

The diversification of social relations in metaverse and the increase of number of users brings a whole new category of perils and threats for humans, jeopardizing their rights and freedoms. While the present criminal regulations tend to cover physical deeds committed in the physical reality, and even the cybercrime rules deal with physical acts committed through computers, the deeds committed in Metaverse have no correspondence with the previous.

The key perils of Metaverse have been divided into three categories named as the three „M" s of Metaverse [9]: monitoring, manipulation, and monetization.

*Monitoring.* Aggressively targeting users for advertising purposes has exploited consumers, caused reduced personal privacy, and has made social media a polarizing force by allowing third parties to deploy customize messaging that is skilfully aimed at very specific demographic groups. This led to the amplification of existing biases in populations and spread misinformation, worsening in the Metaverse. The technology in Metaverse will not just track where users click, but where they go, who they are with, what they do, what they look at, even how long their gaze lingers, it will also track facial expressions, vocal inflections, and vital signs, while intelligent algorithms use such data to predict each person's real-time emotional state.

*Manipulating.* Nowadays custom targeted advertising has greatly increased the persuasive ability of promotional messaging and in Metaverse, such targeting will get far more personal, and the content will get much harder to resist.

*Monetizing.* Platform providers are commercial entities requiring substantial revenue to support the interests of the employees and shareholders. Until now, only a small part of the public has paid subscriptions for access to online platforms, so they must rethink their business model to increase the number of paying users. It was suggested that the most common industry model is to provide free access in exchange for widespread advertising, focusing largely on targeted ads that can be precisely delivered based on the unique behaviours and interests of individual users. That is why the platform providers are pursuing extensive tracking and profiling of their users.

Because the underlying technologies of the Metaverse are specifically designed to trick the senses, deliberately blurring the line between authentic and fabricated experiences, we can expect deceptive abuses of social media to be greatly amplified.

This context triggers the question: does Metaverse worth it?

Despite the risks, the immersive technologies of virtual and augmented reality have the potential to make our lives magical, unleashing creativity more powerfully than ever, even expanding what it means to be human. Still, to avoid potential problems, governments and industry players need to consider significant strict regulations.

In addition, a regulation of Metaverse should be considered promptly, before profound effects on Metaverse's infrastructure and business models be caused, so that they become difficult or even impossible to solve.

As shown in the previous section of the present study, users of Metaverse are extremely vulnerable. Their vulnerability is the result of multiple factors, among which two are popping: new types of deeds adapted to the specifics of the XR and VR realm and the lack of legal rules. The vulnerability of the users in the metaverse asserts the need for the immediate discourse around the rules, regulations or laws that would be implemented in these virtual worlds before the embodied internet materializes [10].

Three directions to address the issue of regulating Metaverse were identified by the scholars, as follows:

a) the harsh modernization of the way crime is viewed through extraterritoriality in the virtual world - including broadening the scope of punitive action and identifying the actors in Metaverse that would have to incur liability; this approach would be a complete review of the current schools of thought pertaining to criminal law and jurisdiction – identifying victims and perpetrators to include AI, AR players and imposition of liability on them.

b) formation of regulatory penal laws of the exact nature and scope of international or transnational laws; this approach is to be materialized after taking into consideration the extent at which activities of criminal nature could take place in Metaverse. In this regard the universal jurisdiction principle has been proposed.

c) decentralizing the criminal legislation process by entrusting the corporations involved with regulatory powers. This third approach focuses on the fact that the regulations are made in effect of existing laws pertaining to technology that will interlink with Big Tech's Terms and Conditions of Service. Regulations acknowledge that criminal jurisdiction is intrinsically connected to state recognition and state sanctioned liabilities. Nevertheless, in technology, the development occurs at a too high rate for state action to respond by designing proper legal rules. For these reasons, the stakeholders should provide Terms and Conditions of use to establish the limits of users' actions, while in other situations are given the role of a mere intermediary.

## 3 Metaverse and Criminal Law

Participating in online games that request the use of avatars sometimes involves committing crimes as part of that game. Metaverse is, manly, a realm of games and entertainment. It is interesting to note that certain deeds are impossible to commit in a virtual world due to code restrictions. In other words, if the designers create such a platform that allows crimes to be committed, they will be committed. On the other hand, the creation of "restrictive" codes regarding criminality does not guarantee that potentially harmful or dangerous acts will not be committed in that environment. The key question that is to be addressed in this matter is: for whom these risks consist of a threat? For the avatar or for the man behind it (using it)? In most cases, if someone commits such acts in a virtual world, they will most likely be warned, suspended, or permanently banned on the platform because, for now, the presence in the virtual world of the Metaverse is based on the idea of the game. However, the development direction of Metaverse with the increase of transactions on virtual properties, moving some businesses into the virtual environment and even creating virtual copies of real cities (such as Seoul [11]) or real spaces (e.g., museums in virtual format whose number of visitors increases every day [12]) shows that the game phase is starting to pass, and things are taking a serious turn. Could such conducts occur in the virtual world being sufficiently harmful to claim the intervention of criminal law and, therefore, the application of punishment in real life? In general, if an incident occurred in a virtual world result in injury, harm or endangerment of a real-life value, there could obviously be legal consequences in real life. But this is extremely difficult to achieve at the present time under the conditions in which the principle of the legality of incrimination forces the verification of the typicality conditions of the concrete act to make it possible to engage the criminal liability.

It has been shown that, „in general, developers of virtual worlds do not want real-world laws applied to their platforms. Mainly because they want to control their world to maximize revenue from users while allowing them to have an enjoyable experience. Users probably feel the same way because they don't want to get, say, a speeding ticket for driving 100 km/h in their virtual Bugatti through a virtual school zone. Whether the laws of the real world could apply to a virtual world will depend on how it is set up. But in general, the more realistic a virtual world is, the more likely it is that disputes will be resolved in a real-life court. But that doesn't mean that real-world law enforcement will solve the problems of the virtual world" [13].

In my opinion, the application of real-world criminal law in the Metaverse space depends on three conditions:

a) the will of the creator and the created code; in other words, The Terms and Conditions established to use the platform become part of the legal frame.

b) the typicality of the act; in this regard, the *nullum crimen sine lege* principle is restricting the intervention of criminal law, since the „deeds" committed in the virtual realm are very difficult to compare with the deeds committed in the physical world.

c) producing a consequence – state of peril or result – in the real world; in other words, it is necessary to admit a connection between Metaverse world and real world.

All these being displayed, certain virtual behaviours, obviously harmful or dangerous, committed in Metaverse cannot be included, now, in the pattern given by the classic criminalization rules: e.g., virtual rape [14, 15], virtual destruction, virtual murder [21].

In addition, it is worth to mention that growth of a specific criminal acts was observed by the users of platforms and scholars: theft and destruction of crypto-assets. For example, Elliptic has revealed that there was already illicit activity regarding the assets used in Metaverse MANA and SAND. Of these illicit activities, 99.5% consist of crypto-assets theft. [4] Thus, the most frequent criminal activity currently in the Metaverse virtuality is highlighted.

Obviously, these facts require criminal intervention, and, at present, this is achieved through inadequate legislation, which is mainly intended to be applied to crimes committed in physical reality, by legal subjects recognized in this reality. In the Metaverse and its virtual worlds, we cannot yet discuss legal subjects because avatars do not have a legally recognized independent existence, distinct from the real-world actor. In this regard, in another study, I have proposed the creation of the meta-criminal law and of the categories of meta-criminality and meta-criminal justice. [16]

Trying to identify which present Romanian criminal rules could be applied to harmful or dangerous acts committed in Metaverse, some legal norms provided by Romanian Criminal Code of 2009 felt more adaptable to the virtual realm: Art. 207 – blackmail, Art. 208 – harassment, Art. 360-366 – Offenses against the safety and integrity of computer data, Art. 368 – public incitement, Art. 370 – the attempt to determine the commission of a crime, Art. 374 – child pornography. Still, reviewing the types of threats occurring or emerging in Metaverse identified by the scholars, one can easily notice they are far of being sufficient or efficient.

The specific threats of Metaverse that could require criminal intervention are categorized as follows [3]:

*A. Threats to Authentication in Metaverse.* In this category the scholars include identity theft in Metaverse, leading to the user's avatars, digital assets, social relationships, and her/his digital life to be leaked and lost; impersonation attack, consisting in pretending to be another authorized entity to gain access to a service or system in the metaverse. It was shown that hackers can invade the helmet and exploit the stolen behavioural and biological data gathered by the in- built motion-tracking system to create digital replicas of the user and impersonate the victim to facilitate social engineering attacks; e.g. avatar authentication issue may appear by creating multiple AI bots (i.e., digital humans) based on facial features, voice, video footage and other authentication items of the real user, which appear, hear, and behave identical to user's real avatar, in the virtual world (e.g., Roblox) by imitating user's appearance, voice, and behaviours .

*B. Threats to Access Control in Metaverse,* including unauthorized data access, misuse of user/avatar data.

*C. Threats to Data Management in Metaverse,* including *data* tampering attacks, false data injection attacks, threats to data quality of user generated content (UGC), threats to UGC ownership and provenance, threats to intellectual property protection.

*D. Privacy Threats in Metaverse,* including pervasive data collection, privacy leakage in data transmission, privacy leakage in data processing; privacy leakage in cloud/edge storage; rogue or compromised end devices; threats to digital footprints; identity linkability in ternary worlds, threats to accountability; threats to customized privacy.

*E. Threats to Metaverse Network.* In this category the scholars include several types of use of malware such as SPoF, DDoS, Sybil Attacks.

*F. Threats to Metaverse Economy,* including service trust issues in UGC & virtual object trading; threats to digital asset ownership; threats to economic fairness in creator economy.

*G. Threats to Physical World and Human Society.* This category is the most important, in my opinion, due to its evident connections between VR/AR and reality and includes threats to personal safety (e.g. an adversary can manipulate a VR device to reset the hardware's physical boundaries, thereby, a user in metaverse can be potentially pushed toward a flight of stairs or misdirected into a crowded street or other dangerous physical situations); *threats to infrastructure safety* by sniffing the software or system vulnerabilities in the highly integrated metaverse. By this way, hackers may exploit the compromised devices as entry points and invade critical national infrastructures via malware attacks.

As regards the complexity of the Metaverse threats and perils presented above, I emphasize once more the imperative need to create a proper legal criminal framework to protect the users of the virtual worlds, their rights, and freedoms.

## 4 The Metaverse and the Criminal Justice System

The creation of new branches of law in general and a new branch of criminal law – the Meta-criminal law - in particular, applicable exclusively to Metaverse realities, is an idea difficult to accept and implement in practice. Still, it is not sufficient to design a new branch of law for Metaverse, we need to design a whole new system to enforce these rules and to punish the criminals who commit meta-crimes.

Will we ever have criminal meta-trials that will involve the administration of virtual evidence exclusively in virtual space, and the punishments will be executed in virtual prisons? This would probably be the natural direction of development. Until then, however, we are already facing a collision of the two worlds in terms of the criminal process, because Metaverse could be successfully used in the instrumentation of criminal cases from physical reality as it allows the virtual reconstruction of the commission of crimes and judicial bodies and jurors, in legal systems who have courts with juries, to ascertain with their own senses how things actually happened and how the crime was physically committed.

For example, in an ongoing trial in Florida, USA, in which a man was accused of trying to kill his neighbour, a motion was filed by the defence attorney asking that jurors hear expert testimony in question using virtual reality glasses. The court was demanded, without precedent, to allow the jurors to be placed „in the driver's seat by using the latest technology – virtual reality headsets that promise to give them a glimpse of the alleged crime from the defendant's perspective". Defence counsel stated that, because the expert testimony was admissible and the virtual reconstruction was merely an extension of the expert testimony, he hoped his motion would be found admissible because it would allow the jury to participate as if they were behind the wheel, and to observe that the defendant „had no intent to commit a crime" [17].

In China, the administration of evidence in the criminal trial using VR technologies was already permitted, since 2018 [18].

Moreover, there are real initiatives of the scholars of advocating for the large-scale use of virtual reality to facilitate the criminal proceedings and the discovery of the truth, as far back as 16 years ago [19].

Even if there are certain preoccupations in the use of VR technologies in the present criminal justice system, this is only the beginning. We will have criminal meta-trials that will involve the administration of virtual evidence exclusively in the virtual space, and the punishments will be executed in virtual prisons.

The benefits of the use of VR in the criminal trial and in the criminal justice system are obvious and numerous: it makes possible to virtually reconstruct of the commission of crimes allowing judicial bodies and jurors (in case of legal systems that have courts with jurors), to ascertain with their own senses how things happened and how the crimes were committed. Another benefit is that VR could be used in training people working in the judiciary or even in re-educating process of convicted criminals, with the aim of their rehabilitation and social reintegration.

Computer simulations are currently used in the criminal justice system for research purposes, but the extensive use of immersive virtual environments offers unique possibilities within the criminal justice system, as it would operate in an environment where operational workers have absolute control over the people's reactions they work with.

## 5 Conclusions

Trying to conclude, several ideas should be remembered. Metaverse represents a new „Wild West" [20] where, for now, intervention by means of criminal law is very limited.

The multitude, complexity, and emergence of social relations in Metaverse generate a whole new category of perils needing to be addressed by the legislators, to ensure the users of the of the virtual platforms' safety. In this regard, I propose a step-by-step approach: in a first phase a set of guiding principles should be established (initial minimum intervention); this first phase should be followed by designing sectoral norms for the regulation of social relations in Metaverse – e.g. specific rules for Meta-data protection, Meta-electronic commerce, Meta-copyright etc. - (intermediate intervention); finally, specific criminal rules frame should be established (maximum intervention).

If we do not act proactively, if we do not accept the (virtual) reality, it is very possible to allow virtual chaos to be installed and cause irremediable harms to our society.

## References

1. U.W. Chohan, SSRN Papers, 1-9, DOI: 10.2139/ssrn.4038770, (2022)
2. S.W. Brenner, Vanderbilt J. of Entertainment & Tech. L., **11(1),** 1-97, (2008)
3. Y. Wang, Z. Su, N. Zhang, R. Xing, D. Liu, T.H. Luan, X. Shen, *A Survey on Metaverse: Fundamentals, Security, and Privacy,* IEEE Communications Surveys & Tutorials, **25,** (1), 319-352, DOI: 10.1109/COMST.2022.3202047, (2022)
4. Elliptic Metaverse Report, URL: https://www.elliptic.co/hubfs/Crime%20in%20the%20Metaverse%202022%20final.pdf, accessed: 14.02.2023, (2022)
5. M. Stephens, *Metaverse Governance*, URL: https://standards.ieee.org/wp-content/uploads/2022/06/XR_Metaverse_Governance.pdf, accessed: 14.02.2023, (Institute of Electrical and Electronics Engineers New York, USA, 2022)
6. L. Rosenberg, Metaverse 101: Defining the key components. VentureBeat, February 5th, URL: https://venturebeat.com/business/metaverse-101-defining-the-key-components/, accessed: 14.02.2023, (2023)
7. Europol, Policing in the metaverse: what law enforcement needs to know, an observatory report from the Europol Innovation Lab, Publications Office of the European Union, URL: https://www.europol.europa.eu/cms/sites/default/files/documents/Policing%20in%20the%20metaverse%20-%20what%20law%20enforcement%20needs%20to%20know.pdf accessed: 14.02.2023, (2023)

8. URL: https://www.gartner.co.uk/en/articles/what-is-a-metaverse, accessed: 14.02.2023, (2023)
9. L. Rosenberg, Regulating the Metaverse, a Blueprint for the Future, DOI:10.1007/978-3-031-15546-8_23, (Springer, 2022)
10. S. Jathavedan, The Buzz Around the 'Metaverse', URL: https://www.khuranaandkhurana.com/2022/10/12/metaverse-blurred-lines-for-criminal-law/, accessed: 14.02.2023, (2022)
11. G. Lawton, How Seoul is creating a metaverse for a smarter city, URL: https://venturebeat.com/ai/how-seoul-is-creating-a-metaverse-for-a-smarter-city/, accessed: 14.02.2023, (2022)
12. A. Romano, These 12 Famous Museums Offer Virtual Tours You Can Take on Your Couch, URL: https://www.travelandleisure.com/attractions/museums-galleries/museums-with-virtual-tours, accessed: 14.02.2023, (2022)
13. S. Chung, The Problems with Trying to Apply Real-World Laws in the Virtual Metaverse, URL: https://abovethelaw.com/2022/02/the-problems-with-trying-to-apply-real-world-laws-in-the-virtual-metaverse/, accessed: 14.02.2023, (2022)
14. W. Soon, A researcher's avatar was sexually assaulted on a metaverse platform owned by Meta, making her the latest victim of sexual abuse on Meta's platforms, watchdog says., URL: https://www.businessinsider.com/researcher-claims-her-avatar-was-raped-on-metas-metaverse-platform-2022-5, accessed: 14.02.2023, (2022)
15. A. Diaz, Disturbing reports of sexual assaults in the metaverse: 'It's a free show', URL: https://nypost.com/2022/05/27/women-are-being-sexually-assaulted-in-the-metaverse/, accessed: 14.02.2023, (2022)
16. L. Stănilă, Dreptul penal al viitorului: spre un meta-drept penal? [Criminal Law of the Future: Towards a Meta-Criminal Law?] in L. Stănilă, (coord), Dreptul penal al Viitorului. Generații [Criminal Law of the Future. Generations], 103-117, (Universul Juridic, Bucharest, 2022)
17. R. Olmeda, Is Virtual Reality the Future of Expert Testimony in Court?, URL: https://www.govtech.com/public-safety/is-virtual-reality-the-future-of-expert-testimony-in-court, accessed: 14.02.2023, (2022)
18. J. Nafarette, Chinese Courtroom Uses VR to Revisit Crime Scene, URL: https://vrscout.com/news/chinese-courtroom-vr-crime-scene/, accessed: 14.02.2023, (2018)
19. J.N. Bailenson, J. Blascovich, A.C. Beall, B. Noveck, Law & Policy, **28(2)**, 246-270, DOI:10.1111/j.1467-9930.2006.00226.x, (2006)
20. A. Woon, The metaverse is not above real-world law. The Straits Times, URL: https://www.suss.edu.sg/docs/default-source/media-coverage/20220125-st---the-metaverse-is-not-above-real-world-law.pdf?sfvrsn=5f6655cb_0, accessed: 14.02.2023, (2022)
21. J. Brassel, Murder in the Metaverse could be a real crime, URL: https://www.beyondgames.biz/21556/murder-in-the-metaverse-could-be-a-real-crime/ accessed: 14.02.2023, (2022)

# Forensic challenges regarding the Internet of Things

*Ancuța Elena* Franț[1*]

[1] Faculty of Law, Alexandru Ioan Cuza University of Iași, Romania

**Abstract.** The Internet of Things brings many benefits to our society, but its advantages come with a price, namely with a huge opportunity for those who want to commit cybercrime. To fight against this kind of criminality, investigators must use appropriate methods. The Forensics of the Internet of Things (IoT) has evolved from "traditional" Digital Forensics, and includes, among other activities, the identification of the devices related to a certain crime, collecting the digital evidence in a form which can be used in front of the judicial bodies, the analysis, and the extraction of all possible information from the collected data, and the preservation of the evidence. The Forensics of IoT must face specific issues, mainly generated by the extraordinary large number of IoT devices and by the great diversity of these devices. An important problem is that data analysis is very difficult to perform, because of different data formats used by the components of IoT. In the forensic investigations related to the IoT, an important concern refers to privacy protection. Overall, IoT Forensics is a challenging field, but we must search for suitable solutions, because ensuring security for IoT is a very important aim.

## 1 Introduction. The importance of a forensic approach to the Internet of Things

The present-day society is becoming more and more dependent on the Internet. This situation is generated by the great advantages which come along with the use of the Internet. People see their lives greatly enhanced with online services, in all areas. But all this comes with a price. The characteristic features of the Internet have made it an appropriate environment for anti-social activities. From fraud to threat, from sexual abuse to blackmail and drug trafficking, an immense variety of crimes can be committed through internet. The possibility for the perpetrators to easily hide their identity and the difficulties which may arise in the criminal investigations, along with the huge potential profits, all are highly tempting for many people, who decide to get involved in criminal activities using the Internet [1], [2].

Among the benefits which are brought in by the Internet, a great part of them is obtained through the Internet of Things (abbreviated IoT). The great importance of this field appears to be obvious, when we think that the IoT literally surrounds us, from the moment we wake up till we go asleep. Even more, we dare to assert that the IoT continues to accompany us while we are sleeping, as lots of devices connected to the Internet continue to function while we are asleep. This area of the Internet has some specific features, which require specific investigation methods,

* Corresponding author: ancuta.frant@uaic.ro

when a crime has been committed in this field. The specificity of the investigation`s techniques and tactics is very important, to have real chances to find the criminals.

Essentially, we aim to highlight the most important aspects regarding forensic methodology applied in cases where the IoT is somehow linked to a crime that has been committed. To reach our goal, we will first present what IoT means and what place it occupies in the Internet universe.

### 1.1 Methodology

In this paper we will present the results that we have achieved through a systematic literature review regarding the meaning of the IoT and the specificity of forensic methodology used in investigating crimes related to the IoT. We will emphasize the difficulties which can be encountered in the criminal investigations regarding IoT, as well as the differences between the so-called "traditional" Digital Forensics and the Forensics used when criminality is related to the IoT. We will analyse the results and we will draw conclusions in refer to the forensic challenges regarding the IoT.

### 1.2 Results

The order in which we choose to present the information we have found is determined by the desire to make a clear presentation of the topic under discussion. Thus, at the beginning we will present the information necessary to understand what the IoT is, highlighting the characteristic aspects of this field. Knowing the specifics of the IoT is a prerequisite to understanding the features of the IoT Forensics, features that clearly distinguish it from other forensic domains.

## 2 Defining the Internet of Things

Explained in a simple manner, the Internet of Things (IoT) is a concept that defines a world where all objects (cars, household appliances, lighting systems, mobile devices etc.) are connected to each other through the Internet or another communication network. The IoT is not only based on computers to exist. Each object, and even the human body, can become a part of IoT if equipped with certain electronic components. The objects which are a part of the IoT must fulfil two conditions: 1.) the object must be able to capture data, usually through sensors; 2). the object must be able to transmit this data elsewhere through the Internet or through another network [3]. According to industry analysts, in the year 2019 there were approximately 8.6 billion IoT devices and, at the end of the year 2022 and in the beginning of the year 2023, there are approximately 13.1 billion IoT devices, with 130 new devices connecting every second. Experts forecast that, in the year 2030, there will be approximately 30 billion connected devices in the IoT network [4], [5].

It is important to highlight that, although the name of the field is Internet of Things, the concept refers to the devices connected through a network, which may or may not be the Internet [6].

Basically, the IoT is a huge network of connected devices which collect and analyse data and perform different tasks in an autonomous manner. The great development of IoT has been facilitated by the improvement of communication technologies (like 5G) and data analysis systems (which use Artificial Intelligence – AI and Machine Learning). All these elements bring a high connectivity and a precise ability to collect and to analyse data, in real time. This enables IoT to apply for a great category of objects, from light, wearable ones (smartphones, smartwatches) to smart cars, smart city infrastructure and smart public utilities (leading to the so-called "smart cities") and industrial equipment [5]. Also, smart services have greatly benefited from IoT. IoT has virtual limitless possibilities, as it can be implemented for an extremely high range of purposes, sometimes in surprising areas. For example, IoT is being used in agriculture, leading to the so-called "smart agriculture". In this domain, IoT applies by monitoring the fields with dedicated sensors, which indicate exactly how much watering and fertilization is needed, depending on the data gathered about a certain field. This helps to obtain better crops, as well as leading to a sustainable agriculture, as water and fertilizers are not wasted, but used only when they are needed [5]. Also, IoT is already used for pollution control, energy saving, smart transportation, and smart industries [7]. Even electronic cigarettes can be a part of the IoT. Overall, it seems that nothing can be surprising in the IoT era, and we can expect that IoT is applied in areas we could have never thought it could be used.

But how did it all begin? The use of connected devices which gather and analyse data in real-time has been a reality for a few decades before the exponential growth of the IoT. For example, smart alarm cars, coordinated traffic lights, electronic wristwatches (to monitor heartbeat) have been in use for some time now [5]. The first encouraging results obtained through such devices certainly determined people to obtain even more benefits. This desire has been also fuelled by favourable conditions, like the evolution of technology and the decrease of the costs of the components. In the evolution of the IoT, researchers have identified three generations: "the first one of tagged objects; the second one of things interconnection through web technologies; the third one of social objects, semantic data representation, and cloud of things" [8].

In search for a definition of the IoT, it is important to pay attention to the definitions given by official authorities. This is why we want to mention the definition given by the European Parliament, which states that "The Internet of Things (IoT) refers to a distributed network connecting physical objects that are capable of sensing or acting on their environment and able to communicate with each other, other machines, or computers. The data these devices report can be collected and analysed to reveal insights and suggest actions that will produce cost savings, increase efficiency, or improve products and services." [9]

It is important to mention that, in some papers, there are specific views (and, hence, definitions), about some elements of the IoT. For example, in *the Report from the Commission to the Council and the European Parliament: Final report - sector inquiry into consumer Internet of Things*, "smart devices" are defined as "wireless electronic consumer Internet of Things devices, such as wearable devices, smart speakers and other smart home devices, capable of connecting to other devices or networks, exchanging data with them, and operating to some extent interactively and autonomously. This definition does not include smart mobile devices (i.e., smartphones and tablets)" [10]. We notice that, in this report, the term "smart device" has a narrower meaning that it is usually understood.

The term Internet of Things has been linked to various concepts and technologies, and sometimes the use of the term has not been very precise. Some authors show that "in spite of its huge success, what IoT really represents is not completely clear" [8]. The evasive meaning associated by some authors with the IoT (especially in the beginning of its use, but not only then) may imply that it is possible that there is a widespread misunderstanding regarding the meaning of the concept. Some authors point out that the IoT is just related to *Radio frequency identification system* (RFID), while others believe it is a web of sensors. Also, some consider that IoT is a sort of Machine-to-Machine communication. Although there is not a unanimous understanding of the IoT, industry takes benefits from the popularity of IoT, due to its solution-oriented profile, which makes it very appropriate to the consumer market. Overall, the scientific literature does not bring much in terms of clarifying the meaning of IoT, as authors offer definitions which are often in discordance [8]. A first step to clarify the significance of the IoT is to understand the differences between IoT and other similar terms.

## 3 Separating the Internet of Things from similar concepts

The IoT is similar to other concepts, and, in the following lines, we will present some of these concepts, namely Internet, Machine to Machine (M2M), Industrial Internet, Industrial Internet of Things (IIoT), Web of Things, Internet of Everything (IoE).

*Internet* is defined by the fact that connections are only made between people, but this simple assertation does not cover all the implications of the Internet. However, the simplicity of such a definition helps to understand what Internet means in opposition to other similar concepts. In the scientific literature there is not unanimity regarding the definition of the Internet. Many authors present the Internet in material terms, as a combination of hardware and software, and see the evolution of the Internet as the spread of these technologies, in space and time. Some authors argue that it is not a problem that many definitions exist but warn that "historians should be aware of the politics of the definitions they use" [11].

*Machine to Machine (M2M)* communication is a communication technology defined by the fact that many smart devices can "autonomously communicate with each other and make collaborative decisions without direct human intervention" [12].

*Industrial Internet* refers to the integration and linking of big data, analytical tools, and wireless networks with physical and industrial equipment [13]. Industrial Internet "is a promising technology combining industrial systems with Internet connectivity to significantly improve the product efficiency and reduce production cost by cooperating with intelligent devices, in which the advanced computing, big data analysis and intelligent perception techniques have been involved" [14]. Unlike Machine to Machine, the Industrial Internet includes not only the connections between machines, but also human interfaces [3].

*Industrial Internet of Things (IIoT)* "refers to the use of smart sensors, actuators, fast communication protocols, and efficient cybersecurity mechanisms to improve industrial processes and applications" [15].

*Web of Things (WoT)* is a concept which refers to the possibility that everyday objects are fully integrated with the Web [16].

*Internet of Everything (IoE)*, although a rather vague concept, refers to all connections that can be imagined, between people, things, data, and processes, with the purpose to offer better experiences and to lead to smarter decisions. The IoE promises to bring fundamental changes to our lives, redefining the way we interact, the way we work, along with a wide range of other benefits [17].

## 4 The deeper meanings of the term Internet of Things

The term *Internet of Things* has been first officially used by Kevin Ashton. He used it as a title of a presentation he made at Procter & Gamble (P&G), in 1999. Through this term, Ashton referred to the network which connects people and objects around them. As it can be seen from the previous information in this article, in the present day, the term is often defined by letting apart the human factor, as it roughly points out to the connection between objects. It is important to say that, in the vision of its creator, the term *Internet of Things* has a slightly different meaning, as we will further show [18].

In 2009, ten years after Ashton first used the term, he highlights that, when he referred to the *Internet of Things* in 1999, he wanted to point out that computers (and other technical devices) need to grow their independence from humans in what regards data collection. He had noticed, at the time when he first used the term, that computers, smart devices, and Internet itself were all depending on humans. In other words, all the information existing on the Internet was, somehow, created by human beings (for example, by taking a picture, typing a letter, or pressing a button). Ashton pointed out that humans are not very good at collecting data, because of specific human features (they don`t have enough attention or precision) and/or because they do not have very much time at their disposal to dedicate it to gathering information complex enough. It is normal for people to not be able to pay enough attention to recording data or to analyse ideas, because real human life and society are based on things, not on information or ideas. In an eloquent example, Ashton points out that humans cannot survive by eating bits or use them as fuel. This is why Ashton expressed his desire that computers become less dependent on people in the process of collecting data. Through this, Ashton believes that we could "reduce waste, lost and cost" [18].

Ashton notices that, ten years after the first use of the term *Internet of Things*, great improvement has been made in empowering computers to gather data by themselves. Now, computers have a very good understanding of the world, without help from humans. But, still, we must deepen our knowledge about what computers can do. Kevin Ashton confidently states that "The Internet of Things has the potential to change the world, just as the Internet did. Maybe even more so." [18]

Furthermore, it is not only about what computers can do, but also about the future implications of the growing *Internet of Things*. The impact is so great, that the European Commission launched a consumer IoT inquiry in 2020, as part of the European Commission digital strategy. The purpose of this inquiry was to obtain a better understanding of what does the *consumer IoT* mean, how does competition work in this domain and what problems may arise concerning competition, and which are the directions of evolution for the consumer IoT. In the final report of this inquiry, published in 2022, it is stated that a growing number of devices and services are becoming part of the IoT and that "overall consumer IoT revenue worldwide will grow from EUR 105.7 billion in 2019 to approximately EUR 404.6 billion by 2030" [10].

## 5 The insights of the Internet of Things

The IoT creates many business opportunities. Many of these opportunities are only known to experts in this domain. Usually, the mass media focus attention on the part of the IoT dedicated to the consumer. There is no doubt that products dedicated to the consumer have an important place in the IoT, but they are only a part of it. Studies indicate that IoT has a lot to offer even to businesses for which, apparently, the IoT doesn`t have much to offer. The IoT has the potential to create important effects on every business activity, regardless the industry type. IoT can solve many problems that businesses have been facing for decades. Along with other technological developments (for example, cloud computing, smart grids, nanotechnology, and robotics), the IoT brings a significant contribution to achieving an economy characterized by increased efficiency, productivity, safety, and profit [3]. Overall, IoT has transformed the traditional way of living into something we can call "a high-tech lifestyle" [7].

We can say that, now, the IoT is no longer an isolated IT segment, but an important factor which sustain much of the world`s economy. The number of industrial activities that are not influenced by the IoT is very small, and the number of industries in which the IoT is vital for performing the specific activities is increasing [3].

Furthermore, favourable conditions must be created in what concerns the radio spectrum, meaning that it must be allocated the needed radio spectrum, in accordance with the rapid growth of the IoT. This is because Radio frequency identification system (RFID) is extremely important in the functioning of the IoT. RFID is an automatic technology which helps computers to "identify objects, record metadata or control individual target through radio waves" [19]. By connecting RFID reader to a certain terminal of the Internet, "the readers can identify, track and monitor the objects attached with tags globally, automatically, and in real time (...)" [19].

According to a study conducted by the Pew Internet Project Research, 83% of technology experts and users of the Internet agree with the idea that the IoT will have widespread benefits by 2025 [3]. The European Parliament asserts that the IoT can thus bring key contributions to implementing the European Union strategy for "smart, sustainable and inclusive growth" [9].

## 6 The essential elements of the Internet of things

Knowing the essential elements which make IoT work is important in our quest, because it allows us to better understand the risks that threaten IoT, and, further, the challenges of the IoT Forensics. This is why we will describe, in short, the essential elements involved in the functioning of the IoT.

*Distributivity* refers to the fact that the IoT works in a highly distributed environment, meaning that data is collected from different sources (the devices) and processed by several entities in a distributed manner [3].

*Interoperability* means that devices from different vendors need to cooperate to achieve the common goals. Systems and protocols must be designed in a way that allows devices made by various manufacturers to exchange data [3].

*Scalability* refers to the fact that the IoT is made up by billions of objects, which means that the systems and applications running on top of the network will have to manage huge amount of data [3].

*Resource deficit* in IoT means that both energy power and computing resources are extremely limited [3].

*Security issues* may arise in the IoT, which can be an impediment for some potential users to buy devices included in the IoT [3].

## 7 The risks faced by the Internet of Things

All opportunities offered by the IoT are linked to a certain level of risk, and, in what concerns IoT, the risks are as important as the rewards. Any object in the IoT world is an entry point through which cybercriminals can penetrate the system. This is why businesses cannot afford to enter the IoT unprepared [3].

As specialists state, the IoT brings major challenges to the human society. An important issue is related to ensuring wide choice opportunities for consumer, and this can be achieved by encouraging competition. Also, innovation must be sustained, because it can bring new technologies, which may be easier to use or may bring greater security. Open standards must be adopted, to offer equal opportunities to all the players in the market [9].

Security comes out as a major concern related to the IoT, because the large number of connected objects makes it easy to steal personal data and use it in illegal purposes. Overall, to enhance the benefits and to reduce the risks of the IoT, a balance must be kept between people`s privacy rights and the gains which can be obtained through the IoT [9].

In a world where machines are starting to replace people and become decision makers, and sensors capture data continuously, questions arise regarding security guarantees, as cyberattacks can seriously affect privacy. Studies point out that the IoT has an impact in every country and economy on planet, even in the developing world. Therefore, appropriate measures are required, especially due to the increasing role which IoT has for industries, as well as for consumers [3].

Some authors bring into discussion another risk related to the IoT. This risk may arise from a poor understanding of the meaning of the IoT, fuelled by the fact that, as we have pointed out before, there is not an unanimously accepted definition of IoT. If the IoT domain is poorly understood (in reference to its meaning, to its technologies, its purposes etc.), IoT may end up being mistrusted by its potential users, which will decrease its application in the human society [8], at least when it comes to consumer IoT.

Studies point out that, usually, IoT is threatened by malware, including ransomware; botnets and Distributed Denial-of-Service (DDoS) attacks; data theft. The phishing attacks are the cause of nine out of ten data breaches [20].

Overall, some specific features of the IoT, like wide distribution and openness, make IoT an ideal target for cybercrime [21]. This is why efficient methods must be taken, to properly respond to the severity of the cyberattacks. The urge for high security in IoT becomes even more clear as studies point out that IoT devices are usually attacked within five minutes after they have been connected to the Internet [22].

## 8 The purpose of IoT Forensics

As a response for the risks confronted by the IoT, a first step is to take protective measures against such risks (which makes the object of IoT security, a distinct scientific field). However, in some cases, such measures do not work, due to various reasons (for example, the superficial implementation of such measures by the consumers or the ingenuity of the perpetrators). In such situations, the infringement of the law must be investigated, to establish the identity of the perpetrator and the exact nature of the crime which has been committed.

The investigation of crimes committed using IoT is performed by IoT Forensics. Usually, IoT Forensics is used to respond to threats like virus attacks, mass surveillance, Denial of Service (DoS) attacks, and disruption of IoT networks [23].

It is important to mention that IoT Forensics can be used not only when a cybercrime has been committed. For example, it can be used in the investigation of a burglary, if the criminal activity of the burglar has been recorded by a video camera connected to the Internet. If the events are recorded by a video camera which has no Internet connection, the investigation is perform by "traditional" Digital Forensics.

The investigations which must be done in the IoT domain have some specific features, which differentiate them from other investigations, even from "classic" digital investigations. The necessity to apply certain methods results from the specificity of the IoT. Thus, even if IoT is depending on computer technology and on the Internet, it has some defining characteristics which bring some prominent changes in IoT Forensics, when compared to forensics applied in other technological domains.

IoT Forensics is a branch of Digital Forensics. IoT Forensics refers to the activities aimed at identifying, extracting, and analysing digital information from devices that are a part of the IoT, which means that the devices must be connected to the Internet or to another network. By comparison, Digital Forensics encompasses the finding and examination of materials found in all devices which can store digital data. The "traditional" Digital Forensics retrieves information by investigating computers, servers, gateways, and smartphones in reference to the data which they can store by themselves, independent from a network connection. IoT Forensics can search for information by analysing devices which are connected to Internet or another network, hence included in the IoT (medical devices, public monitoring devices, traffic lights, smart cars, smart home appliances etc.). IoT Forensics also differs from Digital Forensics in what regards the type of evidence which is examined. IoT Forensics analyses data available in any vendor-specific format, while Digital Forensics analyses data mostly available in electronic documents or standard file formats [23], [24].

Summarizing, while Digital Forensics is any forensic investigation dealing with digital evidence, IoT Forensics is a specialized branch of Digital Forensics which investigates devices connected to the Internet or to another communication network.

## 9 The difficulties confronted by IoT Forensics

IoT Forensics faces many challenges, because of the specificity of the IoT, which brings new problems, which do not exist in the "classic" Digital Forensics. Most frequent issues are related to huge amount of data; complicated network topology; the specificity of the devices which form the IoT; the relation between the IoT and the cloud; lack of data standardization across vendors;

difficulties in decryption; data corruption; the need to respect privacy laws. In the following lines we will give a few details about each of these potential issues.

One of the main problems comes from the fact that IoT devices generate a huge amount of data. This brings difficulties in choosing the sources of evidence which are relevant for the case, and, in establishing the amount of data which will be further used in the investigation.

Another important issue in IoT Forensics comes from the complicated network topology existing in the IoT. Recognizing the network topology of the endpoints is a complex challenge in IoT Forensics [25].

The physical accessibility of the devices can be a real problem for IoT forensic investigators. This comes from the fact that the devices connected on the same network might be in different places, and, even more, at great distances one from each other [26].

The specificity of the devices which form the IoT adds other issues to IoT Forensics. IoT is formed by a high number of devices. Most of these devices do not carry out complicated tasks, as they are designed to perform simple tasks and exchange data between them. Many of the devices which are a part of the IoT have a small amount of storage [26]. This means that the information extracted from a single device usually does not offer much evidence, so it must be coordinated with other information.

The emphasis on the relation between the IoT and the cloud is another specific aspect. This means that it is not unusual to find the cloud as the base of the IoT network, or as a companion which performs the more complex tasks [26]. Such a situation requires a specific forensic approach.

A problem for IoT forensic investigators can be the lack of data standardization across vendors [27].

Also, difficulties in decryption may cause important problems, especially because some data is heavily encrypted. If the encryption has been done with an atypical method or if the decryption token has been lost, it can be very hard to perform decryption [28].

Data corruption is another issue, as data can be corrupted during transfer or as vendors store it over extended periods [29].

IoT forensic investigations can be subject to restrictions when data protection laws and privacy laws are challenged. Some legislations allow storage companies to preserve data for a specific period and to make the data available to those who meet the legal requirements [30].

Of course, labelling such elements as difficulties may be caused by the fact that IoT is a relatively new domain, and forensic investigators have not yet found proper solutions for all the problems raised by the IoT. In other words, the present-day difficulties may be caused by the fact that "classic" forensic tools and methodologies are not suitable for the challenges raised by IoT. However, IoT forensic experts have developed various automated methods to simplify the investigation and make it more efficient. This leads to "clean" data that can be extremely useful for solving a judicial case. Furthermore, we believe that, in the future, forensic investigators will do more and more adjustments to forensic tools, according to the specificity of IoT to improve the results of the investigation.

## 10 The basic notions regarding the IoT Forensics

In IoT Forensics it is essential to trace data because this can be used as evidence in a judicial case. Depending on the level upon which the examination takes place, an IoT forensic investigation may be composed of three types of examinations, corresponding to the structure where data is sought, namely the device, the network, or the cloud. This means that, basically, IoT Forensics implies a combination of three fields: IoT Device Level Forensics, Network Forensics, and Cloud Forensics [31].

IoT Device Level Forensics refers to collecting evidence directly from the device. This process is often hard to accomplish, because of the wide variety of hardware and functionalities, and because some devices store information only for a short period of time. Also, the data traces which can be found on devices may be corrupted [32].

Network Forensics is founded on the ability of networks used to transfer data to keep data traces for a period. Network Forensics tries to identify and extract information from network log, devices traffic traces and communication patterns. The process is not always prone to success, as data traces in networks are fragile and volatile. Also, difficulties may arise from the fact that networks use varied encryption methods, so investigators must use the appropriate network protocol [33].

Cloud Forensics is very important for IoT Forensics because most information collected by devices is stored in cloud. This is because the memory of the devices is usually limited. The result is that the cloud contains a massive amount of data. Cloud service vendors can provide data to those who have a legal right to ask the permission to collect evidence [31].

## 11 How the IoT Forensics works

Both IoT and IoT Forensics rely on sensors, which are installed in various smart devices (for example, a smart washing machine or a fitness tracker bracelet). These sensors collect data and, usually, the device transfers the data to the cloud. Here, the information is examined, stored, or prepared for other purposes. Because of the way that IoT works, IoT Forensics overlaps with Cloud Forensics, as the data has been transferred from the IoT devices to the cloud. As data travels through various networks and implies multiple sources, all these specific aspects lead to differences regarding the methods which are used to localize important digital evidence. Generally, any Digital forensic investigation must include provisions for multiple data formats and for multiple standards.

IoT forensic investigators usually must follow a list of six standard steps. This procedure is necessary, to maximize the results obtained through an investigation. These steps are Evidence Identification, Evidence Collection, Evidence Preservation, Evidence Analysis, Attack and Deficit attribution, Evidence Presentation [21].

*Evidence Identification*, the initial stage of the IoT forensic investigation, is very important and must be done with extreme accuracy, because the success of the whole investigation is rooted in it. This first step can be challenging, because many of the devices which form the IoT are small (for example, a medical bracelet), as they must not create difficulties for people wearing them [21]. As we have already said, most of the data collected by IoT devices is usually sent to cloud servers, because of the very limited memory of the device itself. This adds new challenges for the forensic investigation, because sometimes it is extremely hard to determine where the data is located, as it is distributed among many servers in multiple data centres [31].

*Evidence Collection* often raises difficulties, as, in most cases, it involves cloud evidence collection, and cloud data can often be located under different jurisdictions. This means that an IoT forensic investigation often involves multi-jurisdiction problems. As regards the device itself, once the IoT device has been identified, evidence should be extracted from its physical memory. As the cloud almost substitutes the storage (ROM) of the IoT devices, most of the physical information can, still, be retrieved from the volatile memory (like RAM). To collect evidence from the physical memory, "traditional" Digital Forensics recommends investigators to turn off the devices, to prevent the data alteration. But, in IoT Forensics, the practice is to try to collect evidence without shutting down the device. In other words, in IoT Forensics it is preferred to collect information through live data acquisition, although this cannot always be performed, because of the limited energy of the device [24], [34]. Specialists have developed some useful tools that can be used by IoT forensic investigators to identify and collect evidence, but these tools usually require proactive process (which means installing the software before the cybercrime is committed) [31].

*Evidence Preservation* means keeping the information that has been gathered and guaranteeing its integrity during the full process. The specificity of the IoT makes the "traditional" methods of preservation used in Digital Forensics inappropriate for IoT Forensics. Usually, blockchain solutions are being used, with the main aim to protect the evidence from cyberattacks [35].

*Evidence Analysis* is closely linked to *Attack and Deficit attribution*. These stages refer to the thorough analysis and corroboration of all the evidence, to reach a conclusion, including to identify the perpetrator. In "classic" Digital Forensics, completing these stages can be easier, because, usually, there is a limited number of suspects, as the evidence is commonly extracted from personal devices (meaning that the owner or the user of the device is easier to establish). This is not the case in IoT Forensics. Here, the huge amount of data makes it very hard to perform an end-to-end analysis. Usually, IoT devices do not store any metadata, including temporal information (such as creation or modification times), and this increases the difficulty to verify the source. Even more, as we have already said, in IoT Forensics evidence is in most cases collected from the cloud, meaning that it can be located in physical servers accessed by several users simultaneously [21], [24]. However, some solutions have been found. For example, in order to analyse the big amount of data collected from IoT, Artificial Intelligence and Machine Learning are being used [36].

*Evidence Presentation* is the last stage of any forensic investigation. Unlike in "traditional" Digital Forensics, in IoT Forensics this step may be difficult. This is because the evidence collected through IoT Forensics has usually an abstract form, which is hard to understand for those who are not specialists in IoT (no matter if they are judges or jurors). Giving such situation, the IoT forensic investigator must present the information in a form which is easy to understand for people who are not IoT experts. By contrary, if the evidence is kept in its abstract form, it may not be considered in court [24].

It is important to highlight the fact that IoT forensic investigations must respect all standard guidelines, meaning all legislation which refers to the forensic procedure, as a condition for the admissibility on the court of the evidence which has been collected [32].

## 12 Conclusions

The Internet of Things (IoT) offers many benefits to the human society, enabling people to have a life greatly improved with the help of high technologies. This is something that, for decades, only writers of science fiction literature have brought into discussion, making people dream of the wonders of such a world. Now, this kind of world has become reality. Even more, it evolves from day to day, because technologies develop very fast, creating new ways to enhance life quality using devices connected to the Internet or to another type of communication network. But IoT does not apply only to individuals. It applies at a bigger scale, in a process which seems prone to creating a high-tech human society. Many cities have already become smart, as they use IoT to solve problems related to traffic and pollution. Even agriculture is becoming smart, with IoT being used to maximize the yield and to minimize the loss. IoT is also used in various industries, helping disadvantaged regions to make significant progress towards a better economy. It looks like there are no limits for the benefits which the IoT can bring for humans, and only time will reveal the true potential of this seemingly fantastic technological domain.

There is only one problem which overshadows the promise of an extraordinary future, based on IoT. This problem is deeply rooted in the human nature and refers to the anti-social acts committed by some people. Along the history, almost every major human achievement has been accompanied by the activity of those who wanted to take undeserved benefits, using that achievement. It is, also, the case with the IoT. The great benefits which IoT bring come with a price, namely the fact that many people are willing to use IoT for malicious purposes, for their own mean interests. These people exploit the specific features of the IoT, which depends on data sharing between various devices. The same characteristics which make the IoT so easy to use by *bona fide* costumers make it an easy target for cyberattacks.

To restore the social order that has been broken by the cyberattack, special methods must be used, with the purpose of identifying the perpetrator and finding out the type of crime and the amount of the damage. These special methods are the object of IoT Forensics, which is a specialized branch of Digital Forensics. IoT Forensics works as a combination of three types of forensic methodologies, depending on the level upon it performs the investigation, namely the device, the network, and the cloud. Because it is hard to find evidence on devices and networks, most evidence is collected from the cloud. IoT Forensics faces many challenges due to various factors like: the limited memory of the devices, which usually share data in the cloud; the huge amount of data found in the cloud, which requires special methods of analysis; the multi-jurisdiction issues which may appear, as cloud data can often be located under different jurisdictions.

Despite all difficulties, IoT forensic investigators have, so far, found efficient methods, to solve judicial cases related to IoT cybercrime. Also, it is important to mention that IoT Forensics is a dynamic field, where experts are permanently seeking for new solutions, better adapted to the uniqueness of the IoT domain. The efforts of the IoT forensic investigators are, undoubtedly, worthy, because their scope is to help people to have faith in the benefits which IoT can bring. And, along with trust in the IoT, people may also gain trust in the fact that the future can, indeed, be a technological utopia.

## References

1. M. Karyda, L. Mitrou, *Internet Forensics: Legal and Technical Issues*, Second International Workshop on Digital Forensics and Incident Analysis, 3-12, DOI: 10.1109/WDFIA.2007.4299368, (2007)
2. B. Martini, Q. Do, K.K.R. Choo, Trends and Issues in Crime and Criminal Justice **512**, 1-16, DOI: 10.3316/agispt.2017556 (2006)
3. D. Savu, M. Tomescu, L. Băjenaru, Revista Română de Informatică şi Automatică, **27(1),** 5-14 (2017)
4. J. Wise, Earthweb, December 4, URL: https://earthweb.com/how-many-iot-devices-are-there/, accesed12.12.2022, (2022)
5. L.S. Vailshery, Internet of Things (IoT) - statistics & facts. Statista, August 1st, https://www.statista.com/topics/2637/internet-of-things/#topicOverview, accessed: 12.12.2022, (2022)
6. M. Shafiq, Z. Gu, O. Cheikhrouhou, W. Alhakami, H. Hamam, Wireless Communications and Mobile Computing, **2022**, 1-12, DOI: 10.1155/2022/8669348, (2022)
7. S. Kumar, P. Tiwari, M. Zymbler, J. Big Data, **6,** 1-12, DOI: 10.1186/s40537-019-0268-2 (2019)
8. L. Atzori, A. Iera, G. Morabito, Ad Hoc Networks, **56**, 122-140, DOI: 10.1016/j.adhoc.2016.12.004, (2017)
9. European Parliament, The Internet of Things. Opportunities and challenges, URL: https://www.europarl.europa.eu/RegData/etudes/BRIE/2015/557012/EPRS_BRI(2015)557012_EN.pdf, accessed: 16.12.2022, (2019)
10. European Commission, Report from the Commission to the Council and the European Parliament. Final report - sector inquiry into consumer Internet of Things, URL: https://competition-policy.ec.europa.eu/system/files/2022-01/internet-of-things_final_report_2022_en.pdf, accessed: 16.12.2022, (2022)

11. J. Abbate, Internet Histories, **1(1-2),** 8-14, DOI: 10.1080/24701475.2017.1305836, (2017)
12. P.K. Verma, R. Verma, A. Prakash, A. Agrawal, K. Naik, R. Tripathi, M. Alsabaan, T. Khalifa, T. Abdelkader, A. Abogharaf, J Network and Computer Applications, **66,** 83-105, DOI: 10.1016/j.jnca.2016.02.016, (2016)
13. J.Q Li, F.R. Yu, G. Deng, C. Luo, Z. Ming, Q. Yan, *Industrial Internet: A Survey on the Enabling Technologies, Applications, and Challenges,* IEEE Communications Surveys & Tutorials **19 (3),** 1504-1526, DOI: 10.1109/COMST.2017.2691349, (2017)
14. Q. Wei, C. Siqi, P. Mugen, Digital Communications and Networks, **6(1),** 1-13, DOI: 10.1016/j.dcan.2019.07.001, (2020)
15. S. Latif, M. Driss, W. Boulila, Z. e Huma, S.S. Jamal, Z. Idrees, J. Ahmad, Sensors **21(22):7518**, 1-45, DOI: 10.3390/s21227518, (2021)
16. D. Guinard, V. Trifa, F. Mattern, E. Wilde, *From the Internet of Things to the Web of Things: Resource-oriented Architecture and Best Practices*, in D. Uckelmann, M. Harrison, F. Michahelles, (eds) Architecting the Internet of Things, 97-129, DOI: 10.1007/978-3-642-19157-2_5, (Springer, Berlin, Heidelberg, 2011)
17. D.J. Langley, J. van Doorn, I.C.L. Ng, S. Stieglitz, S., A. Lazovik, A. Boonstra, J. Business Research, **122**, 853-863, DOI: 10.1016/j.jbusres.2019.12.035, (2021)
18. K. Ashton, RFID Journal, **22**, 97-114, (2009)
19. X. Jia, Q. Feng, T. Fan, Q. Lei, *RFID technology and its applications in Internet of Things (IoT)*, 2nd International Conference on Consumer Electronics, Communications and Networks (CECNet), 1282-1285, DOI: 10.1109/CECNet.2012.6201508, (2012)
20. Cisco Umbrella, https://umbrella.cisco.com/info/2021-cyber-security-threat-trends-phishing-crypto-top-the-list, accessed: 18.12.2022, (2021)
21. M. Conti, A. Dehghantanha, K. Franke, S. Watson, Future Generation Computer Systems **78, (2)** 544-546, DOI: 10.1016/j.future.2017.07.060, (2017)
22. B. Jovanovic, Internet of Things statistics for 2022 – Taking things apart. DataProt, May 13, URL: https://dataprot.net/statistics/iot-statistics/, accessed: 20.12.2022, (2022)
23. I. Yaqoob, I.A.T. Hashem, A. Ahmed, S.M.A. Kazmi, C.S Hong, Future Generation Computer Systems, **92**, 265-275, DOI: /10.1016/j.future.2018.09.058, (2019)
24. M. Stoyanova, Y. Nikoloudakis, S. Panagiotakis, E. Pallis, E. Markakis, *A Survey on the Internet of Things (IoT) Forensics: Challenges, Approaches, and Open Issues*, IEEE Communications Surveys & Tutorials, **22(2),** 1191–1221, DOI: 10.1109/COMST.2019.2962586. S2CID 213028057, (2019)
25. H.F. Atlam, E. El-Din Hemdan, A. Alenezi, M.O. Alassafi, G.B. Wills, Internet of Things **11**, 1-10, DOI: 10.1016/j.iot.2020.100220, (2020)
26. J.M. Castelo Gómez, J. Carrillo Mondéjar, J. Roldán Gómez, J.L. Martínez, Forensic Science International: Digital Inv., **36, Supplement,** 1-3, DOI: 10.1016/j.fsidi.2021.301114, (2021)
27. M.S. Gal, D.L. Rubinfeld, NYU Law Rev., **94,** 737-770, DOI: 10.2139/ssrn.3326377, (2019)
28. T. White, Educational St. in Mathematics, **72,** 17–37, DOI: 10.1007/s10649-008-9180-y, (2009)
29. T. Das, *Data Corruption: What is it and How to Prevent it?,* Data Management, December 23, URL: https://geekflare.com/data-corruption/, accessed: 14.01.2023, (2022)
30. M.B. Seyyar, Z.J.M.H. Geradts, Forensic Science International: Digital Inv., **33,** 1-9, DOI: 10.1016/j.fsidi.2020.200906, (2020)

31. S. Zawoad, R. Hasan, *FAIoT: Towards Building a Forensics Aware Eco System for the Internet of Things,* IEEE International Conference on Services Computing, 279–284, DOI:10.1109/SCC.2015.46, (New York City, NY, USA: IEEE, 2015)
32. J. Hou, Y. Li, J. Yu, W. Shi, IEEE Internet of Things J., **7(1),** 1-15, DOI: 10.1109/JIOT.2019.2940713, (2019)
33. U. Karabiyik, K. Akkaya, *Digital Forensics for IoT and WSNs,* in: H. Ammari (eds) Mission-Oriented Sensor Networks and Systems: Art and Science. Studies in Systems, Decision and Control, **2,** 171-207, DOI: 1007/978-3-319-92384-0_6, (Springer, Cham, 2018),
34. S. Mrdovic, *IoT Forensics,* in: G. Avoine, J. Hernandez-Castro, J. (eds), Security of Ubiquitous Computing Systems, 215–229, DOI: 10.1007/978-3-030-10591-4_13, (Springer, Cham., 2019)
35. S. Brotsis, N. Kolokotronis, K. Limniotis, S. Shiaeles, D. Kavallieros, E. Bellini, C. Pavue, *Blockchain Solutions for Forensic Evidence Preservation in IoT Environments*, IEEE Conference on Network Softwarization (NetSoft), 110-114, DOI: 10.1109/NETSOFT.2019.8806675, (2019)
36. L.F. Sikos, Forensic Science International: Digital Inv., **32,** 1-12, DOI: 10.1016/j.fsidi.2019.200892, (2019)

# The implications of cybercrime for national security

*Ioan Dumitru* Apachiței[1*], *Codrin Sîrcu* Ichim[2]

[1]Faculty of Law, Alexandru Ioan Cuza University of Iași, Romania
[2]Faculty of Law, Alexandru Ioan Cuza University of Iași, Romania

**Abstract**. This study aims to identify the general aspects concerning the elements of correspondence between the notion of cybercrime and the field of national security by analysing the regulatory and institutional framework. Electronic information concerning national security requires concrete measures for its identification and control, as its alteration, theft, or modification may constitute a source of vulnerability for the security of the State and its citizens. In this respect, the architecture of the regulatory framework we are considering concerns national security provisions and the protection of classified information.

## 1 Introductory consideration

The significant implications of information systems concerning social relations have led to the emergence of legal mechanisms to prevent and punish criminal phenomena that take advantage of the vulnerabilities of information systems. A first step in this direction was the adoption in 2001 of the Convention on Cybercrime, Ratified by Law no. 64/2004, published in O.J. no. 343 of 20 April 2004. The preamble to the Convention states that the term "computer-related crime" refers to those actions "*against the confidentiality, integrity and availability of computer systems, networks and computer data as well as the misuse of such systems, networks and data by providing for the criminalisation of such conduct*".

As the applicability of computer data has expanded, it has also become applicable in the field of national security, creating a source of vulnerability. Thus, digitising information relevant to national security requires appropriate measures to prevent and remove the consequences of cybercrime.

The *National Strategy for National Defence for 2020-2024,* approved by Parliament Decision no. 22/2020, published in O.J. no. 574 of 1 July 2020, indicates the threats that may directly or indirectly target national security, including cyber-attacks and cybercrime. Regarding cyber-attacks, reference is made to the risk of damage to "*critical information and communication infrastructures*". The Strategy's drafters also understand cybercrime to refer to the actions of criminal groups, which can consist of unauthorised access to or infection of information systems, unauthorised interception of computer data, or illicit transactions with virtual currencies [1].

* Corresponding author: ioan.apachitei@uaic.ro

Similarly, the new *Cyber Security Strategy for 2022-2027,* approved by Government Decision no. 1321/2021, published in O.J. no. 2 of 3 January 2022, identifies cyber threats from state actors as one of the essential sources of threats to national cyber security, which also affects national security. Such threats target information systems operating in the diplomatic, economic, military, and social sectors, all of which are critical to national security. Similarly, the *Strategy* unequivocally states that cyber security is "an integral part of wider national security".

The management of computer data requires the existence of a computer system, *i.e.*, a computer program that processes the data. These concepts are defined in Article 35 of Law no. 161/2003, which regulates the legal mechanisms through which computer crime is prevented and combated: "*a) computer system means any device or set of devices which are interconnected or in a functional relationship, one or more of which provides for the automatic processing of data by means of a computer program; b) automatic data processing means the process by which data in a computer system are processed by means of a computer program; c) computer program means a set of instructions which can be executed by a computer system in order to obtain a given result; d) computer data means any representation of facts, information or concepts in a form which can be processed by a computer system. This category also includes any computer program that can cause a computer system to perform a function.*" (Translated from the original version in Romanian: "*a) prin sistem informatic se înțelege orice dispozitiv sau ansamblu de dispozitive interconectate sau aflate în relație funcțională, dintre care unul sau mai multe asigură prelucrarea automată a datelor, cu ajutorul unui program informatic; b) prin prelucrare automată a datelor se înțelege procesul prin care datele dintr-un sistem informatic sunt prelucrate prin intermediul unui program informatic; c) prin program informatic se înțelege un ansamblu de instrucțiuni care pot fi executate de un sistem informatic în vederea obținerii unui rezultat determinat; d) prin date informatice se înțelege orice reprezentare a unor fapte, informații sau concepte într-o formă care poate fi prelucrată printr-un sistem informatic. În această categorie se include și orice program informatic care poate determina realizarea unei funcții de către un sistem informatic*").

At the same time, the law mentioned above also enshrines several provisions on the institutional framework with powers in the field of national security, thus Articles 39 and 40 stipulate that the Ministry of Justice, the Ministry of Internal Affairs, and the intelligence services must set up and update databases on cybercrime, as well as to carry out "*special training programmes for personnel responsible for preventing and combating cybercrime*".

## 2 Protection of state secret information

### 2.1 General framework for the protection of state secret information

The reference regulatory framework, applicable to the protection of classified information at the level of national legislation, is represented by Law no. 182/2002, Published in O.J. no. 248 of 12 April 2002. The first article of this law states that the protection of classified information is carried out by the *national information protection system*. The link between this category of information and the sphere of relations within the field of national security can be seen from the content of Article 4 of the same law; thus, classified information is protected against acts of espionage, compromise, and unauthorised access, alteration, or modification. The integrity of the systems responsible for storing and transmitting classified information is also ensured.

The notion of protection of classified information is within the legal, physical protection of persons who, by law, may have access to such information and of the sources generating classified information.

In Article 15 (b) and (d) of Law no. 182/2002, the Romanian legislator defines the terms "classified information" and "state secret information". The first term refers to "*information, data, documents of interest for national security, which, due to their levels of importance and the consequences that would occur as a result of unauthorised disclosure or dissemination, must be protected*", while the second refers to "*information concerning national security, the disclosure of which may prejudice national security and the defence of the country*". The distinction between the two terms is from general to special, in the same sense para. (1) of Article 178 of the Criminal Code indicates that "*state secret information is information classified as such*".

According to Article 236 of the *National Standards for the Protection of Classified Information,* approved by Government Decision no. 585/2002, published in O.J. 485 of 5 July 2002, the measures for protecting classified information in physical format are similar to information in electronic form. Annex 10/C of the document mentioned above indicates the primary sources of danger that may affect computer systems storing, processing, or transmitting classified information. Regarding the subject under consideration, threats of unauthorised alteration or destruction of data, programmes, or equipment, unauthorised access, interception of transmissions, and unauthorised copying of data are relevant. In this respect, the provisions of Article 288 of the *National Standards* stipulate that the media on which information is stored shall be kept in such a way as to correspond to the highest level of classification of the information, with protection always ensured.

All public authorities and institutions dealing with state secret information must take the necessary measures to protect it. In this respect, the provisions of Articles 24 and 25 of Law no. 51/1991, republished in O.J. 190 of 18 March 2014 establish that these bodies are obliged both to draw up their programmes to prevent the leakage of information, which is a state secret, and to request the support of the bodies responsible for national security.

## 2.2 General considerations regarding the correlation between cybercrime and national security from the perspective of existing incriminations in the Romanian Criminal Code

Law no. 161/2003 regulated in Chapter III of the Third Title a series of incriminations regarding cybercrime that was subsequently adopted with amendments in Chapter VI of Title VII of the Special Part of the current Romanian Criminal Code.

Cybercrime may affect national security, for example, when the purpose of the crime is to procure or transmit or disclose state secret information. In other words, cybercrime is the means of committing a national security offence. At the same time, if we consider the broad meaning of the concept of national security, we can also consider that the commission of some of the offences against the integrity of information systems and data can lead to the impairment of national security, for example, the severe disruption of the functioning of an information system (Article 363 of the Criminal Code) used within the critical national infrastructure. According to art. 3 letter a) of the Government Emergency Ordinance no. 98/2010 with subsequent amendments and additions (published in O.J. 757 of 12 November 2010), the notion of critical national infrastructure (CNI) is defined as "an element, system or component thereof, located on national territory, which is essential for the maintenance of vital functions of society, health, safety, security, the social or economic well-being of persons and whose disruption or destruction would have a significant impact at the national level as a result of the inability to maintain those functions, as well as the project of a strategic objective of national interest whose construction is imperative to safeguard the national interest".

The correlation between the security of information systems and acts that may harm national security can be seen through the role of classified information. For example, Article 4 of Law 182/2002 states that the protection of classified information aims to prevent espionage and the security of information systems and their transmission. The same perspective is also apparent from the content of the Explanatory Memorandum to Law no. 182/2002, in which the legislator expressly indicated that one of the objectives of the draft law was to "*protect classified information against espionage, compromise or unauthorized access*". It remains to be established whether the commission of both the crimes as means and crimes as purpose will be held to be concurrent or whether they will be absorbed. For example, the offence of unlawfully intercepting a transmission of computer data (Article 361 of the Criminal Code), by means of which confidential information is communicated, will be absorbed into the crime of treason by transmitting information (Article 395 of the Criminal Code) or espionage (Article 400 of the Criminal Code) in the form of procuring "*documents or data constituting state secret information*", provided that the other conditions of the criminal law are met. The perpetrator's action could represent a similar hypothesis in seriously disrupting the functioning of computer systems (Article 363 of the Criminal Code), an act which, in time of war, is "*likely to favour the activity of the enemy or weaken the fighting power of the Romanian or allied armed forces*" (Article 396(d) of the Criminal Code).

## 3 Bodies with duties in fighting cybercrime that concerns national security

At the national level, other bodies have responsibilities in the cyber security and cybercrime field, but they are separate from the institutional framework for national security. One such example is the National Cyber Security Directorate (established by Government Emergency Ordinance no. 104/2021, published in the O.J. 918 of 24 September 2021), a body under the Government and coordinated by the Prime Minister. According to Article 5 point c) point 9 and Article 20 para. (1) of Government Emergency Ordinance no. 104/2021, the provisions of the Ordinance do not apply in the area reserved for national security, but the Directorate may cooperate with "institutions of the national defence, public order, and national security system".

### 3.1 Supreme Council of National Defence

The regulatory framework governing the organisation and functioning of the SCND (C.S.A.T. in Romanian) is represented by Law no. 415/2002, published in O.J. 494 of 10 July 2002. According to Article 119 of the Fundamental Law, the central role in coordinating and organising activities in the field of national security lies with the SCND [2], defined as an autonomous administrative authority whose activity is verified by employing parliamentary control.

Regarding the protection of national security data, we refer to the provisions of Article 14 of Law no. 182/2002, which stipulates that the SCND is also responsible for coordinating programmes for the protection of classified information throughout the country; however, this responsibility is expressly stated in Article 4 of Law no. 415/2002, which lists the primary responsibilities of the Council. However, the leading role in the general coordination and control of measures for protecting state secret information falls to the Romanian Intelligence Service (RIS), according to Art. 25 para. (1) of Law 182/2002. Para. (2) of the same Article also requires the intelligence services, the Ministry of Internal Affairs, the Ministry of Justice, and the Ministry of National Defence to establish concrete measures for coordinating and controlling activities to protect classified information. The fact that governing bodies of these institutions are members of the SCND, according to para. (3) of Article 5 of Law no. 415/2002 explains how the Council coordinates measures for the protection of classified information.

An analysis of the SCND 's reports reveals several measures that directly concern the Council's role in combating cybercrime. For example, the SCND report on the activities carried out in 2009 [3] mentions the approval of the organisation of the Anti-Fraud Task Force, which had both operational powers and the power to promote legislative projects targeting the threats posed by cybercrime. The report also refers to the role of RIS in the fight against cybercrime, mainly through the National CYBERINT Centre set up in 2008 [4].

### 3.2 Intelligence Services

Intelligence services are state bodies that carry out intelligence activities to protect national security and are under parliamentary control [5]. Per the provisions of para. (1) of art. 8 of Law no. 51/1991, the Romanian Intelligence Service is responsible for obtaining internal information, while the Foreign Intelligence Service (S.I.E.) is responsible for obtaining data concerning national security from abroad. At the same time, the Protection and Guard Service (S.P.P.) ensures the protection of Romanian dignitaries and foreigners on the country's territory, namely the guarding of their work premises and residences.

The legal framework regulating the activity of the RIS is represented by Law no. 14/1992, published in O.J. 33 of 3 March 1992, the first article of which defines the RIS as being specialised in the field of national security information, and the activity of the service is organised and coordinated by the SCND and under parliamentary control. According to Article 2 of Law no. 14/1992, RIS "*organises and executes activities for the collection, verification and exploitation of information necessary to know, prevent and counteract any actions which, according to the law, constitute threats to the national security of Romania*".

Regarding the protection of classified information, the role of RIS is to protect state secrecy and prevent the leakage of such information. In this respect, the provisions of para. (1) of Article 3 of Law no. 14/1992, corroborated with art. 34 of Law no. 182/2002 provides for the following tasks of the RIS. with regard to the protection of classified information: "*shall draw up, in cooperation with the public authorities, national standards for classified information and the objectives for their implementation; shall supervise the actions taken by the public authorities for the application of the provisions of this law; shall give expert opinion on the programmes for the prevention of leaks of classified information, drawn up by public authorities and institutions, autonomous regions and companies holding such information; verify how the legal rules on the protection of classified information are respected and applied by public authorities and institutions; carry out on-the-spot checks and reviews of programmes for the protection of classified information; cooperate with the Office of the National Register of State Secret Information and the National Security Authority in all matters relating to the application of this Law; assists in the determination of targets and locations of particular importance for the protection of classified information, at the request of the heads of public authorities and institutions, economic agents and private legal entities, and submits for the Government's approval a centralised record of them; organises and is responsible, in accordance with legal provisions, for the collection, transport and distribution in the country of State secret correspondence and official correspondence of a secret nature; analyses and determines the measures to be taken in relation to complaints or suggestions concerning the way in which the programmes for the protection of classified information are applied; detects non-compliance with the rules on the protection of classified information and applies the contravention penalties provided for by law, and, when the facts constitute offences, refers the matter to the criminal prosecution authorities*".

The *National Centre Cyberint (Centru Național Cyberint)* operates within the RIS. Its role is to use information capabilities to protect technical systems concerning defence to provide relevant information to prevent, limit, and stop the effects of aggression against information systems.

Regarding the powers of the S.I.E. in the field of protection of state secret information, the existing regulations are brief; Law no. 1/1998 itself, which provides for the organisation and functioning of this public authority, deliberately omits to set out the general framework of the powers of the Service [6]. In this regard, we note that the provisions of Article 26 of Law no. 182/2002 establish that the S.I.E. is obliged to coordinate the activities and control the measures concerning the protection of state secret information with which Romania's representatives abroad operate.

All persons authorised to handle or come into possession of state-secret information are obliged to ensure its protection. At the same time, the protection of classified information, according to Article 9 (d) of Law no. 182/2002, also implies the protection of the persons who have access to this information. In this regard, by the decision of the SCND, the persons and objectives whose protection and guarding are ensured by the Guard and Protection Service are established. The S.P.P. is also obliged to organise its own activities to protect state secrecy to prevent any leakage of data or information that is not intended for the public. To achieve this aim, the S.P.P. is part of the national defence system and has a military structure, according to para. (2) of Article 1 of Law no. 191/1998, published in O.J. 402 of 22 October 1998.

### 3.3 Public Ministry – Public Prosecutors Office

The role of the Public Ministry is to protect the general interests, *i.e.*, the fundamental rights and freedoms of citizens. The *Directorate for the Investigation of Organised Crime and Terrorism,* established by the provisions of Government Emergency Ordinance no. 78/2916, published in O.J. 938 of 22 November 2016 (abbreviated to DIICOT) is also part of the Public Ministry – Prosecutor's Office next to the High Court of Cassation and Justice structure.

Per Article 2 para. (1) point f) and art. 11 para. (1) point 2 of the Government Emergency Ordinance no. 78/2016, DIICOT is responsible for prosecuting cases involving the commission of cybercrime offences and those directed against national security. In this regard, the institution's organisational chart provides for the functioning the *Section for Combating Terrorist and Cybercrime Offences*, which includes the *Service for Combating Terrorist and National Security Offences* and the *Service for Combating Cybercrime* [7].

The reports on the activities of DIICOT for 2020 [8] and 2021 [9] provide relevant information on the national development of cybercrime [7].

Thus, during 2020, 1675 new cases were registered, more compared to 1484 the previous year. Thus, the total number of cases to be solved in 2020 was 4874. A total of 267 cases were settled following an indictment or the conclusion of a guilty plea agreement, resulting in a charge of 387 defendants out of the 1335 cases settled.

In 2021, the number of new cases registered increased (by 6.03%) compared to the previous year, reaching 1776 out of a total of 5052 cases in progress. Also, the number of cases solved following the issuance of indictment or the conclusion of the plea agreement was up (by 1.12%) compared to the previous year, consisting of 270 cases and 402 defendants, out of 1623 cases solved. It is also indicated in the report for 2021 that most of the offences concern the e-commerce regime, child pornography, computer fraud and fraudulent financial transactions.

## 4 Conclusion

The digitisation of information contributes to the speed of information transmission and processing. It is a source of strategic and financial interest, which is why cybercrime is rising.

As classified information and critical national infrastructure exploit the means of storing and transmitting information, there is a means-to-an-end link between the acts that compromise information systems and the actions that may compromise national security. This link is usually achieved by absorbing the offence of means into the constitutive content of the violation of national security.

As for the institutional framework, we have shown that the national security authorities also have powers to combat cybercrime. In this respect, the acts that fall within the concept of cybercrime can potentially constitute a source of threat to national security.

## References

1. Presidential Administration, National Strategy for National Defence for the period 2020-2024, Bucharest, URL: https://www.presidency.ro/files/userfiles/Documente/Strategia_Nationala_de_Aparare_a_ Tarii_ 2020_2024.pdf, accessed: 15.10.2022 (2020)
2. T. Toader, M. Safta, Constituția României, [The Romanian Constitution], (Hamangiu, Bucharest, 2019)
3. Supreme Defence Council, Activity Report, 2009, URL: https://csat.presidency.ro/files/documente/Raport_CSAT_2009_5727ro.pdf, accessed: 15.10.2022 (2009)
4. D. Panc, Securitatea cibernetică la nivel național și international, [National and international cyber security], (Hamangiu, Bucharest, 2017)
5. D.C. Mâță, Dreptul, **9**, 76-79, (2015)
6. D.C. Mâță, Securitatea națională. Concept. Reglementare. Mijloace de ocrotire, [National security. Concept. Regulation. Means of protection], (Hamangiu, Bucharest, 2016)
7. Directorate for the Investigation of Organised Crime and Terrorism: Structure, URL: https://www.diicot.ro/prezentare/organigrama, accessed: 15.10.2022 (2022)
8. Directorate for the Investigation of Organised Crime and Terrorism, Activity Report 2020, URL: https://www.diicot.ro/images/documents/rapoarte_activitate/raport2020.pdf, accessed: 15.10.2022 (2020)
9. Directorate for the Investigation of Organised Crime and Terrorism, Activity Report 2021, URL: https://www.diicot.ro/images/documents/rapoarte_activitate/raport2021.pdf, l accessed: 15.10.2022 (2022)

# The collecting of consent to the processing of children's personal data, between volatility and disobedience

*Juanita* Goicovici[1*]

[1] Babeş-Bolyai University of Cluj-Napoca, Romania

**Abstract.** The paper addresses the problematics of collecting consent to the processing of children's personal data, observing the connection between granularity and the specificity of consent and insisting on the triple level of granularity which may be seen as applicable: (i) the granularity of the first degree, relative to the delimitation by reference to the consent granted at the formation of the main contract; (ii) secondary degree of granularity, relating to the sequencing of processing purposes; (iii) tertiary granularity, regarding the taxonomic specificity of the processing operations; in the case of children's consent, this specific protection is expected to apply particularly to the use of children's personal data for marketing or profiling purposes and to the collection of personal data when using services directly offered to children, whose capacity to exercise rights in this matter can be established in national law as beginning at the age of 16, without being able to go below the 13-year threshold, as provided by Article 8, para. (1), second thesis of General Regulation 2016/679. Related to the purposes of the processing, the data operator must inform the child, in an unambiguous and structured way, of the purposes of the processing of personal data, so that the latter were able to express the consent for each of the purposes, in a differentiated manner without being forced to accept them in their entirety, a requirement that functions as a safeguard against the gradual expansion or blurring of the clarity of the processing purposes. In relation to the holder of responsibility or parental authority, Regulation (EU) 2016/679 imposes on the data controller an obligation of diligence, in order to verify whether the holder of responsibility or parental authority has granted or authorized the granting of consent, taking into account the available technologies (as selected by the parent), which is a requirement that implies, for data controllers, the fact that they are expected to check not only the existence of consent (when processing the child's personal data), but also the provenience of this consent.

* Corresponding author: juanita.goicovici@law.ubbcluj.ro

# 1 Introductory Remarks

Children's vulnerability, in terms of personal data collecting and processing, represents a saliently problematic legal territory, constantly alimented by the increasingly augmented appetite for social media exposure, the risk-plethora of which is often ignored, either by the child or by the legal representatives of the latter (parents and tutors). This study approaches the issue of the requirement of granular consent, legitimating the processing of children's personal data and as the basis of the legitimacy of the data collecting and data processing operations in which the data controllers are engaged. The central point of this twofold approach is represented in Article 5, 1st para., let. (b) of Regulation (EU) 2016/679, which imposes additional requirements on the manner of collecting personal data, specifying that these data can be collected for specific, explicit, and legitimate purposes, without being subject to processing operations which are incompatible with these primary goals. Highly provocative, the subject of collecting the consent to the processing of children's personal data continues to generate legal controversy, especially in terms of transparency of consenting. As pointed out by recent specialised scholarly analyses [1], in the perimeter of the obligations incumbent on professionals / data controllers to transparently inform data subjects, three cardinal rules can be distinguished: (I) the resecting of the exigencies derived from principle of informational amplitude, which requires that the information provided to the data subjects is expected to be complete, without omitting essential information; (ii) the principle of intelligibility of information, which refers to resorting to a comprehensible form of providing informative details; (iii) the principle of loyalty, from which the condition of correctness of the provided information follows, as an element of contractual loyalty [2], [3]. This 'tripod' on which the obligation to inform the data subjects is placed remains in the centre of the discussions on the legitimacy of the children's data collecting and processing, as an essential pillar which can be found, with prominent outlines also in the matter of data collecting and processing [4], [5]. On the other versant of the discussions, the inferior capacity of younger children in terms of deciding on their personal data exposure generated privacy concerns, which have led the European legislator to establish a limited timeframe of a minimum of 13 years-old for the child's expressing consent to personal data processing [2], [5].

Underpinning sequential issues on the manners under which children's data collection and processing is managed in the perimeter of children accessing health services, for example, or educational services, the interrogations on the legitimacy of data processing remain complex, due to the envisaged fact that, in a plethora of cases, it can be acknowledged that the data subjects under both categories (children and parents or legal guardians) are underestimating the implications of the manner in which their data are being captured and used, nor are the latter completely conscient of the prerequisites of risks associated to children's data processing or data transfer [6].

European data protection regulation reflects a pointillistic approach to regulation of children's data collecting and processing, while allowing the national legislator to establish time limits for the validity of child's consent expressed without the assistance of the adult guardian, yet not permitting the national frame of each member-state to lower the protection standards under the limit of 13-years old children, whose consent must be replaced by the adult guardian's agreement to the personal data collecting and processing [3], [7]. Nevertheless, the optimal legal protection of children's data gained attention particularly catalysed for hypotheses in which these sets of data were altered or ported to subsequent data controllers, in a context in which these conceptual themes are continuously provocative for legal practitioners [8], [9], [15].

Accommodating the solutions on the adequacy of the processing of children' personal data on the occasion of child-oriented services, the provisions of Regulation (EU) 2016/679 on the pertinency of the parental responsibility holder's consent (excepting the cases of preventive or counselling services) are centred on the transparency exigencies resorting to easily readable language [2], [7]; particularly, in consent-based hypotheses of data processing, the adequate identification of the purposes set for data processing becomes of a more stringent nature in the perimeter of children's data collecting, even in cases in which it is the adult guardian or parent that is called to decide on the agreeing to child's data exposure [6], [10].

# 2 Specific requirements applicable to the collecting of consent for the processing of children's data

## 2.1 Assertions on children over 16 years old's consent to the processing of personal data

In the case of children's consent, the specific protection is expected to apply particularly to the use of children's personal data for marketing or profiling purposes and addressing the private information collected in hypotheses in which digital services were directed towards users under 16 years old. Their capacity to exercise rights in this matter can be established in national law as starting with the age of 16, without being allowed to lessen below the 13-year threshold, provided by Article 8, para. (1), second thesis of General Regulation 2016/679. Related to the issue of purpose selection, the data operator must inform the children, in an unambiguous and structured way [11], on the data collecting process, so that they would be able to express the consent for each of the purposes, in a differentiated manner without being forced to accept them in their entirety, a requirement that functions as a safeguard against the gradual expansion of initial purposes or altering the clarity of the processing purposes [17]. In relation to the holder of responsibility or parental authority, Regulation (EU) 2016/679 imposes on the data controller an obligation of diligence, in order to verify whether the holder of responsibility or parental authority has granted or authorized the granting of consent, taking into account the available technologies (as selected by the parent), which is a requirement that implies, for data controllers [13], the fact that they are expected to check not only the existence of consent (when processing the child's personal data) [14], but also the provenience of this consent [18], [19], [20]. The data controller's possibility to invoke the 'legitimate interest' excuse for the broader expansion of the use of children's data remains marginal and is expected to be used in a parsimonious manner. In such instances, the individual (child) user would have to learn the importance to change the account settings to 'private', otherwise permitting or facilitating third-parties access to personal information such as phone number and/or email address, thus considerably rendering the children vulnerable to malicious or malevolent actions [15], [16].

## 2.2 Parent's liability for the posting of excessive content, comprising the exposing of children's images on social media

Currently, there is no specific national legislation intended to establish pertinent general rules in case parents post (excessive) content including children's images on social media, nor is the mentioned issue specifically addressed under European Union's regulations on data protection and privacy [22]. As resulting from the judicial practice at a national level [3], in cases of shared custody, the plaintiffs were requesting that the defendants be obliged to stop posting/distributing images, photos, videos, on social media platforms, at least not without the other parent's prior consent, until the age at which minors acquire the capacity to exercise their rights to privacy, a request which has been founded admissible in a court of law [3], on considerations pertaining to the other parent's right to oppose to the excessive exposure of children's images by the parent having legal custody [3]. The main reasons for the applicant addressing the court were based on elements such as the fact that the parent sharing custody did not want children to be excessively exposed on social networks, since, in such situations, parents must give mutual permission to post photos of their children. Specifically, the judge may order the defendant (children's parent) to remove the photos of the children from parent's account on the social media platforms and forbade the defendant to post, show or otherwise distribute photos of the children on social networks, unless both parents reach a mutual agreement on the posting of each set of images.

As it has been emphasised in specialised literature [3], there is a salient distinction to be made between the hypotheses in which the dispute arose between the parents, and when the courts will be able to settle it by applying the rules regarding the content of the notion of 'parental authority' under national law, and, on the other versant of the discussion, the hypotheses when the dispute is established between the parent/parents and any other third party, even another family member (grandparents, collateral relatives etc.), the legal basis for solving the dispute concerning the use of children's data is found in the GDPR provisions [24], [25]. Doctrinal previous work established that, in the case of a dispute between parents, the dispute concerns the way of exercising the parental authority, namely the manner under which each parent decides in the interest of his/her own child. A dispute between the parents, on the one hand, and the third-party who processed the child's image, on the other hand, becomes a dispute regarding the processing of personal information [3].

The issue of clarifying the existence of the legal guardian's consent to the posting of children's images on social platforms, it has been pointed out in scholarly analyses, that these types of situations impose the clarification that, if photos are taken at the birthday parties that take place in the playgrounds, it will not suffice for the organizer to obtain the consent of the parents of the child who is being celebrated, yet will have to obtain the consent of all the other legal guardians of children who appear in the photos that the organiser (the services provider) intends to use for advertising and publicity purposes [21], [22]. The assent may be requested in advance or post-event; yet, it remains mandatory to collect this type of assent prior to the posting of images. Similarly, the publication of photos of other children, by a parent, on social networks, should be done only after the latter obtains, in advance, the consent of all the other parents/legal guardians. To the extent that the posting is made in the absence of the specified consent, should there be a parent who requests the removal of the child's image, the parent who posted the images must comply with the request. Otherwise, the controller will be expected to delete the images and to compensate the parties the privacy interests of whom has been compromised [3].

The need for recalibrating the transparency exigencies incumbent to data controllers, to adapt these exigencies to the particularities of children's level of understanding the risks and reverberations of personal data exposure on digital platforms has been accentuated by previous scholarly work [29]. Concerning the validity/invalidity of implicit (tacit) consent to the use of minors' personal data (including in cases in which the data controller invoked reasons pertaining to journalistic freedoms), several jurisprudential benchmarks were proven to be pertinently set, establishing the need for expressly-emitted consent, in hypotheses where the risks for prejudicial effects on the child's legal interests arose [23], especially in terms of respecting privacy preferences [30].

Along with the concerns for lack of transparency, the use of profiling techniques generating derived data while using as a primary source behavioral information collected from children (in the case of digital services targeting children under 16 as main users), may be identified as a pivotal risk, thus rendering more salient the need for imposing on the data controllers specific obligations, such as the duty to 'relational disclosure', implying the obligation to disclose to the users, prior to the collecting of their consent to data processing, the manner in which certain (potentially) disequilibrated general clauses have been accepted/rejected during a selected period of time; as emphasised in specialised literature [31], these aspects render 'relational disclosure' (the peer-to-peer evaluation of certain disequilibrated clauses, based on previous consumer choices) even more stringent [31]. We believe that, for consolidating the level of protection when collecting children's over 16 years old assent to the use of private information processing techniques, 'relational information' disclosure would be useful, by ensuring an indirect link with other consumers. The latter would be more attentive and cautious in making decisions should it was signalled to them, for example, through online banners, the problematic aspects noticed and contested by other consumers or even the highlighting of an acceptance/refusal percentage (for example, consumers should be presented, prior to requesting their consent, a message in which they are warned that 'This clause has been accepted by 32% of consumers in the last 3 months'). We therefore believe, especially in the perimeter of younger users, between 16 and 18 years old, that it is effective for the data subject to know how other consumers (for instance, adult consumers) have reacted to the B2C (problematically imbalanced) clause [27]. Specifically, it might be saliently relevant to disclose the history of the choices of average previous consumers, in order to ensure that minor under 18 years old would be able to analyse, compare and accept or reject the general terms and conditions, in full knowledge of the case and by referring to the factual reality, considering that the latter need to be sufficiently informed, understanding not only the literal meaning, but also the core meaning of the accepted terms [29]. Nevertheless, the numerous nuances revealed when collecting the data subject's assent [32], as well as the several progressive stages for consenting to the processing operations on which the data subject may be embarked when contracting online [33], are calling for the exposing of regulatory disquietudes which became characterizable as 'intrinsic' to the subject of children's data protection [34].

Finally, it is worth mentioning that an adequate digital literacy, although highly important and extremely vital, does not necessarily result in the responsibility to mitigate against these risks being placed on the shoulders of children, in their capacity of social platforms users, especially in terms of correctly evaluating the risks associated to privacy breaches and excessive data exposure [35].

### 2.3 Legal nuances of the data controllers' obligation of verifying the source of (parental) consent

In the case of minors, giving consent is even more problematic, due to the inherent intricacies in terms of establishing adequate control mechanisms for verifying the expressing of the parent/legal guardian's consent to data processing, for minors under 13 years old (respectively, for minors under 16 years old, under current Romanian legislation), to the extent that the consent cannot be considered validly given by the minor, the latter being deprived of the capacity to make valid decisions, thus the agreement will have to be collected from a person with parental responsibility. Practically, the solution to these problems consisted in transferring the responsibility from the child user to the parent. The last-mentioned aspect plays a decisive role in the protection of private information and privacy of minors, although often they are unclear when making decisions about their own personal information; yet, even in these circumstances, the right of the minor to withdraw his/her consent becomes incidental as soon as the age limit for legal competency is reached. GDPR imposes on the controllers an obligation of diligence to verify whether the holder of the parental legal responsibility of the parental authority has granted or authorized the granting of consent to children's personal data processing, while adapting these exigencies to the available digital technologies. Synthesized in terms of 'pertinent diligence', the data controllers' duty refers to the fact that the latter are obliged to verify not only the existence of consent, but also its source.

Reasonable processing, in terms of checking whether the user has reached the minimum age necessary to express his/her own consent or checking whether the person expressing consent genuinely acted in the capacity of legal guardian of the child/s interests, may depend both on the specific risks of the processing and on the technology used to verify the holder, respectively the consent of the parent; in most of the cases a verification by e-mail using parent/legal protector's contact data appears to suffice, although certain cases require more evidence so that the data controller can establish the existence of parental consent and the provenance of the agreement. Thus, based on the provisions of Article 7, 1st para. of General Regulation, it is worth highlighting that, if the processing is based on consent, the controller is expected to be able to demonstrate that the assent to the use of children's data processing techniques originated in parents or legal guardians freely expressed intent. The pertinency of the techniques used by the data controller when establishing child user's age or the recording of email correspondence between the controller and the parents are usually considered to be decisive in litigious contexts.

## 3 Particularities and incidental features of the collector's duties when processing children's data

Several features are used to describe the substantial sphere of incidence of the precautionary measures the selection of which is incumbent on the data controller in hypotheses in which the latter intend to process private information on under-age users, especially those precautions resulting from Recital 38 GDPR, according to which:

(i) the collecting of parents' consent remains a necessary task in cases in which private information collecting techniques are intertwined to the direct offering of digital services to users under 16 years old (respectively, to users under 13 years old in EU member-states where the national legislator reduces the time bars); for other types of services (not targeting under-age users), the data collector may resort to one of the other five fundamental choices extracted from the provisions of Article 6, par. (1), letter b) to f) of the GDPR for offering legal basis to data processing operations (for instance, the performance of contractual obligations may be selected as a legal basis for private information processing, even in cases in which the *in facto* user is a child under 16, since the service was not directly targeting under-age users);

(ii) exceptions are admissible to the above-mentioned rule in cases where the data controller, who is acting in its capacity of service provider, directly targets child users, yet the nature of the service is exempt from the supplementary (mandatory) precautionary measures, namely the service provider is offering the child preventive counselling or other type of specialised advise as a type of autonomous services targeting young users and adolescents; in these hypotheses, the recording of the holder of parental responsibility' assent would not be compulsory for the data collector / the service provider;

(iii) the types of processing operations which necessitate a higher degree of precaution for the data controller, in terms of adequacy of measures selected for ensuring the respecting of parents' choice, include the processing of private information on children serving to further elaborate personalised marketing announcements to further generate user behavioural profiles the finality of which is represented by the recourse to personalised commercial advertising; in these cases, which particularly imply the constant monitoring of the child's or adolescent's behaviour and preferences in order to create a potential profile, collecting parent's consent necessitates particular attention from the service provider; for users between 16-18 years old, when private information is processed for profiling purposes, the transparency principle and the use of clear language represent the major provocative aspects that the data collector is expected to address;

(iv) when addressing the transparency issues, it is worth noticing that, in hypotheses where the private information processing concerns a child's data, and the service providing was directly oriented towards children or adolescents, as users, there is a specific obligation incumbent on the controller, namely the duty to resort to transparent terms, formulated in plain language adapted to children's capacity of understanding, while avoiding extra-technicality or hyperabundant information, as specified in Recital 58 GDPR;

(v) the exercising of the data subject's right to oppose to further processing of private information and the subjacent right to obtain erasure of the processed data (namely, 'the right to be forgotten') is impregnated with special valences when the data subject consented to the use of the data during childhood or during adolescence, not being completely and accurately aware of the legal implications of his/her assent, as emphasised in Recital 65 GDPR.

When services addressed mixed audiences (users enrolled in different age groups), while the transparency information incumbent on the data controllers is concerned, it remains important to incorporate clear, non-abundant and easy to absorb information, using a language that is sufficiently simple for individuals in different age groups to easily digest and comprehend. Facilitating children's acquaintance to data protection and privacy rights, and familiarizing young users to accessible information may involve examples on the previous manner personal information has been used [36]. When granularity of choices is concerned, as well as the granular exercise of control over personal data, data controllers are expected to accurately describe the manner under which children may resort to data control prerogatives, namely the exercising of the withdrawal right or of the right to object to further processing, right to obtain confirmation on data storage and the soliciting of data portable formats or data erasure requests [11].

Avoiding opaque phraseology remains crucial when addressing minor's capacity of understanding pieces of information on personal data storage and data controllers are expected to adapt consistency of informative measures to the evolving capacities of the child [36].

## 4 Precautionary addressing of automated decision making concerning a child

The data controller's recourse to automated decision-making techniques (ADM) when using a child's data is restricted on grounds of the best interests of the child, as specified in Recital 71 GDPR; decisions made by solely using automated means without any human involvement, and profiling of child's preferences (profiling operations integrated in an automated decision-making process or, conversely, autonomous profiling operations) are raising issues of legitimacy; automated processing of personal data to gain a certain level of predictability for future conduct and future commercial choices, when the targeted individual is a child, represent major concerns in discussing the pertinency of security measures and the adequacy of transparent information delivered to the data subject. Using algorithms to make decisions concerning a minor, to predict a minor's behaviour or to control a minor's access to a digital service necessitates the implementing of data security measures every time IA techniques involve drawing inferences form the minor's previous preferences; these aspects become salient especially when using on-by-default settings, or failing to implement adequate transparency or 'by-design' safeguards (preventing child exploitation or abuse online), or using behaviour-assessing techniques which are not in 'the best interests of the child'.

## 5 Selecting adequate measures of collecting the legal guardians' assent

In terms of assessing the lawfulness of processing, in cases when the data controller intended to rely on 'legitimate interests' for justifying the processing of children's data as stipulated in Article 6, 1st par., letter f) GDPR, thus arguing that the processing operations were indispensable for reaching specific purposes of the legitimate interests pursued by the data controller or pursued by a third party, the legitimacy of the processing will be evaluated through the prismatic of the balanced interests: are data controller's 'legitimate' interests overridden by the interests or fundamental rights and freedoms of the child, in the capacity of a data subject whose necessity in obtaining the protection of personal data would remain essential? What would be the most adequate matrix for the informing of the vulnerable data subject on the essential rights available under GDPR, and the special features of the exercise of pre-contractual information duties by the digital services provider? Are there distinct mechanisms describing the remedies available to the child's parents / legal guardians and addressing the subject of modifications made on the general terms of providing the digital services and digital content by the professional trader (the provisions on the latter being further scrutinized and developed, in accordance with specific exigences of transparency, as described in Article 12 GDPR)? Ostensibly, the manner under which the consent of the holders of parental responsibility over processing of children's data was obtained by the data controller may be subject to codes of conduct, should these be elaborated and adopted when intended to contribute to the proper application of the GDPR standards of transparency towards the data subjects.

Data controllers are expected to obey to specific rules regarding the age threshold for solicitating parental / legal representative consent, since the age on which the child becomes legally capacitated to decide on the pertinence of involving in personal data processing operations varies between 13 and 16 years, depending on the age limits set in each EU Member State.

Implementing age-verification measures remains crucial for data controllers when processing children's data, and these measures may take the form of selecting control questions, or designing actions for the parents / legal guardians willing to approach the invitation addressed by the data controller to give assent to data collecting. The reasonableness of taken measures by the implementing of which the data controller addressed the issues of collecting parents' consent is assessed by the considering of the efforts made towards the identifying child's age and the contacting of the legal guardian. Considering the availability of technology, data controllers are expected to identify pertinent techniques when requesting the minor to provide the parents' email or mobile contact data, thus enabling explicit assent to the minor's data collecting.

Data controllers may select as legal grounds for the running of minors' data processing operations the existence of the data subject's consent or the purpose of (objective) performing of the obligations that certain mandatory normative provisions would place on the data controller; symmetrically, it can be selected as legal grounds the fact that data processing would be indispensable for the exercise by the person concerned or on the latter's initiative, of individual rights or legal prerogatives, recognized in positive law (for instance, accessing certain social services when children are targeted). The existence of the data subject's consent (minor over 16 years old or the legal guardian's assent) could not be invoked, in these cases, as a basis for the processing, since by completing and signing the declarations regarding interest in accessing social services, the data subject does not pretend to be the issuer of a genuine consent to the further processing of data (for instance, for personalized advertising and marketing purposes).

Similar prerequisites remain incidental in the case of subsequent withdrawal of the parent / legal guardian's consent to the processing of the minor's personal data, in accordance with art. 7, 3rd par. GDPR, the data subject being able to withdraw consent to the processing of personal data without affecting the legality of processing based on consent prior to its withdrawal); subsequent processing of the minor's data remains possible if based on the necessity of performing contractual obligations, without having the user's consent as a legal basis.

The using of collected data for performance purposes while engaging in direct marketing operations is covered by the provisions of art. 21 of the GDPR. Thus, in situations where the processing of children's personal data is aimed at direct marketing, the data subject (or the legal guardian, in the case of minors) has the right to object at any time to the processing, including to the generating of profiles, insofar as it is related to marketing operations directly targeting children; the consumer opposes to the processing pursuing direct marketing purposes, the possibility of further processing minor's personal data based on those commercial purposes ceases to be available to the data controller.

When the data controller or platform service provider decided to recourse to user age thresholds for accessing services, these mentioned disclaimers are not exempting the data controller from abiding to the under the GDPR standards in hypotheses where 'underage' users are directly targeted as data subjects [36]. For instance, under the provisions of art. 483 to 507 of the Romanian Civil Code, there is no rebuttable presumption on parents / minor's legal guardians acting in the best interest of the child (obviously, nor is a irrefutable presumption of this sort); therefore, it must be noted that organizations and data controllers may be able to process minor's data either on the grounds of child's vital interests where at stake (as in the case of situations presenting a certain degree of urgency) or on consideration of the sensitive nature and confidentiality of the minor's personal data. Data controllers might face the necessity of further processing available information on the existence of court orders relating to parental access or responsibility, shared custody etc., as to be able to assess the pertinence of the parent's choice on the legal treatment of child's data; this type of mission might involve non-facile tasks, in respect of the principle of data minimization, since the data controller would have to further collect personal data on the minor's legal guardians' prerogatives.

## 6 Processing data of vulnerable persons, particularly of children and the prerequisites: pre-evaluation of data-safety risks

Negative scenarios on data safety would necessitate the adapting of data security measures in order to meet the safety requirements that the data subject is legitimately expecting to be met [28].

For the data controller, the electing of pertinent storage intervals, correlated to the nature of the respective data (ordinary data *versus* sensitive data) remains crucial, the storage duration of the children's personal data having to be viewed as sparingly as possible, in order not to enter in disagreement with the generic terms of the processing, postulated by the processing purposes. At the same time, the pertinent selection, with parsimony, of the purposes of processing children's data (from the angle drawn by applying the principle of 'limitation of purposes') remains central to the discussing of pertinent measures; equally important or 'vital' in this area is the establishing, by the data controller, of sufficiently and carefully calibrated measures for data storage review (for reviewing the relevance of the preservation of children's data), so that the private information can be erased or deleted or, depending on the circumstances, by subject to anonymization [26]. Same parsimony should be manifested when deciding whether children's data would be subject to pseudonymization, and to the using of decrypting keys as means to reestablish the identifying functionality of processed data. In the perimeter of processing operations concerning children's data, a processing operation may be considered by the data controller as being "likely to result in a high risk", thus necessitating an ex-ante evaluation carried out by the data controller or on the latter's behalf, meant to assess the likelihood of occurrence for the major scenarios of data security breaches and the appropriateness of protocols established to manage these types of risks.

Running an *ex-ante* Data Protection Impact Assessment (DPIA) impacts the manner of selecting adequate means of processing, as well as the excluding or the including of purposes of processing on the list of purposes set by the data controller when deciding on the finalities and the duration or time bars for the collecting and the storage of personal information concerning children as data subjects.

Congruently, as specified in Recital 76 of the RGPD, the *ex-ante* assessment of the risks associated with the processing of minors' data would involve the granularization of processing operations or their regimentation by risk categories, starting from those that would present minor risks or medium risks and up to operations that would be likely to generate a high risk for the fundamental freedoms of the individuals targeted by the respective processing or would present a considerable risk of data exploitation with discriminatory effects; such a probability should be highlighted in the *ex-ante* evaluation reports or in the internal risk management protocols, implemented by the data controller prior to the start of minors' data collection and data storage procedures.

In hypotheses when children's data are subject to collecting operations, the defining of clear, non-evasive purposes of the processing operation should remain the aspect around which the processing operations will pivot, given that the requirement of proportionality of personal data processing expresses the necessity for an indispensable link between the objectives pursued by the data controller (especially, when marketing strategies targeting minors are used) and the means employed to achieve these objectives; such interference risks being qualifiable as exorbitant or disproportionate by reference to the principle of minimization of processing or to the commands deriving from the exigencies applicable to the processing of children's data, so as not to endanger privacy components.

Verifying users' age for emitting digital consent necessitates carefully calibrated strategies (by design and by default), while parents questioned on the pertinency of such verification measures previously "referred to neutral age gates used in conjunction with a second validation methodology while others emphasized that age gates should be designed to avoid 'back buttoning' and re-entry of dates of birth" when describing the spectrum of methods available to data controllers [36]. Intrusiveness of age-verification methods represent another vividly debated topic, since data controllers would manifest the tendency of over-loading information on the assessing of digital consent [36].

Further discussing points may address the issue of managing situations when the children declare to be under 16, in which case data controllers might consider implementing appropriate measures, such as zero collection of personal data during the minor's online session and the using of appropriate filtering (for listing search results) until parent's or legal guardian's consent is properly obtained [36]. Importantly, further expanded use of minor's personal data that where initially collected for limited purposes would be considered incompatible with the 'purpose-limitations' principle as described in art. 5, 1st par., letter b) of the GDPR, the respecting of which is incumbent on data controllers. Such prerequisites are equally important for data controllers intending to extrapolate initially selected data processing purposes, as to incorporate further processing purposes concerning child's personal information, as for offering personalized advertising messages and marketing-oriented profiling techniques which would involve the processing of children's data [37]; data controllers might be held liable for transgressing the precautionary regime applicable to the processing of 'under-age' users' personal information as 'derived data' (from the taxonomy of profiling operations). Requesting consent to the receiving online direct marketing communications targeting adolescents and children is subject to the 'granularity' and 'specificity' standards described in art. 4(11) GDPR on the definition of 'consent' and art. 7 GDPR on conditions for consent validity; yet, the peculiarities of young users' limited life experience must also be considered when calibrating consent collecting methods; importantly, assent to direct marketing communications can only be collected from individuals over 16 years, otherwise, parents 'consent becomes indispensable for further processing of these types of personal information. Users' right to object to the processing of data for direct marketing purposes will also activate in such cases, according to art. 21, 2nd and 3rd par. GDPR and to Recital 70 GDPR.

## 7 Sensitive data collected from children

The processing of sensitive data is subject to considerably stronger rigors and demands than those generally incident to the processing of usual personal data, hence the importance of a *reductio ad minimum* practiced in the perimeter of this category of processing. The peculiarity which makes processed personal information to be categorized as 'sensitive', selected from the category of 'usual' or typical personal data, as a special category, is the aptitude, ostensibly more accentuated, in these cases, to endanger the privacy rights of the data subjects, uncovering elements of their private life that could make them significantly vulnerable, subsequently placing them in the position of potential victims of discriminating decisions, damaging their reputation, facing professional/social marginalization or damaging social relations, as facts facilitated by third-parties accessing 'sensitive' information [34]. As resulting from Recital 75 GDPR, in the perimeter of processing children's sensitive information, particularly medical information and data relating to health pathologies, the severity of the privacy risks associated to these types of data processing becomes significantly higher than in the case of adults consenting to the use of their medical data.

In the context of conducting the risk assessment for the processing of children's sensitive personal data, namely for the profiling based on the processing of sensitive data which may have potential negative effects on the data subject's privacy rights, it renders necessary the selection of sufficiently pertinent and adequately tailored guarantees, while the establishing of legal remedies available to the data subject for the legal rebalancing of the privacy prerogatives remains crucial. When processed, personal data whose nature, intrinsically, implies the existence of potential risks for privacy rights, will require the selecting, by the data controller, of internal protocols regarding data processing, which allow specific protection, based on the desirability of preserving their integrity in the face of malware-type attacks or other types of security breaches, since minimizing the importance of processing could generate considerable risks to privacy rights. Similarly, it is important to highlight that either the data controller or the persons authorized by the latter are required, in imperative terms, to establish appropriate guarantees, in a consistent manner, in addition to the usual organizational measures, considering the heightened level of risks associated with the processing of children's sensitive data; thus, on a first level, the measures aimed at minimizing the amount of processing data or reducing the categories of processed data would have to be implemented accordingly to the meta-rule bearing the desiderata of minimizing the processing of personal data; for concentric reasons, it remains vital, within the perimeter of sensitive data processing, to employ technical or organizational measures aimed at ensuring that the data controller respects the principle of the integrity of the processed data, respectively the principle of the confidentiality of the processed data [35].

As postulated in the text of art. 9, 1st par. GDPR, the data controller is placed under a ban on processing data from the categories of 'sensitive' personal information, which would have the potential to be exploited in a discriminatory manner or could, in other ways, alter the exercise of fundamental freedoms; included in these categories are the data that reveal the political, trade union or religious options of the individuals, respectively their sexual orientation; on another level, the processing of genetic data and, similarly, those that exploit biometric data (being targeted, however, only biometric data exploited for the purposes of identification/establishing the identity of natural persons), respectively data that reveal aspects regarding the health status of the individuals [34].

As outlined in Recital 75 of the GDPR, the data controller's failure to assimilate additional security measures for the treatment of sensitive data, the failure to conduct or the improper conduct of the *ex-ante* impact studies on the potential risks which are located on different levels and presenting differentiable gradients, in terms of the extent and in terms of the probability of occurring, and which the processing of sensitive data could generate for fundamental freedoms, as well as slippages in maintaining the records of sensitive data processing (especially through the prism of the prohibition aimed at their non-selective processing) represent culpable behavior (impermissible actions or omissions); such actions/omissions of the data controller may generate either physical (bodily, biological) damages to the minors whose sensitive data were subject to improper processing, or emotional damages, being listed as examples of the categories of situations in which such risks inevitably affect the minor's rights, the sensitive data of whom was subject to processing, both in online and offline contexts.

Listed in Recital 75 of the GDPR are also the situations of processing by operators of minors' data or of sensitive information collected from other vulnerable categories through the prism of age or the absence of life experience that would suffice when estimating the risks associated to the data collecting. The last on the list of situations that fuel high levels of risk regarding the processing of personal information are the cases in which the processing (of sensitive data) is extensive from a quantitative or volumetric point of view, involving consistent amounts of processed data (even if coming from a limited number of minors, in their capacity of users of digital services).

## 8 Conclusive Remarks

Seen as a genuine 'cornerstone' in the legal architecture of data protection, the legal mechanism of consent withdrawing to data processing is directly connected to the fulfilment of the obligation incumbent on controllers in terms of informing the parent (in the latter's capacity of adult guardian of the child whose data are collected and processed) regarding the existence and the ways of exercising this faculty of consent retract. Consequently, the approach of the gradients of good faith in the execution of the (pre-contractual and/or contractual) obligation to inform becomes indispensable to discern the contours, not necessarily volatile, but certainly versatile, of withdrawing data subject's consent in contracts formed on virtual platforms.

The General Regulation preserves the possibility for Member States, through the adapting of national law, to opt for regulating a lower age for children's data processing purposes, of at least 13 years, and imposes on controllers the obligation of verifying in such cases that the parent has granted or authorized consent, while considering the particularities of available technologies. Therefore, after reaching the digital age, at 16 years at the latest, children themselves become responsible for the content they post on social networks, thus rendering the 'granularity of consent' exigencies even more stringent.

Addressing the issue of the 'granularity of consent' in terms of collecting and processing children's data, there is a miscellany of convergent and non-convergent answers, hence the importance of methodical approaches and of the practitioner's commitment to use clear legal mechanisms. As a rational secondarily derived argument, the necessity for a clear and unambiguous action, resulting in parent's granularly obtained assent becomes even more stringent in the perimeter of the protecting of children's data, especially on social networks, but, more largely, in B2C relationships involving personalised advertising based on profiling. Legal answers to these key issues are invariably imbued with references to the discretionary nature of the assent, namely the adult guardian/parent's decision concerning the processing of under the age of 16-child's data.

Specifically, the solutions to the interrogations on the respecting of the 'granularity of consent' principle, more stringently in the sphere of collecting children's data, are inspired or permeated with references to the general rule according to which, for any processing of children's images in an educational context or entertainment services addressed to children under the age of 16 (or 13 years old, in member-states in which the national legislator opted for lowering the time frame to 13 years old), the consent of the parents or representatives of the parental authority is required, regardless of whether the images are posted on social networks by the employer who organized the event or by the third party who took part in the event, such as the owner of the playground, suppliers or party entertainers, during educational events meant to promote children-addressed products or services.

Finally, in terms of assessing the absence of the elusive effect on civil liability for the prejudicial processing of children's data, it is worth emphasising that precautionary measures on parents' consent collecting become non-compulsory for the data controller in situations where the service provider is offering the child preventive counselling or other type of specialised advise, and these types of autonomous services were targeting young users and adolescents; in these hypotheses, the recording of the holder of parental responsibility' assent would not present a mandatory nature for the data collector / the service provider.

## References

1. D. F. Barbur, Protecția datelor cu caracter personal, 2nd edition (C.H. Beck, Bucuresti, 2002)
2. J. Goicovici, Analele Universității de Vest din Timişoara, Seria Drept, **2**, 7-24 (2019)
3. D. F. Barbur, Pandectele Române, **5**, 63-72 (2021)
4. L. Archbold, D.- Clifford, M. Paterson, M. Richardson, N. Witzleb, University of New South Wales Law Journal, **44(3)** (2021)
5. M. Arenas Ramiro, A. Ortega Giménez (eds.), Tratamiento de datos personales en centros educativos. Cuestiones prácticas, (Editorial Sepin – Servicio de Propiedad, Madrid, 2021)
6. S. Grimes, EDPL, **8(1)**, 14-18, DOI: https://doi.org/10.21552/edpl/2022/1/5. (2022).
7. J. Dolan, EDPL, **8(1)**, 7-13, DOI: 10.21552/edpl/2022/1/4 (2022)
8. J. Goicovici, Dreptul relațiilor dintre profesioniști și consumatori (Hamangiu, Bucuresti, 2022)
9. J. Goicovici, Revista Română de Drept Privat, **1**, 304-328 (2022)
10. J. Henrich, EDPL, **5(1)**, 78-79, DOI: 10.21552/edpl/2019/1/12 (2019)
11. J. Goicovici, Analele Științifice UAIC, SSJ, **Tomul LXVII/2,** 57-80, DOI: 10.47743/jss-2021-67-4-4 (2021)
12. J. Goicovici, Revista Română de Drept Privat, **2**, 399-415 (2019)
13. R. Gola, Droit du e-commerce et du marketing digital (Gualino, Paris, 2019)
14. S. Van der Hof, S. Ouburg, EDPL, **8(1)**, 61-72, DOI: 10.21552/edpl/2022/1/10 (2022)
15. I.-F. Popa, Revista Română de Drept Privat, **1**, 153-184 (2018)
16. E. Kaiser, EDPL, **6(4)**, 607-610, DOI: 10.21552/edpl/2020/4/19 (2020)
17. E. Lievens, EDPL, **7(3)**, 423-428, DOI: 10.21552/edpl/2021/3/11 (2021)

18. I. Milkaite, R. De Wolf, E. Lievens, T. De Leyn, M. Martens, Children and Youth Services Review, **129**, DOI: 10.1016/j.childyouth.2021.106170 (2021)
19. M. Macenaite, E. Kosta, Information & Communications Technology Law, **26(2)**, 146-197, DOI: 10.1080/13600834.2017.1321096 (2017)
20. N. Martial-Braz, J. Rochfeld, Droit des données personnelles. Les spécificités du droit français au regard du RGPD (Dalloz, Paris, 2019)
21. F. Mattatia, RGPD et droit des données personnelles, Fifth edition (Eyrolles, Paris, 2021)
22. M. Maxim, Răspunderea civilă contractuală în domeniul protecției datelor cu caracter personal în contextul noului Regulament general (UE) privind protecția datelor 2016/679, (Universul Juridic, Bucuresti, 2021)
23. E. Politou, E. Alepis, C. Patsakis, Journal of Cybersecurity, **4(1)**, 5-18 (2018)
24. K. Poludniak-Gierz, European Review of Private Law, **26(3)**, 297-309 (2018)
25. OECD, *Children in the digital environment: Revised typology of risks*, OECD Digital Economy Papers No. 302, OECD Publishing, DOI: 10.1787/9b8f222e-en (2021)
26. OECD, *Protecting children online: An overview of recent developments in legal frameworks and policies*, OECD Digital Economy Papers No. 295, OECD Publishing, DOI: 10.1787/9e0e49a9-en (2020)
27. ***, *Limits to Journalistic Freedom in Reproducing the Image of a Hospitalized Minor – Italian case law* Journal of European and International IP Law – GRUR International, **71(1)**, 82-87, DOI 10.1093/grurint/ikab132 (2022)
28. A. Davola, I. Querci, S. Romani, *No Consumer is an Island – Relational Disclosure as a Regulatory Strategy to Advance Consumers Protection Against Microtargeting*, SSRN, DOI: 10.2139/ssrn.4068548 (2022)
29. M. Dumitru, C. Pristavu, Revista Română de Drept al Afacerilor, **1**, 26-49 (2021)
30. M.-C. Dobrilă, Analele Științifice UAIC. SSJ, **LXVII, Supplement**, 211-225, DOI: 10.47743/jss-2021-67-3-15 (2021)
31. P. Borzykh, *Concept of Personal Data in Social Media Environment: Effect of General Data Protection Regulation and Trade Secrets Directive*, SSRN, DOI: 10.2139/ssrn (2021)
32. G. Buttarelli, EDPL, **3(2)**, 155 – 159, DOI: 10.21552/edpl/2017/2/5 (2017)
33. A. Vogel Y, EDPL, **8(2)**, 238-249, DOI 10.21552/edpl/2022/2/10 (2022)
34. J. Goicovici, Studia Universitatis Babeș-Bolyai Iurisprudentia, **67(4)**, 13-54, DOI: 10.24193/SUBBiur.67(2022).4.1 (2022)
35. T. Tombal, I. Graef, *The regulation of access to personal and non-personal data in the EU: from bits and pieces to a system?*, SSRN, DOI: 10.2139/ssrn.4304148 (2022)
36. Data Protection Commission (DPC), *Fundamentals for a child-oriented approach to data processing* (Dublin, 2021)
37. J. Goicovici, InterEULawEast: Journal for the International and European law, economics and market integrations, **9(2)**, 43-68, DOI: 10.22598/iele.2022.9.2.2 (2022)

# Competition and sustainability - the avatars of the modern world

*Lucia* Irinescu [1*]

[1]Faculty of Law, Alexandru Ioan Cuza University of Iasi, Romania

**Abstract.** Environmental protection and climate change are by far the hottest topics in contemporary competition policy. In fact, sustainability and competition often go hand in hand. All companies should compete for the most favourable and best solution for customers. In turn, consumers are immersing themselves deeper in the magic of consumption, and the pandemic period has led to the growth of online commerce in all markets. In the present study we aim to analyse to what extent consumer behaviours and competitiveness affect sustainability.

## 1 Introduction

### 1.1 The legislative batch

In December 2019, the European Commission presented the European Ecological Pact [1], through which it proposed new strategies leading to the transformation of the EU 'into a fair and prosperous society, with a modern, resource-efficient and competitive economy where there are no net emissions of greenhouse found in 2050 and where economic growth is decoupled from resource use'.

In this context, competition policy must constitute one of the basic pillars of these transformations and strengthen the transition towards a greener, more digital economy. The application of competition policy and legislation aims, as a last strategy, to contribute to the effectiveness of the European Green Deal by maintaining efficient, fair and innovative markets.

Thus, the General Directorate of Competition focused mainly on the way in which environmental and climate policies could be correlated with those existing in the field of antitrust, economic concentrations and state aid. All these efforts have been concretized by the General Directorate of Competition in an analysis named 'Competition Policy in Support of Europe's Green Ambition' [2] which provides examples of concrete reforms of competition policies.

On 4 February 2021, the Directorate-General for Competition organised a conference hosted by Executive Vice President Margrethe Vestager to discuss how competition policy can contribute to the Green Deal. '*Competition Policy is not in the lead when it comes to*

* Corresponding author: lirinescu@yahoo.com

*fighting climate change and protecting the environment – there are better, much more effective ways, such as regulation and taxation. However, competition policy can complement regulation and the question is, how could it do that most effectively*?'.

As a result, during 2021, the Commission adopted a series of measures aimed at supporting the transition to a green economy of the European Union, including: European Battery Innovation in the field of state aid and continued to approve a series of aid schemes state to the member states (Romania, Germany, Denmark, France) intended to contribute to the European objective of achieving climate neutrality by 2050, without justifiably distorting competition. In parallel, the Commission launched a series of investigations and applied antitrust and merger control rules which played a part in the transition to a green economy.

All these actions of the General Directorate of Competition are part of a wider legislative package of the European Commission, entitled 'Fit for 55?' which constitute a set of proposals for new European Union legislation aimed at achieving the 2030 climate objective and which refer, among other things, to:

- the EU system for trading emission certificates;
- EU's Effort Sharing Regulation;
- land exploitation and forestry;
- infrastructure for alternative fuels;
- the carbon border adjustment mechanism;
- the fund for mitigating the social impact of climate actions;
- ReFuelEU in the aviation field and FuelEU in the maritime field;
- standards regarding CO2 emissions for cars and vans;
- energy taxation;
- energy from renewable sources;
- energetic efficiency;
- energy performance of buildings.

These are joined by a number of other strategies aimed at tackling the environmental crisis and achieving a circular, clean and resource-efficient economy:

- A Farm to Fork Strategy for a fair, healthy and environmentally friendly food system [3];
- A new circular economy action plan for a cleaner and more competitive Europe [4];
- EU Biodiversity Strategy for 2030 [5];
- Pathway to a Healthy Planet for All. EU Action Plan: 'Towards Zero Pollution for Air, Water and Soil' [6].

Moreover, the Commission highlighted in the Report on Competition Policy 2021 [7] all the efforts of the General Directorate of Competition, underlining the fact that 'the application of the policy in the field of competition stimulates competition with a view to a post-pandemic recovery and a greener, more digital economy, more resilient and more favourable to inclusion in the EU'. In this report, the Commission says it will carry out an unprecedented review of EU competition policy to ensure that EU competition policy instruments remain future proof.

The revision of the main antitrust, merger and state aid rules will consider market developments that have transformed the way businesses operate, including the development of e-commerce and online platforms.

Antitrust enforcement ensures that businesses only enter into agreements that benefit the market at large and consumers, and that dominant businesses do not use their position in a market to eliminate competitors or exploit customers. Merger control must ensure that enough competitors remain in a market so that competition is not distorted by a merger or acquisition. State aid rules must support Member States' efforts to invest in the national economy and help businesses transition to a green economy. In this sense, we can appreciate that through the Guidelines on state aid for environmental protection and energy [8], the first steps have been taken towards achieving the climate objectives by increasing the use of renewable energy sources.

However, we must add that only the efforts of the states and the European Union are not enough. Something more is needed: businesses must understand that they must also contribute to this endeavour, through innovation and investment, in order to be able to compete better in a globalized economy that wants to be a green one. In turn, consumers must change their consumption behaviours to prepare for the transition to a greener economy.

Therefore, the competition rules will complement the 'Fit for 55' legislative batch by creating a competitive, investment-based market to ensure the transition to a green economy. The Commission has estimated that at least 30% of Europe's long-term budget will be allocated to combating climate change.

### 1.2 Revision of the rules on the definition of the relevant market

The starting point will be the definition of the concepts of the relevant market, the product market and the geographic market, which will respond to the current demands and to include the digitization of the markets, but also all the changes that have taken place in the last 20 years in the competitive environment [9]. In this sense, the Commission launched a consultation of the national competition authorities of the member states and the business environment. It also requested an external evaluation that took into account four specific aspects of market definition, namely: innovation, digitization, geographic market definition, and quantitative techniques. The definition of the market must reflect the its current demands and allow the identification of potential competitors at the local or national level.

The evidence gathered in the evaluation revealed several issues that should be updated when defining the relevant market. These include the digital ecosystem, the assessment of geographic markets under globalization, non-price competition (including innovation), the calculation of market shares, and the use and purpose of the SSNIP test (small significant non-transitory increase in price) [10].

Executive Vice-President Margrethe Vestager, responsible for competition policy, said on this occasion: 'We need to look at the market and the boundaries of the market in which companies compete (...) The basic principles of the Communication on market definition, based on the jurisprudence of the EU courts, remain sound and today. At the same time, the assessment indicates that the Notification does not fully cover recent developments in market definition practice, including those related to the digitization of the economy. We will now consider whether and how the Notice should be revised to address the issues we have identified' [11].

## 2 State Aid

The review of state aid rules is intended to support the Commission's environment, climate and energy objectives. Competition policy, and in particular State aid rules, have an important role to play in enabling and supporting the Union in meeting its Green Deal policy objectives. Thus, state aid that will ensure climate neutrality will be able to be declared compatible with the internal market under Article 107 paragraphs (2) and (3) of the Treaty of the Functioning of the European Union.

In November 2021, the Commission adopted a revised Communication on State aid rules for important projects of common European interest (the PIIEC Communication), which applies from 1 January 2022 [12]. The 2021 Communication aligns its objectives with the priorities of current EU's policies to support environmental strategies and accelerate the green transition. At the same time, in order to meet the EU's climate and energy objectives for 2030 and 2050 such as decarbonisation of industry, supporting all technologies that can implement the European Green Deal, energy performance of buildings, biodiversity, zero emissions, clean mobility, the Commission launched a series of public consultations to review State aid rules: Public consultation on the Framework for State aid for research, development and innovation [13], Public consultation on the Guidelines on State aid for broadband networks [14 ].

Also, the General Block Exemption Regulation was amended in July 2021 to allow Member States to grant State aid for the digital and green transition. The scope of the Regulation will be extended to areas such as the energy performance of buildings, recharging and refuelling infrastructure for clean mobility, efficient use of resources and biodiversity, investments in new technologies such as hydrogen and the capture, storage or use of carbon dioxide.

In February 2022, the Commission published the Guidelines on State aid for climate, environmental protection and energy 2022 [15]. The document provides guidance on how the Commission will assess the compatibility of environmental protection measures, including climate protection, and energy aid that are subject to the notification requirement under Article 107(3)(c) of the Treaty. A measure of aid can be declared compatible with the internal market if it fulfils two conditions: the aid facilitates the development of an economic activity and does not adversely affect trading conditions to an extent contrary to the common interest.

The Commission establishes the categories of state aid that are subject to these guidelines, namely:

- aids for renewable energy;
- aids for the improvement of the energy and environmental performance of buildings;
- aids for clean mobility;
- aids for resource efficiency and for supporting the transition towards a circular economy;
- aids for the prevention or the reduction of pollution other than from greenhouse gases;
- aids for the remediation of environmental damage, the rehabilitation of natural habitats and ecosystems, the protection or restoration of biodiversity and the implementation of nature-based solutions for climate change adaptation and mitigation;
- aids in the form of reductions in taxes or parafiscal levies;
- aids for the security of electricity supply;
- aids for energy infrastructure;
- aids for district heating and cooling;
- aids in the form of reductions from electricity levies for energy-intensive users;
- aids for the closure of power plants using coal, peat or oil shale and of mining operations relating to coal, peat or oil shale extraction;
- aids for studies or consultancy services on matters relating to climate, environmental protection and energy.

Recently, on the basis of these Guidelines, the Commission approved the modification of two German state aid schemes to contribute to the achievement of Germany's energy and environmental objectives and the EU's strategic objectives related to the European Green Deal.

The first scheme aims to support the production of electricity from renewable energy sources, by reaching a share of 80% of electricity produced from renewable energy sources by 2030, with a view to achieving climate neutrality by 2045 [16]. The second scheme is intended to support the production of offshore wind power in Germany [17]. In both cases, the Commission found that the positive effects of the scheme, in particular the environmental ones, outweighed any possible negative effects in terms of distortion of competition.

In conclusion, state aid has the capacity to accelerate the transition to a green economy. It is particularly important that the State aid is properly granted and does not distort competition. For example, aid in the form of research and development expenditure is essential for the energy transition, in the sense that it could contribute to the reduction of business risks and the promotion of green initiatives. So, it is noticeable that we are witnessing the transition to a new era of state aid evaluations, through the lens of environmental protection objectives.

# 3 Agreements between enterprises

## 3.1 Vertical agreements

Article 101(1) TFEU prohibits anti-competitive agreements between enterprises that have as their object or effect the prevention, restriction or distortion of competition within the common market. Article 101 (3) TFEU provides for their exclusion if they contribute to the improvement of the production or distribution of products or to the promotion of technical or economic progress, at the same time assuring consumers a fair share of the benefit obtained and which: (a) do not impose on the companies in question restrictions that are not indispensable for achieving these objectives; (b) does not give undertakings the possibility of eliminating competition in respect of a significant part of the products in question.

New market developments, such as the emergence of online markets, the development of e-commerce, sustainable development have led to the replacement of Regulation (EU) no. 330/2010 [18] with Commission Regulation (EU) 2022/720 of 10 May 2022 on the application of Article 101 paragraph (3) of the Treaty on the Functioning of the European Union to categories of vertical agreements and concerted practices starting on 31 May 2022. [ 19]

The notion of sustainability is defined in the Guidelines on Vertical Restrictions [20], in the sense that it 'includes, but is not limited to addressing climate change (for example, by reducing greenhouse gas emissions), limiting the use of natural resources, reducing waste and promoting animal welfare'. Vertical agreements that pursue sustainability objectives or contribute to a digital and resilient single market are not exempt from the application of competition rules, therefore they must be assessed on the basis of the principles set out in the Guidelines.

Therefore, the exemption provided for in Article 2(1) of Regulation (EU) 2022/720 applies to vertical agreements that pursue sustainability, resilience and digitization objectives if they meet the conditions laid down in the Regulation. Vertical sustainability agreements are not subject to express exemptions, but they may be subject to individual exemptions in accordance with the provisions of Section 8 of the Guidelines. Companies can invoke the benefit of Article 101(3) TFEU and have the burden of proving that the conditions set out in this provision are met. When it is shown that the agreement may produce anti-competitive effects, undertakings can demonstrate the existence of efficiency gains and set out the reasons why a particular distribution agreement is indispensable to bring likely benefits to consumers without eliminating competition.

For the exception to apply, the vertical agreement must meet the following four cumulative conditions:

- to produce objective economic benefits - an evaluation of the objective benefits reflected by increases in efficiency due to the vertical agreement is required. In the case of this condition, a delimitation must be made between economic benefit and technical progress. Many sustainability agreements will comply with this requirement. For example, if an agreement turns into the productions of a car with the same costs but with much lower carbon emissions, will this condition be considered fulfilled? In our opinion, the Commission's Guidelines should have clarified whether environmental benefits can be considered 'objective economic benefits' or indirect economic benefits. Over time, the Commission has appreciated that the improvement of the environment is considered a factor that contributes to the improvement of production or distribution or promoting economic or technical progress.

- a fair share of the benefit must go to consumers - they must at least be compensated for the negative effects of the agreement on prices, production and other relevant factors - environmental benefits benefit society as a whole, not just a small group by consumers. But what do we mean by 'fair share' and how can we assess whether it has reached consumers? When assessing whether consumers receive a 'fair"' share of the benefit, we might consider, for example, that the price paid after the agreement may be closer to the 'true' price of the product than before the agreement. [21]. The term "customers" includes potential and/or existing customers of the parties to the agreement.

- the restrictions on competition must be indispensable for obtaining these benefits - the Commission will examine, in particular, whether each restriction allows the production, acquisition or (re)sale of contractual goods or services to be carried out in a more efficient manner than in the absence of the restriction in question. For example, in the case of motor vehicle emissions, the Commission found that the conduct of car manufacturers Daimler, BMW and the Volkswagen group (Volkswagen, Audi and Porsche) was, by its very nature, capable of restricting competition in terms of the characteristics of new diesel car models, regarding AdBlue tank sizes and filling intervals. Smaller AdBlue tanks presented advantages in terms of use, vehicle weight (and therefore fuel consumption and CO2 emissions) and available construction space. Carmakers have conspired to stymie the full potential of a jointly developed technology to limit harmful emissions from diesel cars by signaling to each other that they will not compete to meet stricter car emissions standards than those imposed by the EU. [22]

'More specifically, Daimler, BMW and Volkswagen group reached an agreement on AdBlue tank sizes and ranges and a common understanding on the average estimated AdBlue-consumption. They also exchanged commercially sensitive information on these elements. They thereby removed the uncertainty about their future market conduct concerning NOx-emissions cleaning beyond and above the legal requirements (so called 'over-fulfilment') and AdBlue-refill ranges. This means that they restricted competition on product characteristics relevant for the customers.' [23]

- the agreement must not enable the parties to eliminate competition on a significant part of the market for the goods or services concerned

Also on the same line, the Commission's decision in the case of the biofuels cartel is also included. They can help promote cleaner transport and reduce greenhouse gas emissions and therefore play a key role in the green transition. Abengoa, one of the largest ethanol producers in the EU, coordinated its commercial behavior with other companies on a regular basis with the aim of increasing, maintaining and/or preventing the artificial lowering of benchmark ethanol levels of Platts.

Therefore, it is quite possible that anti-competitive agreements are often hidden behind green initiatives. In these situations, competition regulations must step in and act to prevent or stop them. For example, in the so-called Consumer Detergents case the Commission issued a prohibition decision under Article 101 of the TFEU against three large detergent manufacturers: Henkel, Unilever and Procter & Gamble, which tried to achieve stabilization of the market position, ensuring that none of the companies will use the environmental initiative to gain a competitive advantage over the others and that market positions will remain at the same level as before actions were taken under the environmental initiative (in particular compaction products).

First, they agreed to raise prices indirectly, that is, not to lower prices when the products were 'compacted' (*i.e.*, when the weight of the products was reduced), when the quantity of the products decreased (*i.e.*, when the volume of the product) or when collective reductions in the number of measures (*i.e.*, detergent doses) per package. Second, the three companies agreed to limit their promotional activity, which is also considered a form of collusion on prices. Third, the parties agreed on a direct price increase towards the end of 2004, which targeted specific markets and was to be introduced in order of market position, *i.e.*, the market leader would be the first to introduce the increase, followed by the other undertakings. [24] Therefore, the Commission found that their conduct has the goal of restricting competition.

All the presented cases illustrate how environmental agreements have taken existing competition instruments into account but without further in-depth assessments, often considering environmental benefits to be complementary to economic benefits but without quantifying them.

## 3.2 Horizontal agreements

With regard to horizontal agreements, the Commission approved on March 1, 2022 the content of the Commission's Communication Draft – Guidelines on the applicability of Article 101 of the Treaty on the Functioning of the European Union to horizontal cooperation agreements[25]. It should be noted that the document regulates, in addition to the most common types of horizontal cooperation agreements, those that pursue sustainability objectives, dedicating them an entire chapter (Chapter 9). The current horizontal guidelines that have been applied since 2011 are set to expire on 31 December 2022, and from 1 January 2023 the new horizontal guidelines will enter into force.

By sustainability agreements we must understand any type of horizontal cooperation agreement that genuinely pursues one or more sustainability objectives, regardless of the form of cooperation. Raise competition concerns under Article 101(1) TFEU only if they involve serious restrictions of competition in the form of restrictions by object or if they produce significant adverse effects on competition contrary to Article 101(1) TFEU. The notion of „sustainability" should be understood in a broad sense, including addressing climate change, eliminating pollution, limiting the use of natural resources, respecting human rights, promoting resilient infrastructure and innovation, reducing food waste, facilitating the transition to healthy and nutritious food, ensuring animal welfare etc.

The guidelines make it clear that agreements which pursue sustainability goals are not distinct types of cooperation agreements. In addition, if a sustainability agreement relates to a specific type of cooperation as defined in other chapters, then its assessment will be governed by those legal provisions.

In principle, sustainability standardization agreements have positive effects on competition, for the most part, but there may also be situations where they can lead to the restriction of competition by coordinating prices, excluding alternative standards and excluding or discriminating against certain competitors.

The Commission identifies three types of sustainability agreements that do not fall under Article 101, namely:

- the agreements that refer to the internal behavior of these enterprises;
- agreements on the creation of a database containing information on suppliers that have sustainable value chains, use sustainable production processes and supply sustainable production factors, or on distributors that sell products sustainably, but do not require the parties to purchase from those suppliers or sell to those distributors;
- agreements between competitors regarding the organization of sector-wide awareness campaigns or customer awareness campaigns regarding the environmental footprint of their consumption, but which do not constitute joint advertising for certain products.

However, a sustainability agreement in breach of Article 101(1) TFEU may be exempted under Article 101(3) TFEU if four cumulative conditions are met, namely:

- increasing efficiency, in the sense that the agreement contributes to the improvement of production, distribution of products or to the promotion of technical or economic progress;
- indispensability: the parties must prove that all restrictions are necessary to obtain the benefits;
- a fair share of the benefits of the agreement to reach consumers, more specifically to all direct or indirect users of the products that are the subject of the agreement;
- maintaining a certain degree of competition on the market covered by the agreement.

Consumer benefits can be individual or collective. Individual benefits can be related to use value or non-use value. Individual value-in-use benefits are those that improve the consumer's experience with the product in question and can materialize in improved quality, product diversification, lower prices, etc. Individual benefits related to non-use value are indirect benefits arising from consumers' appreciation of the environmental impact of their sustainable consumption. These refer to the voluntary and altruistic choices of consumers. For example, consumers may prefer a particular car simply because it pollutes less. These indirect benefits of non-use can be measured by surveys that show that customers are willing to pay more for these benefits. In any event, the parties to an agreement must provide convincing evidence demonstrating actual consumer preferences.

In the case of collective benefits, they can be materialized only through a collective action. For example, not all consumers may be willing to pay a higher price for a car that does not pollute the environment; but if only electric cars were to be manufactured, as a result of an agreement to phase out the polluting technology, the benefits would be felt by all consumers in that relevant market. The Commission points out that a distinction must be made here between consumers and citizens, *i.e.* when the sustainability benefits (of cleaner air in this case) are significant enough to compensate consumers in the relevant market for the harm suffered, the agreement may be exempted under Article 101(3) TFEU. In these situations, the parties to the agreement must prove that the clearly described benefits have already occurred or are likely to occur; to clearly define the beneficiaries; demonstrate that consumers in the relevant market substantially overlap with or are part of the beneficiaries and demonstrate the extent to which collective benefits occurring or likely to occur outside the relevant market will be felt by consumers of the product in the relevant market .

## 4 Economic mergers

Sustainability and climate change issues can and should be taken into account by the Commission in its merger assessment. Article 2(1) of the Merger Regulation (EC) No 139/2004 sets out the criteria that the Commission must take into account when deciding whether or not to approve a concentration. These criteria include, inter alia, 'the development of technical and economic progress, provided that this is to the advantage of consumers and does not constitute an obstacle to competition' [Article 2(1)(b)].

At the end of March 2021, the Commission published a Communication [26] through which it provided a series of guidelines on the application of the referral mechanism provided for in Article 22 of the Regulation on economic concentrations to certain categories of cases. Article 22 of the Merger Regulation of one or more Member States to require the Commission to examine, for those Member States, any concentration which is not EU-wide, but which affects trade between States and threatens to significantly affect competition in the territory. the requesting Member State or States. Although the Commission's recent policy has been to discourage referral requests from Member States, market developments, particularly in the digital economy or others where innovation is an important competitive parameter, have generated transactions involving innovative companies carrying out projects. research and development and with a strong competitive potential [27].

This situation will include all the causes where the turnover of at least one of the enterprises involved in the transaction does not reflect its current or future competitive potential and would include, for example, a new enterprise or a new entrant with a significant competitive potential that does not has yet developed or implemented a business model that generates significant revenue, a major innovator, or conducts major potential research [28]. This could also include companies whose main activity is environmental protection or sustainability and which notify the competition authorities or the possibility of a merger or safety. In their case, no specific economic value can be assigned. On the other hand, the Commission will have to take into account the environmental impact of an agreement. For example, the Commission approved, with certain conditions, in the Suez area by Veolia. The 2 companies operate in the water treatment and waste management sectors and offer a wide range of municipal and industrial services. As a result of the concentration, the Commission concluded that it would have been faced with a reduced range of service solutions, with no real bargaining power. To meet the tasks, Veolia has offered a package of commitments that includes the divestiture of almost all of Suez's French non-hazardous and regulated waste management activities and municipal water management activities to a newly created entity called 'New Suez' . Veolia is further committed to divest the mobile water services activities in the EEA, almost all of its industrial water management activities in France and part of the hazardous waste activities of Veolia and Suez.

In another case, Bayer/Monsanto [29], the Commission considered that it does not analyze environmental and climate risks in a merger, although there was widespread opposition to the agreement between the two companies from NGOs environmentalists and a wider public, based on concerns about the environment and climate change. In the Commission's "Monsanto/Bayer Letter" to the petitioners, Commissioner Vestager responded that "while these concerns are of great importance, they do not form the basis of a merger review," arguing that such concerns "are handled by my colleagues and the authorities national and are subject to European and national rules to protect food safety, consumers, the environment and the climate". [30] Specialists in the field of competition have criticized this position, in light of the fact that it is contrary to the provisions of art. 2 of the Regulation on economic concentrations. [31]

Later, in the Aurubis/Metallo case [32] Margarethe Vestager stated that: *„a well-functioning circular economy in copper is important to ensure a sustainable usage of resources in the context of the European Green Deal. This is why we carried out an in-depth investigation of the merger between Aurubis and Metallo*". One of the important aspects brought to the attention of the Commission in this case was "greening of competition policy".

Aurubis, based in Germany, is a worldwide provider of non-ferrous metals and the largest integrated European copper producer. Aurubis processes copper concentrates and copper scrap and produces copper cathodes and by-products of the copper refining process. The company also supplies copper shapes and semi-finished copper as well as copper alloy products such as flat rolled, bars, rods and wires. Metallo, based in Belgium, is active in the recycling, processing and trading of non-ferrous metals. In particular, Metallo refines copper scrap to produce copper anodes, copper cathodes, tin, lead and other by-products of the refining process.

In conclusion, we can see that merger control could become one of the most effective ways that competition policy has to promote the sustainability objectives established in the Green Deal, which would stimulate the European transition towards a greener economy.

## 5 Conclusions

Through the European Ecological Pact, the European Commission announced its intention to lead the competition provisions on the sustainability line. The efforts of the competition authorities in the member states to update their work agenda with legislative proposals based on ecological policies also follow the same direction. In this sense, we welcome the steps taken by the national competition authority in the Netherlands — Autoriteit Consument & Markt, ACM, which launched the proposal that competition assessments should focus, in the future, on the benefits for society as a whole and not only on those of to a certain group of consumers in that market.

For their part, private companies have begun to give signals that they will support these efforts either through individual or collective actions. However, companies sometimes claim that the collective initiatives they would like to undertake are prevented by competition rules. It is therefore necessary to adapt the competition rules so that the interests of society can be taken into account when assessing cooperation between firms.

## References

1. Communication from the Commission, *The European Green Deal*, COM (2019) 640 final, URL: https://eur-lex.europa.eu/legal-content/RO-EN/TXT/?from=RO&uri=CELEX%3A52019DC0640, accessed: 5.01.2023 (2019)
2. European Commission, *Competition policy contributing to the EU Green Deal*, COM (2021) 713 final, URL: https://eur-lex.europa.eu/resource.html?uri=cellar:77b87fe6-4856-11ec-91ac-01aa75ed71a1.0001.02/DOC_1&format=PDF, accessed: 5.01.2023 (2021)
3. *A Farm to Fork Strategy for a fair, healthy and environmentally-friendly food system*, COM (2020) 381 final, URL: https://eur-lex.europa.eu/legal-content/RO-EN/TXT/?from=RO&uri=CELEX%3A52020DC0381, accessed: 5.01.2023 (2020)
4. *A new circular economy action plan for a cleaner and more competitive Europe, COM (2020) 98 final, available*, URL; https://eur-lex.europa.eu/legal-content/EN/TXT/?uri=COM:2020:98:FIN#:~:text=COM%20%282020%29%2098%20final%20COMMUNICATION%20FROM%20THE%20COMMISSION,THE%20REGIONS%20A%20new%20Circular%20Economy%20Action%20Plan, accessed: 5.01.2023 (2020)
5. *EU Biodiversity Strategy for 2030*, COM (2020) 380 final, URL: https://eur-lex.europa.eu/legal content/EN/TXT/?uri=CELEX%3A52020DC0380#:~:text=COM%20%282020%29%20380%20final%20COMMUNICATION%20FROM%20THE%20COMMISSION,OF%20THE%20REGIONS%20EU%20Biodiversity%20Strategy%20for%202030, accessed 5.01.2023 (2020)
6. *Pathway to a Healthy Planet for All. EU Action Plan: Towards Zero Pollution for Air, Water and Soil*, COM (2021) 400 final, URL: https://eur-lex.europa.eu/legal-content/EN/TXT/?uri=CELEX:52021DC0400#:~:text=COM%20%282021%29%20400%20final%20COMMUNICATION%20FROM%20THE%20COMMISSION,%282021%29%20140%20final%7D%20-%20%7BSWD%20%282021%29%20141%20final%7D, accessed: 5.01.2023 (2021)
7. *Report on Competition Policy 2021*, COM (2022) 337 final, URL: https://eur-lex.europa.eu/legal-content/EN/TXT/PDF/?uri=CELEX:52022DC0337, accessed: 5.01.2023 (2022)
8. *Guidelines on State aid for environmental protection and energy 2014-2020*, JO C 200, 1-55 (2014)
9. *Commission notice on the definition of relevant market for the purposes of Community competition law*, JO C 372, 5 (1997)

10. *Commission staff working document evaluation of the Commission Notice on the definition of relevant market for the purposes of Community competition law of 9 December 1997*, SWD (2021) 199, URL: https://eur-lex.europa.eu/legal-content/RO/TXT/?uri=celex%3A52021SC0199, accessed: 5.01.2023 (2021)
11. *Competition: Commission publishes findings of evaluation of Market Definition Notice*, Press release, Brussels, URL: https://ec.europa.eu/commission/presscorner/detail/en/ip_21_3585, accessed: 5.01.2023 (2021)
12. *Criteria for the analysis of the compatibility with the internal market of State aid to promote the execution of important projects of common European interest*, JO C 188, 4-12 (2014)
13. *Communication from the Commission-Framework for State aid for research and development and innovation*, JO C 198, 1-29 (2014)
14. *Communication from the Commission: EU Guidelines for the application of State aid rules in relation to the rapid deployment of broadband networks*, JO C 25, 1-26 (2013)
15. Communication from the Commission, *Guidelines on State aid for climate, environmental protection and energy 2022*, JO C 80, 1-89 (2022)
16. SA.102084 EEG 2023 - Erneuerbare Energien Gesetz, URL: https://ec.europa.eu/competition/elojade/isef/case_details.cfm?proc_code=3_SA_102084, accessed 5.01.202 (2022)
17. SA.103069 Offshore Wind Energy Act - amendments 2023, URL: https://ec.europa.eu/competition/elojade/isef/case_details.cfm?proc_code=3_SA_103069, accessed: 5.01.2023
18. Commission Regulation (EU) 2021/1237 of 23 July 2021 amending Regulation (EU) No 651/2014 declaring certain categories of aid compatible with the internal market in application of Articles 107 and 108 of the Treaty, JO L 270, 39-75 (2021)
19. Commission Regulation (EU) 2022/720 of 10 May 2022 on the application of Article 101(3) of the Treaty on the Functioning of the European Union to categories of vertical agreements and concerted practices, JO L 134, 4-13 (2022)
20. Communication from the Commission, *Guidelines on vertical restraints*, JO C 248, 1-85 (2022)
21. S. Holmes, Journal of Antitrust Enforcement, **8**, 354–405, DOI: 10.1093/jaenfo/jnaa006 (2020)
22. European Commission, Decision of 8.07.2021, Case AT.40178, *Car emissions*, JO C 458, 16-19, URL: https://ec.europa.eu/competition/antitrust/cases1/202146/AT_40178_8022289_3048_5.pdf, accessed: 5.01.2023 (2021)
23. Press release, Brussels, 8 July 2021, URL: https://ec.europa.eu/commission/presscorner/detail/en/ip_21_3581, accessed: 5.01.2023
24. European Commission, Decision of 13.04.2011, Case COMP/39.579, *Consumer detergents*, JO C 193, 14-16 (2011)
25. Communication from the Commission, *Approval of the content of a draft for a Communication from the Commission – Guidelines on the applicability of Article 101 of the Treaty on the Functioning of the European Union to horizontal co-operation agreements*, JO C 164, 1-121 (2022)

26. Communication from the Commission, *Guidance on the application of the referral mechanism set out in Article 22 of the Merger Regulation to certain categories of cases*, JO C 113, 1–6 (2021)
27. Point 9 of Commission Communication, 31.03.2021
28. Point 19 of Commission Communication, 31.03.2021
29. European Commission, Decision of 11.04.2018, Case M. 8084, *Bayer/Monsanto*, URL: https://ec.europa.eu/competition/mergers/cases1/202150/M_8084_8063748_12985_9.pdf, accessed: 5.01.2023 (2018)
30. Petition letter in Monsanto/Bayer case, Brussels, URL: https://ec.europa.eu/competition/mergers/cases/additional_data/m8084_4719_6.pdf, accessed 5.01.2023 (2017)
31. A. Bertuzzi, , S.T. Blanco, R. Bove, L. Forestier, M. Goppelsroeder, C. Hariton, A. Impellizzeri, D. Kovo, G. Notaro, M. Ramondino, J. Tew, S. Vande Walle, T. Deisenhofer, *Bayer/Monsanto - protecting innovation and product competition in seeds, traits and pesticides,* Competition merger Brief (2), 6-12, URL: https://ec.europa.eu/competition/publications/cmb/2018/kdal18002enn.pdf, accessed: 5.01.2023 (2018)
32. European Commission, Decision of 04.05.2020, Case M. 9409, *Aurubis/Metallo Group Holding*, JO C 13 URL: https://ec.europa.eu/competition/mergers/cases/decisions/m9409_3908_3.pdf, accessed: 5.01.2023 (2020)

# The average consumer standard - an assessment of the challenges of e-commerce

*Diana-Raluca* Fofiu[1*]

[1]Faculty of Law, West University of Timişoara, Romania

**Abstract.** With the signing of the Treaty of Rome and the regulation of the single market, the European Union must continue its efforts to modernise and update the legislation governing the free trade area. It is not enough for the single market to exist, but it must be functional, competitive, and at the same time, secure and balanced, in order to support sustainable economic and social development. In this respect, greater attention must be paid to the digital internal market, which operates using new and complex instruments that can deepen the existing imbalance between the trader and the consumer. In the context of this digital asymmetry, the portrait of the average consumer needs to be analysed in relation to these new tools, as this standard generates new legislative directions and influences the way consumer protection policies are applied.

## 1 Introduction

The consumer protection legislation acts as an intermediary between suppliers of goods and services and those who want to purchase them for personal use – the consumers. However, this intermediary appears to be manifestly biased, in order to protect the economic and social interests of the buyers. Nevertheless, the road to legislation that protects a vulnerable category of people must be paved with the utmost caution. The business-to-consumer (B2C) relationship must remain an effective one. At the same time, it must not constitute an unreasonable burden on traders, but rather compensate for the intrinsic disadvantages affecting consumers, that might prevent them from having certain social and economic needs met.

The aspiration of some European countries to create a single market to achieve economic and social progress was realized in 1957 with the signing of the Treaty of Rome, which established common policies in key areas such as trade. Since then, important steps have been taken to achieve an efficient single market that serves the interests of the Member States, and efforts have been made to remove all barriers to the free movement of goods, services, capital, and people. Once the preliminary step of regulating the common market has been completed, the next steps involve constant efforts to modernize and update this common commercial area. It is therefore not enough for the single market to exist; it must be functional and highly

* Corresponding author: diana.fofiu97@e-uvt.ro

competitive to support sustainable economic and social development. A market cannot perform if the parties to the legal relationships that arise within it do not have confidence in this newly created system, so it is necessary to create a secure and accessible European trading area, to identify the potential vulnerabilities and to provide guarantees. The first section of the article aims to identify the trends governing the digital environment and the new commercial practices whose fairness and trustworthiness is in question. Once the picture of the digital internal market is sketched, it is essential to have a good understanding of the digital consumer's portrait as a beneficiary of this market. Thus, the second section examines the dynamics of the notion of consumer and the applicable standards, around which the whole consumer law policy is built. Finally, within the second section there will also be identified the elements that should be considered when assessment of the consumers' standards is made, especially in the digital world.

## 2 An overview of the digital internal market

The architecture of the digital environment is changing the relationship between the consumer and the trader. Traditionally, in 'classic' business-to-consumer relationships, the consumer finds himself in a disadvantaged position, inferior in terms of knowledge and bargaining position, in relation to the purchased good or service. Given the complexity of the tools used in the digital environment (such as innovative payment methods or commercial marketing tools), but also the peculiarities of a distance contract (lack of physical interaction with both the goods and the supplier of the goods), it is reasonable to assume that the imbalance is deepening in the digital environment. To confirm this assumption, it is necessary to analyse the complexity of the existing tools and products in the digital internal market and to examine the profile of the digital consumer, to see whether the existing digital environment generates an asymmetry strong enough to represent the basis of the current and future legislation. All the tools, communications and behaviour of the trader in the digital environment, aimed at providing or promoting goods or services, represent commercial practices under Directive 2005/29 on Unfair Commercial Practices (UCPD), and are subject to legislative censorship when they are 'produced' in a way that may influence the economic behaviour of the average consumer. Thus, current European legislation seeks to prevent traders from taking advantage of their economically superior position and greater volume of information in order to sell their products. At the other end of the scale, an absolute presumption of inferiority is established in the case of the consumer, which operates independently of the actual knowledge that the person concerned may have or the information that he or she has [1].

The law is based on the idea of fairness, which must exist not only during the contractual relationship between the parties but also before and after it, just as in the case of the obligation of good faith during the pre-contractual negotiation stage. As will be shown in the next section, fairness is usually assessed by reference to a fictional standard, that of the average consumer. However, given the architecture of the digital environment, it is essential to also consider that it subtly but significantly influences consumer reactions and can even create digital vulnerabilities. Thus, consumers can be considered digitally vulnerable when they are susceptible to commercial exploitation, which is achieved by new technologies and commercial marketing tools [2] such as algorithmic profiling, automated decisions, or behavioural analytics based on which strategic predictions are made. The problem with this terminology lies in the fact that the UCPD and Directive 2011/83/EU on Consumer Protection (CPD) use the notion of vulnerability to designate a category of people who are disadvantaged due to their intrinsic characteristics (such as age or the existence of a physical or mental disability), thus excluding external aspects (the systemic configuration of the digital environment and the way technology shapes the relationship between consumers and traders).

The architecture of the digital environment is based on the study of affective and cognitive judgments, anticipating the behaviour of Internet users to influence and direct them towards commercial decisions that satisfy the trader. Accordingly, the Commission confirms that the notion of vulnerability should be revised to also include external factors such as the specificities of the digital environment. In general, a person can be said to be vulnerable when he or she is unable to collect and assimilate information, understand the characteristics of certain products and the effects of certain marketing techniques and is therefore particularly vulnerable to making decisions that are economically disadvantageous and do not contribute positively to the person's quality of life [3]. We are therefore talking about a variable, situational concept, where people can be vulnerable in relation to one product or situation, and 'non-vulnerable' in relation to others. However, external factors do play a role in establishing the standard of the average consumer, as it will be shown in the next section.

The architecture of the choice in the digital environment raises issues of fairness in particular because of the three basic characteristics by which it operates [2]:

1. It is based on data, namely the fingerprints left by consumers online (user X is interested in buying a pair of shoes and has spent a lot of time looking at a particular retailer's website for a particular pair Y);
2. It is dynamic in the sense that it adjusts and reconfigures itself according to the information collected, trying to anticipate future behaviour in order to influence it in a certain direction (when using the search engine again to look for shoes, user X will see as first search results the website of the retailer selling pair Y);
3. It is personalized (user X may receive a personalized price offer, given his interest in pair Y).

These features reinforce the idea that the legislator's attention should (also) focus on the vulnerabilities generated by commercial marketing practices in the digital environment. The complexity and subtlety of some practices can leave the average digital consumer as exposed as a child in a 'normal', non-digital environment. Children are vulnerable precisely because they fail to understand the role and consequences of an advertisement and are more likely to react to emotional stimuli and make irrational decisions based on superficial and induced needs. Precisely the same effects can be produced by some of the tools used in e-commerce and the standard provided for in current legislation and developed by the case-law may no longer correspond to digital realities. In any case, the intrinsic traits of a given individual also dictate their ability to manage some external elements, in particular to identify and not fall into the trap of certain unfair practices. If we hit two people with the same intensity, one may bruise and feel pain ('vulnerable consumer') and the other may not feel pain and does not bruise ('average consumer'). In the context of digitization, this should not mean that the hit is illegal only as far as the 'bruised' consumer is concerned, but it should be universally labelled as illegal.

In the current legislation, a commercial practice is either presumed to be absolutely unfair (those listed in Annex 1 of the UCPD) or its unfairness must be established by an authority or by a judge, by assessing the degree of influence on the economic behaviour of a consumer prototype. In the latter case, as will be shown in more detail in the next section, a practice may be considered unfair in relation to a vulnerable consumer (such as a child), but fair in relation to the average consumer (a reasonably attentive and circumspect adult), the decisive factor being the standard reference which has been used. A digital consumer could therefore be saved from a unfair practice in two situations:

- **if it is on the list of practices considered unfair in any circumstances, namely Annex 1 of the UCPD**. Currently, the list also includes certain practices that are prevalent in the digital environment (e.g., the prohibition of false reviews or the absence of mechanisms to control the veracity of such reviews, or the obligation to mention that the ranking of the results of an online search is based on paid advertising). However, to keep pace with the new digital reality, this list should be completed. For example, it could include the application of differentiated pricing based on profiling, in particular where differentiation is done to the disadvantage of the consumer because an urgent need or particular interest in the product or service has been identified. In this case, it is the European legislator who must intervene, as the directive's completion will also have the effect of harmonizing all the laws of the Member States.

**- if the assessor considers it likely to influence consumers' economic behaviour**. In this case, since the effects of the judge's decision are limited to the borders of the Member State concerned, there is a risk of non-uniform practices at European Union (EU) level. Given the cross-border nature of businesses conducted in the digital environment, heterogeneity in this case would mean that a practice is considered fair in one State and unfair in another, which would be an obstacle to intra-community trade.

Such heterogeneity has been in the past the subject of references to the European Court of Justice for preliminary rulings: in the Clinique case, Germany held that the name Clinique used in relation to cosmetic products was misleading, as it could give consumers the impression that the products were having medicinal effects. This led the company to market its products under a different name in Germany, thereby incurring additional costs, which the court considered to constitute a barrier to the free movement of goods. Naturally, the court first examined whether the restriction was proportionate and justified by a legitimate interest, namely the protection of consumers against misleading practices which may harm their health or economic well-being. Thus, it took into account the fact that the average consumer could have realized that the product did not have medicinal properties because, firstly, that was not stated on the product and, secondly, they were available in cosmetic shops and not in pharmacies [4]. This case is an example of the risk that the UE takes when it leaves it to the courts to determine the legality of a practice instead of determining it itself by means of an European legislative act. Of course, for practical reasons, it is impossible to list all unfair practices in advance, and in this case the solution is, on the one hand, to regulate at European level the practices that are frequent in the market and which have a considerable impact on consumers, and, on the other hand, to give the judge the clearest possible criteria for assessing the impact of the other practices. In this second hypothesis, the criteria should be drawn up bearing in mind both the characteristics of the digital environment and the impact on the market in general. Applying the average consumer standard is a good solution in two respects. Firstly, it prevents over-protection, ensuring a balance between the interests of consumers and traders. Secondly, it allows the market to self-correct in relation to those practices which may harm consumers who are below the average of due diligence and circumspection required by law, in the sense that they will not buy a second time from a trader who has misled them with deceptive practices, therefore the bad reputation will drive that trader out of the market [5]. However, this standard, without clear criteria for its application, runs the risk of assessing desirable rather than actual behaviour. From a legal and economic point of view, in assessing the fairness of practices, consumer detriment should be assessed in terms of how consumers actually are and act, not how they could or should act [6].

Finally, the UCPD allows for heterogeneous assessments as it considers that the standard of the average consumer cannot be set correctly without taking into account social, cultural and linguistic factors. Therefore, a linguistic aspect may categorize a commercial practice as fair in one State and misleading in another, as was the case in the Graffione case. In this case, given that *'cotone'* means cotton in Italian, the Court held that a mark named Cotonelle could mislead Italian consumers into believing that goods marketed under that mark were made of that material [7]. In the absence of such an association between the name and the material, there would have been no case of deceptive practice. Since the Graffione judgment dates from 1996, a similar interpretation today would raise two problems. On the one hand, it contradicts the objective enshrined in the consumer protection directives, which is to create a uniform system of protection at EU level and to remove barriers to cross-border trade. On the other hand, it challenges certain characteristics of the average consumer, who is presumed to study product labels (including the list of ingredients) before making a purchase [5]. In the digital context, it seems disproportionate to oblige a trader to market products under different names in order to prevent confusion, given that online shops may target consumers in different Member States.

The digital internal market is very crowded. On the positive side, this ensures the high degree of competitiveness that the Union wants. From 2017 to 2021, global e-commerce sales have almost doubled (from $2.382 billion to $4.938 billion in 4 years [8]) and the trend remains ascendent. The downside is that in the battle for consumers' attention, the techniques being used cause consumers to act against their will and are built into the very design of the platforms (the so-called dark patterns). Examples of such practices are the placement of banners that do not offer the option to refuse the usage of online identifiers, such as cookies, or platforms that make it difficult for consumers to make decisions that are contrary to the interests of the trader (for example, in order to delete a user account on the Amazon platform, the procedure is not intuitive at all, with the person having to go to 'Help' → 'More help' → 'Contact us' → 'Something else' → 'Login and security' → 'Close my account', and then send a message to the platform asking to deactivate the account). Another example of a dark pattern is the use of font colours or sizes to direct the consumer to the merchant's desired decision, relying on the fact that the user does not have time to read every message on the website, but rather navigates intuitively and reflexively. In this respect, the concept of clickbait has emerged, which encompasses all content on the internet designed to attract attention and encourage internet users to click on a particular link.

Platforms have become particularly creative in this regard, with examples of banner ads that have integrated a design element representing a speck of dust to generate a click when the person actually intended to wipe their phone or tablet screen. One last example of cleverly designed marketing communications are ads placed in the inbox of email service users, which mimic an email very well. This example raises discussions around protection of individuals against unsolicited communications, as advertising materials stored on users' terminals have a special regime, regulated by Directive 2002/58/EC on privacy and electronic communications (ePrivacy Directive). According to this Directive, direct marketing consisting of placing advertising materials in people's inboxes can only be carried out with their prior consent, the rationale being that unsolicited advertising material appearing on users' terminals is an intrusion into their privacy. In practice, marketers capture this consent in many forms, such as by offering free products or a discount on the first order in exchange for subscribing to the company's newsletter. Although the conditions for placing advertising material by email seem clear, they made the subject of a preliminary referral to the Court of Justice of the European Union (CJEU) in late 2021. Thus, in case C-673/17 StWL v. ePrimo GmbH, the Court examined to what extent a communication for marketing purposes made through email complies with the requirements of the Directive. In fact, users of an email service received in their inbox advertisements relating to the supply of electricity by the company ePrimo. These materials were not visually distinguishable from other e-mails but were inserted among them and marked as 'advertisements'. Therefore, although the ad had the form of an email, it was not in fact clear to the referring court whether such a message fell within the concept of electronic mail, since the applicant argued that such advertisements may constitute unsolicited communications for which the express consent of the person concerned is required. The CJEU indeed held that the use of banner advertisements in such a manner is exactly the type of intrusion that the European legislature intended to prevent through the ePrivacy Directive. Therefore, the consent of the holder of the e-mail address was required for the display of this advertisement and no other legal basis was allowed. However, the e-mail service was a free service, financially supported by advertisers and users had the possibility to pay for an ad-free e-mail service. In this case, it can be argued that the user was informed in advance of the marketing practices used and consented to them when deciding to use the free e-mail service. This once again reinforces the theory that personal data has become a mean of payment for various goods or services. Consequently, the CJEU has ruled that although consent must exist, it is for the referring court to verify that this condition is met [9], and under the relevant legislation, the burden of proof of consent lies with the issuer of the advertising material, namely the trader.

The above examples of dark patterns represent subtle practices, and their categorization as unfair requires a rather difficult assessment, given that the second situation above is involved, when the assessor must analyse abstract aspects, i.e., the reaction of an imagined character to a practice with a psychological substrate that is not necessarily manifestly illegal. At the opposite end of the spectrum are those practices whose illegality is obvious. The sneak into basket technique involves inserting unwanted products into a shopper's basket. If he does not want them, he must remove them himself. The term 'products' also includes additional services, such as inserting travel insurances automatically when the consumer wants to buy airplane tickets. This practice is also common in relation to placing online identifiers in users' browsers for various purposes such as marketing. In Case Planet49, the court held that a consent cannot be considered valid if it has been given following the placement of a box expressing consent to the placement of cookies, if this box is pre-ticked, so that in case of disagreement, the user should untick it. The situation is also the same as regards the active conduct that the consumer must have if he does not want to purchase the products added by default to the basket. The Court emphasized that remaining passive cannot be an expression of valid consent, since in order to meet the requirements of clarity, specificity and lack of ambiguity, it must be the product of 'a clear affirmative action' [10].

Regulation 2022/2065 on digital services (DSR) confirms the concern of the Union's legislative bodies about these manipulative design practices. The Regulation was published in the Official Journal of the European Union on 27.10.2022, with most of its provisions to apply from 17.02.2024. This legislation defines dark patterns as practices that 'distort or significantly impair, either intentionally or through their effects, the ability of recipients of the service to make informed and autonomous choices or decisions', prohibiting platforms from containing such elements. Unfair commercial practices, on the other hand, include any act, omission, course of conduct, representation or commercial communication made by a trader, and which is directly connected with the promotion, sale, or supply of a product to consumers which, being contrary to professional diligence, is likely to materially distort the economic behaviour of the average consumer. It thus follows that sometimes dark patterns, if they originate from a trader and possess the related characteristics, may constitute unfair commercial practices, and may be invalidated under the UCPD. Such manipulative designs may also fall under the General Data Protection Regulation (GDPR), as in the case of Planet49 mentioned above. Moreover, the European Data Protection Board (EDPB) published a guide on dark patterns in social media platform interfaces in which, in addition to identifying and classifying a multitude of dark patterns, it also indicated how exactly the GDPR is incident in such cases. Thus, *'the principles of accountability, transparency and the obligation of data protection by design stated in Article 25 of the GDPR are also relevant regarding design framework and dark patterns could infringe those provisions'* [11]. For all other situations where the practice does not fall under any of the above-mentioned laws, the DSR becomes applicable, and Member States must establish and apply sanctions to platforms containing elements of manipulative design.

Every action taken online generates data and its processing is done to ensure the functionality of the platforms but also to personalize the content displayed to users. In both cases, certain data files are stored in the browser (e.g., cookie identifiers, which assign each visitor a unique string of numbers and characters). In the first case, these identifiers help e-commerce platforms to recognize a specific user to provide useful functions, such as remembering login credentials or products added to the shopping cart. Accordingly, only the platform that placed the identifiers in someone's browser after obtaining their consent may use the information stored in them (first party cookies). In the second case, however, the use of identifiers for the purpose of providing personalized advertising material is the starting point for a discussion with legal relevance, both from the perspective of consumer and personal data protection. Thus, in addition to the identifiers described above, e-commerce platforms may also place identifiers such as cookies from third party platforms, like Google (third-party cookies), which will retain information about the user's behaviour on the site. Specifically, an e-commerce platform selling books stores a Google cookie in the user's browser, which stores data confirming that the user is interested in a particular book. When the user accesses Google, he will be recognized as 'that user interested in books' and will consequently fill in the empty advertising space on the platform with an ad for products which shall interest readers. This process is known as profiling, which is defined in the GDPR as *'any form of automatic processing of personal data consisting of the use of personal data to evaluate certain personal aspects relating to a natural person, in particular to analyse or predict aspects relating to that person's performance at work, economic situation, health, personal preferences, interests, reliability, behaviour, location or movements'*. Figure 1 illustrates the phenomenon in 3 general steps:

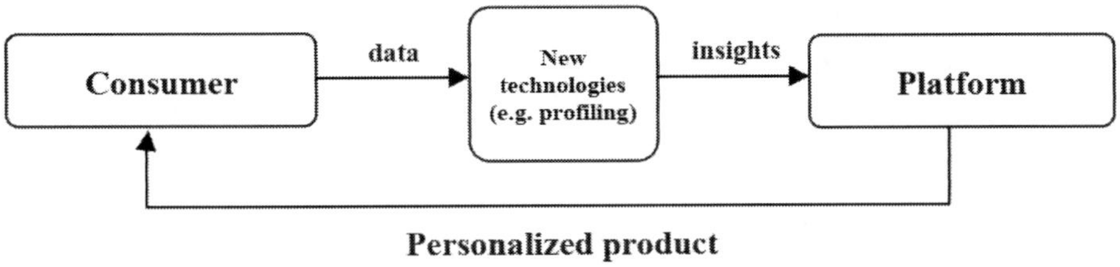


**Fig. 1.** Illustration of profiling phenomenon.

Profiling involves combining information collected through cookie identifiers (individual user preferences) with individual characteristics of each person, such as date of birth, age, place of residence, the latter being information that is personal data within the meaning of the GDPR. Thus, each user ends up with a digital *alter ego*, which is seen by marketers as a valuable product[2], and the more accurately this *alter ego* reflects the real consumer, the more likely is that the marketer's advertising will be successful. From a consumer protection perspective, this phenomenon is relevant firstly because it can generate the development of unfair practices that can influence the consumer's economic behaviour in directions that can affect him financially and secondly because it can give rise to discrimination, in particular when age or material circumstances lead to differential pricing for the same goods or services.

To highlight the scale and subtlety of these practices, it is also important to recognize that they have consequences which go beyond commercial interests. As the information that reaches an individual is filtered and adapted to match and constantly reconfirm their preferences [12], there is also recognition at the level of the EU of the effects that targeted political propaganda can have on people, with the aim of providing each user the information that is most likely to convince them, with the consequence that citizens can no longer rely on a common set of facts, but rather a harmful polarization is created [13]. While it may seem that such arguments are too extreme, it is the courts themselves that have confirmed the impact of algorithms on major political events, such as the Brexit.

As far as the protection of personal data is concerned, it represents the currency paid for certain facilities offered on the internet. Thus, 'free' services involve advertisements or even direct collection of personal data (e.g., offering digital products or services in exchange for an e-mail address and agreement to provide marketing materials). The interchangeability of price and personal data in the context of the provision of digital services has been recognized by Directive 2019/2161 (the Omnibus Directive), stating that the CPD rules should also apply under the same conditions when the price for certain digital services consists of personal data. However, particular attention should also be paid to the actors involved in the online marketing activity to establish who bears responsibility for the processing of consumer data. The trader usually outsources this activity to an advertising agency, which will take care of the dissemination of advertisements through the processes described in the lines above. In this context, who is a controller and who is a processor, within the meaning of the GDPR? Intuitively, given that the advertising agency is processing data at the request of a company that wants to promote its products or services, one might think that the agency is the processor, with the responsibility falling on the 'shoulders' of the company that determines that customer data will be used for advertising purposes. This reasoning is correct, up to a point. The margin of discretion that an advertising agency has can push it into the realm of controllers, since although the final purpose of the processing is determined by the company, the modalities of processing, the categories of data, and the places where the advertisements will be displayed, are determined by the agency. Even if the entity acts in a similar capacity as a processor, it will no longer be considered a mere processor in the terminology of the GDPR if it has a significant degree of influence over the processing arrangements [14]. When the agency and the company share the purpose and means of the processing, as is often the case for profiling advertisements, they are joint controllers and are responsible for compliance with data protection provisions.

The technological progress that has shaped e-commerce has not been ignored by the Union's legislative bodies. In 2019, the CPD, the UCPD, Directive 93/13/EC on unfair terms in consumer contracts and Directive 98/6/EC on price indication were amended and supplemented by the Omnibus Directive, with these changes due to take effect in all Member States from May 2022, but the updating of the legislation does not stop there. The ePrivacy Directive is also in the process of being transformed, with a draft regulation still on the table of the European Parliament to better protect electronic communications. In addition, once the DSR becomes enforceable, several commercial practices which are harmful to consumers will become illegal, such as targeted advertising based on sensitive data and that related to minors. Despite the subtlety that characterizes the architecture of the digital environment and irrespective of all the rights that have progressively been granted to consumers over time, the mechanism available to authorities and judges to invalidate commercial practices (including digital ones) involves the application of the fictitious average consumer standard. It is therefore necessary to establish who falls within the notion of consumer and what criteria shall be applied for identifying the average consumer in the digital context presented in this section.

## 3 The creation of a digital consumer standard

E-commerce, by its particularities, defies the definition of the consumer under European law. An essential element that places individuals under the umbrella of consumer law is the purpose of the purchase of the good or service. Thus, to enjoy the privileges granted by the laws that operate with this notion, a person must act for purposes which are outside his trade, business, craft or profession. Naturally, for practical reasons, this purpose is verified in a superficial way. Thus, the purchase of a product or service as a natural person is absolutely presumed to be for personal purposes. Conversely, if the same natural person makes purchases through the company they manage, the purpose condition will no longer be met. By way of example, if a laptop is purchased by a teacher to prepare lessons for the students, the purchase falls within the scope of consumer protection law, even though it is to be used for professional purposes. On the other hand, the same purchase made by a teacher organised as a legal person (such as an authorised natural person) does not benefit from the protection of this legislation.

Since this situation may ultimately place a natural person at a disadvantage, it is natural to wonder whether there are situations in which a legal person could be a consumer. Although the definition of consumer in all the European directives is limited to natural persons, this does not rule out the possibility of granting a certain form of organisation the protection conferred by consumer law. Two perspectives must therefore be considered:

## 3.1 The perspective of equality of persons before the law

This equality seems to be breached by the different legal regime applicable to the two teachers in the above example. In this respect, a company has lodged an exception of unconstitutionality with the Constitutional Court of Romania (CCR), arguing that the exclusion of legal persons from the umbrella of consumer protection constitutes discrimination and violates constitutional principles. Overlooking the procedural irregularities of this referral, the CCR justifies the rejection of the exception with two main arguments. On the one hand, the differentiated treatment does not concern comparable situations, since *'professionals who conclude contracts within their field of activity are not in the same situation of vulnerability as persons who do not normally conclude such commercial contracts, so that they cannot invoke the discriminatory nature of the provisions of Article 2 of Law 193/2000 (n.n. Law on unfair terms in contracts concluded between professionals and consumers, which transposes the UCPD)'* [15]. On the other hand, a legal person can only rely on the principle of equality when the legal regime applicable to it affects a group of citizens, thereby creating inequality between them. Such a situation arises in Case C-329/19 *Condominio di Milano via Meda v. Eurothermo SpA*, discussed in the next sub-section.

Consequently, from the point of view of the equality, the two professors are not in comparable situations, since organisation in the form of a legal person gives rise to an absolute presumption of possession of additional knowledge of a possible commercial relationship and of the power to negotiate the contract giving rise to that relationship. Thus, from a legal point of view, the teacher-natural person and the teacher-legal person are two different entities, who 'judge' differently and to whom different standards apply. In the first case, the legislator's expectations are average, all lack of knowledge and bargaining power being supplemented by law. In the second case, the expectations are high(er), as legal persons are *ex officio* 'smart' from an economic point of view. In conclusion, at least as far as European consumer protection law is concerned, as a rule, the corporate veil is not lifted so that the natural person behind a company can be identified with it.

## 3.2 The perspective of ensuring a high level of consumer protection through homogeneous legal regimes

This level is itself an aim of the Union, declared and assumed by the Treaty on the Functioning of the European Union (TFEU). As the Constitutional Court of Romania pointed out in the above-mentioned decision, not granting a legal person the status of consumer may, in some cases, deprive of rights natural persons who are acting for personal and not professional purposes and who compose that entity. This would result in discrimination between consumers simply because some of them have associated themselves in some legal forms/structures.

This situation was the subject of a preliminary reference to the CJEU, as the Italian courts wished to clarify whether a legal entity similar to an association of owners (in Italian law, *condominio*) can be qualified as a consumer. That association, the *condominio*, concluded through its administrator a contract for the supply of energy with a company, which contained unfair terms whose usage in consumer contracts is prohibited by Directive 93/13/EEC on unfair terms in consumer contracts (UCTD). However, for such terms to be invalidated by the court, a consumer must be a party to that contract. Although the final beneficiary of these clauses is still a natural person (a tenant of a common property) the party to the commercial relationship does not fulfil the condition of being a natural person and therefore, according to the European directives, cannot be regarded as a consumer. However, Member States have the power to change this as both the CPD and the UCTD allow them to extend the application of the rules contained in these legal acts to other legal entities. In *Condominio di Milano via Meda v. Eurothermo SpA*, the CJEU recognises this power even to the courts, which have the power to interpret the transposing laws extensively and to create a practice that offers more protection than that in the Directives [16]. The reasoning of this decision is also valid in relation to the CPD, meaning that a transposition law or even the practice set by the courts can recognise an entity such as *condominio* the right to withdraw from a distance contract for instance, or the right to be provided with a certain set of information. This broad interpretation does not enter into conflict with Article 4 CPD, which provides that Member States may not introduce into their national law *'provisions diverging from those laid down in the Directive, including more or less stringent provisions, to ensure a different level of consumer protection'*. The scope of the CPD is limited to natural persons, therefore the regime applicable to other entities remains to be determined by the Member States, which may decide to assign them the same regime as the one set by the Directive itself, without this amounting to a change in the provisions applicable to natural persons. However, if a Member State chooses not to confer the protection of the Directive to entities like the Italian *condominio*, the issue of discrimination discussed in the previous sub-section becomes relevant. In these situations, since such entities are groups of natural persons not acting for professional purposes, it is questionable whether it is appropriate to assimilate them with a typical legal person, which is presumed to have advanced knowledge and bargaining power and presumed to be on an equal footing with its contractual partner.

Once the categories of persons who may be consumers have been established, the next important point concerns the standards with which the legislator operates and which the judge is called upon to apply when dealing with consumer protection claims. Thus, in C-210/96 *Gut Springenheide*, the CJEU validated the profile of the average consumer: a sufficiently attentive, informed, and circumspect person [17] without advanced knowledge of the product he is buying. By reference to this standard, the courts were to conclude whether a particular commercial practice was misleading. As a decision of the CJEU was unable to ensure uniform application of this standard across the Member States, the standard was codified, but not in the form proposed by the Court. The European Economic and Social Committee, an advisory body of the Union, the European Parliament and the Council of the European Union, as legislative bodies, have argued that this standard does not offer sufficient protection, in particular in relation to vulnerable groups of persons, such as children or persons with certain disabilities [5]. The current law on unfair commercial practices therefore provides that the standard set by the Court must be applied taking into account *'social, cultural and linguistic factors'*, the yardstick being the average member of the group to which a particular practice is directed. In conclusion, in order to assess the fairness (and therefore the legality) of a commercial practice, the assessor will have to go through two steps:

### *3.2.1. The identification of the target group of the practice*

This step is essential as the standard to be applied depends on it, but it is not easy, especially as neither the legislation nor the case law provides much guidance. Thus, the UCPD provides in Art. 5(2)(b) that a practice is unfair if it *'materially distorts or is likely to materially distort the economic behaviour with regard to a product of the average consumer whom it reaches or to whom it is addressed or of the average member of a group where a commercial practice is directed at a particular group of consumers'*.

The court must therefore first ascertain whether the product or service has features which suggest that it is not addressed to everyone, but to a specific category of consumers. Thus, an advertisement for robes specific to the legal professions may be addressed to a particular group, namely certain legal professionals, such as judges and lawyers. Thus, to be able to impact the assessment of the fairness of a practice, the group must meet three conditions: it must be *'sufficiently identifiable, limited in scope and homogeneous'* [18] , otherwise the judge must look at the general benchmark. The geographical criterion, although it delimits a group which shares a set of common characteristics (cultural, social, or linguistic), it does not meet the condition of having a limited scope but even so, it influences the portrayal of the average consumer and can work in parallel with a specific group. Thus, if the specific group under consideration is pregnant women, and pregnant women in a particular State are affected to a greater extent by a practice given a linguistic particularity similar to that in the Graffione case, the standard of the average consumer applied in that State must be related to an average pregnant woman who is a national of that State. Secondly, Art. 5(3) UCPD provides for a specific kind of group, namely that of persons who are particularly vulnerable because of intrinsic characteristics such as age or infirmity. In order to ensure that the protection of vulnerable categories of persons does not turn into unreasonable obligations for traders, the Directive lays down the condition of foreseeability of the negative impact on vulnerable persons. In addition, as explained in the previous section, vulnerability is situational: a person with a physical disability may be particularly vulnerable in relation to one product (such as medicines or treatments for that disability) and not vulnerable at all in relation to other products (such as food or clothing). Therefore, the intrinsic characteristic of the group member must be relevant to the practice whose fairness is being assessed, otherwise the standard may be the general one.

Relevant for the digital environment, however, is the following question: can digital consumers be considered as belonging to the specific group in the sense of Art. 5(2)(b) CPD or to the vulnerable group of consumers in Art. 5(3) CPD? In the first case, a group consisting of persons who have in common only the fact that they are digital consumers does not meet the criterion of homogeneity and limited scope, so the answer would be a negative one. In the second case, as the intrinsic characteristics listed in the UCPD are not exhaustively listed, the Court could establish the existence of other personal elements that make a group of consumers particularly vulnerable and consequently apply a lower standard. As in the first case, the group of vulnerable persons should be clearly identifiable, so that it is still not possible to speak of digital consumers as a group in its own right, but rather as a group of digital consumers sharing certain common features. Thus, people who have a chronic alcohol addiction which is known by algorithms that deliver personalised advertising could be considered as representing a group of vulnerable digital consumers and therefore, the standard will be set accordingly. It is important to note that applying the standard by reference to the target group does not always mean lowering the benchmark. In the case of the marketing dental cutters for instance, it is clear that the product is aimed at dental experts, so a reasonably informed and knowledgeable dental practitioner, and not an ordinary person, will be considered. Finally, even in the absence of a specific group, the external elements that characterise the digital environment should be considered in determining the behaviour of the average user, as explained in the next sub-section.

### *3.2.2 The identification of the average consumer's reaction to the practice, analysing to what extent their economic behaviour could be changed*

In deciding how the fictional average consumer would have behaved in each case, the court must take into account a variety of factors. As we have seen in cases Clinique and Graffione, an average consumer would be misled by a trademark called Cotonelle, since it would suggest to him that the products marketed were made from cotton, but not by a Clinique trademark, since he could reasonably identify from all the circumstances that the products in question were not medicinal products but cosmetics. Although the two cases appear to betray an inconsistency in the application of the average consumer standard, the conclusion to be drawn is that conjunctural factors are particularly relevant.

The legislation proposes general formulations in this respect, stating that in assessing the misleading or aggressive character, account should be taken of the facts, characteristics and circumstances of the particular case, the limitations of the medium used, and the fact that Article 114 TFEU establishes a high level of consumer protection. More specifically, the assessor must consider factors such as:

- the presumed expectations which a reasonable person might have of a product and its characteristics, [19]
- the complexity of the product or service, with the average consumer's level of expectation and attention varying according to the value of the good purchased,
- the categories of information that have been made available to the consumer, including information conveyed through advertising,
- the manner in which the information is provided, including the clarity of the language used,
- the general context of the purchase, such as the specifics of the shop from which a product is purchased,
- market conditions, such as political or economic phenomena (e.g. the influence of energy market liberalisation on electricity supply services),
- findings and studies in the field of behavioural economics,
- the impact on free trade and the movement of goods and services, in which case a proportionality test must be carried out,
- the architecture of the digital environment, including the algorithms that generate a particular practice,
- the social, cultural and linguistic characteristics of the state where a particular practice is implemented,
- consumer protection must not place an unreasonable burden on the trader, so a new proportionality test must be made.

The assessment of the practice in accordance with the above-mentioned factors must be made *in abstracto*, by taking into consideration the potential harmful effect of the action or omission under review. Accordingly, there is no need to have a person who was actually affected by a practice in order to apply the standard. In addition, the notion 'commercial decision' does not refer only to the decision regarding the purchase of a particular product, but it also includes whether or not the consumer is persuaded to enter a shop or spend more time on a website engaged in a booking process [20]. Therefore, from the perspective of the UCPD, there is no formal impediment for assessing the fairness of the dark pattern practice described in the previous section.

Case law has not provided specific guidance for the digital environment, nor has it (yet) created a portrait of the digital consumer. Given the list of factors to be taken into account when setting this standard, we can conclude that the particularities of the digital environment significantly influence the assessments made by judges. Thus, certain traits and behaviours established as belonging to the average consumer in the offline environment do not remain valid in the online environment. For example, generalizing CJEU's findings in *Clinique*, the average consumer can determine the category to which a product belongs and identify its general characteristics by reference to the general context of the purchase (such as the specifics of the shop) and additional information on the packaging, even if the product name or pictures on the label suggest otherwise. In the online environment, a marketplace may sell products from different categories and there is no physical access to the good to study its packaging or label. According to *Concord*, the average consumer perceives a brand as a whole (global appreciation) and does not proceed to analyse its various details, so there is a likelihood that he or she will not distinguish between two similar brands and thus confuse them [21]. This issue becomes more acute in the online environment, where the digital representation of the brand, the photos and the presentation of the product sometimes make it impossible to distinguish between an original product and an imitation. Splitting the price of a product into several elements and highlighting only one part of the price [22] in order to arouse the user's interest can very easily lead to consumers accessing the platform and researching the offer, which already influences the consumer's behaviour without having to materialise into a purchase. In the online environment, these practices are very common, therefore the insertion of false or unreasonable incomplete information in advertising banners should be considered unfair practice. In addition, taking into account the architecture of the digital environment, profiling techniques, differential pricing policies, dark pattern designs and other similar factors, we can conclude that the average consumer's standard is lower in the digital environment and, at the same time, the number of elements that the court must take into account when making its assessment is higher.

The usefulness of the standard goes beyond helping authorities or courts to enforce consumer protection policies, it also has legislative relevance for the development of these policies themselves [23]. For example, if we were to consider a hypothetical statistic in which 8 out of 10 young people aged between 18 and 21 who have a credit card end up taking on excessive debt, thus engaging in financially irresponsible behaviours, the legislator could restrict access to such products up to a certain age, just as in the case of the sale of alcoholic beverages to minors, which is prohibited.

## 4 Conclusions

The EU is trying to update consumer protection legislation to make e-commerce and online navigations a safe option for all internet users, tendency proved by the Omnibus Directive, the draft of a Electronic Communications Regulation and the new regulations on digital services and markets. From 02 May 2023, Regulation (EU) 2022/1925 on contestable and fair markets in the digital sector (Digital Markets Act - DMA) became applicable and aims to better control the large platforms that support the digital infrastructure and the space where traders meet consumers, such as Google. For example, DMA states that any consumer profiling techniques these big platforms apply to their core platform services will be subject to independent audit and transparency obligations in relation to these techniques. This aims to allow the users to act in an informed way when engaging in certain economic behaviour.

However, there are currently two certainties. The first is that the digital sector is specifically designed to attract and hold the attention of the consumer, the digital *alter ego* is traded between different platforms to identify the consumer's profile and to provide advertising material of interest. These techniques, practised within certain limits, based on legal grounds, and governed by principles such as transparency, have no harmful effects and enhance the digital consumer experience. However, for those situations where the digital architecture generates unfair commercial practices based on the vulnerabilities of internet users, remedies must be put in place. The second certainty is that in order to remove an unfair practice, the judge (and the legislator, when crafting certain policies) must determine the behaviour (the reaction) of the average consumer - a person who is *'reasonably critical, aware and knowledgeable in his or her behaviour in the marketplace'* [18]. Therefore, in order to be able to provide a protection at least as robust as in the offline environment, the assessor must also consider certain subtle characteristics of the digital environment, understand the algorithms behind the operation of certain platforms and must consider the collection and processing of socio-demographic and psychological characteristics of the users. For example, a gambling platform identifies the interest, weakness and/or history of a loyal player and displays an offer presented as exclusive to him/her and whose validity is limited to the next two hours. When assessing the aggressiveness of such a practice, consumer profiling should also be considered, as this impacts the standard used. Thus, the wording of Art. 5(3) UCPD regarding vulnerable subjects should not be restricted to intrinsic characteristics such as age, but all dimensions of this notion should be recognised.

From the perspective of equality of persons before the law, consideration could be given to extending the notion of consumer to those groups of natural persons who act jointly for a purpose which is not related to their professional, commercial, industrial or craft activity, such as a *condominio*. The fact that Member States have the power to make such an extension in their national law may lead to situations where an Italian co-owner is exempted from paying excessive penalties because the clause establishing them was unfair and has been invalidated, whereas a co-owner from another Member State will be obliged to pay those penalties because the contracting was done through the administrator of the association, so that the condition of being a natural person is not met and the consumer protection legislation cannot apply.

In order to ensure the greatest possible degree of harmonisation, EU legislation should supplement the annexes to the UCPD by including more unfair digital practices. In this way, the assessor will be relieved of having to identify the reaction of the average consumer, which can imply analysing subtle factors and can be done differently within the Member States. For other practices, the law should provide clear criteria to be applied by all judges in all Member States. Such approaches are not only to the benefit of the consumer, but also to the benefit of traders who should be subject to as few differences in standards as possible within the EU.

## References

1. Court of Justice of the European Union, Advocate General's Opinion, Case C-110/14, *Horațiu Ovidiu Costea v. SC Volksbank România SA*
2. N. Helberger, O. Lynskey, H. Micklitz *et. al., EU Consumer Protection 2.0. Structural asymmetries in digital consumer markets*, A joint report from research conducted under the EUCP2.0 project (2021)
3. Consumers, Health, Agriculture and Food Executive Agency, *Consumer vulnerability across key markets in the European Union: final report,* Publications Office, URL: https://data.europa.eu/doi/10.2818/056024, accessed: 14.10.2022 (2016)
4. Court of Justice of the European Union, Judgement of 02.02.1994, Case C-315/92, *Verband Sozialer Wettbewerb eV v Clinique Laboratoires SNC et Estée Lauder Cosmetics GmbH*
5. B. Duivenvoorde, The Consumer Benchmarks in the Unfair Commercial Practices Directive, Vol. 5 (Springer, 2015)
6. F.Gomez Pomar, *The Unfair Commercial Practices Directive: a law and economics perspective*, InDret 1/2006 (2006)
7. Court of Justice of the European Union, Judgement of 26.11.1996, Case C-313/94, *Fratelli Graffione SNC and Ditta Fransa*

8. https://www.statista.com/statistics/379046/worldwide-retail-e-commerce-sales/, accessed 15.10.2022
9. Court of Justice of the European Union, Judgement of 25.11.2021, Case C-102/20 *StWL v. eprimo GmbH*
10. Court of Justice of the European Union, Judgement of 01.10.2019, Case C-673/17, *Bundesverband der Verbraucherzentralen und Verbraucherverbände — Verbraucherzentrale Bundesverband v. Planet49 GmbH*
11. European Data Protection Board, Guidelines 03/2022 on Dark Patterns in Social Media Platform Interfaces: How to Recognise and Avoid them (2022)
12. E. Pariser, The Filter Bubble: What The Internet Is Hiding From You (Penguin Books, 2011)
13. G. Sartor, *New aspects and challenges in consumer protection: Study for the committee on the Internal Market and Consumer Protection*, Policy Department for Economic, Scientific and Quality of Life Policies, European Parliament, Luxembourg (2020)
14. European Data Protection Board, Guidelines 07/2020 on the concepts of controller and processor in the GDPR (2021)
15. Constitutional Court of Romania, Decision 360/2013 on the rejection of the exception of unconstitutionality of the provisions of Article 2 of Law 193/2000 on unfair terms in contracts concluded between traders and consumers
16. Court of Justice of the European Union, Judgement of 02.04.2020, Case C-329/19, *Condominio di Milano via Meda v. Eurothermo SpA*
17. Court of Justice of the European Union, Judgement of 16.07.1998, Case C-210/96, *Gut Springenheide GmbH and Rudolf Tusky*
18. Guidelines on the interpretation and application of Directive 2005/29/EC of the European Parliament and of the Council concerning unfair business-to-consumer commercial practices in the internal market, Official Journal of the European Union, C 526/1
19. Court of Justice of the European Union, Judgement of 13.01.2000, Case C-220/98, *Estée Lauder Cosmetics GmbH & Co. OHG and Lancaster Group GmbH*
20. Commission Staff Working Document, Guidance on the Implementation/Application of Directive 2005/29/EC on Unfair Commercial Practices, Brussels, 4.12.2009, SEC(2009)
21. Court of Justice of the European Union, Judgement of 23.10.2002, Case T-6/01, *Matratzen Concord v OHIM – Hukla Germany*
22. Court of Justice of the European Union, Judgement of 26.10.2016, Case C-611/14, *Criminal proceedings against Canal Digital Danmark A/S*
23. L. Bercea, *Standardul „consumatorului mediu" şi consimţământul pentru prelucrarea datelor cu caracter personal*, Revista Română de Drept Privat, **1** (2018)

# The legal framework of data subject representation

*Andreea* Şerban [1*]

[1]Faculty of Law, Alexandru Ioan Cuza University of Iasi, Romania

**Abstract.** The GDPR provided for new rules on the right of the data subjects to an effective judicial remedy against a controller or a processor where they consider that their rights have been infringed under the Regulation as a result of the processing of personal data. Art. 80 of the GDPR, on the representation of data subjects, is intended to favour private enforcement of EU data protection law, providing for the representation of data subjects by a body or entity which must meet specific requirements in order to exercise the rights conferred to the data subject regarding an effective judicial remedy. The representation of data subjects by a third party in legal actions is possible in two cases: on the one hand, the situation where a data subject mandates the body or organization to represent them or, on the other side, when a body or organization, has the right to lodge a complaint and exercise the rights to effective judicial remedies provided by the GDPR independently of a mandate. This paper will detail the legal framework of this private enforcement tool and analyse the links between data protection and consumer protection from the perspective of collective redress and representation of the interests of a data subject.

## 1 Introductory considerations

In its ambitious intent, the General Data Protection Regulation (hereinafter, the GDPR) aims to empower the data subjects to the extent of(re)establishing the balance where their rights to data protection are concerned.

The rapid pace of technological development saw the privacy laws fall far behind their times, as legislators needed to catch up with the ever-accelerating digital revolution. At the European level, standing firm for over 15 years as the central legal instrument of the European Union (EU) in this field was Directive 95/46/EC. However, almost two decades later, the Directive barely scratched the surface. Despite its valid and sound legal principles, the Directive has become outdated and insufficient to meet the needs and demands of the

* Corresponding author: andreeaserban20@yahoo.com

21st-century digital environment, with enforcement becoming increasingly challenging given the rapidly evolving technological and digital realities.

The aim of the GDPR has been, since the time of its legislative proposal, the protection of the data subject against unlawful data processing by a controller or a processor [1]. Advocate General Sánchez-Bordona, in his latest opinion on case C-300/21 [2], stated that 'the GDPR does not seek to increase the control of individuals over information concerning them, by merely giving way to their preferences, but rather reconcile each person's right to protection of personal data with the interests of third parties and society'.

The GDPR represents the beginning of European data protection and its framework for privacy reform. The EU has since proceeded to build on the concept of privacy, proposing additional legislation meant either to complement, clarify or apply to more specific situations the basic principles first dignified by the GDPR. The latest examples of the EU's very own 'digital revolution' are key pieces of legislation destined to revamp the European digital legal framework and the sectors that rely on it today, such as the Digital Services Act (Regulation (EU) 2022/2065 of 19 October 2022), Digital Markets Act (Regulation (EU) 2022/1925 of the European Parliament and of the Council of 14 September 2022), Data Governance Act (Regulation (EU) 2022/868 of the European Parliament and of the Council of 30 May 2022 ), and Data Act [3].

The key aspect of the coming of age of EU privacy laws was the dawn of private enforcement made possible in the wake of GDPR. Soon after the enforcement date of the GDPR, NOYB (None of Your Business, Austria) filed the 101 'dalmatians' complaints [4] against controllers from EU member states on Google Analytics and Facebook Connect integrations. The complaints were filed with the national data protection authorities (hereinafter, DPAs) from Austria, France, Spain, and others, as the criteria for determining the competent filing authority being either the establishment of the controller or the residence of the data subject. The complaints were filed following article 80 (1) of the GDPR. More recently, the Court of Justice of the European Union (CJEU) ruled in judgment C-319/20 *Meta Platforms Ireland Limited* [5] on this precise matter focusing on the article80 of the GDPR and looking at the link between the legal remedies for data protection, commercial practices, and consumer protection law. With the GDPR providing a solid legal basis for the triggering of a growing number of litigations regarding the infringement of the right to data protection, it is worth taking a closer look at the EU rules that govern data protection enforcement, especially the provision enshrined in article 80 of the GDPR, focusing on the representation of the data subject.

The line between data protection and consumer protection is relatively thin. It becomes increasingly blurred in the digital age as it becomes ever more challenging to tell apart "users" and 'consumers'. An individual in the capacity of a data subject should have the right to redress under the rules provided by the GDPR; an individual in the ability as a consumer will have the right to redress under the consumer protection acquis [6]. In a business-to-consumer relationship, a data subject that is also a consumer may exercise their rights twice in both capacities [6].

This paper aims to take a closer look at the data subject representation, analysing the remedies provided by the GDPR and the specific circumstances where article 80 is applicable. Our primary research questions regard the definition of data subject representation, the parties involved in the representation of the data subject, the mandate, the purpose, and the impact of this legal tool.

## 2 GDPR remedies

The purpose of the GDPR is to empower the data subjects and to arm them with the necessary tools to confront the potential infringements of their data protection rights: where the controller and/or the processor fail to comply with the rules regarding the right to data protection or the rights derived from the GDPR [7], the data subject can address the competent authority, which is determined by the chosen legal remedy. Thus, the GDPR provides two ways of remedies in articles 77-82: the administrative and the judicial path. The judicial path can occur independently or simultaneously with the administrative way [8], following the application of administrative remedies.

According to article 77 of the GDPR, the data subject has the right to lodge a complaint with a supervisory authority. Where a controller and/or a processor has infringed any of the rights of the data subject regarding their data, it is recommended that the data subject first exercise their rights by contacting the competent controller and/or processor, as it is relevant to have a clearer view of how the data is being dealt with and how the data subject's rights have been infringed [9]. Yet, such a step is not compulsory as the GDPR does not provide for it. While a lack of answers or resolution on behalf of the controller/processor might provide additional support for a legal claim in the respective case, the data subject has the power to address their case directly to the data protection authority. It must be noted that some authorities require data subjects to provide supporting evidence. For example, correspondence with the controller, contracts, or screenshots could be *supporting evidence*. Nonetheless, it is possible to lodge the complaint without such supporting evidence.

There is a divide between DPAs concerning the requirements that complaints must observe, as well as the necessity for prior documented correspondence between the data subject and the controller: data subjects are encouraged to first bring the data protection issue to the attention of the relevant controller, or they receive an indication in the complaint form to do so, without being made clear to them whether it is a mandatory condition or not.

For example, the Hamburg Data Protection Authority recommends that the data subject first contact the data controller as there frequently is a data protection officer who provides independent consultancy regarding the protection of data – this step may occasionally prove itself to be a faster way to find a solution fit for the interests of the data subject [10]. On the other side, the Irish Data Protection Commissioner, in its contact form, only allows the finalization and submission of the complaint form provided if the data controller has been priorly contacted, inviting this way the data subject to first raise their concerns with the data controller [11]. In the latter case, the data subject may only contact the DPA following a previous inquiry with the respective data controller and only after receiving a negative reply to their claim. – *e.g.,* the data subject requests a data controller to delete their data, and the controller refuses. Per the Decision of the Romanian Data Protection Authority, no. 133/2018, regarding the procedure for receiving and handling complaints, according to article 5(1), when lodging a complaint, it is mandatory to specify the subject matter of the complaint in detail, as well as the steps taken by the complainant concerning the controller and/or controller targeted by the complaint or, where is the case, the information available to support the allegations, and to attach the conclusive evidence, where available.

The judicial path is multiforme. It must be noted that this path can be taken following a decision of the supervisory authority or directly against the controller or processor, thus independently and without prior informing or addressing the data protection authority. The GDPR further details the judicial instruments that the data subjects have at their disposal: article 78 details that the data subject has the right to an effective judicial remedy against a supervisory authority, and article 79 establishes an effective judicial remedy of the data subject against a controller or processor.

These provisions enshrine the EU legal framework for effective judicial remedies in data protection, while the procedural rules remain a competence of each Member State. The Romanian Data Protection Authority stated in its Decision no. 133/2018, art. 5(2), that if the complainant has lodged a complaint with a national court with the same subject matter and against the same controller or processor, the data subject must bring the complaint to the attention of DPA. Art. 8(2) of this Decision further states that the Romanian Data Protection Authority may close or suspend the complaint where a similar complaint was lodged with a national court, while art. 8(3) states that the competent court is the one from the establishment of the controller or processor or the habitual residence of the data subject.

Article 79 of the GDPR has a broader application than article 78. The obligation foreseen in article 78 to provide an effective judicial remedy against a legally binding decision of the DPAs does not guarantee an effective judicial remedy" in itself. There are claims that cannot fall under the remit of the DPA [12].

As the right to data protection is not new, nor is the GDPR a legal innovation anymore, it is now litigation that steals the spotlights: over the past years at the EU level, the attention of the data subject to data protection issues has intensified due to the rise of cases at the CJEU. With jurisprudence highlighting growing loopholes and showcasing the rigid incapacity to adapt to current times - thinking of *Google Spain* [13] or *Schrems* [14] cases - new calls for improving the European legislation are made for supporting the role of the data subjects and the underlying the importance of providing alternative courses of action to promoting adequate protection [15].

However, there is a fundamental problem of affordability and accessibility of legal counsel and the legal capacity for data subjects to engage in litigation to defend their rights effectively. The lack of understanding of data protection matters or financial or legal support for the act in situations where data protection rights are infringed might prove to be one bridge too far for the average data subject. Therefore, the GDPR, unlike its predecessor, Directive 95/46/CE, provides for new legal instruments regarding data subject representation, ultimately drawing inspiration from the consumer protection law.

## 3 Collective redress in data protection matters

Before diving into the data subject representation and collective redress in data protection matters, it is worth considering the legal notion of collective redress and defining the terminology in both the data protection and the consumer protection context.

Initially created as an instrument to avoid repetitive litigation in 17th-century England, collective redress has evolved since its Elizabethan days to become a much more modern tool. The mechanisms for collective redress and class action are developing rapidly at the global level due to multiple reasons: on the one side, there is a shifting attitude toward favouring these types of collective claims; on the other side, the rights of individuals have expanded in many areas together with the number of civil society organisations with resources to take such initiatives on, allowing litigants being more interested and aware about their rights nowadays [16] – a clear example of how the data protection rights provided the foundation for an increasing number of litigation cases.

In short, a 'class action is a legal procedure which enables the claims (or part of the claims) of a number of persons against the same defendant to be determined in the one suit' [17]. The complex nature of this procedural instrument has been the subject of controversy over time, having been described either as a 'Frankenstein monster' or 'one of the most significant procedural developments of the century' [17].

Collective redress refers to any legal mechanism that provides a possibility to collectively claim cessation or prevention of unlawful business behaviour or collectively demand compensation in mass harm situations when two or more natural or legal person claim to have suffered damage resulting from the same illegal activity. Harm could be material or immaterial – the latter being the case with privacy and data breaches.

Over the past years, class action cases concerning data protection and privacy before the Courts in the United States and the United Kingdom have been rising steadily. In the US, LinkedIn had to make settlements on weak password security and the scanning of its users' contact lists [18]. In the UK, a class action was filed against a supermarket chain over mass personal data theft [19].

The collective redress mechanism has been developing in a fragmented fashion in the European Union, both at the national and the EU level, as well as sector-wise. In the Commission Recommendation of 2013 on common principles for injunctive and compensatory collective redress mechanisms in the Member States concerning violations of rights granted under Union Law [20], collective redress is defined as '(i) a legal mechanism that ensures a possibility to claim cessation of illegal behaviour collectively by two or more natural or legal persons or by an entity entitled to bring a representative action (injunctive collective redress); (ii) a legal mechanism that ensures a possibility to claim compensation collectively by two or more natural or legal persons claiming to have been harmed in a mass harm situation or by an entity entitled to bring a representative action (compensatory collective redress).'

The Recommendation further defines representative action as "an action which is brought by a representative entity, an ad hoc certified entity or a public authority on behalf and in the name of two or more natural or legal persons who claim to be exposed to the risk of suffering harm or to have been harmed in a mass harm situation whereas those persons are not parties to the proceedings".

Collective redress was under the spotlight before the CJEU. In the *Maximilian Schrems v Facebook Ireland Limited* [21] case, the questions regarding the role of class action within the legal framework of the EU further developed the discussion, with broad implications for data protection and consumer rights alike [22]. Two issues were of relevance for the data protection representation matter: (1) on the one side, the activities of Max Schrems in data protection and privacy matters and the fact of being assigned the claims of numerous consumers for the purpose of law enforcement entailed the loss of his private status as a consumer within the meaning of the Regulation on judgments in civil and commercial matters. The Court concluded that while the concept of the consumer must be strictly construed, excluding the activities of Schrems would prevent an effective defence of consumer rights and thus, as per point 41 of the Court decision, "the activities of publishing books, lecturing, operating websites, fundraising and being assigned the claims of numerous consumers for the purpose of their enforcement do not entail the loss of a private Facebook account user's status as a 'consumer' as understood within the meaning of art. 15 of Regulation (EU) 44/2001; (2) on the other side, the Court was asked if a consumer could assert in the courts of the place where they have domiciled not only their own claims but also the claims assigned to them by other consumers, possibly domiciled in the same Member State, other Member State, or in 3rd countries. The Court concluded that the fact that consumers could bring proceedings where they are domiciled 'does not entail the jurisdiction of this court for similar claims assigned to the consumer' [23]. This means that, in this case, Schrems could enforce his claims before the court relevant according to his domicile, but not the claims of other consumers.

While it represents a milestone for the evolution of consumer rights enforcement, the judgment underlines the law's current state through the Court's refusal to create a new consumer forum – the current legislation does not yet support trans-border consumer actions [23]. The European Consumer Organisation (BEUC) noted that 'with this judgment, the European Court of Justice has made expectations collapse that consumers can join forces in one court to achieve redress in mass harm claims.' [24] BEUC also noted that this judgment was a call to action for the EU for a collective redress tool to shift the balance in favour of the consumer and produce effects at the European level.

Looking back at the state of the collective redress legislation in Member States across the EU before 2018, we can observe discrepancies and significant differences between Member States [25]: while some countries did not provide any type of collective actions for damages, others provided within their framework very complex procedures that rendered the collective redress mechanism highly expensive, burdensome and inaccessible for consumers in different matters, let alone consumers as data subjects in data protection matters.

The Austrian Constitutional Court accepted the admissibility of the joint individual applications in the constitutional action brought by Mr. Tschohl with 11128 other applicants on the compatibility between the Federal Constitutional Law and the transposing the directive on Data Retention into Austrian Law. The action served as the origin of the request for a preliminary ruling in Case C-594/12 before the CJEU [26].

In *Fashion ID* [27], it was asked whether the Data Protection Directive precluded national legislation from granting standing to consumer protection associations to bring actions against infringers of data protection laws. The Court interpreted the provisions of art. 22-24 of Directive 95/46 as 'not precluding national legislation which allows consumer-protection associations to bring or defend legal proceedings against a person allegedly responsible for an infringement of the protection of personal data.' The Court noted that article 80(2) of GDPR reflects the intention of the European legislation by expressly authorizing 'the bringing of legal proceedings by such an association', confirming that Directive 95/46 did not preclude such an action [27].

## 3.1 Collective actions according to GDPR

One of the novelties of the GDPR was the provision for collective redress in art. 80. Per art. 80 (1) of the GDPR, 'The data subject shall have the right to mandate a not-for-profit body, organization or association which has been properly constituted in accordance with the law of a Member State, has statutory objectives which are in the public interest, and is active in the field of the protection of data subjects' rights and freedoms with regard to the protection of their personal data to lodge the complaint on his or her behalf, to exercise the rights referred to in Articles 77, 78 and 79 on his or her behalf, and to exercise the right to receive compensation referred to in Article 82 on his or her behalf where provided for by Member State law.' Art. 80 (2) of the GDPR provides that 'Member States may provide that anybody, organisation or association referred to in paragraph 1 of this Article, independently of a data subject's mandate, has the right to lodge, in that Member State, a complaint with the supervisory authority which is competent pursuant to Article 77 and to exercise the rights referred to in Articles 78 and 79 if it considers that the rights of a data subject under this Regulation have been infringed as a result of the processing.'

For further interpretation of art. 80, GDPR provides recital 142. While not a binding provision, recital 142 reiterates the right of the data subject 'to mandate a not-for-profit body, organisation or association which is constituted in accordance with the law of a Member State [...]'. Additionally, recital 142 provides that 'body, organisation or association may not be allowed to claim compensation on a data subject's behalf independently of the data subject mandate'.

Other related provisions can be found in the EU's Law Enforcement Directive 2016/680, respectively in art. 55 – representation of data subjects, art. 52 – right to lodge a complaint with a supervisory authority, art. 53 – right to an effective judicial remedy against a supervisory authority, and art. 54 – right to an effective judicial remedy against a controller or processor.

Why was this article needed in the GDPR? In a report of the European Union Agency for Fundamental Rights (FRA) on access to data protection remedies in EU Member States [28], addressing the protection of personal data as enunciated by art. 8 and the right to an effective remedy as provided for by art. 47 of the Charter, it was shown that broadening collective action in data protection matters was relevant for increasing accessibility and efficiency of the remedies in the data protection area [28]. Intermediaries and legal professionals interviewed for the report from most of the EU Member States have suggested a class action type of procedure, arguing that these 'are related to the correction of power relations in the proceedings and possible reduction of costs for the individuals subjected to the data protection violations'. In the absence of such procedures, such affordability and accessibility issues, among others, represent veritable barriers that are significantly off-putting in certain sensitive sectors, in particular small commerce and individual consumers. Thus, in the data protection field, a collective redress mechanism is a valuable tool concerning the number of potentially affected people, reducing significant individual costs, promoting accessibility, and creating a more efficient procedure for effectively protecting rights. The European Commission, in its Recommendation [29], recital 7, states that 'amongst those areas where the supplementary private enforcement of rights granted under Union law in the form of collective redress is of value, are consumer protection, competition, environment protection, protection of personal data, financial services legislation and investor protection.'

Art. 80 GDPR is a novelty in data protection, having no equivalent in Directive 95/46, Convention 108, or Modernised Convention 108 (Convention for the Protection of Individuals with regard to Automatic Processing of Personal Data). As the previous legal framework for data protection was based on a directive, Member States had the competence to transpose these provisions into their national legislation and thus determine how they would work in practice, ultimately resulting in different national approaches across the EU Member States.

The title of art. 80 GDPR regards the 'representation' of data subjects, with this provision establishing 'a number of rights or modalities of a single right, and foreseeing the possibility, at national level, of others' [12].

Looking at its first paragraph, it should be noted that data subjects can mandate bodies, organizations, or associations that comply with the following requirements: (1) not-for-profit – e.g., the organization is not constituted for commercial gain, its purposes are to benefit the public; (2) properly constituted per national legislation; (3) has statutory objectives in the public interest - e.g., a precondition for allowing Member States to provide for the possibilities of these entities to act without an individual mandate [12]; (4) to act in the field of data protection – e.g., the activities of the entity should concern the promotion of data protection rights and freedoms.

The qualifying criteria have been subjected to criticism in recent literature, having been considered limitative, in practice posing more questions than answers [22], as the aim of these criteria 'can be inferred' in national legislations of some Member States.

The mandate that article 80(1) GDPR refers to concerns the right of the data subject to mandate any of the entities that cumulatively meets the criteria to lodge the complaint on his or her behalf and to exercise the rights referred to in articles 77-79, and the right to receive compensation referred to in article 82 [...] where provided for by Member State law.

This first form of class action provided for in art. 80(1) is similar to the opt-in class action as understood in common law [30]. It is conditioned by a manifestation of will that results in the mandate given by the data subject or data subjects to an entity established per the criteria mentioned above. Where more data subjects express their will in this sense, the mandate is common for all of them, and the mandated entity will commonly represent them.

As a rule, all data subjects can mandate. In practice, though, this will depend on the existence of entities properly established according to the legislation of a Member State that could exercise the data subject's right of representation as foreseen by art. 80(1) GDPR. The existence of the mandate determines a choice of forum restriction by the jurisdictional provisions relevant to the content of the mandate [12].

As for the last part of the 1st paragraph of art. 80 GDPR, the right to receive compensation as provided by art. 82 GDPR, the intention of the legislator is clearly to leave to the legislative framework of each Member State to provide for compensation rules concerning data protection matters. In the sense of the line to exercise the right to receive compensation referred to in Article 82 on his or her behalf where provided for by Member State law, the exercise of this right is not established as a rule but rather as a possibility that is provided only in the case of this type of class action. As we will see in art. 80(2), the same possibility is not provided for the opt-out type of class action.

Looking at the wording of art. 82 GDPR, we note that this provision leaves no room for interpretation or discretion in its implementation by the Member States. The article, titled right to compensation and liability, has a direct effect regardless of its implementation in the respective national legal orders [12].

Yet, concerning the mandate for representation given to an entity, as established in art. 80(1) GDPR, the right to compensation has a differentiated approach, which differs depending on the national legislative framework of each Member State.

As mentioned above, a closer look at art. 80(2) GDPR reveals an opt-out form of class action [30]. An entity established under the criteria set out in this paragraph may lodge a complaint, independently of a data subject's mandate, with the data protection authority and/or exercise the rights provided by articles 78-79 GDPR.

Regarding this paragraph, we note that it is not an obligation or a rule to be followed but rather an option that the Member States can further provide for in their national legislation.

As for the entities subject to this provision, they can refer to anybody, organisation, or association, as mentioned in paragraph (1). Therefore, those properly established and respecting the criteria abovementioned. These entities do not act on behalf of a data subject or with a mandate. At the same time, their interest in acting must not be manifested in abstracto or as a theoretical public interest concern. The entities may act only if they consider that the rights of a data subject […] have been infringed as a result of the processing. Thus, the entities may even represent an unidentified yet presumably affected data subject [12].

Compared to the 1st paragraph, this provision raises questions regarding the forum. The entity may bring the complaint to the competent data protection authority as provided by art. 77 GDPR, yet not having an identified data subject could mean that the possibility of predicting the possible forum is considerably decreased. Thus, the competent data protection authority can also be the one in the Member State where the alleged infringement took place. In Weltimmo [31], the Court decided that the Hungarian DPA was competent to hear the claims against a Slovakian company that targeted its data processing in Hungary and affected data subjects from Hungary.

Deconstructing art. 80 GDPR, we see that, in practice, its application might lead to the increased involvement of consumer protection associations and, as noted by Gierschmann [32], increased pressure on controllers/processors to reach compliance, as well as a rise in the number of complaints that have their legal basis on this art.

Also, concerning the application of paragraph 2 of art. 80 GDPR, it depends on the will of each Member State to provide a rule that ensures the application of this form of class action, as well as the interest and devotion of entities to pursue such actions without a mandate.

### 3.2 Brief considerations on Directive 2020/1828 on representative actions for the protection of the collective interests of consumers and its connection to GDPR

With the Representative Actions Directive (Directive (EU) 2020/1828 of the European Parliament and of the Council of 25 November 2020 – 'RAD'), a new era of European class actions began.

In 2017, *the European Commission announced a new deal for consumers* in the aftermath of the Dieselgate scandal [33]. This new deal also included the proposal for the directive on representative actions that was later adopted in 2020.

This new instrument is the result of a legislative evolution at the EU level in response to the issue of limited resources of representative entities that prevented the initiation of mass claims [34].

In brief, RAD requires Member States to adopt at least one efficient collective action mechanism that aims to enable entities to bring representative actions against traders concerning infringements of EU law in matters such as data protection, product liability, telecommunications, financial services, etc [35].

RAD grants standing to *qualified entities*. These are being defined in art. 3(4) RAD as 'any organisation or public body representing consumers' interests which has been designated by a Member State as qualified to bring representative actions'. Art. 4(3) RAD further states the criteria to be met for the qualified entities: (a) *legal person* – constituted in accordance with the national law and *can demonstrate 12 months of actual public activity in the protection of consumer interests prior to its request for designation*; (b) *statutory purpose* that demonstrates the entity's *legitimate interest in protecting consumer interests*; (c) non-for-profit character; (d) not subject of insolvency proceedings and not declared insolvent; (e) *independent and not influenced by persons other than the consumers*; (f) ensures transparency – making publicly available information that demonstrates the compliance to the criteria as mentioned above.

RAD also lays down the redress measures defined in art. 3(10) as measures that 'require a trader to provide consumers concerned with remedies such as compensation, repair, replacement, price reduction, contract termination or reimbursement of the price paid, as appropriate and as available under Union or national law'.

At first sight, the interplay between the GDPR and RAD is a complicated relation up for interpretation. On the one side, art. 80 GDPR establishes an exclusive framework, and all representative actions must necessarily respect its requirements. Thus, should there be no mandate, as art. 80(2) does not provide for it, representative entities cannot request compensation. Therefore, art. 80 GDPR would always apply, while RAD provisions would be seen as devalued in data protection matters [36]. On the other side, another question that might raise concerns is the possible parallel litigation channels. In this case, actions that do not fall within the scope of art. 80(2) GDPR could be pursued under national law following its transposition of the provisions of RAD. Therefore, the issue stands in the fact that RAD appears to impose even stricter conditions than GDPR [36].

### 3.3 Brief considerations on CJEU C-319/20 Meta Platforms Ireland Limited

The European discussion around class actions in data protection matters significantly increased with the Judgement in the C-319/20 *Meta Platforms Ireland Limited* case before the CJEU. The Federal Union of Consumer Organizations and Associations (Verbraucherzentrale Bundesverband - vzbv) brought an action for an injunction before the Regional Court in Berlin, Germany, against Meta Platforms Ireland for the infringement of rules concerning certain users' data. The action was brought *independently of a specific infringement of a data subject's right to protection of his or her data and without being mandated to do so by such a person* [5]. The action reached the Bundesgerichtshof, the German Federal Court of Justice, which voiced its doubts concerning the admissibility of a consumer group bringing a claim on behalf of a group of users, questioning whether German national law provisions which allowed for consumer protection associations to bring these claims were indeed compatible with the GDPR [5].

The question referred to the Bundesgerichtshof regarded whether the provisions of arts. 80 and 84 GDPR precluded the national rules which empower competitors, associations, entities, and chambers entitled under national law to bring actions independently of an infringement of specific rights of data subjects and without a mandate from a data subject [5].

The Court confirmed that art. 80(2) GDPR is not '*precluding national legislation which allows a consumer protection association to bring legal proceedings, in the absence of a mandate conferred on it for that purpose and independently of the infringement of specific rights of the data subjects, against the person allegedly responsible for an infringement of the laws protecting personal data, on the basis of the infringement of the prohibition of unfair commercial practices, a breach of a consumer protection law or the prohibition of the use of invalid general terms and conditions, where the data processing concerned is liable to affect the rights that identified or identifiable natural persons derive from that regulation*'. [5]

The Court confirmed that vzbv could bring the claim independently of the infringement of specific rights and regardless of a particular mandate from a data subject. The immediate impact of this confirmation is the bringing of a broader protection net for consumers, who can now be offered a more significant number of tools to defend their rights.

## 4 Concluding remarks

The data protection framework is still a veritable construction site, an ongoing process of construction and reconstruction of an evolving framework in a revolutionary world. The class action mechanism is only one representation of this constant evolution, a necessary tool now reinvented to keep up with the pace of the digital world, ensuring that the protection of rights is effective and does not leave out those most vulnerable.

The provisions of the Representative Actions Directive confirmed and doubled down by the most recent jurisprudence, together with the GDPR provisions for redress, stand to create a solid basis for private enforcement, promoting increased levels of litigation from consumer groups, thus keeping pressuring controllers and processors accountable and providing the right incentives for these entities to focus even more on adequate compliance.

Nonetheless, even with an improved and updated legal framework, it is still very much up for discussion how the provisions of art. 80 GDPR will be ultimately implemented, given that there is still enough room for interpretation and for Member States to choose the option to (not) legislate in this matter.

## References

1. D. Hallinan, EDPL, **5 (3)**, 293–99, DOI: 10.21552/edpl/2019/3/5 (2019)
2. Court of Justice of the European Union, Opinion of the Advocate General Campos Sánchez-Bordona delivered on 6.10.2022, C-300/21, *UI v Österreichische Post AG* (2022)
3. Proposal for a Regulation of the European Parliament and of the Council on harmonised rules on fair access to and use of data (Data Act), COM/2022/68 final (2022)
4. EU-US Transfers Complaint Overview, URL: https://noyb.eu/en/eu-us-transfers-complaint-overview, accessed 10.01.2023
5. Court of Justice of the European Union, Judgment of 28.04.2022, Case C-319/20, *Meta Platforms Ireland Limited*
6. M.R. Leiser, *Dark patterns': The case of regulatory pluralism between the European Union's consumer and data protection regimes*, in E. Kosta, R.Leenes, I. Kamara (eds.), *Research Handbook on Eu Data Protection Law*, Research Handbooks in European Law, 265 (Edward Elgar Publishing, United Kingdom, 2022)
7. A. Serban, Analele Ştiinţifice UAIC, SSJ, **64**, 167 (2018)

8. C.T. Ungureanu, Revista „Dreptul", **10**, 85 (2018)
9. *Exercise Your Rights – Article 77 – complain to your DPA*, URL: https://noyb.eu/en/exercise-your-rights-article-77-complain-your-dpa, accessed 10.01.2023
10. *Elektronische Beschwerde*, URL: https://datenschutz-hamburg.de/beschwerde/, accessed 20.10.2022
11. *Data Protection Commission – Contact Us*, URL: https://forms.dataprotection.ie/contact, accessed 20.10.2022
12. C. Kuner, L. A. Bygrave, C. A. Docksey. Commentary on the EU General Data Protection Regulation, 1135 (Oxford University Press, 2018)
13. Court of Justice of the European Union, Judgement of 13.05.2014, Case C-131/12, *Google Spain* (2014)
14. Court of Justice of the European Union, Judgement of 06.10.2015, Case C-362/14, *Maximillian Schrems V Data Protection Commissioner* (2015)
15. P. Hustinx, *The role of Data Protection Authorities*, in S. Gutwirth, Y. Poullet, P. De Hert, C.De Terwangne, S. Nouwt (eds.), Reinventing data protection?, 136, 137 (Springer Science & Business Media, 2009)
16. *Collective redress class actions 2021*, URL: https://practiceguides.chambers.com/practice-guides/collective-redress-class-actions-2021, accessed 20.10.2022
17. R. Mulheron, C. Baudenbacher, P.Tresselt, T.Orlygsson, *The class action in common law legal systems: a comparative perspective,* 3 (Bloomsbury Publishing, London, 2004)
18. J. Roman, *LinkedIn Settles Data Breach Lawsuit*, URL: https://www.bankinfosecurity.com/linkedin-a-7229, accessed 23.10.2022
19. *English High Court Finds Supermarket Liable for Data Breach by Employee in First Successful Privacy Class Action*, URL: https://www.insideprivacy.com/data-security/english-high-court-finds-supermarket-liable-for-data-breach-by-employee-in-first-successful-privacy-class-action/, accessed 23.10.2022
20. Commission Recommendation of 11 June 2013 on common principles for injunctive and compensatory collective redress mechanisms in the Member States concerning violations of rights granted under Union Law, OJ L 201 (2013)
21. Court of Justice of the European Union, Judgement of 25.01.2018, C-498/16, *Maximilian Schrems v Facebook Ireland Limited* (2018)
22. L. Jančiūtė, International Data Privacy Law, **9 (1)**, 3 (2019)
23. J. Haslach, Common Market Law Review, **56, Issue 2**, 570 (2019)
24. *EU top court ruling exposes need for European collective redress tool*, published on January 25, 2018, URL: https://www.beuc.eu/press-releases/eu-top-court-ruling-exposes-need-european-collective-redress-tool, accessed 23.10.2022
25. BEUC, *Where does collective redress for individual damages exist?*, Updated in October 2017, BEUC-X-2017-117
26. Court of Justice of the European Union, Judgment of 08.04.2014, C-293/12 and C-594/12, *Digital Rights Ireland Ltd* (2014)
27. Court of Justice of the European Union, Judgment of 29.07.2019, Case C-40/17, *Fashion ID* (2019)

28. European Union Agency for Fundamental Rights, *Access to data protection remedies in EU Member States* (2013)
29. Commission Recommendation of 11 June 2013 on common principles for injunctive and compensatory collective redress mechanisms in the Member States concerning violations of rights granted under Union Law, OJ L 201 (2013)
30. C.T. Ungureanu, Drept internaţional privat european în raporturi de comerţ internaţional, 154 (Hamangiu, Bucuresti, 2021)
31. Court of Justice of the European Union, Judgment of 01.10.2015, Case C-230/14, *Weltimmo* (2015)
32. Gierschmann *apud* P. Voigt, A. von dem Bussche, The EU General Data Protection Regulation (GDPR), A practical guide, 1st Ed., 216 (Springer International Publishing 10, no. 3152676, 2017)
33. European Commission, *Dieselgate*, URL: https://commission.europa.eu/live-work-travel-eu/consumer-rights-and-complaints/enforcement-consumer-protection/coordinated-actions/dieselgate_en, accessed: 10.02.2023
34. A. Biard, *Collective redress in the EU: a rainbow behind the clouds?,* in ERA Forum, vol. 19, no. 2, 189-204 (Springer Berlin Heidelberg, 2018)
35. F. Rielaender, ICLQ, **71, no. 1**, 108, DOI: 10.1017/S0020589321000403 (2022)
36. A. Pato, *GDPR Collective Litigation Against Facebook*, URL: https://verfassungsblog.de/gdpr-collective-litigation-against-facebook/, accessed 10.02.2023

# AUTHOR INDEX